WORKING WOOD 1&2

The Artisan Course with Paul Sellers

WORKING WOOD 1&2

The Artisan Series with Paul Sellers

Master Woodworker, Paul Sellers presents the Working Wood series, teaching you the application of his woodworking principles.

Working Wood 1 & 2 provides a structured series of seven films (available on DVD and for download) and accompanying 320-page, full-color book with 880 color photos and diagrams.

This series of structured and integrated training courses will enable woodworkers of all ability levels to easily master Paul Sellers' essential skills that can be used for a lifetime of woodworking projects.

The series is produced at the Artisan Media studios in Penrhyn Castle, a prestigious, historic property in North Wales.

Published 2011 by Artisan Media Ltd

13b Chestnut Court, Parc Menai, Bangor

Gwynedd LL57 4FH

United Kingdom

Printed in the USA by unitedgraphicsinc.com

ISBN: 978-0-9569673-0-5

Acknowledgements

Working Wood 1&2 in both written and video format, has been produced through the dedicated commitment from a skilful team of writers, technical editors, 3D animators and designers, filmmakers, videographers and film editors as well as graphic artists and creative sound specialists.

I have worked alongside the team as close friends, rather than mere associates, but I would first like to thank my closest team players, my sons Abraham, Joseph, Jonathon and Peter, who cut their teeth in my workshop and gave me the desire to create this course for others, who never complained in my all too frequent calls for help at difficult and sometimes intrusive times. I especially thank my wife Elizabeth, who bore the late nights and early starts almost every day, through years of work that went into preparing the curriculum. To Joseph, my thanks for his kindness, patience and skill in assisting with the technical edit of this book.

Without Simon James, my close friend and fellow director, who tore into the pages of the manuscript with dogged determination, none of this book would make any sense. To Dave and Lynwen Brown, two close friends, film makers and directors who invested in the unknown and stepped out in faith to embark on this exciting project.

Roy Parkinson, for his incredible sound and video editing skills, attention to detail and endless enthusiasm and energy.

Toby Niesser for his commitment to designing and producing high quality 3D animations.

I must thank Eifion Williams for searching beyond the limits of his camera lens, to capture the hidden details that bring this course to life.

My apprentice and friend John Winter for his aid in photography and woodworking

Jean Sherry for her design input and digital processing.

Peter Wood for his professional publishing consultancy.

Matthew Mortimer (Mortimer Design) for his input with design concepts and graphic layout.

To Iestyn Lloyd and Tom Pollok for their graphic layout work, and to Gemma Jones for taking care of the Project Administration.

Also to Galen Walters, for his encouragement and contagious enthusiasm.

I promised my family that one day, my books would be on bookshelves throughout the USA and around the world, and I am grateful to all those named above, who have enabled me to fulfil this. I also thank the three thousand five hundred students and friends that proved the efficacy of this course.

Contents

Series 1

Series 2

Contents *continued*

Series 2

Contents

Foreword

The art and craft of working wood have existed for thousands of years. But it's been only in the last 100 years or so that the use of machines has significantly replaced what was formerly done with manual tools alone. This shift is significant because, while it certainly has raised levels of productivity, it also separated the worker from the very material to be worked. This alienation has been exacerbated by the rise of a large woodworking tool industry continually offering new devices and increasingly complex machines which further contribute to the isolation. An all-important hand/eye/brain coordination link is thus broken and modern woodworkers are often left with a feeling of dissatisfaction. Meanwhile, industrialization has also given rise to a larger leisure class, allowing the development of woodworking as an avocation or hobby. However, the vast array of tools and machines available are daunting to the novice searching for advice and direction while being bombarded by commercials and advertisements offering the latest often expensive solutions.

In 2003 I had an experience that profoundly changed the way I work with tools. I attended a class taught by Paul Sellers, an incredibly skilled Master Woodworker with over forty years of working and teaching experience. Paul has the fantastic ability to distill those decades of experience down to the very essence of woodworking. Paul delivers this information through an expertly devised set of basic skills, one building upon the other, so that in a very short period of time one learns how to use a really minimal set of tools to produce wonderful objects of function and beauty. As with any true expert, it is evident that Paul cares very deeply about his craft. He combines this with concern about the future, and delivers not just content on the technique of woodworking but the philosophy of such as well, giving tremendous depth and support whether one is using these lessons in a quest for a vocation or just as a hobby.

Having read or scanned hundreds of woodworking books myself, I have been waiting for nearly a decade for Paul to write his own. You hold the results in your hands. As I tell my students at Stanford University, give woodworking a try. Wood is warm to the touch. It often has a wonderful smell. Working wood with manual tools strengthens the hand/eye/brain coordination while producing objects of utility, art, or both. Hand woodworking is a contemplative process requiring concentration and attention that can touch the heart and soul. This book represents the very best of what a Master Woodworker can offer and once started will provide years of joy and a real connection to our human history, present, and future.

Craig Milroy
Palo Alto, CA. 2011

Craig Milroy serves as Senior Lecturer at Stanford University in the Design Division of Mechanical Engineering.

Preface

In some ways writing this book was more by serendipity than intent, yet it was truly borne out of a desire to help future woodworkers discover the essential elements to become creative artisans in their own right.

Of all the enterprising creative ventures developed through the centuries, none prove more vibrant and compelling than those whereby hundreds of thousands of inventions we today take for granted were born. Without the carpenter no tall ships would have ever traversed the oceans, and the pumps that enabled man to search out ore and coal from the bowels of the earth, began with great baulks of timber and a handful of simple carpenter's tools. No other craft birthed more invention than that of the carpenter. From his planes and saws, chisels and shaves came the moulds and flasks for cast wheels and cogs. Pump casings and bearings, huge flywheels and sprockets helped birth the age of invention and the revolution by which British industry would advance irreversibly into centuries of commerce and trade and an end of which seems to us so boundless.

Little did those men of old know that one day the tools with which they worked, simple tools of seasoned beech, oak, hard maple and mahogany; tools of steel, of brass and of bronze, would one day be rendered obsolete by the machines their hands were facilitating the making of.

At first, craftsmen marvelled at the machines, in awe and amazement at the power and laboursaving productivity of their creations of wood and steel. The demand for machinery soon led to ingenious manufacturing systems, eventually controlled by computers and only serviced by specialists.

The age of the machine had rapidly replaced hand skills and in the same breath, tolled the bell for the warm and vibrant interpersonal relationships by which craftsmen shared with others the work of their hands and the life they worked productively and honourably in.

A new genre artisan

My generation has seen the fading days of skilled, creative handwork across many sectors of manufacturing. It seems to be in its final diminishing phase, replaced by digital creativity in a world that does not exist.

At first, the decline was slow, and went seemingly without notice. It is only today, looking at the skilled work that once provided every city, town and village, every home, farm and hamlet with the essentials for life, that this may well seem all but gone.

I see around, more than a glimmer of hope worth fanning into flame; a new emerging genre that seems boundless in child-like energy, inquisitiveness and enthusiasm and unrestrained by protocol and tradition. It is a genre resolved to grasp its rightful inheritance of fine and inspired work with a resolve to pay the price. It's this emerging artisan that first stood with unending questions around my bench some twenty years ago that deserves the best of the past to conserve the core essentials for future generations to learn from and master.

It is this generation for whom I have spent the last 20 years filtering the mass of information, and misinformation, to rediscover the simplicity and contentment of hand craftsmanship, and present this in a new way.

The course, starting with this book, and the supporting DVDs, contains those elements I consider essential to every apprentice in the formative years of developing skill.

Many of my perspectives have changed as I developed this course, distilled through determination and adversity, and I am now convinced, more than ever, that simplicity is the key. Living in the USA for many years, I produced new designs for a wide range of discerning collectors including Senators and even for the Permanent Collection of the White House. I have made and sold pieces for four decades, and I can say that today, thousands of woodworkers around the world have followed much if not all this very course to its conclusion—they are the new genre artisan.

Where this book sits in your future course is rightly placed at the very beginning. My hope rests in the secure knowledge that through the following pages you will quickly discover the art and craft of hand tool woodworking and by its fullness displace those myths and mysteries that once held in fear, craftsmen and women, living and working in the dark ages of times past. I ask only that you pass on your newfound knowledge and skill, to those searching the same paths that brought you to follow the course you are about to embark on. This will ensure that the craft of woodworking continues to grow and flourish through the planting of seed in the fertile soil of the new genre artisan.

1 Introduction

New genre woodworking

Many mysteries surround the different crafts that rely on the use of wood, which the secrecy of the early guilds and a century of innovation did nothing to demystify. Add to this the diminishing skill levels in modern society and it is easy to see how the fine handwork and craft values that for centuries supported the way we live and work, have come under increasing threat.

Surprisingly though, despite the loss of working knowledge and skill, most woodworking can still be rediscovered from the legacy left by our forebears who mastered highly accomplished standards with just a handful of basic tools.

The course you are about to embark on unlocks the secrets of the past to demonstrate proven methods handed down from father to son and master to apprentice. It is a journey of discovery; a rite of passage for anyone who wants to become a skilled artisan. It is the path I took from boyhood to become a master furniture maker and woodworker. It is the path you are about to take, and I will pass on all that I know to help you.

I've used the same hand tools for over forty-five years. My craft has sustained me through each of those years and I have enjoyed every challenge along the way. I have not known a day's true unemployment and I have trained each of my sons to be just as creative and capable with their hands. This course works.

My first Stanley plane cost me a week's wages, so too my tenon saw and my brace and bits. Using these tools, and others, to create and refine my work, I've made well over 100,000 woodworking joints in thousands of pieces ranging from walking canes and timber-framed roofs to complex carvings and even cabinets for the White House.

The more I work wood, the more I realize how complex a craft it is. But despite this complexity, at its heart is a simple yet profound truth: almost everything ever made from wood can be made using no more than three joints and around ten hand tools. There are two or three variations to each of these joints, but the methods of construction vary only slightly. Once you've mastered one, you can make any of the others. There are also a handful of key techniques, that not only ensure total accuracy, but surprisingly can be mastered in a relatively short time.

Hand tool woodworking is precise and accurate once you learn the techniques.

Some might say it's over simplistic to suggest that the violin maker and the furniture maker rely on so few tools and techniques to create the masterpieces we so respect and admire. It's not. Look back through history and read of the ancient masters: Amati, Stradivarius, Hepplewhite, Sheraton. For three centuries and more, the matchless pieces they produced came from the same modest range of hand tools. Their ancient works, still unequalled in quality, have survived the test of time in the form of violins, cellos, desks, chairs, beds and others too numerous to list.

Learning from these masters, discovering how they worked by studying the marks left by their tools, I find myself in constant search of the deeper insights they sought in perfecting their craft. The more I work with my hands, the more conscious I become of the whole grain, the tree that grew, the tools I choose and how I use them. Soon, the piece I imagined in my head takes form beneath my gouge and chisel. The more my senses engage with the task, the more my awareness heightens. I become ever more immersed in the elements surrounding my work and my work becomes more cohesive and challenging.

Losing myself in my work is a vital part of the process. It creates the increased awareness I need for what is directly before me, the same way we tune in to a conversation with a friend, even while the noise of the crowd grows ever louder around us. Tuning in to the essentials filters out the distractions.

These distractions are all around and it's the same for all woodworkers, regardless of professional status or ability. There is so much woodworking information available that it is becoming more difficult to know what the most pivotal elements of knowledge and skill are.

How do you know what is essential to becoming a skilled and competent artisan? Is it the finest tools and equipment, top quality machines, prime cuts of well-seasoned wood? Just ask yourself this question. How did Stradivarius plane his highly figured cello bouts so thinly and perfectly with wooden-bodied planes? How did he carve the scroll and neck of his highly perfected 'Messiah' violin without a power router or copy carver? No power machines in his workshop, a few homemade hand tools wrought by his own hand: scrapers, planes, saws and splitting tools to rive the wood to rough size.

What you will learn on this course

If you have never picked up a sharp hand tool and used it with confidence, or known the satisfaction of crafting beautiful furniture, this course is for you. If you have worked with wood for decades, but never mastered hand tools, this course is for you, too. If you want to rely less on your machinery and aspire to establish faster, better techniques, that put you in control through the development of real skill, this course will offer you that opportunity.

I developed the course to teach my own sons, apprentices and anyone else interested in working with wood. The principles you will follow have trained over 3,500 woodworkers from around the world. It worked for them and it will work for you. Start with the spatula and the wooden spoon and then, one step at a time, add new skills and techniques as you learn the art and practices of the masters. This course could take those who persevere all the way to the level of a Master Craftsman.

As you work through the pages and follow the course through the DVDs, your patience and determination will be rewarded with attaining levels of skill and confidence that will astound you.

I hope, like me, you find yourself on an exciting journey of discovery.

Working with my son.

Mesquite veneers.

The newly installed cabinets in the White House.

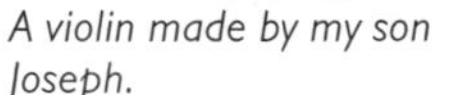

A violin made by my son Joseph.

Working with wood fascinates me.

"How do you know what is essential to becoming a skilled and competent artisan? Is it the finest tools and equipment, top quality machines, prime cuts of well-seasoned wood?"

Apprenticing today's woodworker

Through the New Legacy School of Woodworking and the courses I teach, I am training the new genre woodworker. These future artisans may never change their jobs or sell their work, but pursue their interest for personal fulfillment.

Aside from anything else, the purpose in my writing this book and filming the course is to dispel the idea that woodworking is not for you. The course takes into account all people from all backgrounds. It provides a logical training program that enables you to gradually gain composure and confidence in your craft. It is designed to help men and women to become not merely amateurs, but skilled amateurs with skill levels that surpass the professionals who pursue woodworking merely for money.

I have taught thousands of people to work with wood and this course has been proven to work by every one of them.

Investing in the future

You will need to invest time, finance and effort to truly master the skills and techniques covered in this course. But it is an investment that will soon show exciting returns.

In about thirty days, you will have made a five-foot workbench, spatula, spoon, cutting board, carved bowl, three-legged stool, dovetailed Shaker-style box, a four-shelf wall unit replete with stopped housing dado joints and through tenons, and a chair-side table in solid oak with fully shaped legs, arched aprons and eight haunched mortise and tenon joints. Add six more days and you will be completing your first oak dining chair, kitchen table or a mahogany desk for your office.

I have tried to minimize your set-up costs and inspire you to tackle concepts you might never have otherwise engaged in. Apart from the saws, all the tools you need will fit into one tool box and the cost to buy them will be negligible compared to the fulfillment you will gain by pursuing this course and following its basic principles.

Investing in the next generation of woodworkers is an important part of what I do. John is my current apprentice.

Reward in handwork

People inevitably compare machine woodworking methods with more traditional hand methods. Of course, a table saw will slice oak down to minute fractions of an inch in seconds and no hand method can compare with the ease with which it cuts. Planers, too, flatten boards and mill foursquare with equal alacrity. So why not rely entirely on machines as some manufacturers and magazines encourage us to?

> *"In practiced hands, hand tools are highly effective, fast, and accurate, especially when it comes to really fine tolerances in demanding work."*

Although working using hand tools is often faster, safer and more reliable for smaller scale work, machines such as bandsaws do have practical uses. The next book in this course, covering Artisan level 3 projects, will take you through the essentials of working with the bandsaw including setup, adjustment and use.

Working with both machines and hand tools, I find it impossible to compare the two. In practiced hands, hand tools are highly effective, fast, and accurate, especially when it comes to really fine tolerances in demanding work. On the other hand, many machines require minimal skill because they were developed for mass manufacturing to deadline. In fact, they generally substitute for skill, even though people often attribute the finished results to skilled workmanship.

Many see machine methods as the modern, natural evolution of traditional hand tool woodworking. They believe many of the tasks accomplished by machine are much harder to achieve, if not impossible, using traditional hand tool methods. This may be true in terms of production speed, where completed units are designed for mass manufacturing and sold at low prices, but the artisan must consider his work according to conscience: There is a dimension to hand tool work, that unites the artisan to his or her work, and not only creates a sense of fulfillment, but releases that sense of inner creativity that brings real and tangible meaning to life as a working artisan.

By way of contrast, production factory workers making products by industrial machine processes only, often find themselves unwittingly on the precipice of demoralization simply because they soon realize that they are little more than a small cog in the overall mechanism of mass manufacture. They see neither the beginning nor the end of what's being made, which reduces, if not totally eradicates, any kind of fulfillment. They never discover the true joy in the actual manual process of creating an individual piece of work from start to finish. Instead of gaining real skills, they become button pushing lever pullers, jig makers and machine operators. Their primary purpose in the process is to feed the machine and make certain nothing goes wrong with the production process.

This often becomes the case in the home workshop, where, in a similar fashion, woodworkers rely so much on machine methods to accomplish their work that the need to develop real skill is lost amidst the manufacturing process and the almost incessant whine of machinery.

There can be no doubt that woodworking by machine has its purpose. No one is suggesting we dig six-foot pits and start slabbing trees by pitsaw just for the fun of it. Machines have eased heavy work, not least in terms of preparing stock for subsequent work. But we should see machines as complementary to handwork, rather than its replacement. Handwork expands the realms of woodworking craft into areas no machine can possibly come close to. Your work is to develop real skill and practice the art and craft of handwork until every stroke accomplishes perfect results. It's an ambition we all strive for and it comes through practice. Once we acquire it, we never lose it. If you are a beginner, the tasks and challenges may at first seem difficult if not daunting, but you will be surprised how rapidly your skills can grow.

Hand tools, when they are well adjusted and well sharpened, are a joy to use.

2 Hand tool woodcraft

The art and practice of crafting wood enables you to create objects of function, beauty and structural significance. Throughout this course, you will see how a simple combination of accuracy, sharpness and technique can build ever-increasing levels of skill.

My creative workspace.

Woodcraft

This diagram is an interpretation of the scope of hand tool woodcraft.

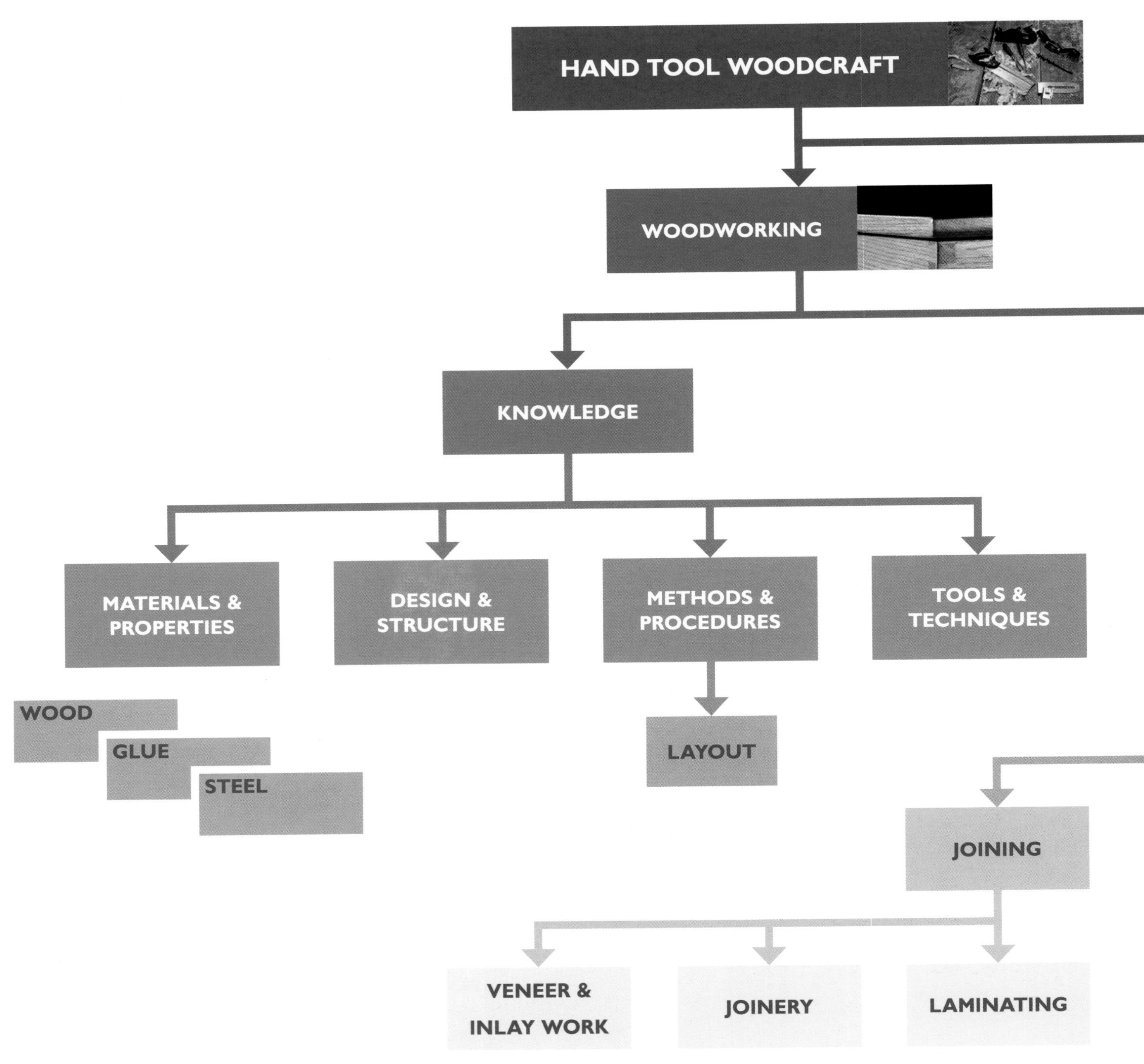

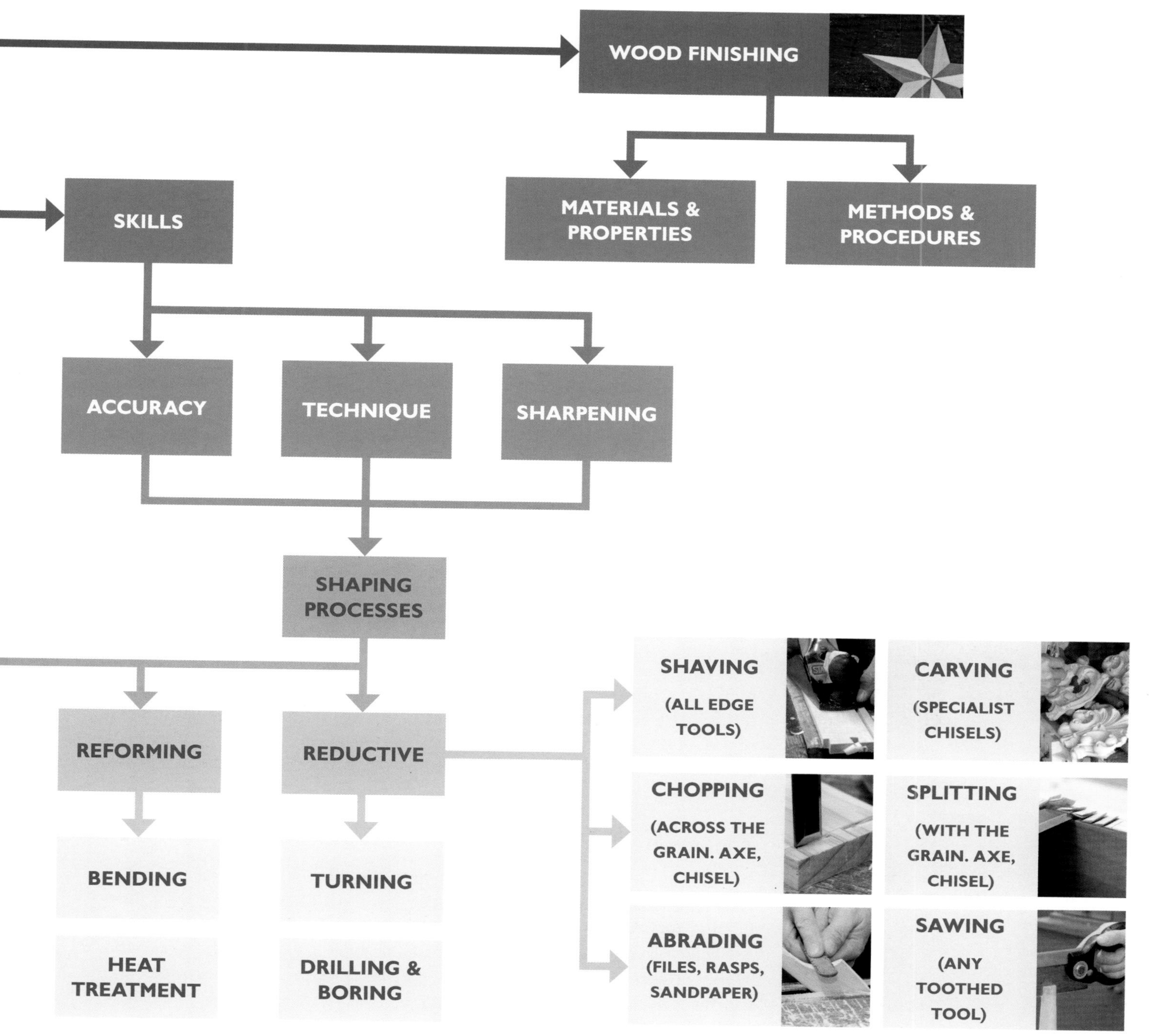
WOOD FINISHING
MATERIALS & PROPERTIES
METHODS & PROCEDURES
SKILLS
ACCURACY
TECHNIQUE
SHARPENING
SHAPING PROCESSES
REFORMING
REDUCTIVE
BENDING
HEAT TREATMENT
TURNING
DRILLING & BORING
SHAVING
(ALL EDGE TOOLS)
CARVING
(SPECIALIST CHISELS)
CHOPPING
(ACROSS THE GRAIN. AXE, CHISEL)
SPLITTING
(WITH THE GRAIN. AXE, CHISEL)
ABRADING
(FILES, RASPS, SANDPAPER)
SAWING
(ANY TOOTHED TOOL)

The basic processes of working wood are ancient.

Tools that seem complex often perform simple tasks.

Applying finish is a simple process.

What is woodworking?

All woodworking begins with the conversion of cut, raw trees into dimensions suited to the different woodworking trades. Though fewer than in past centuries, there remain several woodworking trades that produce non mass-made products: musical instruments, barrels, furniture, buildings, joinery products and vessels ranging from ships to canoes. Some of the more demanding and highly specialized trades have remained essentially the same for centuries. Despite their different objectives, all these crafts are based on similar techniques and processes, which form the basis of this course. Mastering these skills will help you determine which areas of woodworking you are most drawn to. No matter the trade, ancient or modern, the general processes remain unchanged.

A note on wood finishing

This distinct area of woodcraft employs processes that are more aesthetic and protective. With the wood planed, scraped and sanded, we no longer work the wood but the finish itself. Veiled for centuries as a secret and mysterious art, this course provides you with the techniques to confidently apply a full range of finishes to any of your projects. My aim in this preparatory part of the course is to provide only the information you need for a limited variety of finishes. A later section of this course will cover this area in detail.

There are four key universal areas of knowledge in woodcraft. All woodworkers must begin with a basic understanding of these areas:

Materials and properties

Fine woodwork, no matter how it is produced always starts with solid wood, not reconstituted wood-based materials like MDF or pressed fiberboard (chipboard in the UK). But whether you use hand or machine methods, key to understanding the many aspects of woodworking is the structure of the wood grain itself and the critical and constant influence moisture plays, regardless of the source or age of the wood.

Woodwork also relies on non-wood materials and as you work through the different projects, you will learn the properties and limitations of commonly used woodworking PVA (polyvinyl acetate) adhesive. You will also learn about the important aspects of tool steel and its characteristics in the sharpening section.

Prepared material.

Design and structure

In these initial stages of learning, design and structural issues are covered from a practical and functional point of view. Learning to work with wood and understanding the grain, the tools and the joints requires considerable concentration, especially during exercises and projects. For this reason, we discuss the creative elements of woodworking in a more advanced level of the course, where you will learn design concepts that allow more complex forms to be woven into a range of projects.

Even basic design features can be beautiful.

Methods and procedures

The methods and procedures you will learn in this course are simple and practical. Although the best ways of doing something can depend on personal taste, you will benefit initially from following the methods that I have adopted and developed throughout my life as a woodworker. By following the step-by-step guidelines, you will establish methodical work patterns that result in predictable woodworking excellence. Throughout each section and with every project and exercise, I explain how to achieve the same levels of accuracy that are attributed to master woodworkers.

Fast. Efficient. Sophisticated?

Tools and techniques

A knowledge of woodworking tools and a knowledge of the use of these tools are inseparable. Within a few hours of starting this course, you will know exactly which tool to choose and how to use it. Choosing the right tools for specific aspects of work should never be underestimated. I value the simplicity of my personal tools, they are non intrusive, efficient and generally cordless. In the following pages I provide a complete explanation of my everyday hand tools, together with the more general equipment essential to hand work. You will learn how to adjust, sharpen and take care of every tool you need to achieve the higher levels of fine craftsmanship you aspire to.

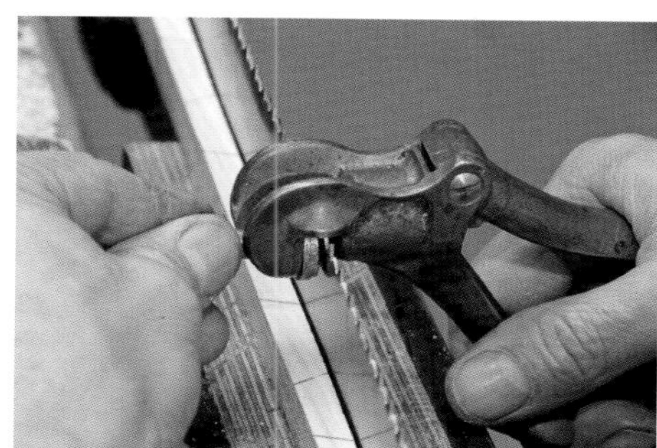

The tools are essential to the process.

Three distinct areas of skill

Accuracy

For any artisan, accuracy is much more than lines or numbers on a page. It is an ethos and goes hand in hand with sharpness and technique. We need to understand that how we work, determines the quality of the outcome. It helps us to better understand that accuracy affects every dimension of the creative sphere we work in. It is therefore essential that we train ourselves to carry out accurate work. The discipline to work with precision places great demands on every artisan. To produce consistently high levels of quality work with high degrees of accuracy takes considerable skill – which in turn, takes time to develop.

Accuracy in our calculations or writing are of course important, but it's how we physically handle tools and the raw material, and it's the way we exercise care and judgment that really counts.

Sharpness

Sharpening is the single skill most lacking among contemporary woodworkers. A dull tool from the barn or garden shed, even off the workbench, can never produce satisfactory results. Anyone exposed to a dull tool will quickly, and mistakenly, dismiss the tools as useless. The validity and value of woodworking hand tools relies on one simple fact: when they are truly sharp, they really work. I have dedicated a large proportion of this book to teaching the skills required to keep your tools in pristine order, and that means reaching levels of sharpness few woodworker's ever reach. Only when you make the decision to sharpen your tools to this demanding level, as frequently as required, will you achieve the results you strive for.

Accuracy and technique both rely on sharpness.

"The validity and value of woodworking hand tools relies on one simple fact: when they are truly sharp, they really work."

Technique

Defining technique can be difficult because many of the woodworking processes once common to daily life, even something as basic as chopping firewood, are now seldom performed or seen. Every hand process has been replaced by a machine method, which in general replaces any need for technique. Because we no longer understand how artisans really mastered technique to accomplish fine levels of workmanship, we fail to understand that technique is not singular but a range of processes that come only through practice. Technique involves all the senses. It is the information we receive through our senses that enable us to micro-adjust the way we work with specific tools, adjusting or adapting them to the task and working with our raw material. The more we work with our hands using hand tool methods, the better our techniques become.

How you swipe a plane across the narrow surface of a wooden box differs greatly from planing a massive planked tabletop of oak, and then again of cherry or of walnut. Just as size and bulk determine which plane you choose and how you use it, so too the wood itself, because no two species of tree have the same grain structure. Technique determines which plane you choose and furthermore the direction you plane and how you set the cutting edge to cope with swirling grain and knots.

There are thousands of techniques to master as you grow and develop your skill. Some are mastered in seconds, while others take many years to fully develop. It is through working with wood that we discover the skills yet to be fully developed. We begin to understand more fully how and why our artisan forebears worked and the techniques they used in accomplishing their work.

These four areas of knowledge and three areas of skill inform and govern the woodworkers' approach to the most comprehensive area in the realm of woodwork, *shaping*.

There are hundreds of simple techniques that have been around for centuries.

Shaping processes

Shaping wood is the most ancient of all woodworking skills. The shaping processes are mostly reductive, for example using a saw or chisel to remove wood for a specific reason. One process, bending, only changes the shape. Other processes involve joining parts after a series of reductive processes. Shaping wood to form interlocking joints is commonly known as joinery. Other joining processes are laminating, veneering and inlay work. Although it is convenient to look at joinery as a form of shaping, I generally see shaping and joinery as being two sides of the same coin. Reductive shaping always precedes any form of joinery, and as you progress, you will appreciate the significance of the following processes in all your handwork.

Reductive shaping processes

This group of processes involves the use of tools to cut, split and remove wood in order to define the shape of the workpiece. The tool lists to carry out the various processes are by no means exhaustive but are limited to the tools that are demonstrated in this book.

The reductive processes are:

SPLITTING—The process of prizing wood fibers apart along the grain. Tools used: Axe, chisel.

CHOPPING—The process of cutting cross grain fibers by successive impacts from a sharp cutting tool. Tools used: Axe, chisel.

SAWING—The use of any toothed tool to divide wood by cutting a narrow slot or passage. Tools used: The entire range of saws, from coarse through to fine.

SHAVING—The process of removing very thin, sometimes transparent, layers of wood fibers, either with the grain or across it. The grain orientation determines the nature of the shaving produced. Tools used: Plane, spokeshave, chisel, basically most edge tools and all scrapers.

CARVING—The process of using specially shaped chisels to cut a particular uniform section or profile according to the shape and size of the cutting edge. Tools used: The whole range of carving chisels and gouges.

ABRADING—The process of removing wood fiber, regardless of grain orientation, by a combination of cutting, grinding and tearing, sometimes at microscopic levels. Tools used: Rasps, files and abrasive papers (usually referred to as consumables).

DRILLING AND BORING—The process of forming cylindrical holes using either a drill bit, or a larger diameter rotary cutting tool. Tools used: Hand drill and bit, battery drill, brace and bit.

Controlled splitting is one way of shaping wood.

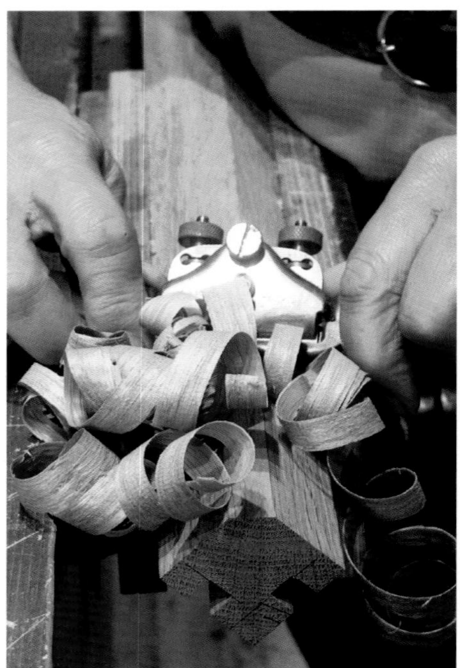

Sometimes working wood looks great.

Reforming processes

In these two processes, no wood is removed and nothing is joined.

BENDING—For centuries, the shape of wood has been permanently changed by woodworkers who have understood the process of heat and steam bending. This is a technique that will be further explained and demonstrated in a later part of the course.

HEAT TREATMENT—This is a process of chemical reformation, or alteration, where the organic composition of the wood is altered by an extended period of high temperature exposure. This is not a practical process for the average woodworker, but is carried out on a large scale universally. The benefits of the chemical changes are a higher resistance to decay and insect attack, and better wearing properties in areas of high traffic, such as decking.

Bent wood is used for many functions such as the sides of this boat

Heat treating is used to make the wood harder and less prone to rot, ideal for decking and other outdoor uses.

Joining processes

When any two separate pieces are joined together in some way, the purpose is either for structural or aesthetic reasons. The most common ways of achieving this are by using a joint and a combination of glue, wedges and pegs. The glue used will depend on the purpose of the finished piece, be it a boat hull, a guitar body or a workbench.

JOINERY—The dominant joining process is the development of joints and it forms a major part of this course. It involves cutting, shaping and fitting separate pieces of wood to create an interlocking mechanical joint. In practice, only a small number of types of joint are used for 99 percent of the structural work carried out in woodworking.

LAMINATING—This is the process of gluing together strips, boards or layers of prepared timber to increase the sectional area, width or strength of the material.

VENEER AND INLAY WORK—In general, these processes originated for more aesthetic reasons than practical ones. Either flat sawn pieces of figured or decorative wood were laminated onto a less expensive secondary wood, or contrasting strips and decorative patterns were glued into slots or recesses of the background wood. In Artisan Level 4, you will learn how to transform your projects with some incredible, but simple, inlay work.

Joints are functional but they can also be beautiful. This is a 'houndstooth' dovetail.

Laminating is the process of joining wood. Here it is being used to make the top of a chairside table.

Mortise and tenon joints are incredibly versatile.

The structure of this course is based on the four key knowledge areas, the three key skills and the shaping processes. You will learn about the nature of wood in the next section, which in turn will form the foundational knowledge required to understand the shaping processes covered in this book.

Progressing through this early part of the course will prepare you for learning more advanced skills in woodturning, wood finishing, veneering, carving, inlaying and more. We have much to work through to get to that stage, but the path is an exciting and rewarding one. And it starts here!

3 Wood and its properties

The wood we work inspires us. It informs our designs and determines the techniques we'll use. As artisans, we need to relate to the physical properties of wood by working it and gaining knowledge of its inner substance. Throughout this course, your knowledge and feel for all the materials you work with will be developed and expanded. From knowledge and experience come capability and well-informed decisions.

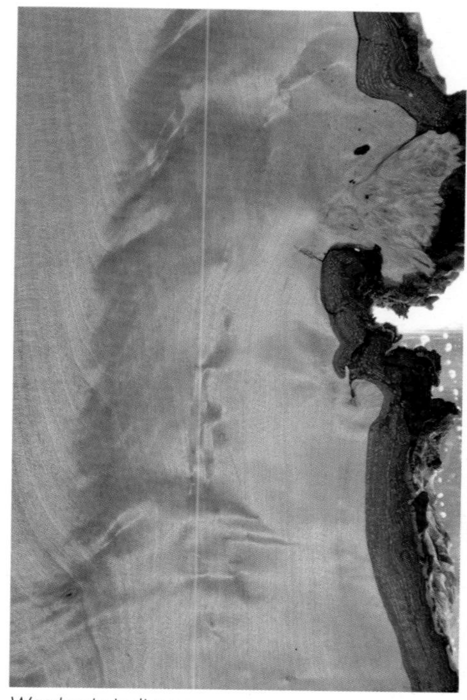

Woodgrain is diverse.

I often walk through these woods on my way to work.

Oak leaves.

Let's start in the woods

Woodlands and forests were once the local storehouses from where artisans cut the oak and ash they needed for their work. I, too, once enjoyed harvesting my wood from local woodlands, but for most of us those days are gone. It was an era when the relationship between an artisan and his material was more direct. They could choose from thousands of trees, consider their growth, compare one to another and relate it to the type of work they were involved in. One tree might yield twenty Windsor chairs. Another might provide half a dozen tabletops. They picked out trees for the length and straightness of their grain, or for their curves to make boat ribs. Trees unsuited to particular tasks were left to grow another ring or two, until large enough for the next project.

It may seem an obvious consideration, but many artisans don't pay close attention to their natural resource until there's a drop in quality or availability. It's as if the woodlands and the wood are two separate entities, rather than two sides of the same coin. Though I've cut hundreds of trees and converted them to workable stock, I find it impossible to fathom the unique relationships between the different plants and animals that all help create the trees we so value; wood-boring insects, grubs and ants that bore deep into the sapwood, fungi tracing subtle webs in shades of green and blue and grey to create astonishing spalted patterns.

It's hard to imagine the wood we work with when it's still a standing tree among thousands of others. What we see in the natural woodland is the raw, growing stock. It is only the very beginning of understanding wood. It's only through experiencing wood through our own eyes, ears, nose and hands that we really begin to understand the structure of its inner fibers. It's the splitting, sawing, gouging, shaving, planing, chiseling, rasping, filing, bending, boring, and sanding of wood at the workbench, at the kitchen table or in the forest that makes the difference

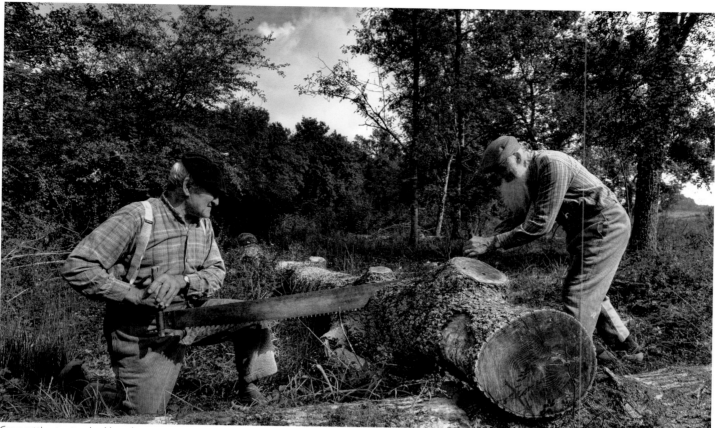

Crosscutting to standard lengths.

Engaging the senses

Our senses transfer information to the brain and it's from this that we make thousands of decisions every day. In a world filled with reproduced imagery and sounds, working with wood and hand tools engages us with palpable reality. It's a reality based on thought, effort and a sense of accomplishment. To be truly creative with wood involves more than merely pressing a button. Creative, practical work engages the senses of touch, taste and smell that together make the essence of what craftwork is really all about and it's when these senses engage that we feel truly involved and in control.

Throughout this course I constantly refer to the need for sensitivity, mainly because it's an area often neglected in favor of power and force. Success and fulfillment in woodworking may be more to do with engaging your senses rather than engaging more horsepower.

As artisans, our heightened sensitivity to the different characteristics of wood help us to make decisions about the design, form and structure of the things we make. In the early stages of training, we must strive to see and understand what these material characteristics are and how they can change.

Hazel leaf from a coppiced stump.

Hardwoods and softwoods

Most people, understandably, think that hardwoods are hard and softwoods are soft. It would be simple if this was true, but balsa, for example, the lightest, softest, least dense wood with the lowest specific gravity of any true wood in the world, is actually a hardwood that grows in South America. Longleaf pine, on the other hand, compares in hardness and density with cherry and oak, yet it's a softwood.

Hardwoods are angiosperms, which means they are broad-leafed deciduous trees like oak, apple, plum and beech that produce seed in some kind of fleshy fruit or nut. Softwoods are gymnosperms. They produce needle-like leaves and are generally evergreens like pines, larches and firs. They don't produce fruit, but dozens of seeds that mature inside cones.

The leaves of a hardwood, oak.

These are the needles typical of softwood.

Looking at the tree—from the inside out

Wood expands and contracts according to changes in the surrounding atmosphere. It also splits readily, whether intentionally or otherwise. You must experience these properties of wood first hand through working with it. As you study wood, under different conditions, your increasing knowledge will allow you to make informed decisions about how you use it in projects. It's only when we delve beneath the rough bark that we begin to discover the incredible structure of wood and the importance of the grain.

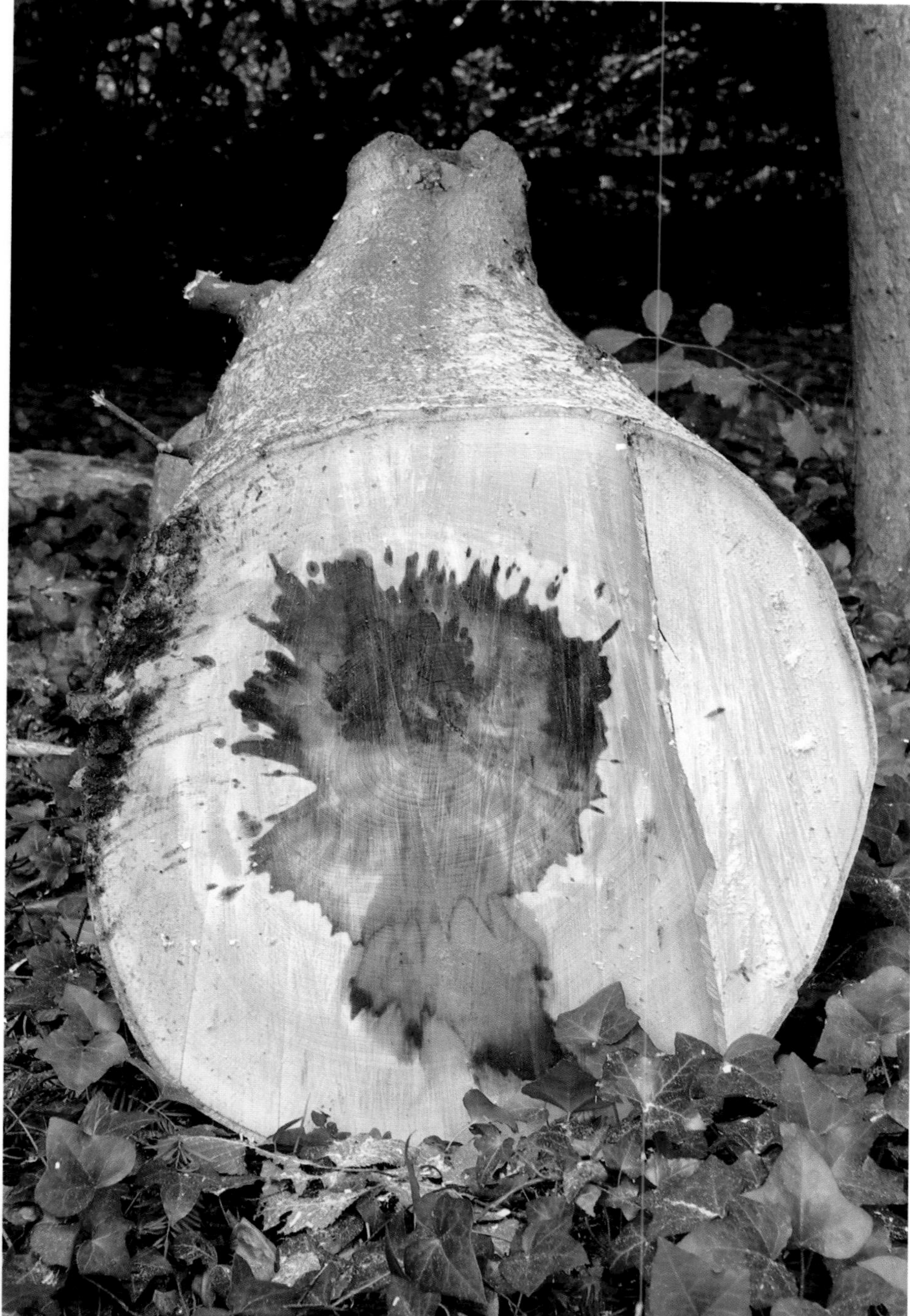

The first stage in the reductive process of woodworking.

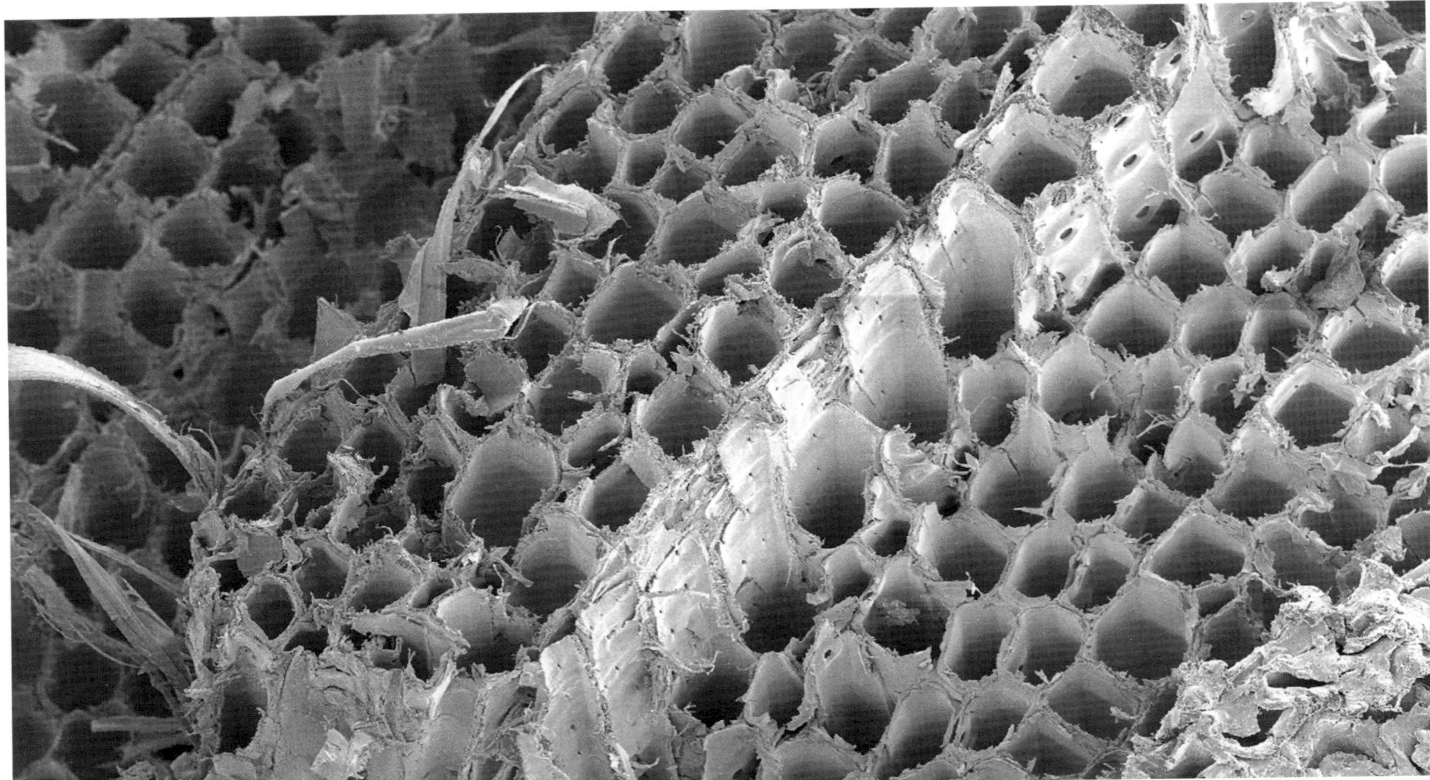

Magnified image of softwood (Sitka spruce) tracheids, copyright and courtesy of Neil Shearer and Thomas Reichert, Edinburgh Napier University.

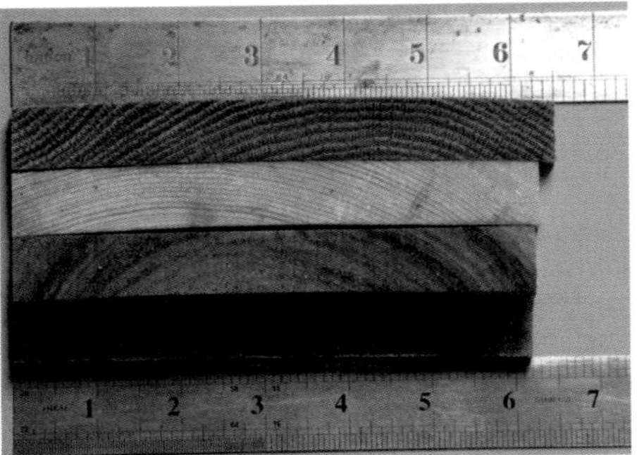

Some woods when resaturated can expand by half an inch over six inches.

Discovering wood's ability to expand and contract

Wood is not a homogeneous solid material. As it grows, the tree carries nutrients and sap up the trunk through elongated cells, much like straws. The long tubular cells are only between 20 to 30 microns in diameter, so you could bundle up about 1600 cells together on a pinhead. A water molecule is a lot smaller still, about 86,000 times smaller in fact. For this reason, water and water vapor can flow in and out of the cells easily. The water molecules actually bind to, and become part of the complex organic structure of the cell walls, and this phenomenon is responsible for causing expansion. It's just like putting dried noodles into boiling water, they absorb water and swell. The process is completely reversible and so, as the cell walls dry out, the result is an overall contraction of the wood.

I carried out a simple but fascinating experiment that you can try for yourself. It will provide a great insight into the effect moisture has on wood.

DRYING WOOD BY HEAT ON A RADIATOR– I cross-cut thin slivers of ¾" x 6" sections of wood, about 3⁄16" long, and dried them on a radiator (any dry heat source will work). This allowed me to establish zero moisture content, shrinking the wood to its minimum possible size.

I dried four samples of different types of wood: Oak, Pine, Poplar and Sapele Mahogany. This enabled me to find the exact dry weight and size of fully dried-out wood. Reintroducing the wood to a normal atmosphere allowed the wood to reabsorb moisture naturally, returning it to its previous size and weight.

EXPANDING WOOD BY RESATURATION–I then took the same thin sections of wood and placed them in water, returning them to the original size and weight of freshly cut wood, before any seasoning and drying. The difference was quite dramatic. In some of the samples I dried, the wood expanded in width by as much as ½".

Even a slicing cut can result in some splitting which you can see in the small checks on this curl.

Wood splitting—all woods split differently

SPLITTING WOOD—Again, using pine, sapele mahogany, poplar and oak, try splitting them and examine the different ways that they respond. I did this and found that the sapele mahogany offered the greatest resistance because of the interlocking nature of its grain. The pine readily split and so did the oak, although it did offer somewhat greater resistance. Surprisingly, the poplar offered much greater resistance than oak or pine. Woods that have tighter and smaller cells are capable of absorbing the axe blows more readily, so splitting the poplar and sapele was more difficult. This is purely for experimentation and is not scientific, but it does help us to understand the nature of the wood.

Most woods smell wonderful.

Wood smells—no two woods smell the same

SMELLING THE WOODS—Sawing, planing and splitting wood helps us to discover the various smells associated with the different species. Oak is as distinctive as pine and rosewood. Species like mesquite are sweet, whereas walnut has a musky smell.

TOXIC WOODS: Most North American woods are non-toxic, as are most native European woods, but you can develop an allergy to any wood if you work with it long enough. Some woods, particularly exotic hardwoods, are very toxic and can cause immediate and prolonged allergic reactions and even serious illness. Make sure that the wood that you are using is safe to work with and will make a safe finished article. This is particularly important when making items for the kitchen.

Two contrasting but complimentary woods.

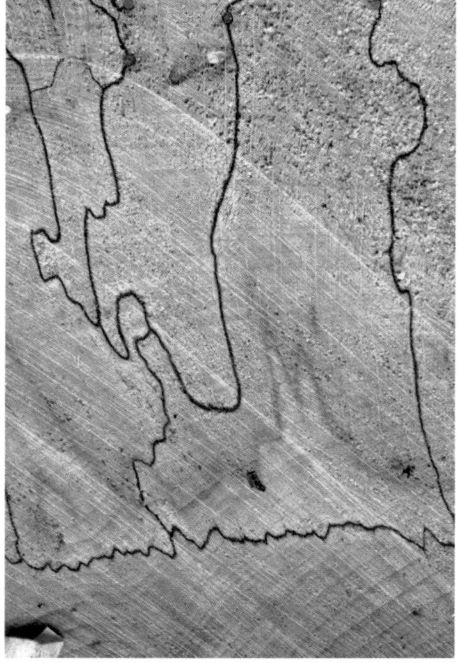

Spalting can create amazing patterns in wood.

Color—all wood species are different colors

Looking at wood—No two species of wood are the same color. Even within the same species colors can vary considerably. The color of some woods will fade in sunlight. Hardwoods such as teak can lose their rich colors and fade to grey if left untreated. Others woods, including most pines, darken when exposed to sunlight. Heartwood and sapwood can change color very differently, especially in cherry and softwoods, a fact, which can determine how we choose wood for furniture. Sometimes, a black fungal growth can occur in rotting or diseased wood, leading to contrasting dark lines, known as 'spalting'. There is an incredible variety of color amongst wood types, and this can be used in both harmony and contrast to create objects that have a beauty which goes beyond the craftsmanship of the artisan. Man made materials rarely substitute for the richness and warmth of natural materials.

Grain—understanding surface texture

Feeling the grain—Most people think the grain is what they see as the surface of wood, in the color and by feeling its texture after it's been sanded and a finish applied. However, as wood fiber comprises millions upon millions of tubular bundles of cells, what we see and feel on the surface can tell us much about what lies beneath. Every characteristic that exists through the depth of the wood is represented on the surface in visible variations of grain pattern, color and the way that the grain reflects light. I refer to a technique called 'reading the grain', which is simply using what you see and feel on the surface to predict how the fibers inside are arranged. This in turn determines how they should be cut, shaved or finished.

Thin wood like this being used to make cello sides can be bent simply with the application of heat.

Wood is flexible and compressible.

All woods will flex and bend. Without this natural property, the trees could not withstand the pressures applied by wind passing through the leaves or the weight of snow on their branches. This flexibility has been used to the advantage of the artisan in making hunting bows, coracles, tents, chairs and many other projects which benefit from using wood in a form other than straight flat boards. Recently felled, 'green' wood, is more flexible than well-seasoned wood, but the application of heat and steam can allow craftsmen to form useful curved shapes in many woods even after they have been seasoned. Most species of wood, especially softwoods, will compress slightly. This must be accounted for in joinery and if used correctly can be of great advantage in projects. An example of this is where wooden wedges are used to introduce intentional compression into a joint, which then holds the joint together for decades and often centuries.

Trees grow—and so does wood

A tree comprises three primary elements:

- Crown or canopy—the umbrella of branches and leaves.
- Trunk—the timber-producing section from where we harvest most of our wood.
- Roots—usually below the ground.

Most timber-producing trees produce growth in the form of concentric outer layers, just beneath the bark. This type of tree is called exogenous. Most of the woods that we use for carpentry, joinery, furniture making and general woodworking are exogenous,

ANNUAL RINGS—Cutting a cross section of almost any tree will reveal circular rings called annual rings. Each year of growth adds a two-part ring that shows two distinct periods of growth in a single year. These parts are known as early-wood (spring-wood) and late-wood (autumn-wood). In some woods, such as oak, ash and elm, there is visible difference between the large porous early-wood and the dense late-wood. By contrast, in many tropical woods there is hardly any seasonal difference in an annual growth ring, resulting in a very even texture. Tree rings record the tree's growth history throughout the seasons and changes in climate. You can read the story of every tree simply by examining its annual rings.

HEARTWOOD—as the name suggests, is at the heart of the tree. It is old growth, fully formed wood that remains unchanged. The heartwood provides the structural strength of the tree, giving it the rigidity required to support its growth. In general, heartwood is the wood we use for woodworking. It is usually darker in color than the sapwood layer that surrounds it. In some woods, the two areas of heartwood and sapwood are easily distinguished, while in other woods there is no apparent difference.

SAPWOOD—is the younger wood, with the primary function of conducting and distributing water and minerals from the roots, and up through the tree. In some cases sapwood is less solid and lacks the hard density of heartwood. Usually, we discard all the sapwood. This is especially true in woods like cherry and pine, where there is a considerable difference in color between the heartwood and the sapwood.

KNOTS—Knots show where the branches grew from the tree. Some branches are very close together, while others spread from the trunk. As the fibers grow to form a branch, they turn and intertwine to support the weight of the branch as well as carrying the sap. It is these intertwined fibers that produce the orderly change in grain direction around the junction. Every branch is connected to the center of the tree, causing most vertical fibers of the main trunk to flow around the branch center, much like water in a brook flows around a rock. Of all the difficulties surrounding any work in wood, knots cause

the greatest variety of problems, causing difficulty in every process of planing, chiseling and sawing. A full understanding of the different types of knots and how they vary between species, comes only through years of experience, as you work around them in the wood you choose.

PITH—The pith is the center of the tree and is formed when it is a sapling. Once the sapling has grown and the tree begins to form, however, the pith has no more use. In making furniture and other aspects of woodworking, we usually cut out the pith because it has no strength and looks inconsistent. It's not much of a problem for structural works such as roofing and stud framing.

ROOT—The root system anchors the tree to the earth and carries the mineral-rich solutions from the surrounding soil. Root systems differ between tree species. Some have deep-reaching roots, others have shallower roots spread over a wider area. In general, the roots of trees have no value to woodworkers as they have no heartwood and are generally too small for most work.

BRANCHES—Branch wood is of equal value to heartwood from the main trunk. The main difference is size and straightness. Chairs, barn crooks, braces and ship parts can be obtained from these ready-formed bowed sections. They are also widely used in woodturning as they are ideal for work such as bowls and turned legs.

CROTCHES—Another problematic area for woodworkers is where the branches diverge to form separate main branches. This is called the crotch. Usually, the trunk splits into two or more divergent branches that give the tree its umbrella shape. It's the crotch area of the tree that produces the figured areas of contrasting patterns and swirling grain, often used to enrich the work of furniture makers, woodworkers and woodturners.

The first step in converting the tree.

Drying or seasoning wood

Moisture content

"The tendency of wood, without fail, is to reach an equilibrium with its surroundings."

Like the ebb and flow of the oceans, wood continually expands and contracts throughout its lifetime. Some seas have massive surges, while others lap gently to and fro. So it is with different woods: some surge, while others creep. This means that wood is hygroscopic. It's why doors stick in the jamb in damp weather and swing freely when it's dry. The amount different woods change varies between species, which often makes woodworking even more unpredictable. One thing you can rely on, however, is that wood moves most of the time.

Often the movement may be a simple expansion or contraction across the width of a board, which is something we can plan for. However, when wood expands and contracts in different amounts within the same piece, the wood can twist, bow, cup or split. The process of seasoning minimizes the likelihood of distortion occurring in the finished project, such as toolboxes, doorframes, doors and tabletops.

The moisture that permeates the wood's fibers, whether from the atmosphere, direct saturation or spillage, will be slowly released until it reaches the same level of moisture content as the atmosphere around it. The tendency of wood, without fail, is to reach an equilibrium with its surroundings. Newly cut (unseasoned) wood is fully saturated to the same level of moisture as the tree it was cut from. It cannot absorb any more moisture. Only after removing the bark and converting the wood into smaller sections will wood fully release its moisture content.

Often we feel wood to gauge its wet or dry condition, but what we feel on the surface may well be different to what's inside the fibers. The weight of wood will provide an indication if wood is wet or dry and we can detect this, after handling the same species on a regular basis. For the main part, the moisture content can best be accurately checked by measuring it with a calibrated electronic meter. This type of meter determines the moisture content of wood by using electric probes to penetrate beyond the surface fibers into the wood itself. Other methods involve calculating the wood density, both before and during project development and construction.

As we know that moisture content is not a stable and fixed value, it won't surprise you that most problems arise when wood, even air dried, top quality timber, is shaped and jointed in one environment (your workshop) and then transfered to a dryer, more controlled situation. This is particularly evident when the outside air is cold and damp, and the inside of your house is warm and dry. You must allow for seasonal changes in humidity and I'll show you how to do this as you progress through this course. However, the most critical factor is to start your project with well-seasoned wood.

Drying wood

Wood is dried either by rapid kiln drying or the more natural process of air drying. Seasoning by air drying causes less internal stress to the wood because it is a gradual seasoning process. Newly cut trees are very high in moisture. Moisture can be above 50 percent in some trees and as low as 10 percent in others. The average water content for living trees is around 25 percent. When seasoned, this is halved.

The process of drying wood starts the moment the branches are severed from the trunk and the trunk from the root. Any exposed end grain will allow moisture to escape, often at a greater rate than the fibers can cope with. It is this internal stress from sudden contraction that causes unwanted tension in the end grain. To prevent the end grain from surface checking, we coat the open grain with paraffin wax or latex paint to slow any rapid release of moisture.

Good quality, kiln dried lumber is readily available from lumber (US) or timber (UK) suppliers. I have slabbed, converted and dried different types of wood with great success for many years. There are several different methods for converting raw trees and stacking them to dry. Most require industrial equipment and machines, space and patience. Although it's an area I'm passionate about, I won't cover the process in detail here, as it's the way we use the dried wood that is important for this course.

Using well-seasoned wood minimizes problems with movement at the outset of any project. It also minimizes future movement in the fibers of the wood, so the wood remains more stable. Another key factor is the reduction in the weight of the wood itself. When you reduce the moisture content of raw, unseasoned wood, you reduce its weight, too. A section of undried wood weighing 100lbs may drop to 78lbs once it has been dried to around 10 percent moisture content.

The amount by which we reduce the moisture content depends on the intended use of the finished project. For furniture making and indoor woodworking projects, 11-12 percent moisture content generally works well, but it depends on where you live. This is particularly true in the USA, where extreme differences in humidity are common between, and even within, states. Even in the UK, where generally atmospheric moisture is fairly constant, it's still a concern between different regions.

Short bursts of heat and direct sunshine, particularly through glass, will often cause cracks and distortions in the wood. That's why I like to keep my work out of direct sunlight as much as possible.

Kiln dried lumber is often touted as being equal to or more stable than wood dried naturally, but this is untrue. The slower process of natural air drying releases stresses caused by drying, so the wood being worked is less inclined to distort. All through my early woodworking days the older woodworkers spoke highly of natural air drying methods, declaring the wood to be more stable than when kiln dried. Fifty years on, I now know that they were right.

This is an industrial wood drying kiln.

"To prevent the end grain from surface checking, we coat the end grain with paraffin wax or latex paint to slow any rapid release of moisture."

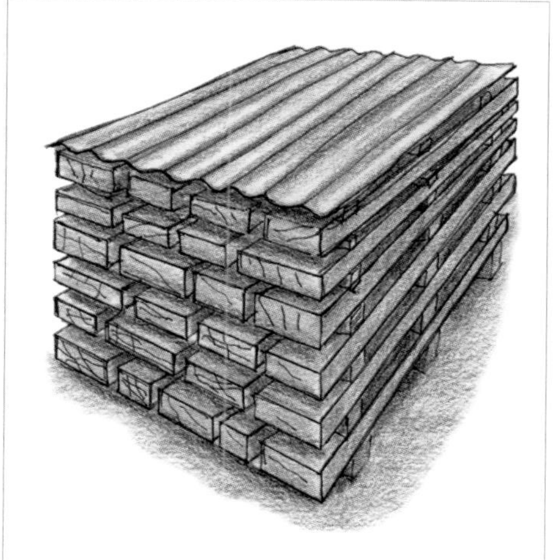
Air drying is my preferred way of drying wood.

NOTE: *The hand drawing above and many more that follow are taken from my personal woodworking journals.*

Working with moving wood

Well-planned joinery takes into account changes in the moisture content over the lifetime of the piece, but, no matter how good a joint, or the glue, wood constantly moves to a greater or lesser degree. As you work through the jointed projects in this course, you will begin to understand how to incorporate joinery into your projects that considers these factors throughout the planning phase of each piece.

Unrestrained and loose, non-joined parts, like tabletops and adjustable shelves, are particularly prone to large-scale movement and distortion. To help combat this, we apply sufficient finish to the piece to slow down moisture absorption. I generally apply the same quantity of finish to both sides of such components and to all the edges, especially the end grain, not to necessarily stop absorption, but to slow down the ingress and egress of water molecules. Few finishes can totally prevent absorption, so it's best to make sure that whatever does enter, enters equally from all surfaces, sides, edges and ends. Wood surfaces also absorb moisture at different rates, something that is evident on flat-sawn stock. To minimize distortion on key components, such as panels and tabletops, it's advisable to use quarter-sawn wood if possible, which allows absorption and release of water equally from both main surfaces of the wood.

The fragility of trees

Taking a walk through woodlands and forests reminds me how increasingly fragile our world is

Man's connection to the land – particularly wooded land – is stronger than we perhaps realize. Whole societies once derived their entire existence from the forests and woodlands that surrounded them. It's a long way from the grey, concrete world most of us live in today.

Man's lack of foresight and focus on short-term gain often plays a critical role in the demise of natural resources, forgetting (or ignoring) that future generations need trees as much as we do. People used to be more directly connected to the land and knew that the consequences of their actions were permanent and irreversible. Woodlands and forests on every continent once sustained centuries-old communities with wood for heat, building and everything from axe handles to furniture and roofing. Trees held within their leaves and branches much of what man needed to support sustainable life. If a local community needed wood to build a new church, they would replace the trees they cut with new saplings. That way, the next generation would have good oak shaped by the same winds that weathered those original boughs.

We rely on trees for life, now more than ever, yet for over 150 years we've steadily depleted the world's forests, replacing them with wastelands. Taking a walk through woodlands and forests reminds me how increasingly fragile our world is: Remove one tree from the forest and it creates a space that wasn't there before. To balance the loss, another tree must be planted, but it will take decades to replace what was there before. Controlled harvesting and replacement planting programs enable us to buy our wood responsibly. But although forest replanting is a positive step, it may take hundreds of years to generate the massive overarching canopy of a fully mature woodland that once existed, and until that happens, the original growing environment is simply lost.

Trees are such an important resource, and we woodworkers must source and use wood wisely.

4 Tools and equipment

General equipment

Quite apart from the specific tool sets I outline for shaping and joinery, you will also require a full set of general purpose equipment. The most important item in this list is the workbench. The ability to hold a workpiece while it is being sawn, shaved or split is often overlooked in a shop packed with machinery. A solid bench to work on is to a woodworker what the forge is to a blacksmith.

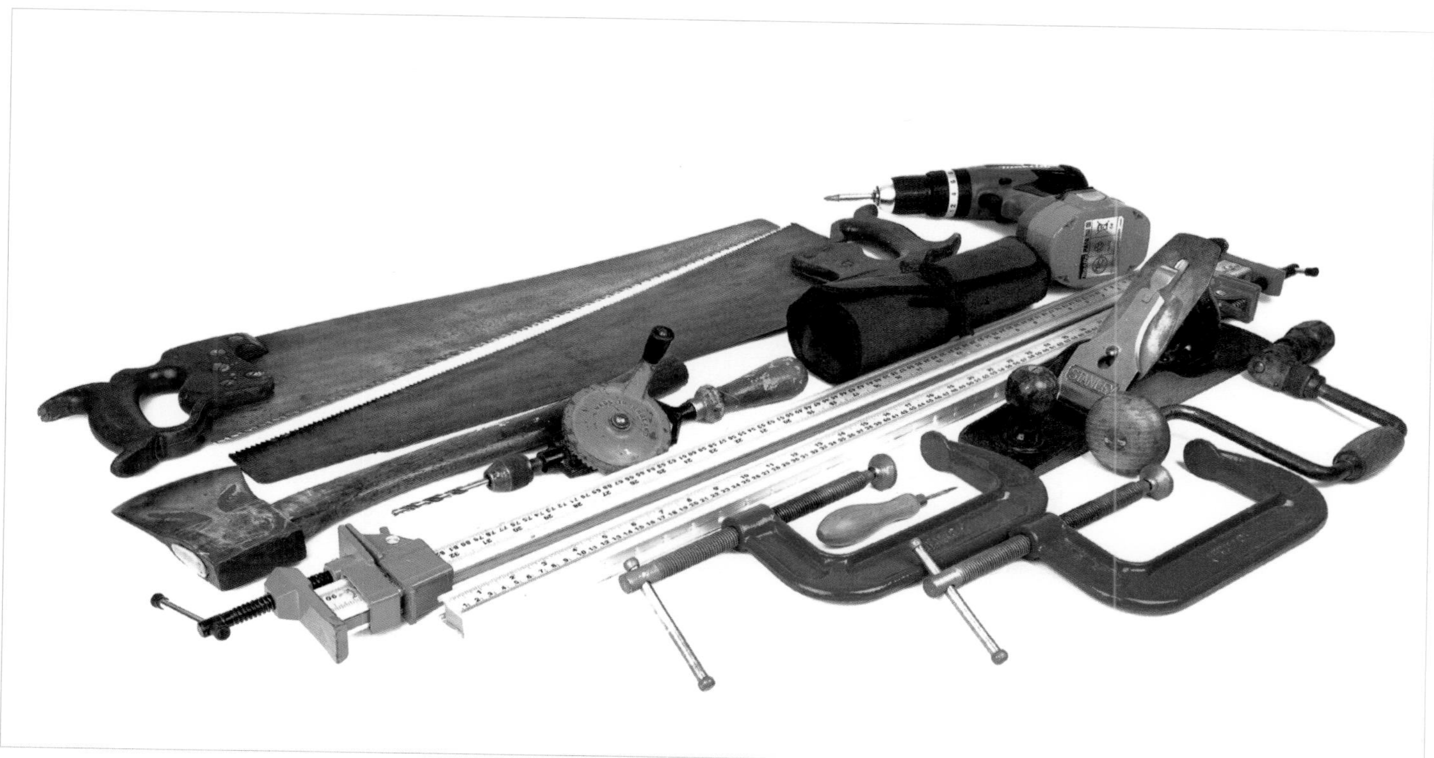

Workbench

If you do not own a well made, solid bench, you can go through the simple step by step process of making your own, following the instructions in chapter 10,page 179. With minimal complexity, this simple bench will last for generations.

Clamps

A good selection of clamps is a non negotiable necessity. Always check the assembly stage of a project to make sure you have sufficient clamps of the right length.

Ripsaw

Ideal for ripping boards to the right width.

Crosscut saw

For cutting to length longer pieces of stock.

Axe

When sharp, and used with care, this tool will remove waste very efficiently, but it's not for the kids.

Hand plane

A Stanley No. 5½ is included in this general list as the longer sole will flatten larger pieces more effectively than the more widely used No. 4½.

Hand brace and auger set

Reliable for quietly boring holes in any wood.

Hand drill and bit set

This tool is ideal for pre-drilling for larger screws, or through hole drilling. The selection of bits must be sharp, and particular care is needed with small diameter twist drills.

Square awl

Unlike the round awl, the square awl actually reams a tapered hole by cutting wood fibres, not just forcing them apart, which can split the wood.

Cordless drill/screwdriver

Although not essential, a cordless screwdriver takes the hard work out of driving screws.

Bench dogs

Bench dogs are simple additions to any workbench. They are usually set at incremental distances from the vise to hold dowels or pegs and against which the work is wedged or clamped.

Screwdrivers

Both cross head and flat head screwdrivers in two sizes will take care of most screwdriving needs.

Granite slab

A true, flat, hard surface is invaluable for flattening plane soles and the flat face of chisels and plane irons. (Page 235)

Electric grinding wheel

These machines are ideal for rapid removal of larger quantities of steel to re-establish severely damaged cutting irons and chisels. (Photo on page 216)

No.80 Cabinet Scraper

For surface finishing, this tool is versatile and invaluable. (Photo on page 294)

Tool storage

Though technically non-essential to working wood the tool chest provides somewhere to safely store your tools. Remember that it must not only protect your tools but ideally it should also be convenient so that you can reach for your tools as you need them. Also remember it's important that the surfaces that your tools touch should not contain metal as this will dull the cutting edges. Line any metal drawers or surfaces around your work area and tool storage with a suitable material to protect your tools.

Shaping tools

Shaping wood is a large section of woodcraft and the tools that we use reflect the diversity of the subject. There are many hundreds of tools that are useful in shaping wood but only a few are truly essential. These are those tools. These tools will allow you to shape pieces from a single piece of wood or shape a part for a larger joinery piece. Whatever your woodworking project, you will find these tools indispensable.

Joinery tools

The tools used in joinery rely on each other for accuracy and efficiency. Most of the tools are never used alone but are used together for many aspects of work. Four of the tools are layout tools which are not used in the active working of the wood but provide critical accuracy for the other tools. These tools are truly a set and each tool is essential to making accurate joints.

Sharpening tools

Most of the above tools need regular sharpening to work effectively. This selection of sharpening tools will cover all of the sharpening needed for your edge tools, scrapers and saws. Sharp tools are a necessity. See chapters 11 to 18 for full sharpening instructions.

5 Introduction to shaping

This first part of the course is derived from a program for training children, my own children. I knew that if they could understand the substance of wood, from the growing tree first, they would better understand what wood is as an organic material. This is an important step to take before moving into the complexities of more advanced woodworking. It's sad that woodwork is often reduced to a production line of machine-made goods. We are learning how to manually work wood rather than just slot it into a precision machine and hit the green button. You'll sweat a little, scab and scar your knuckles, and may even work up a blister or two—but you'll be working the wood with your own hands and be in touch once again with real life. Wood has more to offer than a warm fire and beautiful grain. Culture is sustained by it, history is recorded in it, and landscapes are defined by it.

The spokeshave is the ideal entry-level woodworking tool for new woodworkers.

Woodworking usually begins with simple projects and builds in complexity the more we learn about it. I've trained children as well as adults to work with wood for more than twenty years, including my own sons. Each began with a spatula and a cutting board and progressed through spoon making and on to higher levels of complexity. By the time they were in their mid to late teens they had learnt the substantive woodworking skills I have enjoyed all my life. Little did I realize back then that when they were making a spatula and spoon they were really learning to make guitar necks and violins. My son, Joseph, now makes fine violins and cellos—arguably one of the highest levels of woodworking crafts.

"You'll be working the wood with your own hands and be in touch once again with real life"

Getting to know your hand tools

Many woodworkers embrace machine-only methods when they begin woodworking, believing that the old hand methods offer little more than poor results and hard work. Little do they realize that using machine-only methods dumbs down woodworking to a mere mechanical process. It denies the heights of excellence only possible when the human hand and eye take control of the hand tool and directs its course.

The list of tools below will enable you to complete all the elements and projects in the shaping section of the course. Planes are initially difficult to master, but through perseverance and practice comes proficiency. Chapter 14 page 231 provides detailed information on setting up and using your plane. You'll be amazed how many projects you can make with just a few basic hand tools. And if you look after them, these tools will last you a lifetime.

Some of these tools when they are well maintained, should be extremely sharp. Care should be taken when using them, and children should always be supervised.

FOUR-WAY RASP—This rasp and file tool has both curved and flat surfaces, cut in coarse rasp and smooth file patterns. It was the basic tool of farriers and blacksmiths for horseshoe fitting and hoof shaping, but woodworkers also rely on its combination of rough and smooth cutting capability in a single tool.

GOUGE—This is the only gouge you will need for these and dozens of other projects. Once sharpened, it will easily carve out scallops in spoons, bowls and chair and stool seats. A well-made gouge can be repeatedly sharpened and used for many decades.

SPOKESHAVE—I love all my woodworking tools, but none so much as the spokeshave. It provides immense versatility and is underestimated by most woodworkers. By removing either fine or thick shavings, it allows many different curved and straight shapes and profiles to be formed. It's also simple, fast and safe.

This is the shaping set

Four-way rasp

A wide gouge works best

Spokeshave

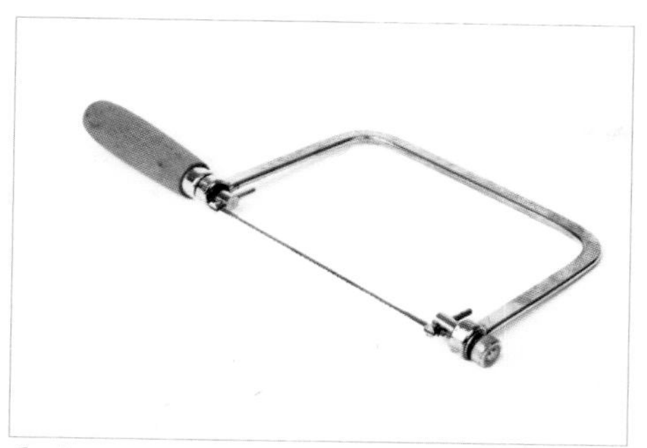
Coping saw

Curved and straight scrapers

This is a great general purpose panel saw

My tenon saw. I have a very fine set on this

My chisel set

My Stanley No. 4½ bench plane

I have dozens of these that all my students use

COPING SAW—A quality coping saw is fairly inexpensive and expands the realms of shaping wood, with its capability to make curved cuts. The back frame must be rigid and strong enough to resist the bending forces as it cuts.

A SCRAPER SET (curved and straight)—This is a tool many woodworkers consider unnecessary and yet those who know its function would never be without one. When sharpened and prepared correctly, these simple tools will deal with any type of wild grain in almost any wood. They can be shaped to specific contours and flexed to cut in small and confined areas. When a plane cannot deal with wild and awkward grain, the scraper can.

HANDSAW—I have included this saw because it aids so many areas of woodworking and is great for general-purpose use. With ten points per inch (10ppi), the teeth are fine enough to cut any wood at any angle, both with and across the grain.

TENON SAW—My favorite tenon saw is far more versatile than its name would suggest and can be used to cut anything that requires precision. For cutting smaller pieces to the right length, you'll find that this fine-toothed saw will cause very minimal splintering where the teeth exit the wood. I've reshaped the handle so it fits my palm perfectly.

CHISEL SET—My chisel set is fairly modern. I like the handle design and the steel quality gives me an edge I can rely on. There are so many makers that it's hard to recommend a particular one. Good, old chisels are available secondhand.

PLANE—Although I own a large collection of planes, my Stanley No. 4½ lives on my bench. This is the plane I reach for throughout my working day.

CHISEL HAMMER—This panel beater's mallet might seem an unusual choice of chisel hammer, particularly for an experienced craftsman. I use this every day and its weight and balance make it a joy to use.

Practice exercises

Before you get started on the projects, try out your tools on scraps of wood to get a feel for the way they cut and how you adjust them. Any scrap of 1" stock will work, but I suggest a softer wood like pine; about 3" wide and 10-12" long.

TECHNICAL POINTER: *New tools are not sharp tools; you may want to visit the sharpening pages before beginning the projects. Only three of the tools should need any special adjustment or preparation; the spokeshave, the plane and the scraper.*

Many of the shaping skills used to complete the following projects use the same tools, methods and techniques. Others are particularly pertinent to specific projects. I recommend that you practice cutting with and against the grain, and also try working the grain around knots with contrary grain. Try changing the orientation of the tools as much as possible to better understand how they affect the wood and how the wood responds.

Using the gouge

Gouges make up a broad section of curved chisels used for carving unique shapes in wood. Though dozens of shapes are available, most people rely on only a handful for most of their work. Make sure the practice piece is held securely in your vise before you start, and that it is held slightly proud of the jaws so you don't damage the cutting edge of the gouge.

Grip the handle firmly, and with the other hand further down the blade, dig lightly into the wood in a scooping movement, rotating slightly in a slicing action. Try cutting with and across the grain in scalloping movements, as this is the action we will use for carving the spoon, bowl and carved seat of the kidney-shaped three-legged stool. Make sure your gouge is well sharpened. Pretty soon you will feel confident as you work.

Using the chisel

Take a piece of pine, maybe 12 inches long and no more than ¾" thick and sketch an arc in the middle, about 1" deep and almost to the outer edges. At one end, sketch a rounded corner, use a teacup as a guide if you like. Using hand pressure and light mallet blows to your 1" chisel, cut to the lines you have just drawn. Keep the bevel up for straight and convex cuts on the corner, or bevel down for concave cuts creating hollows. Always work towards the middle of the arc.

Experiment with narrower chisels, too. Try chopping a series of cuts with a mallet to see how the cuts affect the wood. Look at the grain; feel how the darker, harder annual rings affect the chisel cuts. It's here that you'll discover the qualities of soft and hard wood growth, results of the changing seasons as the tree grew.

Using the spokeshave

To get a feel for the spokeshave try using it to smooth out the arc you just made with the chisel. Chamfer the corners and follow the arc. Adjust the depth of cut and take light and heavy passes. This tool takes a little mastering, but you can start tweaking the adjustments to suit the task.

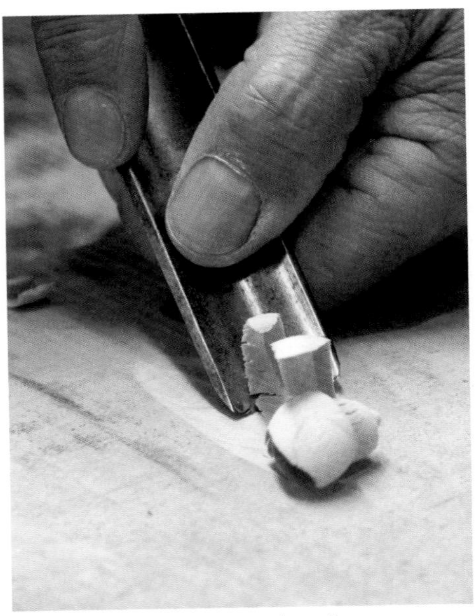

A sharp gouge leaves a smooth surface.

Mark the board to look something like this.

Practice carefully and stay above the line.

Continue to shape the board using the spokeshave.

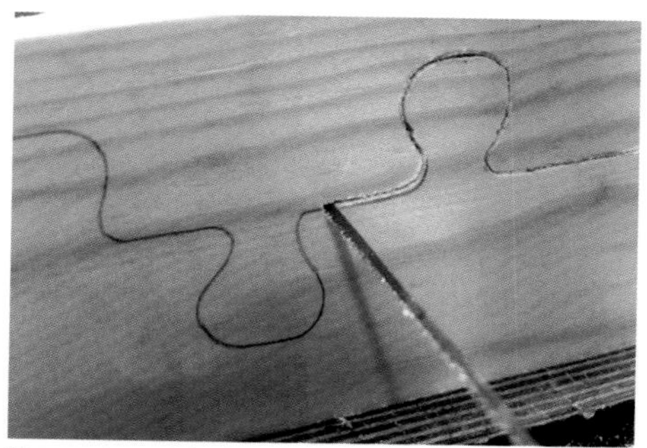

Try cutting to the lines.

If your spokeshave leaves marks on the wood it probably needs adjusting.

The vise is essential for almost all woodwork.

> *"You must sharpen all your edge tools regularly"*

Using the coping saw

It's generally accepted that a coping saw blade is installed in the frame with the teeth pointing toward the handle. I find it more practical to point the teeth away from the handle so that it cuts on the push (forward) stroke and this was the common practice of every furniture maker and joiner I ever knew. Try cutting using forward strokes first and then reverse the blade and use the pull strokes. The direction of cut depends on how the blade is installed in the saw frame—with teeth facing towards or away from the handle. The best practice technique is to free-cut, attempting turns and curves. If the teeth are not too large, these saws cut easily with or across the grain. Using the chisel to cut across the grain is sometimes difficult but a coping saw easily handles any shaped cross grain cuts. It's always best to mark the wood where you want to cut. Although this saw is designed to cut curved shapes, you'll find it equally valuable for cutting straight lines too. So, why not mark your wood with a few interesting shapes and try following the lines? You can turn the blade on its axis to cut sideways or upwards too. Enjoy experimenting.

Adjusting the tools

The tools you use require constant adjustments depending on the grain, grain direction and wood type. In these early stages, it's always good to practice adjusting the tools. Adjustments can be as simple as raising or lowering the angle of the chisel, or altering the depth of the spokeshave for light and heavy cuts. Exact adjustments are critical for precise workmanship so get used to how the tools respond by practicing on bits of scrap wood. Spokeshaves especially must be carefully adjusted or they dig in and gouge the work (see Chapter 14, page 255, for full instructions on troubleshooting your spokeshave). Work the spokeshave with and against the grain to gain a better understanding of what this means. You will see how going against the grain has a 'stroking-the-cat-backwards' effect on the wood. Also, note how angling the spokeshave to 45 degrees from the direction of travel changes how it cuts.

Edge tools must be sharpened frequently. Many woodworkers overlook this important preparation. It's only by using sharp edge tools regularly that we recognize when they are too dull to give truly pristine cuts.

Making templates

We make templates (or patterns) to trace around so we can be sure of accurate cut lines. It's a good idea to keep your templates in case you want to repeat a project. The set of templates included here may be photocopied, or traced over and transferred to a piece of card, thin plywood, or a rigid plastic. The plastic I often use comes from local sign writers. It snaps readily along scored knife lines and gives a clean line.

Holding your work

Vises, clamps and other devices such as bench dogs, holdfasts and hold-downs, will help hold your work securely as you chisel and shave the wood. Most hardware stores carry a variety of generic products, so balance value for money and suitability for the tasks you have in mind. Remember, they must be large enough and strong enough to provide both holding power and weight. Mail order catalogues offer a wide range of vises, clamps and dogging systems.

Making spatulas

Though totally functional, spatulas can also be admired as works of art. In fact, people are often reluctant to use them because of their beauty, especially with foods that raise and stain the grain. But beauty can be as much about function as aesthetics. Any well-used utensil develops value through use.

You can use just about any wood for making spatulas, but research to check it's safe for use with food as there are a few woods that can leak toxic substances. I stick with the fruitwoods, such as cherry or apple and pear, and also native woods such as oak, ash, bois d'arc, mesquite and a dozen or so others. Mesquite is my favorite. It has beautiful characteristic grain, as well as being twice as hard as oak and extremely durable.

Spatulas are useful kitchen tools that make great gifts for friends and relatives. You can complete one in an hour and it should last for 100 years. I use this project to introduce shaving and shaping skills. There are a couple of varieties for you to choose between. It's best to make the templates you need before you begin.

Quadrant spatula

To make the quadrant spatula, you will use many of the grain-tackling techniques we need for other projects, from spoons to violins, so it's useful to start here.

The quadrant spatula has a comfortable handle and is shaped around the head on one side only. It can be made as a left or right-handed spatula. This design came from one of my customers twenty-five years ago and I have been making them ever since. The quadrant shape fits the edge of bowls so is ideal for deep mixing and scraping. The hole is optional, but helps to disperse the ingredients being mixed more efficiently.

1. Begin by making a template. Cardboard will work fine if it's only going to be used for a few projects. For permanent templates I use the thin plastic used by commercial sign makers.
2. With a sharp pencil, draw around the template onto the blank.

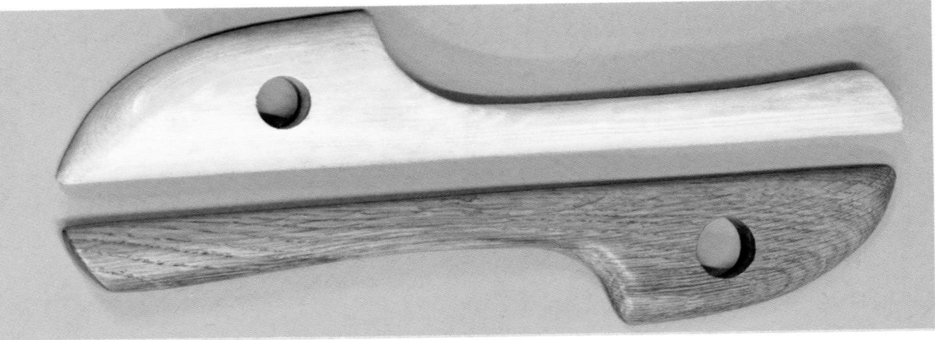

Use any non-toxic wood to make spatulas from.

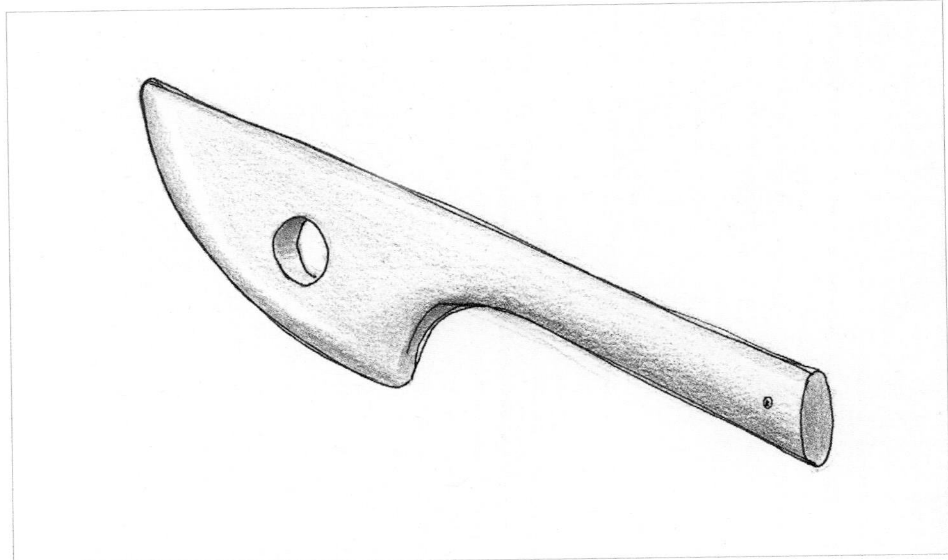

Shapes are unlimited once you master the skills.

Cut out the template with a sharp knife.

Trace the shape onto the spatula blank.

The coping saw cuts short cross grain well.

TECHNICAL POINTER: *Sawing close down to a line with a series of parallel saw cuts and removing the waste with a sharp chisel is what I refer to as the 'stop-cut' method.*

SAFETY TIP: *If you want to avoid younger children using a sharp 1" chisel, you can use the coping saw for initial shaping.*

Cut stop-cuts down to just above the depth line.

Remove the waste wood with the chisel.

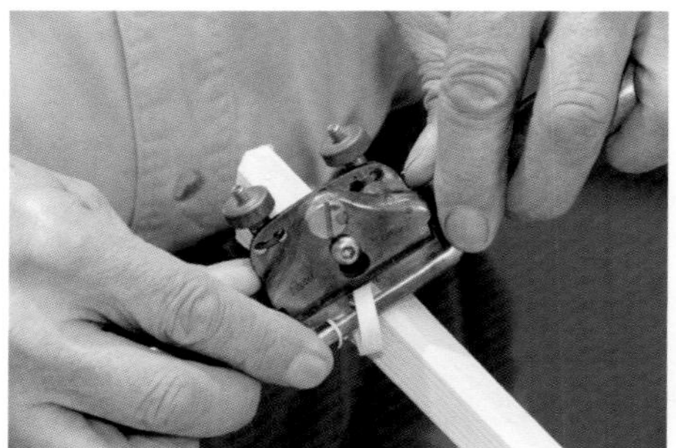
Remove the corners with the spokeshave…

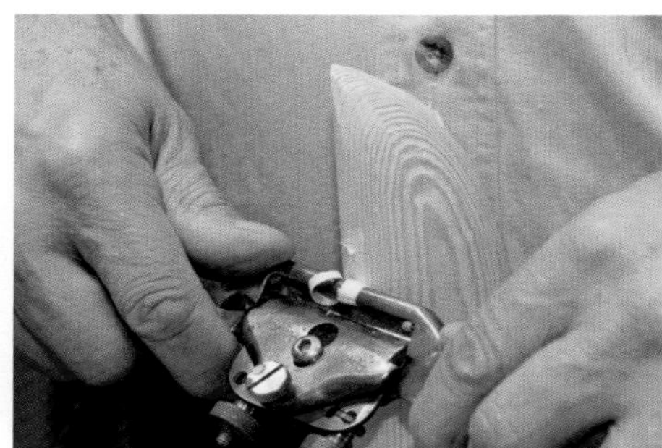
…and define the overall shape.

Refine the shape with a finely set spokeshave.

The four-way rasp is ideal for awkward end grain.

Bore with the brace and bit, but…

…only until the point of the snail protrudes.

Sand the final shape with 240 grit sandpaper.

Apply a suitable food-safe finish.

3. To cut out the shape, you can either use the coping saw and follow the profile lines, or you can make stop-cuts with the tenon saw—cutting close to but not into the profile lines—and then use the 1" chisel to cut away the waste. Remember, bevel down for concave cuts, bevel up for convex cuts. Look closely at the grain to determine which way to direct your chisel.
4. Use the spokeshave to remove the corners and shape the contours, choosing your direction by looking at the grain. Try not to cut the wood all the way to the flat face, stop maybe $\frac{1}{16}$"short. You can draw a pencil line around the edge using your finger as a guide, about $\frac{1}{16}$ from the edge, if that helps. Start with the head of the spatula and shape it fully before moving on to the handle. Once the head is shaped, wrap it in non-slip rubberized shelf liner to prevent movement in the vise.
5. Further refine the shape with a finely set cutting iron. Frequently alter the presentation of the spatula in the vise so you are always working comfortably. You can also use the four-way rasp in areas that are more difficult to reach with the spokeshave.
6. If you choose to bore a hole, make sure you don't go all the way through from one side, or the grain will tear out and look ugly. As soon as the threaded part of the bit protrudes slightly out of the other side, back off and reverse the presentation of the spatula in the vise. Locate the tip of the bit in the small hole and with care, finish the hole off.
7. With the shape finished, sand the final surface with 240 grit sandpaper.
8. Apply a little vegetable oil to bring out the color of the grain. Rub it vigorously with a clean cotton cloth to remove any excess oil.

You should now see how the skills learned here can be readily used to shape other kitchen utensils, and indeed create curved surfaces on all manner of other projects.

Making a round cutting board

Like spatulas, cutting boards can be any shape or size you like. I have provided a couple of examples, which will present some challenges. I suggest you work these shapes first and then expand the range with new designs of your own. The round cutting board is the first one to tackle. This project will help you understand the nature of grain, the versatility of the spokeshave and reinforce the stop-cut method you have learned.

1. Find the center of your square blank by making two diagonal marks from one corner to form an X. Create a circle onto the wooden blank with a compass and pencil. Make this circle as large as the size of the wooden blank will allow.
2. Use a 1" wide chisel and follow the profile, beginning at the lowest point on the long grain. You can of course use a coping saw for this too—in fact, it can be easier when removing sections directly across the grain. It's important to look closely at the grain to determine in which direction to direct the chisel.
3. If you need to use the four way rasp to remove any surface marks from the edge, use the smooth, flat file section to get a smooth polished finish all the way round. At this point, you can either go to the next step with a spokeshave or go to page 68 and see how you can use the round blank to make a three legged stool.
4. Use the spokeshave to round off all of the corners and contour the edges on both faces of the cutting board.
5. Sand the final surface with 240 grit sandpaper.
6. You can apply a little vegetable oil to bring out the color of the grain.

I use the same techniques used to make this round cutting board, for creating even complex shapes on fine furniture pieces. The stop-cut method is fast and accurate so always pay close attention to the direction of the grain.

A round cutting board made from softwood.

Lines from corner to corner cross at the center.

Use the compass to draw the circle line.

Align the chisel and cut following the line.

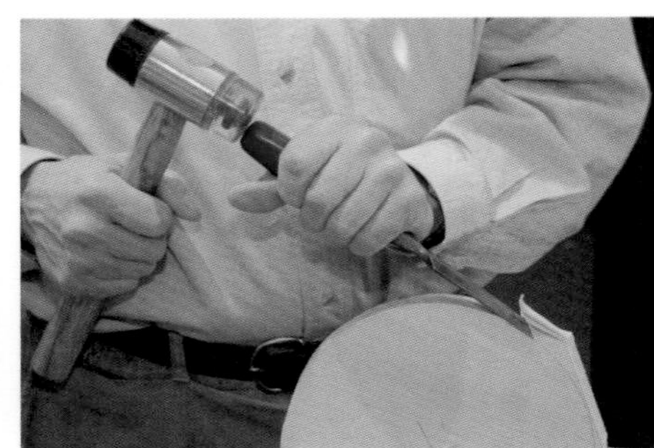

Repeat to each corner.

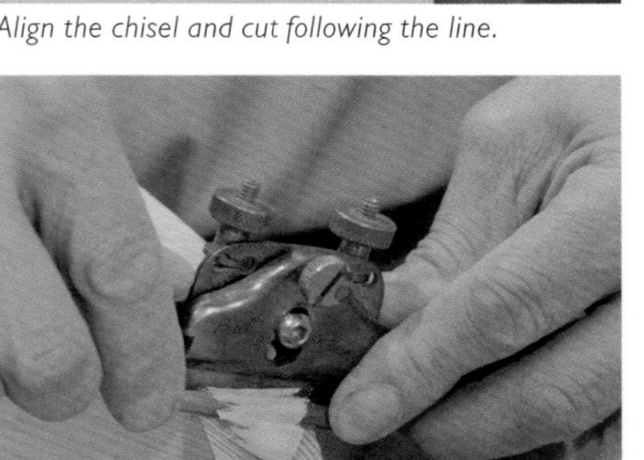

Use the spokeshave to remove any unevenness.

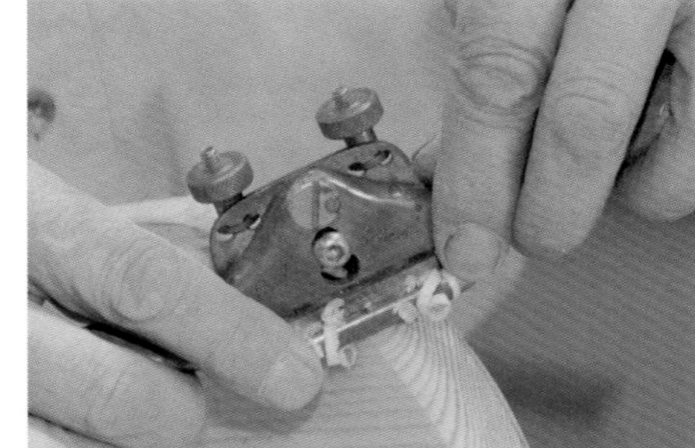

Round over the corners with the spokeshave.

Draw around the template.

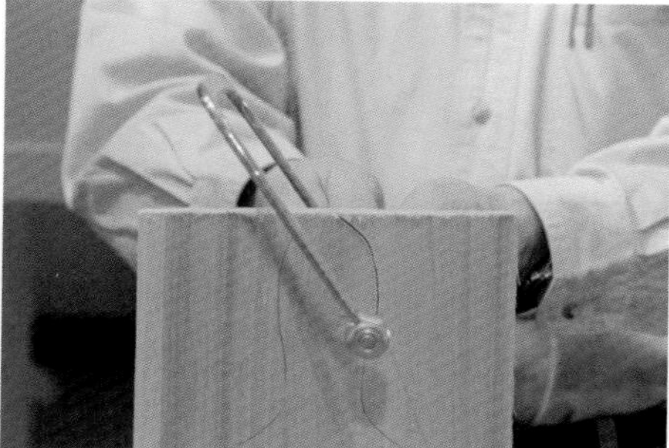
Use either the coping saw...

...or the stop-cut method to remove the waste.

Chop the waste with the 1" wide chisel.

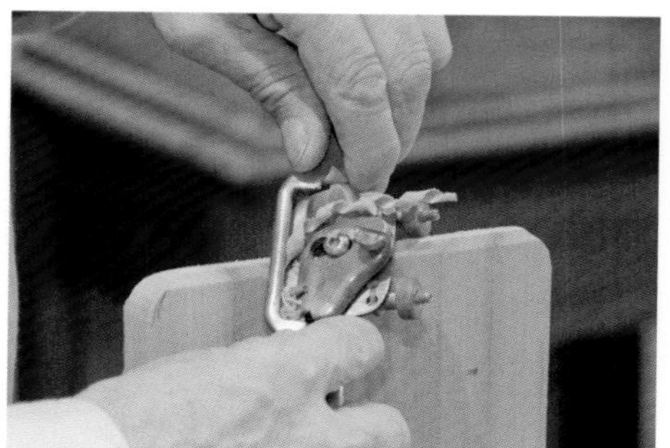
Round over the corners with the spokeshave.

Use the four-way rasp for awkward inside corners.

Sand with 240 grit sandpaper.

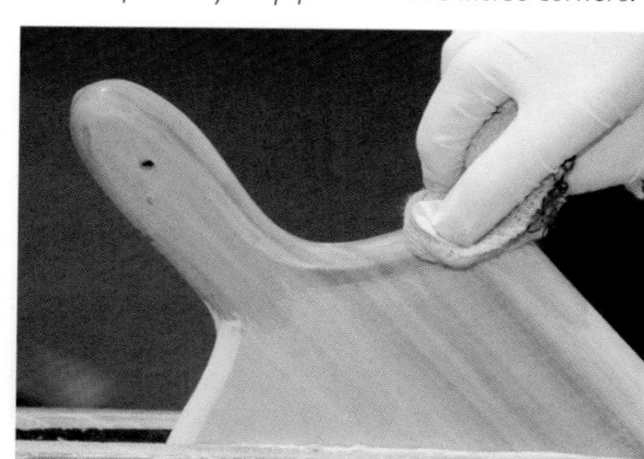
After sanding, apply a coat of food safe finish.

Making a rectangular cutting board

The handle makes this project more complex, but you will see how we use the 1" chisel to its fullest advantage. We also use the four-way rasp to deal with awkward internal corners and radiuses.

Shaping the cutting board is straight forward, but the handle adds an additional complexity. This will help you engage in more complex shapes used in more advanced projects. Begin by making a template from the pattern on page 320. An enlarged photocopy (200%) will give you a pattern of the right size.

1. With a sharp pencil, draw around your template onto the blank.
2. Cut out the shape using both the coping saw and the stop-cut method. Use a 1" chisel to follow the profile, beginning at the lowest point on the long grain. The coping saw can be easier when removing sections directly across the grain.
3. Use the spokeshave to round all of the corners and contour the edges on both faces of the cutting board.
4. For the internal corners, use the four-way rasp to tackle the awkward grain on the tight corners. The four-way rasp will also deal with all the end grain, allowing you to get a smooth finish.
5. With the shape finished, sand the final surface with 240 grit sandpaper and apply a little vegetable oil.

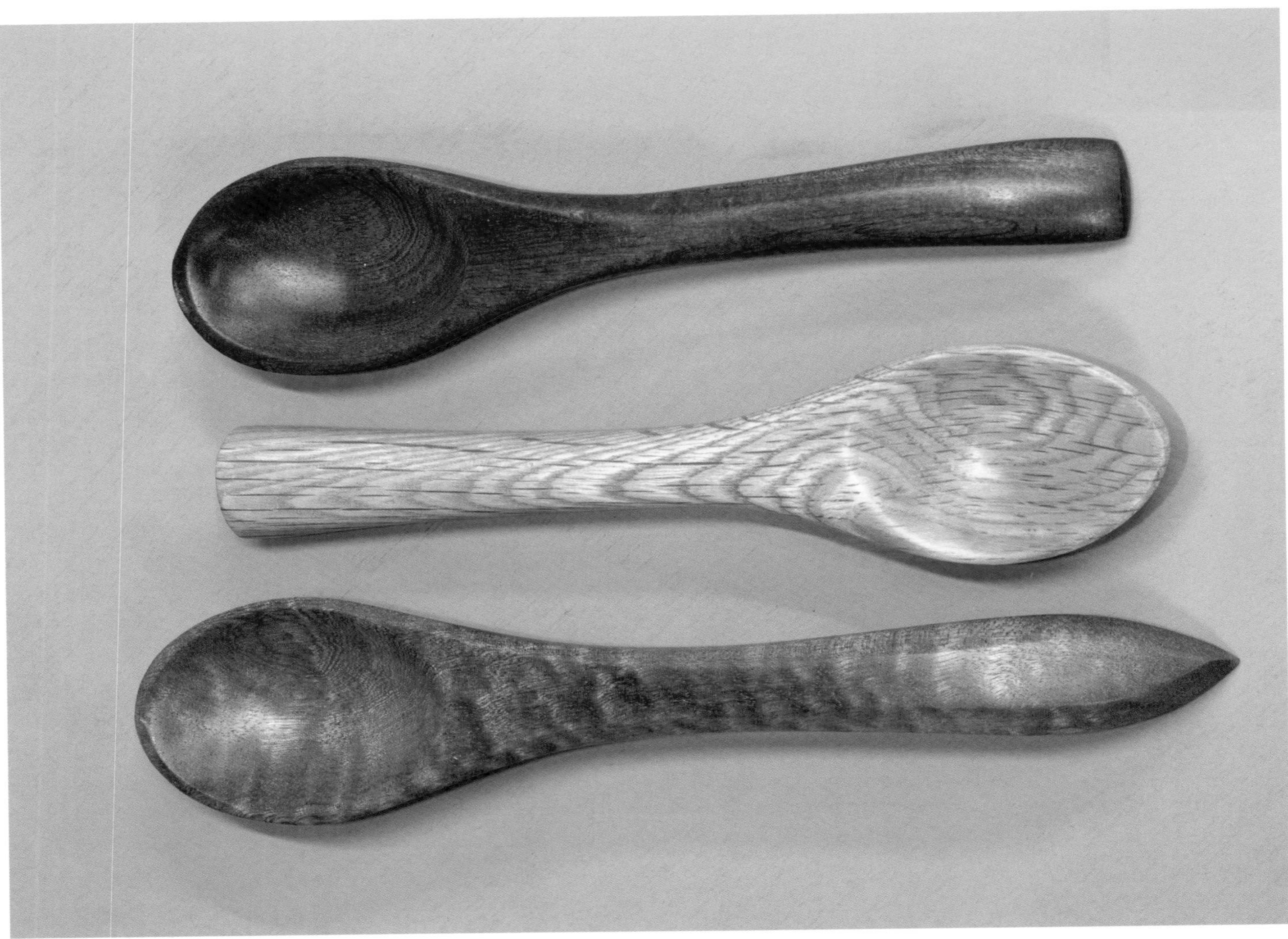

Making spoons

Spoons can be deep-bowled or shallow, and any size you like, depending on their intended use. The basic concepts remain the same for similar utensils such as dippers, ladles and salad servers. Working on spoons will present some challenges, but remember you are developing skills that will last a lifetime, including sharpening gouges and scrapers. If this is the first time you have used a gouge on a project, make sure it is razor sharp or you will tear the grain rather than slicing through it cleanly. If you are in doubt, go to the section on Sharpening Gouges on page 227.

Carving and shaping the bowl and the back of a wooden spoon is a great introduction towards eventually carving violin tops (belly) and backs. These skills are developed fairly rapidly; so don't be afraid to experiment working with the grain, changing the direction of your cuts.

You can use both the coping saw and the stop-cut chisel method to roughly shape any wooden spoon. Compare both alternatives, both going with and against the grain, as this will help you to understand grain structure and how best to tackle grain with hand tools. Be sensitive and ready to change direction if the cutting edge grabs and tears the grain.

Begin by making the template (see page 320) and drawing around it onto the blank. You must then mark the elliptical shape of the concave hollow (scallop) that you are about to carve.

TOP TIP: You may be tempted to make the spoon super thin and delicate, but in practice it will last longer if no part of the spoon is less than ¼" thick.

Begin by carving the bowl first. Work across...

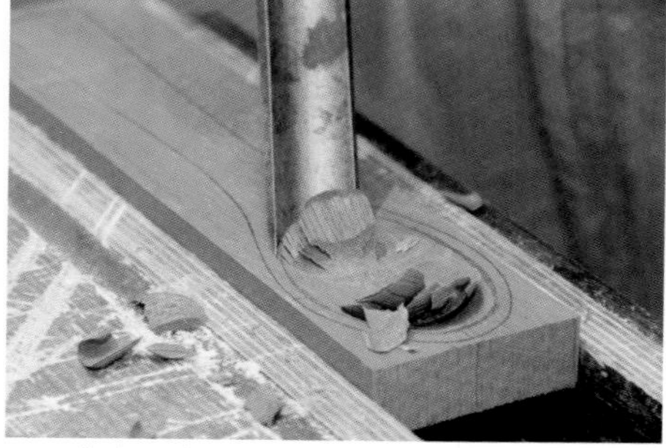
...and along the grain from both ends.

Use the round scraper to even out the bowl shape.

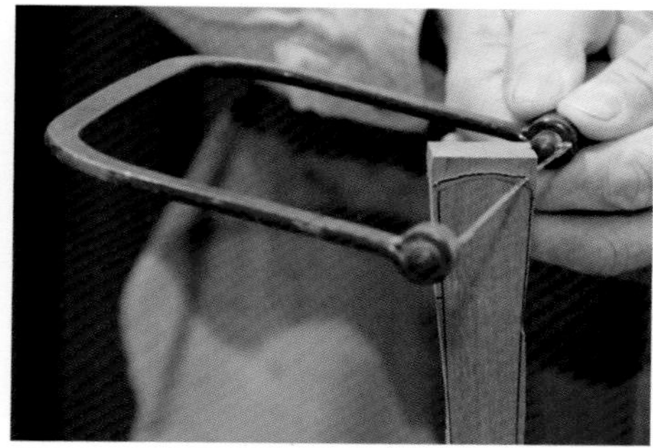
Shape with the coping saw and stop-cut methods.

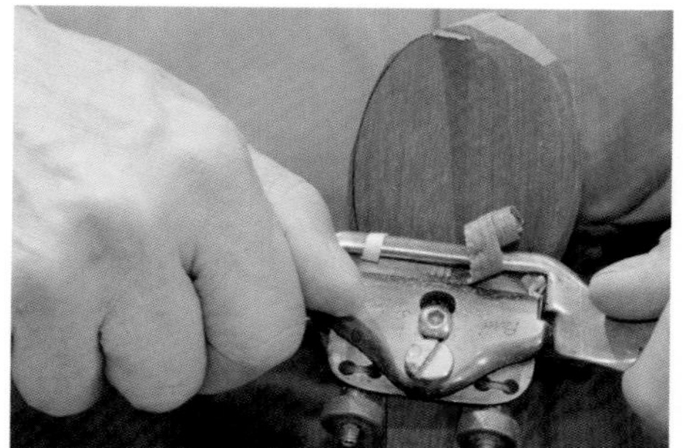
Spokeshave the spoon back with a heavy set...

...and further refine with a finer set.

Sand the overall spoon and apply vegetable oil.

Making carved bowls

The basic concept of carving bowls follows the same patterns as carving the spoon, but on a much larger scale. In carving and shaping this bowl you will use the same techniques violin makers use to carve a violin belly (top) and back. Begin by making an elliptical template (based on the curved line labeled 'Nut Bowl' on page 320) and drawing round it onto the blank. The project is scaleable so the absolute dimensions are not critical.

TOP TIP: Carving and shaping the bowl and the back of the bowl can require substantial pressure so be careful not to crack the bowl. Take care to apply as little pressure as necessary. I use a rubberized non-slip shelf lining on both sides.

Use a template to trace the corner of the ellipse.

Use the gouge across the grain to remove waste.

Work with the grain to refine the bowl shape.

The scraper evens out uneven cuts quickly.

Chisel the outside shape with a 1" chisel.

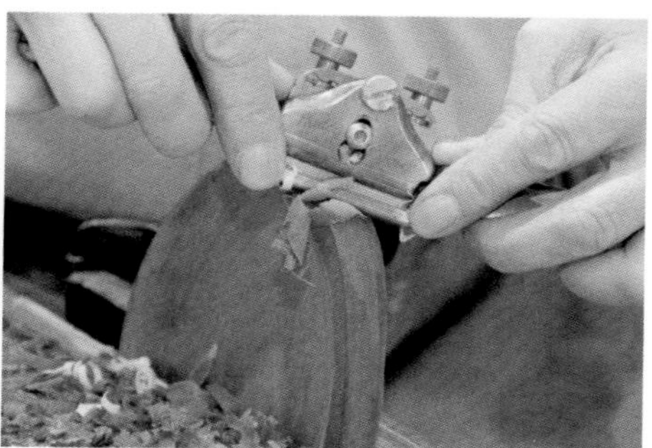
Spokeshave the shape evenly.

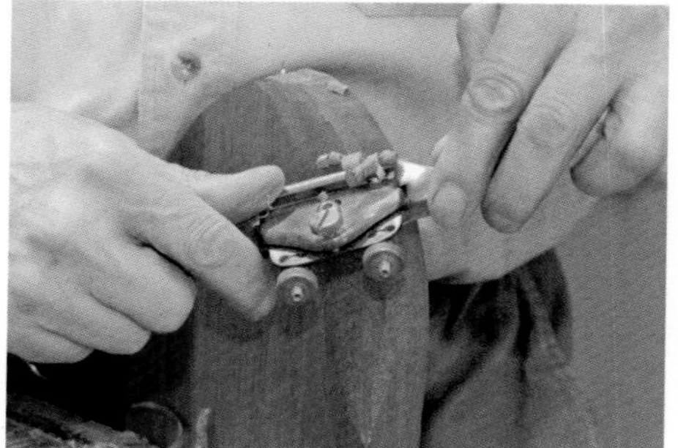
Refine further with a finer setting.

Sand inside and out before applying any finish.

1. Clamp the bowl blank in the vise and start cutting the bowl, initially by scalloping across the grain. You must work carefully and feel for the grain. Work down towards the center as you deepen the bowl. Try to work as evenly as possible and let the bevel of your gouge 'ride' the wood as you go deeper. You can work in all directions, providing you are working downhill towards the center, throughout the lower areas of scallop.
2. Use a curved scraper or sandpaper to smooth all unevenness in the bottom of the scalloped bowl and work through to 250 grit for the finished effect.
3. Cut out the shape with both the coping saw and the stop-cut method, using the same techniques and principles as for the spoon.
4. Use the spokeshave to remove all of the corners, perhaps using your file to smooth out the edges.
5. To shape the back, clamp the bowl in the vise firmly but with care and shape the contour of the back of the bowl. Slowly rotate the bowl in the vise so as to work on each section in turn.
6. When finished, sand the bowl all around, gradually progressing from 80 grit up to 250 grit sandpaper. Vegetable oil will bring out the color of the grain.

Making the three-legged stool

This traditional three-legged stool requires a variety of new skills. First, we will use the round blank described in step 3, page 62 to make the seat, laying out the position of the holes and boring them at an angle with the brace and 1" bit. Shaping the legs requires a first-level use of the plane, and we must learn how to set it up and use it.

Make a circle 1½" from the edge of the seat.

Use the same setting and step off six points.

Connect every other line to the centerpoint.

The layout will look like this.

In the vise, underside facing you, align the seat...

...and bore the holes from the same angle point.

Stop when the point of the snail pokes through.

Allow for the angle, and bore from the other face.

Making the seat

1. Take the round blank, set your compasses to 1½" from the edge of the seat, and draw a concentric circle on the underside of the seat, using the center point defined by the X. This circle ensures the legs will be equidistant from the center.
2. Use the same compass setting to step marks round the circle you have just made. Erase every other one of the six marks, which will accurately divide this circumference into three equal parts. These three points are the positions for the 1" diameter holes to be bored for the legs. Now mark a line between the center and each of these three marks.

> **TECHNICAL POINTER:** *Notice the position of the holes in relation to the grain. The first hole should be centered along the grain line, with subsequent holes corresponding to this first hole position.*

3. Clamp the seat blank in the vise. The three marks for the holes are in the shape of a triangle. Arrange the first mark as the uppermost apex of the triangle.
4. Working from the underside of the seat, position the point of the auger on the first mark. Start by holding the brace and auger horizontally and **lifting the pad of the brace about two inches**. Bore the first 1" diameter hole. **Do not bore all the way through from this side**. When the thread (snail) of the bit shows, turn the blank around and, allowing for the angle of the hole, complete the boring of the hole from the topside of the blank.
5. Repeat for the other two holes, rotating the blank so that the marks are at the apex before boring the holes. Remember to lift the pad by two inches before you start each hole. This will ensure the legs have all got a symmetrical splay.

6. You now need to chamfer both top and bottom edges of the seat. The chamfer on the top edge needs to be about ¼" and on the underside, make it about ½". This lightens the appearance of the stool and makes it look less 'clunky'. You can mark lines to guide you by just using your finger as a guide and running pencil lines accordingly.
7. Use the spokeshave to remove the corners and create a very even chamfer all the way around both edges of the seat. This lightens the appearance of the stool.
8. Use the hand plane or sandpaper to smooth both surfaces.

The angle at which you bore is open to personal preference. To save time, I generally position the pad (handle) of the brace at a point on my stomach or chest, as shown on the previous page. I use the same method on all the legs, this ensures that they come out at the same angle.

Gauge a ½" parallel line on the underside face...

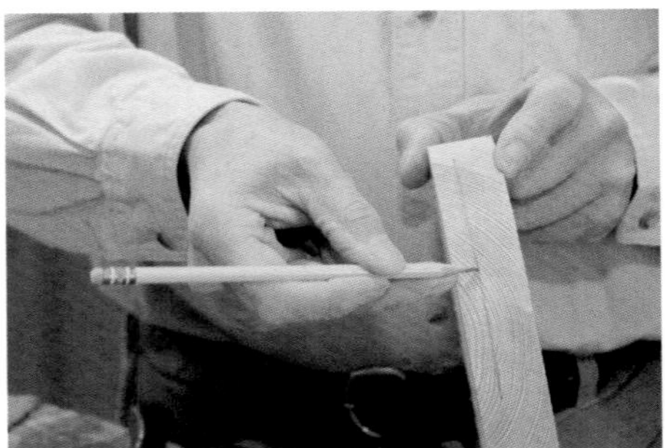

...and also onto the edge.

Do the same on the topside corner, this time ¼".

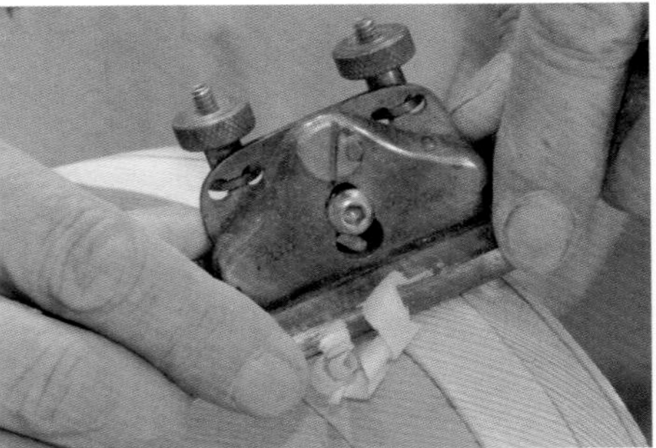

Chamfer the under edge with the spokeshave.

Work with the grain, all around, following the lines.

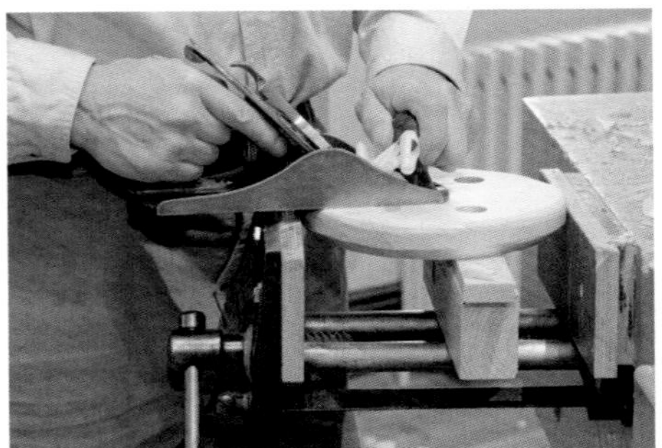

Surface plane the seat if needed to remove marks.

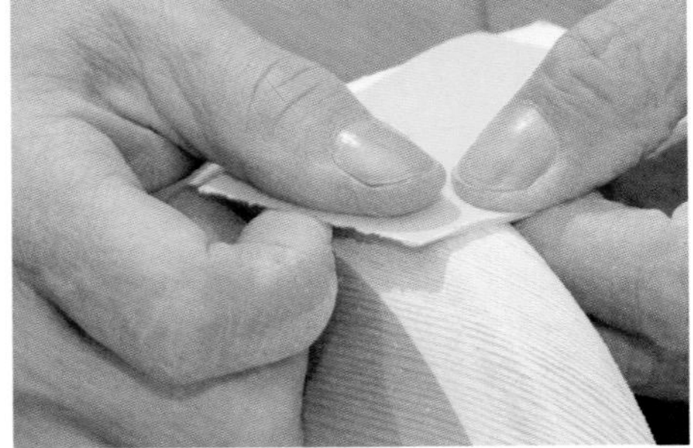

Now sand all the surfaces to a smooth finish.

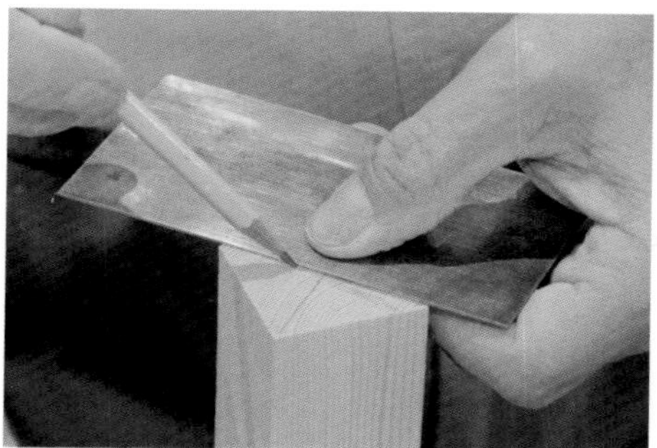
Corner to corner lines give the center of each end.

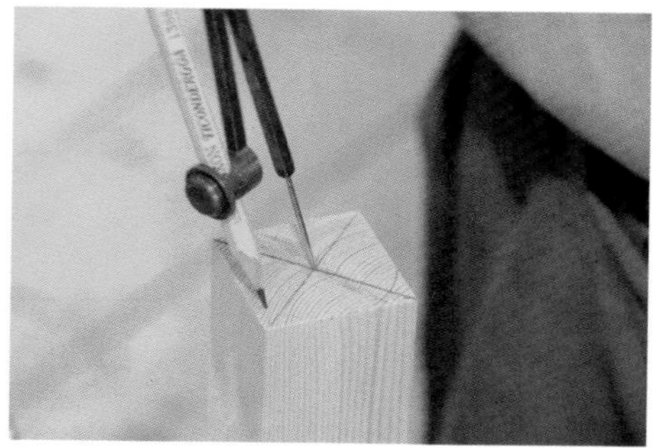
On one end of each leg make a full diameter circle.

On the other, a 1" diameter disc works best.

Make parallel lines to each edge of the circle.

Lay out the taper on two opposite faces only.

Taper the legs with the axe...

...the saw...

...or the plane. Plane all surfaces straight.

Set up a clamp in the vise as shown.

Tapering the legs

1. Find the centers of the top and bottom of the legs by drawing lines from corner to corner.
2. Use the compass to draw a circle onto one end of the leg. This circle is the full width of the leg.
3. On the opposite end, because the legs will be tapered, the circle diameter should be 1". You can either set the compass to 1" diameter, ½" radius, or use a 1" diameter coin or washer.
4. Using your finger as a gauge, draw lines across the end grain, parallel to each edge and just touching the 1" circle.
5. Using a straight edge, draw the taper onto two opposite sides of the leg and on both opposite faces.
6. Now taper the leg. There are three ways to do this: Using an axe, a saw or a plane. If using the axe or the saw, you must plane the rough surface smooth, right down to the lines.
7. Do the same to the adjacent faces so that all four faces taper the same. The leg is now tapered and therefore more difficult to hold but by clamping one end in the vise and placing a scrap under the other end, you can successfully plane the opposite faces.

The legs should now have a taper to all four sides. The next step is to chamfer the corners and round them completely to a perfectly tapered leg. Holding a tapered shape in a vise is difficult, so place a long clamp in the vise to grip the leg from each end.

Final shaping of the legs

1. Chamfer the corners along the length using the hand plane. Because the legs are tapered, you will need to plane a narrower chamfer towards the narrow end. To do this, simply start at the narrow end and take successively longer strokes all the way up to the wider end. Plane down to the circle guidelines on each end.
2. Work all of the corners until they are round and evenly tapered along the length.
3. It's important that you fit the end of the leg into the hole without creating too much taper. Offer the tapered end into the hole to check for fit, and remove just enough material from the round to accommodate it. Once it fits fairly tightly and enters the hole by about ¼", begin shaving the round to create a parallel end that will fully enter the hole. To do this, work from the main body of the leg towards the end, but raise the heel of the spokeshave so you don't take off any shaving towards the end of the cut so that you do not make the rounded end too small.
4. Keep offering the tapered leg into the hole, looking for shiny bruise spots to guide you. These shiny spots are the 'high spots' that must be reduced slightly. The end of the leg should fit tightly, only protruding enough to allow for a flush-cut after wedging and gluing.

Remove the corners with the plane.

Use the end circles as a guide for the plane.

From the end, spokeshave the leg to fit the hole.

Offer the leg into the hole.

Bruising from the hole guides further shaping cuts.

Make a saw kerf in the tenon end of the legs.

Cut long tapered wedges from 1" stock.

Glue the tenon and insert in the seat with a twist.

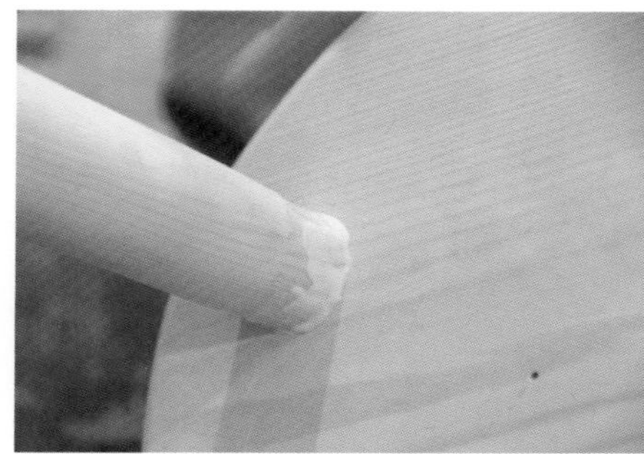
Tap home with the hammer, aligning the kerf.

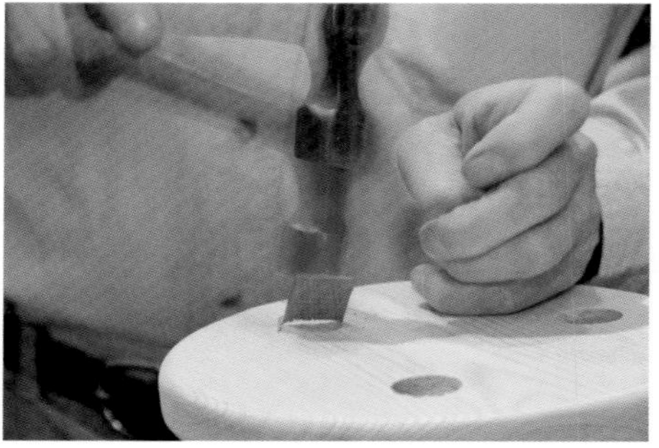
Check kerf alignment and drive the wedges home.

Wedged legs look like this.

Remove the protruding end with a sharp chisel.

Apply a sealer coat of shellac and finish to suit.

Gluing up

1. We secure the legs using wedges. Mark each leg with a single line across the diameter, and extend the lines down the leg about 1⅛" Cut down these lines with a tenon saw. The wedges should be cut from 1" thick stock and about 1½" long. You can use a contrasting wood for appearance, but any wood will suffice.

> **TECHNICAL POINTER:** *The wedges must be orientated at 90 degrees to the grain run of the seat or they will split the seat.*

2. With the saw cuts completed, apply a film of glue to the end of the leg and insert it fully into the hole. You can tap the foot of the leg with a swift knock to fully position the leg and express any excess glue. Line up all the saw cuts at 90 degrees to the grain of the seat.
3. Turn the stool over and, with the foot of the leg on a firm surface, apply glue to both sides of the wedge and drive it in until it feels solid. Watch out—if you drive the wedge in too hard, it can split the seat.
4. Use the tenon saw to cut the leg down. I suggest you cut slightly above the surface of the stool and plane it down flush; otherwise you will dig into the surface of the seat with the saw teeth.
5. The next day, trim off any glue residue with a sharp chisel, and give the stool a good sanding, always in the same direction as the grain.
6. Apply a protective finish of your choice. I use shellac as a sealer coat for applying all other finishes including water-based paints and varnishes.

Making a kidney-shaped three-legged stool

The kidney-shaped three-legged stool requires the same skills learned in making the round three-legged stool, with the added techniques of shaping a scalloped Windsor chair-type seat. We will show how to lay out and bore the angled seat holes and align them for boring with the brace and 1" bit. Instead of using shaped inshaves to shape the scalloped seat area, we will use the gouge; a common method used in chair making.

Materials list:

SEAT: 1 @ 1½" x 10" x 15"

LEGS: 3 @ 1½" x 1½" x 11"

Use a template to layout the seat shape.

Use a 1" chisel to remove the waste.

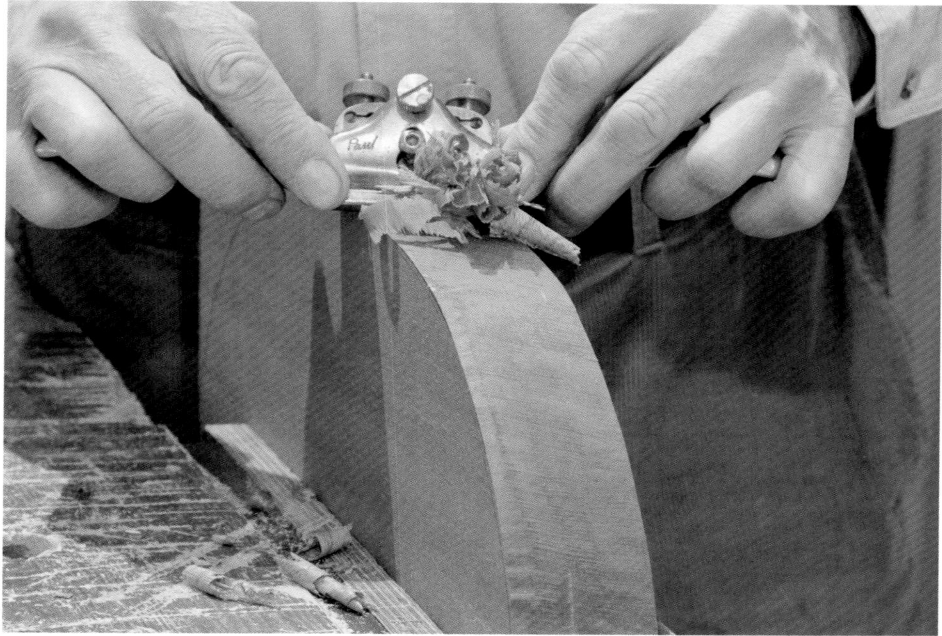

Refine the shape using the spokeshave.

Run a pencil line 1½" from outside corner edge.

Square a line from front to back in the center.

From the center of the seat, draw two lines.

The layout lines look like this.

Making the seat

1. Begin by drawing a symmetrical shape onto your blank. The front corners are quadrant and the back corners are elliptical. The exact shape is not critical. With the seat blank clamped securely in the vise, cut it to shape.

TOP TIP: *When using the spokeshave to shape the seat of this stool, try to develop your spokeshaving technique as you work towards the line. Don't take off too much wood at first and if you are not getting a smooth surface, back off the blade to take a finer shaving. Make small adjustments as you work and if the spokeshave is not moving smoothly and evenly over the surface of the wood try moving the spokeshave at an angle to direction of the cut. You can also make small adjustments by slightly lifting the heel of the spokeshave so that you are reducing the amount of material you are taking off.*

2. Use a flat-bottomed spokeshave to level and even out the chisel cuts as you work down to the line.
3. To prepare for boring the holes, measure 1½" in from the rim of the seat and use your finger to draw an offset line following the shape of the seat blank—on the underside only. This marks the distance from the edge for the leg holes.
4. Square a line in the center of the seat blank from front to back. The point where this line intersects the offset line gives you the position of the back leg hole.
5. Next, take a piece of wood with a straight edge and place it so as to join the dead center to the front corner of the stool. Draw a heavy pencil line. Repeat for the other side. The front leg holes will now be bored where these lines intersect the offset line.

6. Clamp the seat blank in the vise, with the hole position mark directly above the dead center mark. This ensures that all the legs splay from the dead center outwards.
7. The angle at which you bore is open to personal preference. To save time, I generally position the pad of the brace on my chest about 2" above the horizontal. When I bore the other holes, I use the same method and the legs come out at the same angle.

TECHNICAL POINTER: *Do not bore all the way through from this side.*

8. Bore the first 1" diameter hole working from the underside of the seat. When the point (snail) of the bit shows, turn the blank around and, allowing for the angle of the hole, complete the boring of the hole from the topside of the seat blank.

Each guide line should be perpendicular.

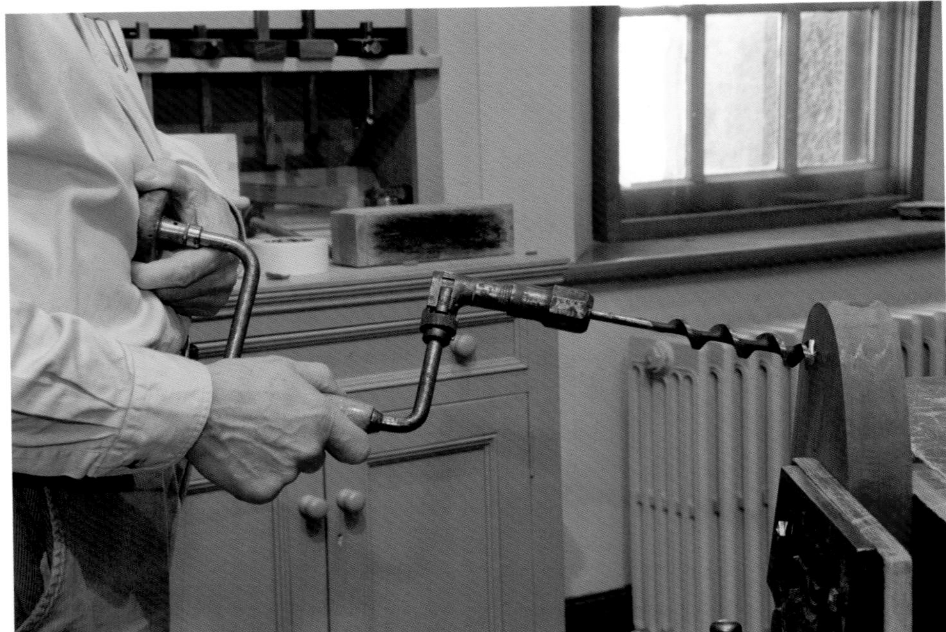

Find a reference point on your body for the brace angle.

Mark a line around the seat, 1" from the edge.

Mark the centerline of the front edge.

Mark ½" down for scalloped leg area of the seat.

Use the gouge cross-grain to cut out the scallop.

Work cross-grain from both sides.

A rounded scraper evens out the unevenness.

Follow steps 7-8 to chamfer the corners of the seat.

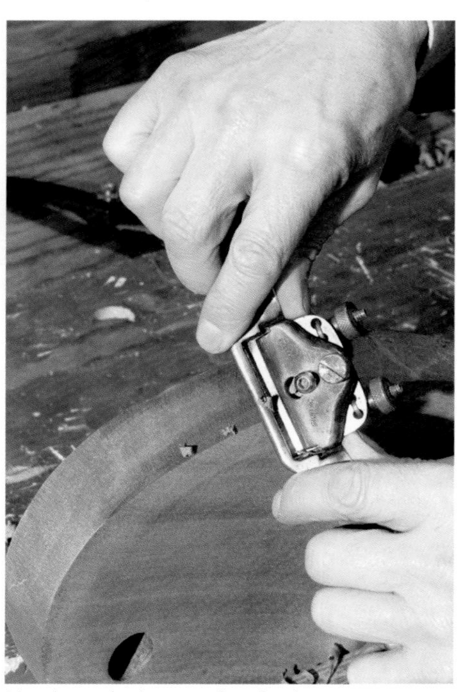
Use the spokeshave to chamfer the seat corners.

Carving the seat scallop

1. Use your finger as a guide to run an offset line around the top face of the seat, 1" from the edge. This marks the outer limit for carving the seat scallop.
2. Find the center between the two ends and square a line across the seat. This line is the centerline for the raised area in the seat carving.
3. Make a depth mark on the front edge of about ½", which gives the depth of the seat scallop, and pencil a curve to make the transition from the seat rim to the ½" depth line.
4. Carve cross-grain with the bowl gouge from one side to the other, outlining the rim of the seat all the way around. Work evenly, as this can be hard to correct later. Refine all of the cuts as you complete the gouge work.
5. Use a curved scraper to remove all gouge marks from the scallop.
6. Sand the scallop with 250 grit sandpaper.
7. Using your finger as a guide, run a pencil mark on the underside of the seat ½" from the edge. Create a second mark on the bottom of the edge, also ½".
8. Repeat this on the top and top edge of the seat but this time at a smaller distance of ¼".
9. These lines mark the size of the bevels on the edges of the seat. To make the bevels use the spokeshave at a 45 degree angle to remove the corners and create a chamfered edge. This lightens the appearance of the stool.
10. Use the hand plane or sandpaper to smooth both top rim and bottom face.

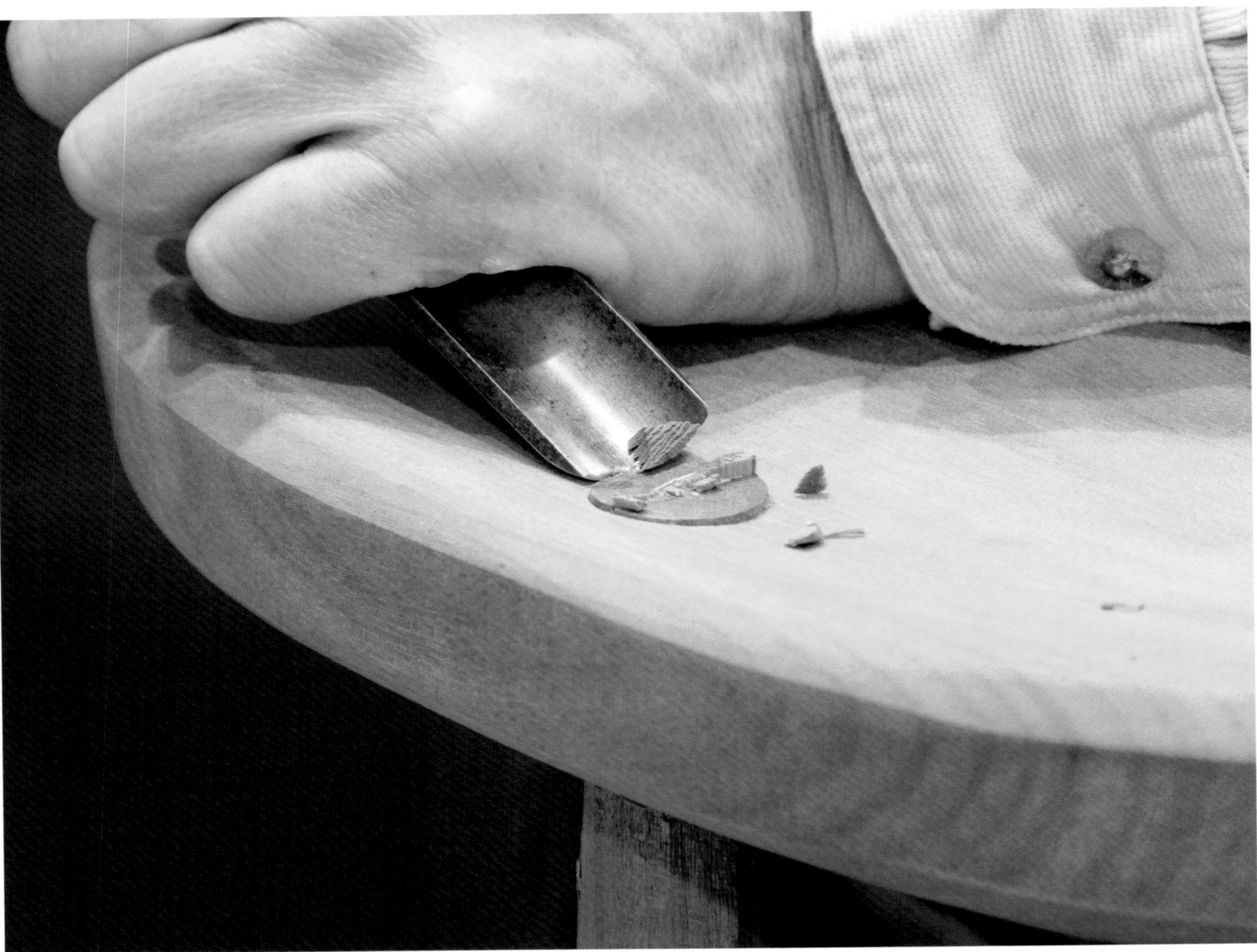

A gouge removes waste from the protruding tenon ends and follows the seat cove too.

Making the legs, gluing up

Use the same process for making, shaping and tapering the legs, and for gluing up, as for the three-legged stool, but when you come to trim off the protruding legs and wedges it is best to use a gouge as shown rather than a tenon saw because of the shape of the curved seat.

We used only three hand tools to scallop the contoured seat.

Conclusion

We commonly refer to three-legged stools as milking stools. Milk barns generally had dirt or cobblestone floors, both uneven. A three-legged stool is steady on a cobbled floor, whereas a four-legged stool will rock unless it's on something dead flat.

Completing this stool provides the perfect introduction to the art of chair making. Although it is still early days, your levels of skill and understanding are already developing. Shaping wood is the essential skill you can now use in most areas of woodcraft. You can practice further by making stools of different proportions, bowls of varying shapes and a range of kitchen implements. Each time, the tools will become more familiar, as will the behavior of the grain. It's liberating to begin imagining how the skills you now have can be adapted for other types of work.

6 Joinery

For centuries craftsmen have used a wide range of joints for thousands of different structures. In choosing which joint to use, they consider the natural properties of the wood, methods of construction, special project features and, most importantly, the mechanical and structural strengths of the joints themselves.

An old kitchen table in Penrhyn Castle

"an interesting journey, discovering skills you thought were unattainable and a confidence you've never before taken hold of."

Though joinery—the craft of joining wood—is recognized as a specialist field throughout woodworking, it forms an important part of woodworkers crafts. Furniture makers, boat builders, violin makers, carpenters and many more tradesmen all use the same tools to make the same joints. Although there are some notable variations, the way we work with tools is governed more by the nature of wood itself, than any personal preferences of the artisan.

Because of the organic nature of wood, which changes with moisture and temperature, joints must be used that not only provide structural strength but they should also allow flexibility and movement. Joints must be either oriented so that they allow all parts to expand and contract equally; or specifically designed as framed structures in which parts move only minimally.

In this section you will learn to create the basic version of every joint that is essential to woodcraft. It will also provide an overview for the application of these joints. This section puts in place a foundation upon which I have built this entire course. These joints, although simple, will enable you to make structural frames, such as those used in chairs, tables and doors, and box frames such as those used in drawers, chests and bookshelves. By using sharp tools, accurate layout, and the techniques I describe, you will soon discover that hand cutting joints is not a time-wasting chore, but an interesting journey discovering skills you thought were unattainable and a confidence you've never before taken hold of.

My ten joinery tools

There are hundreds of different types of tools available to woodworkers—including some that were developed or partially developed centuries ago. Because old tools often work as well or better than their modern-day counterparts, we cannot simply dismiss them as archaic or obsolete. For new woodworkers, it's not so much a question of deciding between old and new, but more a question of what's practical. Some better quality modern tools are less problematic for those starting out in woodworking. I use both modern and old tools (some ancient), because I choose them according to how they feel and behave, not according to how they look.

The most important realization for any woodworker embarking on this course, is that a relatively small number of tools will enable you to carry out all aspects of joinery work. If you have the following tools, sharpened up as required, all within easy reach on your workbench, you are ready to learn to tackle any joinery work for any project.

Combination square

Measuring tape

Sliding bevel

Layout tools

My layout tools account for half of my joinery tools. It is with these that I establish the basic dimensions of components, their relative positions within each project and the joint details that will give the project strength, shape and structure. Each tool is indispensable.

Combination square

The square is the ultimate reference tool. It can be used to create reference marks using the pencil or knife, or it can be used as a gauge to check that components are square and whether they are correctly aligned. The combination square has the added advantages of having faces aligned at 90 or 45 degrees, and the hardened beam means you can run a marking knife along the edge without cutting into it or causing undue wear to the edge. The beam also has a graduated ruler, which is useful for measuring and layout.

This, my first entry in the list of essential tools, may at first glance seem to be of low priority, but all other tools take their reference from the square. Without perfect accuracy, it is of little use to a craftsman. A square must be accurate, finely crafted and totally reliable.

Measuring tape

Tapes have replaced traditional flat, rigid rules. A craftsman working alone can tolerate minor inaccuracies because his measurements come from the same reference point. That said, find an accurate measuring tape so that every measurement you make is as accurate as possible. Tapes made by Starrett and Veritas have always proven accurate in my experience.

A steel retractable tape measure is compact, precise and versatile. I find that a 10' (3m) tape takes care of most of my work. Longer tapes are often too cumbersome for bench work. Different tapes are available for left and right-handed people, and with large numbers for ease of reading.

Sliding bevel

We use sliding bevels to establish and transfer angles to the workpiece and check the angles correspond to the design. I often use two or three on the same project, so most woodworkers own more than one.

In the same way that we use a square to establish true 90° or 45° angles, we use a sliding bevel for tasks where any other angle is required. This is the most efficient means of accurately laying out angled shoulder cuts, dovetails (unless you have a template), and to ensure that angled components correspond perfectly. I have a few with a composite plastic stock. They work fine, but I still prefer the solid wood stock over any other type because I like the balance between the wood and steel blade.

As with many tools, a range of sizes is available, according to the task in hand. I often need to measure angles in confined spaces, so I prefer smaller sizes. A 6" sliding bevel makes a good starter size.

Layout knife

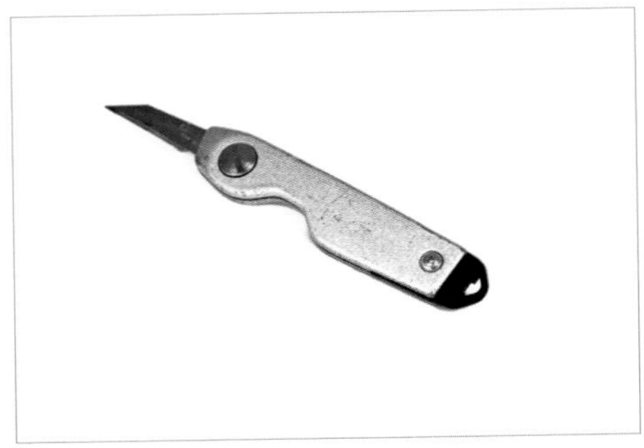

Layout knife

We use layout knives to establish all cross-grain cut lines, generally known as shoulder lines. These knife cuts must be absolutely accurate, and the only way we can guarantee this accuracy is if the knife-edge and point are surgically sharp.

My favorite layout knife is the Stanley 10-049 pocketknife. It has a long finely pointed blade that's adequately strong and ideal for cutting knifewalls, and its length makes it perfect for reaching into tight spaces to create marks for tail and pin recesses for dovetailing. Regular utility knives also work, but are too cumbersome for finely detailed work and visibility is restricted due to the size of the blade, and the stout, bulky handle.

Straight chip-carving knives also work well. I have a few home made ones and I occasionally use these, too.

Combination gauge

Combination gauge

This gauge combines the two most commonly used gauges into a single tool, which works well and is perfect if you are beginning in woodworking. Later on, for convenience, you'll find a few dedicated gauges work best simply because most projects require gauges to be set and left unaltered throughout the duration of a project.

People often find the gauge awkward in the hand. It feels very different to a hammer or a screwdriver, which most people are generally familiar with. Practice on a scrap of wood. See how much pressure it takes to lightly mark the surface rather than gouge it. Get used to holding it and using it effectively. Be careful not to dig the points in as hard as possible on your first pass.

Other Tools

You may have noticed that the photo showing all my essential tools and equipment (Chapter 4, page 53), separates the shaping tools from the joinery tools. However, the following tools (apart from the router plane) are actually common to both sets and I will discuss them here in the context of joinery work.

Tenon saw

Tenon saw

Most tenon saws are between 8" and 16" long, but they can be even longer. Different lengths of saw are generally used for different functions. We sharpen these saws to cut both with (along) and across the grain. I use a tenon saw for most of my tenon and dovetail joints. Brass-backed saws usually have thicker spines than those with steel ones, so tend to be heavier than steel-backed versions, but there is minimal difference in functionality. I like to use both steel and brass-backed saws. This one has 14 points per inch (See Chapter 15, pages 260 and 275 for more information on this), which I find ideal for nearly all of my joinery work.

Chisel set

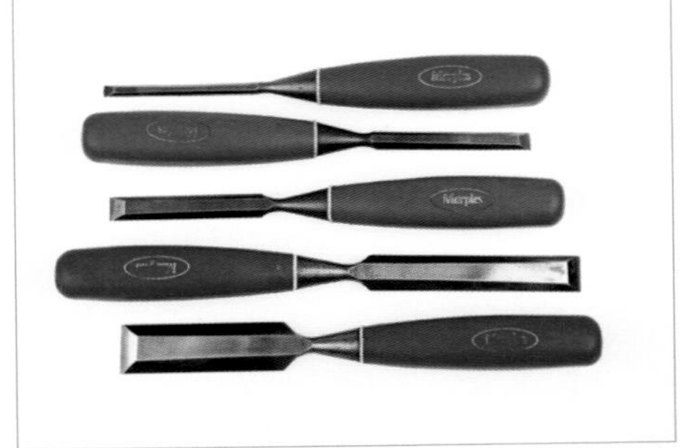

Chisel set

A chisel set usually comprises a set of five chisels, with a handle and a steel blade. They are typically sized in ⅛"increments between ⅛" and 1", the most common sizes are ¼", ⅜", ½", ¾", and 1". We use them for splitting, chopping and paring actions, to shape wood and cut joints.

Though a few manufacturers still produce wooden-handled chisels, most now use plastic. New woodworkers find the vast array of chisels confusing, so let me simplify exactly what you need. For forty-five years I've used only bevel-edged chisels for all my work. I own many chisels and have fine mortise chisels that chop mortises very well, but I still prefer bevel-edged chisels simply because they take half the effort to cut twice as deep in half the time. Steep angled, full mortise chisels will take a good beating, but more often than not, beating isn't really what is needed. See chapter 11, page 203 , on sharpening hand tools, and you will understand why more force is not the answer.

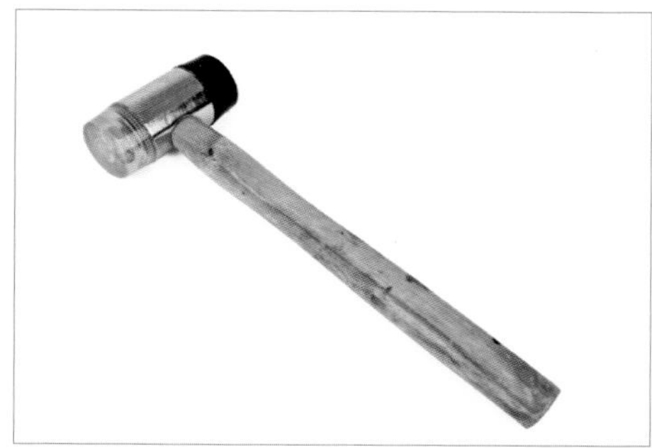
Chisel hammer

Chisel hammers

Many years ago, I would use a hard wooden mallet as my only tool for striking chisels, and I still use a mallet these days for heavier work. Some time back, however, I reconsidered my traditionalist view. After experimenting with different mallets and hammers I found that the best one was an inexpensive panel-beater's hammer, like the one shown.

Today, I like the versatility of this type of chisel hammer, so this is what I recommend. Hammers like this usually have a softer face, ideal for project assembly. The hard, shatterproof plastic face works well for direct impact with minimal absorption, which means it delivers the full and direct energy to the chisel for chopping mortise holes. Look for a chisel hammer that has a good weight and balance with a well-shaped oval handle. About a 20-24oz weight seems best for furniture making.

My Smoothing plane

Smoothing plane

Smoothing planes are centuries old and span many woodworking crafts. They are short-soled planes that require super-sharp irons to cut surface fibers to a pristine finish. We also use smoothing planes for a wide range of support tasks, from localized surface leveling between jointed components to rounding over the edges of shelves, windowsills and box lids. No single other plane can perform all the tasks of the smoothing plane, and today this plane has become the refined thoroughbred to replace a host of other bench planes.

I've used the same Stanley No. 4½ throughout my woodworking life and it's better now after forty years of use than it's ever been. Older models are generally better quality. They have wooden handles instead of plastic and are usually worn, which means that they have that 'old-slipper' comfort and they adjust smoothly. I've written chapter 14 on tuning up your hand plane, to make sure you can get the very best out of this fine, indispensable tool.

Router plane

The router plane

I somehow regret that we now associate the word router with the word power, but my router needs no motor, it delivers the cutting edge exactly where I need it at just the right pressure.

Most modern woodworkers have never seen or used these wonderful tools, but at one time they were as common as the bench plane. In fact, it's from this humble tool that the modern day industrial router takes its name. For leveling the bottoms of housing dadoes and inlay recesses, no other tool gives greater depth control and safety.

The router plane is included in my ten joinery tools because it gives me a speed and efficiency for cutting housings that is hard to match. The router shown here is my choice for everyday work. However, I own and use a range of hand routers. I enjoy my Veritas hand router plane, which has very fine and sensitive adjustments. Smaller versions are handy for tight spaces and close work. We generally chisel the waste wood from housing dadoes to within 1⁄16" of the depth gauge line and then use the router to establish the final depth across the whole width of the dado and length of the housing.

Quick fix router: To create a temporary router, I have on occasion used a simple method I learned as a boy. Simply bore an undersized hole at any angle around 45° through a 1" block of wood, so the sides of a chisel bed into the walls of the hole slightly. For example, for a 3⁄8" chisel bore a 5⁄16" hole. Tap the chisel into the hole until it protrudes to the required depth, bevel down, and you have your router plane.

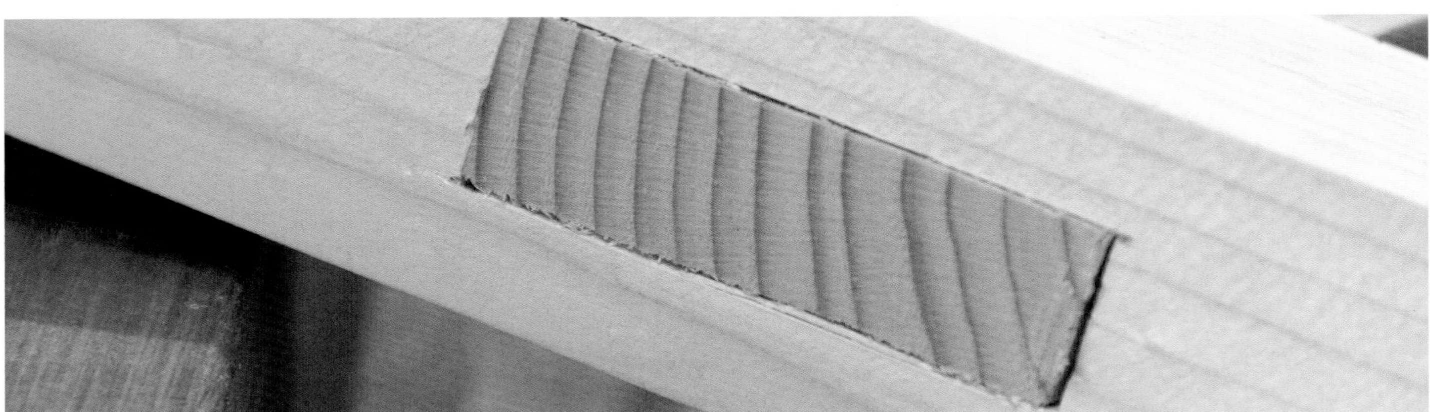

The three joints and where to use them

There are some 3,000 joints used around the world, but throughout my woodworking life I've used mostly three main types—the housing dado, mortise and tenon, and dovetail joints. I've made about 120,000 joints in my lifetime, at least half of which I made completely by hand using only ten hand tools. In forty-seven years I cannot recall a single joint ever failing.

Many new woodworkers believe making joints must be complicated, because they see the numerous jigs and guides needed to control the machines. In fact, these three joints are simpler made by hand. This chapter explains the housing dado, mortise and tenon and dovetail joints in more detail, so you can better understand how to use them for different applications in woodworking and furniture making.

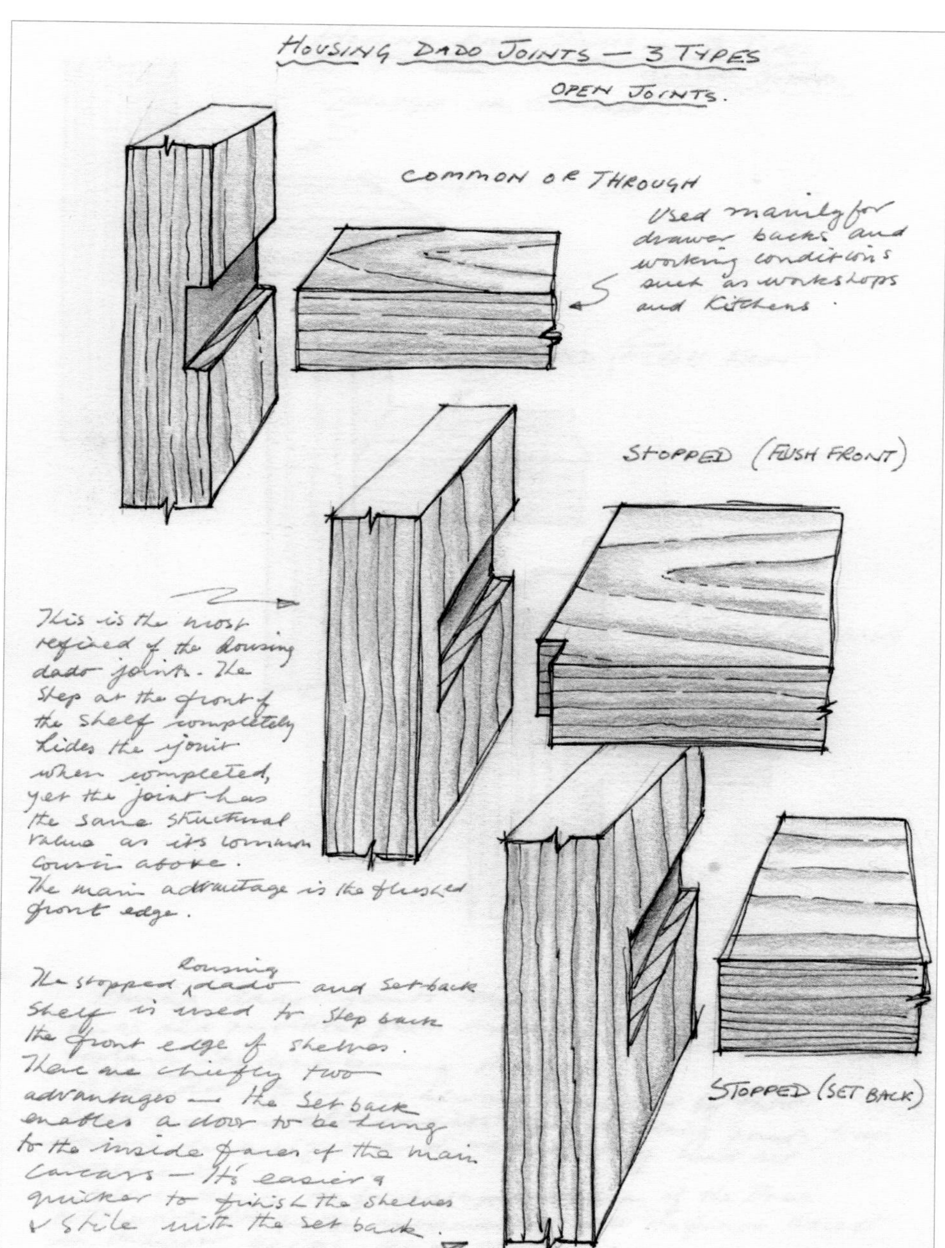

HOUSING DADO JOINTS — 3 TYPES
OPEN JOINTS.
COMMON OR THROUGH
Used mainly for drawer backs and working conditions such as workshops and kitchens.
STOPPED (FLUSH FRONT)
This is the most refined of the housing dado joints. The step at the front of the shelf completely hides the joint when completed, yet the joint has the same structural value as its common cousin above.
The main advantage is the flushed front edge.
The stopped housing dado and set-back shelf is used to step back the front edge of shelves.
There are chiefly two advantages — the set back enables a door to be hung to the inside faces of the main carcass — It's easier & quicker to finish the shelves & stile with the set back.
STOPPED (SET BACK)

Housing dado joints

No other joint can replace the housing dado joint as the ideal shelving or bookcase joint. It houses the ends of shelves and connects them into the vertical side pieces. It keeps each shelf perfectly flat while supporting the extreme weight of downward pressure associated with books. These joints provide almost no mechanical strength when pulled apart, but combining them with joints such as mortise and tenon and dovetail joints—or using plywood panels to 'skin' the back of the case—ensures the integrity of the whole project. We also use this classic joint for drawer backs and dividers, chests, boxes, cupboards, and several other applications.

There are three types of housing dado joint:

- Through housing dado (common)
- Stopped and stepped (flush front)
- Stopped (stepped back)

Dovetail joints

Dovetail joints appear complex because they involve angled cuts interlocking several times in a single joint. Sometimes the dovetails vary in size and often the joint is hidden from sight. It's no wonder therefore, that this joint confuses so many woodworkers. However, made properly with hand tools, the tails and pins interlock to provide a strength no other joint offers.

Millions of boxes are resolutely held at the corners because of this humble joint. Pioneers and settlers created their log cabins and barns using axe-hewn dovetails. Thousands of structures worldwide have withstood the elements for centuries with simple dovetailed bracings to roof trusses, anchor walls and tie beams.

There are two basic types of dovetail joint:

- The through dovetail

  This version is the most straightforward to make, and you will use this for your project work covered in this book.

- Half-blind (or half lapped) dovetail

  This variation is used for drawer making, which is covered in a later part of the course.

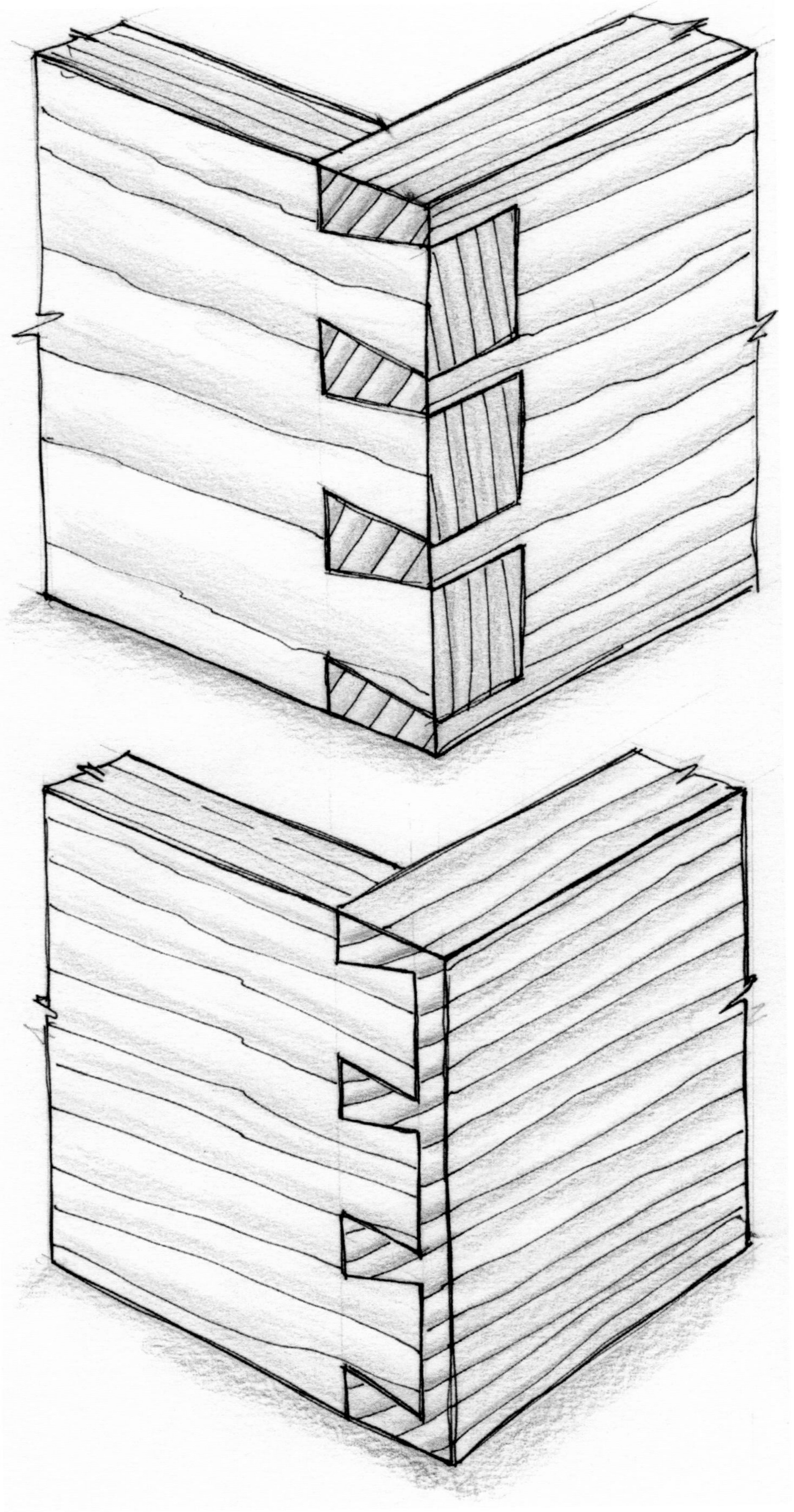

Beams in the roof structure of Penrhyn Castle.

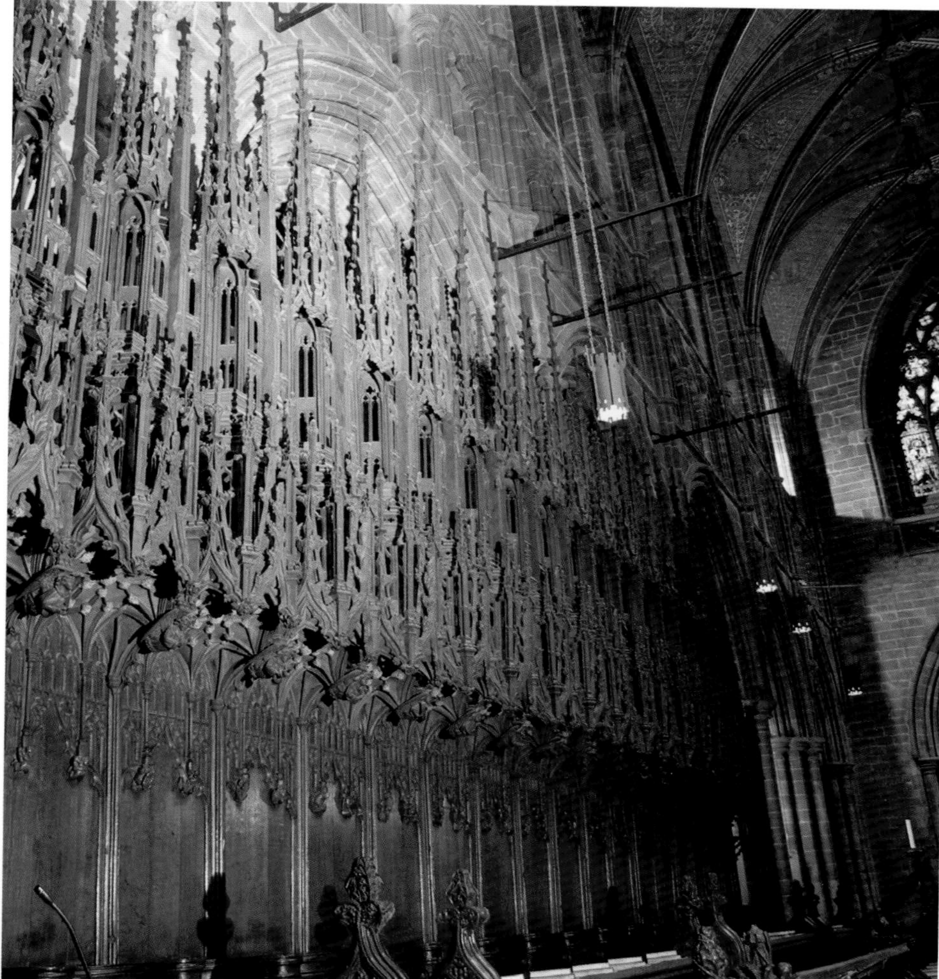

Beneath the ornate carved facade, thousands of intricate mortise and tenon joints provide the structural integrity for this 15th century masterpiece, the choir of Chester Cathedral, England.

Mortise and tenon joints

I find the mortise and tenon joint the most fascinating of all joints. It is by far the most common joint ever made and yet, through its unobtrusive nature, you rarely detect its presence. From minute tenons in Chinese lanterns to the massive barns throughout the eastern seaboard of the US, the mortise and tenon joint is universally used as the frame joint. Chairs, tables, desks, window frames, doors, doorframes, beds, ladders and hundreds of other framed projects wouldn't hold together without this versatile joint.

There are three types of mortise and tenon joint:

- The through mortise and tenon
- The haunched mortise and tenon
- The mortise and stub tenon

You will be making each of these types of joint in this course, and I'll show you the differences in their use and construction. The following page shows the interlocking nature of this joint. Undoubtedly, these three types are the most widely used mortise and tenon joints of all.

Terminology of Joinery

This haunched tenon is about twelve inches wide. It is for one of the doors in the castle.

This is a traditional English garden bench for the grounds of Penrhyn Castle. I have used stub tenons and blind mortise holes.

Dovetail Joint

1. Shoulder
2. Tails
3. Pins
4. Tail recess
5. Pin recess

Housing Dado joint

1. Recess
2. Shoulder

Haunched mortise and tenon joint

1. Mortise
2. Mortise haunch
3. Tenon
4. Tenon haunch
5. Shoulder

Crisp, sharp edges are the hallmarks of accuracy and care.

Accuracy

For many years in my early apprenticeship training, I did not practice the real accuracy necessary for creating pristine work. It was my loss. When some years later I needed my work to match the standards set by the craftsmen of old, I realized many things must change. I had to discover how they accomplished such fine and detailed work, without the modern tools available to me. I came to understand that accuracy doesn't happen by accident; it involves developing sensitivity to the whole work process. It takes a determination to work with precision and care.

Accuracy is more than just square cutting or keeping to the line—it comes from a state of heightened consciousness and awareness. This awareness tells us when and where to flex tool and muscle to wood. It's as much about the sharpness of the knife's blade as the angle and length of the pencil point, and the pressure you apply to both. But the first thing we must hone is our layout skill.

I will now teach you three techniques that are common to all aspects of joinery, and are fundamental to the concept of accuracy.

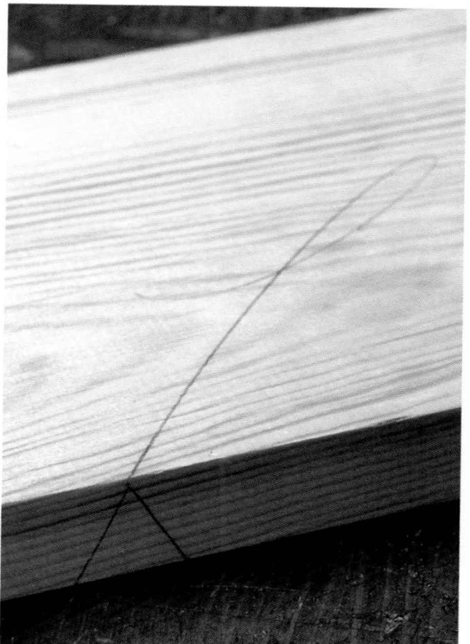
The face and face-edge reference marks.

Make a small nick in the corner where you need your shoulder line to begin.

Register your cut against the square at all times.

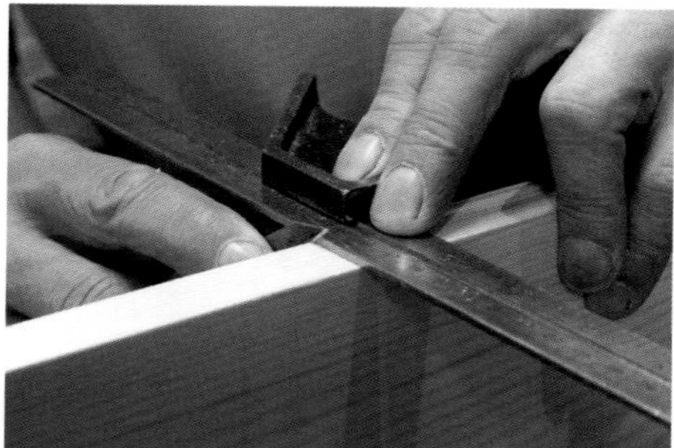
Always register against the edges you have marked as face and face-edge.

Face/Edge marking

At this early stage of the course, I would expect you to use machined stock that has been cut and planed before you buy it. The procedure of producing uniform, planed and trued stock (planed foursquare), by hand, requires both skill and confidence. For this reason, I suggest that you choose wood that has at least one edge and one face that are both fairly clear from defects and perfectly square to each other. You need to check the angle, just in case the stock has been machined badly.

Face/face-edge marking is a simple method for referencing your wood that you should use whenever you are preparing to cut joints. Choose an edge and a face that you want to use as reference faces, first checking for surface defects and distortion by sighting along the corner and surface by eye, and then, with your square, making sure that the corner is dead square at 90 degrees. Assuming the length is straight and each face and edge has been machined square, mark on the chosen flat face with a cursive '𝒻' (face mark) and on the face-edge with a ^ (face-edge mark). These marks now prove the two absolute reference faces that, from now on, no matter which way you turn this piece of wood, you will always reference from this face and edge. This is a traditional method and you will see how important it is as you work through this course.

Transfer of shoulder lines

When joint making, it is important to establish corresponding reference points on all edges and faces for the shoulders. The shoulder line is the most important reference line for both the dovetail joint and the mortise and tenon joint. This is an absolute reference for any cross grain cut you will make on any face or edge of your workpiece. A shoulder line, when transferred around all faces and edges of a workpiece, should meet perfectly with no mismatch whatsoever on any of the corners. To achieve this, we must always reference our square from the same face and the same edge. A pencil mark is simply not precise enough and so we use our marking knife instead. The pencil lines marking shoulder lines are simply to indicate a close approximation of where the knife line will go. The knife line itself is definitive.

Start by making a small knife nick on the corner. Don't worry if you can't see it, you don't need to. By lightly tracing the knife blade of your marking knife over the nick, you will hear a light 'tick' or clicking noise, which tells you the knife has found the mark. Do this a few times until it seems easy. This is a first step.

Next, place the stock of your square against the edge (marked ^), near to the pencil line, with the blade of the square placed across the face (marked with the cursive f). Find the nick with your knife, and hold your knife in place. Now, carefully move the square up to the knife, at which point hold the square steady and immovable, applying pressure to the stock with your thumb.

Now you can reach across the face with your marking knife and make another nick on the other corner of the face. By using the same process of making the nick, moving the square, finding the nick, you can transfer the nick all the way round your workpiece. Make sure your stock is always against either the face or the edge with the face and face-edge mark. Any shoulder lines can be referenced to the invisible nicks.

I know of no method more accurate than knifewall woodworking.

Using a knifewall

"the knifewall creates shoulder lines wherever we cut across the grain."

Using a knifewall is an ancient technique that has largely fallen into disuse, primarily because most woodworkers today use machines to make their cuts. However, industrial machines stymie the art and craft of woodworking, and I know of no safer or more accurate method for creating hand cut joints and crosscutting wood than the knifewall method. For every joint described throughout this course (and on through the more advanced levels), we will always use the knifewall method for setting exact shoulder lines to follow when cutting across the grain.

In the initial layout, lines that run along or with the grain are usually laid out with marking gauges. The cross-grain cuts are first marked out with temporary pencil marks. Only with the first pass of the knife along the square does the position of the cut become permanent. Put simply, the knifewall creates the shoulder lines wherever we cut across the grain. It prevents unsupported fibers from tearing and gives supreme accuracy to your work.

Good registration against the square is vital.

Take care not to break past the wall.

Keep the chisel square and vertical.

The final knifewall need not be very deep but this shows the shape and configuration.

Steps for making the knifewall

Regardless of the joint type, the opening cross-grain cut starts with the square and a sharp, pointed knife. With a sharply defined boundary, we can further define this line by deepening the recess on the waste side of the line using a chisel in an angled horizontal position as shown. The recess we create will then guide subsequent deepening cuts, regardless of which tool we use to cut down the wall.

By combining the two processes of transferring shoulder lines and creating the knifewall, it is possible to work with absolute precision. It does however take a little practice to become proficient.

For the following exercise I suggest that you use a piece of softer wood such as pine, about 8" long and 4-5" wide. You will also need your marking knife, combination square, a finely honed 1" chisel and a sharp pencil. Begin by making a fine pencil line across the board.

1. To learn to work accurately, you must get used to registering your square. Place the very point of the knife anywhere along the pencil line and hold it there.
2. Slowly and carefully advance the square up the workpiece, controlling it with your thumb, until it just touches the knife. Now increase your grip pressure on the square and workpiece to lock it to the wood so that it's immovable.
3. Now, take your knife to the corner of the stock farthest away from you and, using the square to guide the cut, carefully and lightly run your knife along the square making a fine surface cut across the wood.
4. Repeat a second pass with the knife, this time applying more pressure with each pass. After the second pass, you can cut with the knife as hard as you like because the knife will not wander from its course.
5. With the workpiece secure in the vise, use a sharp 1" chisel to further define and deepen the knifewall. Incline the chisel on the waste side of the line towards the knifewall, about the same angle you see here. Firmly press or chop towards the knifewall until the surface fibers separate by the knifewall. You will see the fibers lift and separate as you near the knifewall cut.
6. Continue across the full width of the board keeping the same angle. Use your fingers to remove the newly cut waste. This splits the wood to the depth of the knife cut.

> **REMEMBER:** *Because the knifewall is at first shallow at the surface level, never chop the vertical cuts with your chisel with full force or the bevel will drive the chisel into the knifewall, compressing the fibers and moving what was an accurate cut line.*

The knifewall gives a pristine and accurate shoulder. You must now deepen the wall with vertical chisel cuts, registering the flat face of the chisel against the knifewall. After each series of vertical chops, again angle your chisel toward the knifewall and deepen the knifewall.

With practice, this method becomes less awkward. The way you grip and move the square and hold the knife will become second nature. Once learned, this is a very fast process guaranteeing total accuracy.

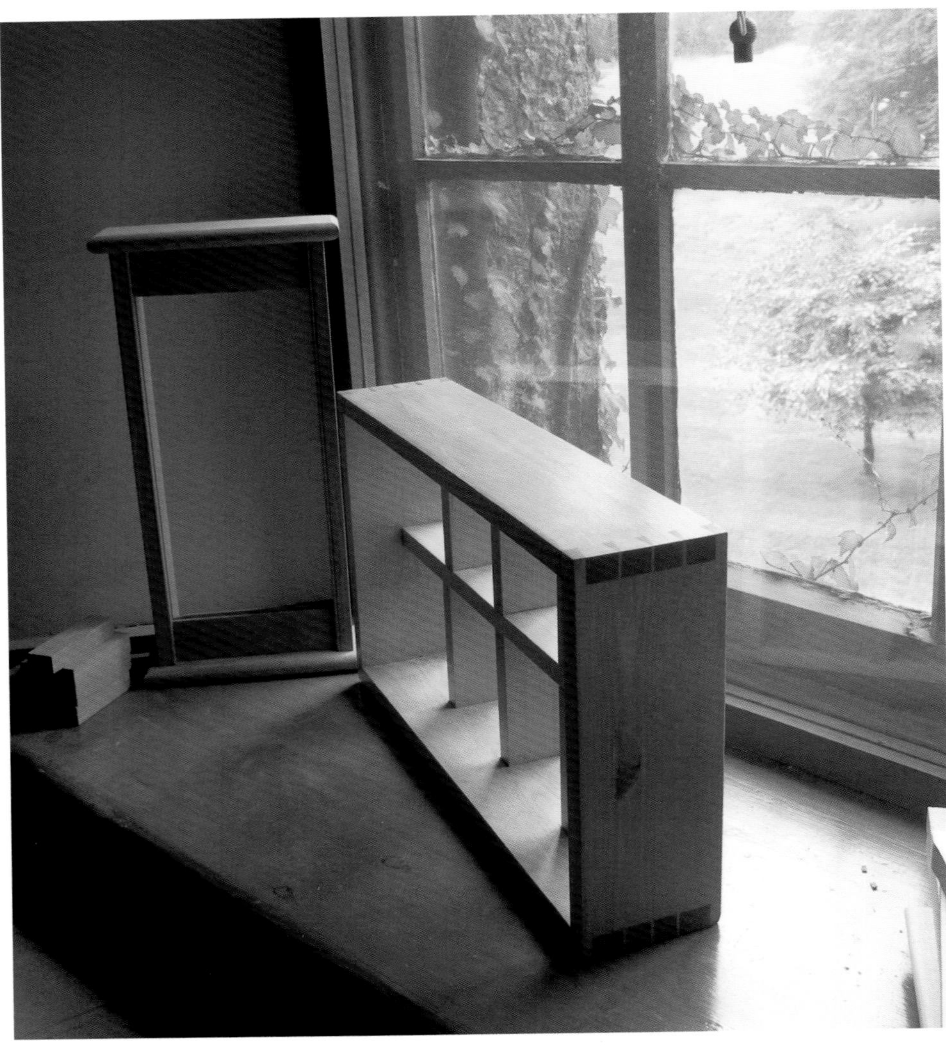

> **TECHNICAL POINTER:** *Make sure you are totally confident in the procedures of transferring shoulder lines and forming knifewalls. These are fundamental to all aspects of joinery work. Also, to reiterate, your square must be perfectly square and your marking knife and chisels sharpened as for surgery.*

Making the three joints

Your choice of stock for these practice joints is entirely up to you. However, there are a couple of important points you should be aware of which are worth a brief mention:

Firstly, take a square with you when you visit your local wood store or lumber yard. Choose your wood by first checking it is not twisted, cupped, bent or cracked. Then, take your square and check the corners are at 90 degrees. They probably will be, but it's still worth checking. I would suggest you buy planed stock at this stage so you can take it home and get to work straight away. Starting with good quality, well-planed wood will eliminate any joint making difficulties that are not your fault.

In a later part of this course you will learn how to produce your own perfectly square stock from any rough sawn lumber, sourced independently or bought commercially.

Housing dado

Most joints rely on the reduction of both parts to make a joint, but in this case we reduce only one. Developing a well-made housing dado depends on the accurate placement of the two knifewalls to house the adjoining shelf or divider. The two walls must correspond perfectly to the dimension of the part to fit into the housing, without excessive tightness and without gaps. Using the following method works well and will produce accurate results, but proficiency comes only with practice. Make sure your tools are in prime condition before starting. Work carefully and think through each of the steps. You'll notice the difference. Also, to make a joint tight but not overly so, you must judge the compressibility of the particular wood being used. I recommend pine as a good starter wood.

Two pieces of wood ⅞" thick, 5" wide and 10" long will work well and will be enough to practice making three or four joints. Throughout this exercise you will use your square, knife, chisel, marking gauge, small tenon or dovetail saw, mallet and hand router. Now for the layout.

1. Using a sharp pencil and square, decide on the location of your housing dado and mark this with a single pencil line.
2. Align the second board on the squared line and mark the position of the second line.
3. Again, use the square and pencil to continue this second line across the full width of the board.
4. Using the square, extend both lines around onto both edges of the board, visibly but lightly
5. Set a marking gauge to ¼" as shown. This guides the depth of cut when you mark the board.
6. Now use your marking gauge to run gauge lines on both edges of the board, just between the pencil lines.

Use a sharp pencil and square to mark the first line.

The second board positions the parallel line.

Use the square to establish all the cut lines.

TECHNICAL POINTER: *Remember that the goal here is not to score a deep groove by pressing hard, but a fine score line using only light pressure with the very tip of the point. Pressing hard will increase the thickness of the line and will make the pin follow the grain, rather than creating the exact line you need.*

Set the marking gauge for the ¼" depth.

Run the gauge line between the pencil lines.

First knifewall:

1. Using the procedure you have learnt, create the first knifewall only. You'll establish the second wall shortly, so don't cut both lines at this point. It may help to clamp the board securely in the vise, with about half the thickness of the board above the top edge of the vise so that the stock of the square is unhindered by the vise jaw.
2. With the knifewall defined, use the chisel to deepen the wall. When using the chisel, take the board out of the vise and place it on the benchtop, using the mallet to drive the chisel deeper. Keep your chisel perpendicular and strike the chisel handle with a firm blow. Listen for the change in the sound as you strike; it will help you judge when to stop. If you use too much force, you risk moving the knifewall, driving it into the original line and compressing the fibers.
3. Continue to sequentially deepen the knifewall, alternating between vertical and angled cuts and also alternating the board between the vise and the benchtop for safety. Carry on until you have a knifewall almost down to the depth line you made with the gauge.

Create the first knifewall only.

Deepen the wall using a 1" chisel.

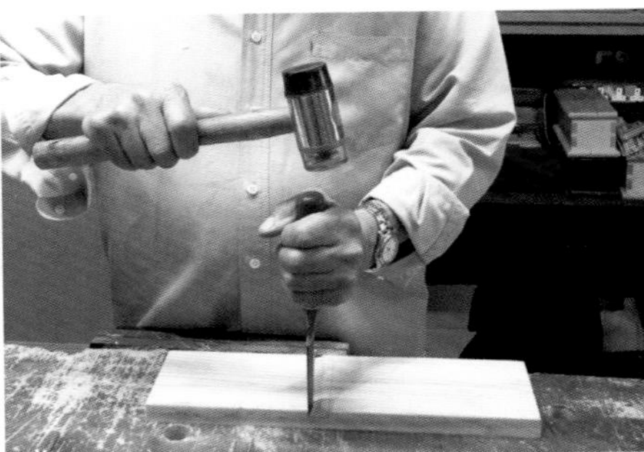

Use the mallet to drive the chisel deeper.

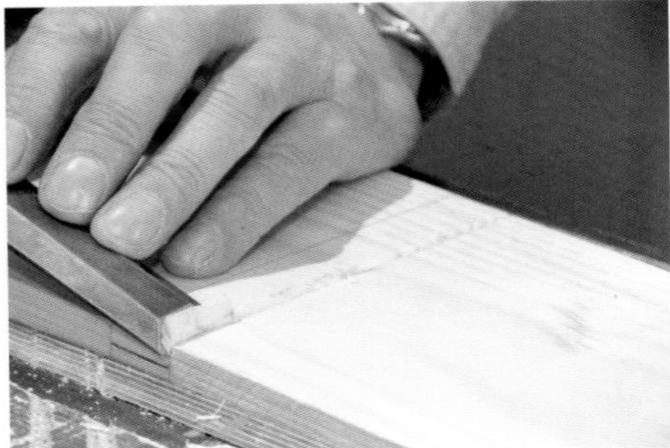

Make deeper angled horizontal cuts.

Work evenly across the full width.

Continue, but stop just above the gauge line.

Your housing dado now looks like this.

Use the board to position the second knifewall.

Square the second knifewall across the board.

Chop down the knifewall with the chisel.

Continue using the same procedure.

Your housing dado now looks like this.

Grip the chisel with a two-handed grip…

…and remove the waste with progressive cuts.

Use the hand router to level the housing dado.

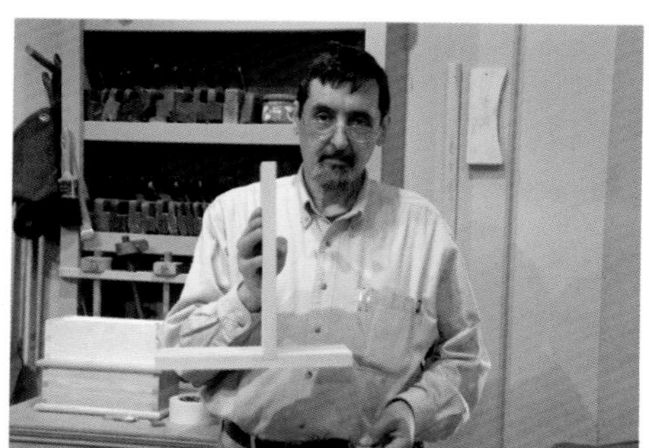
A housing dado should be self supporting.

Second knifewall:

1. With the first wall cut, you can now focus on the opposite knifewall. Place the second board tight up against the first knifewall and, using the sharp point of your knife, make a small mark on the other edge of the board. Use the square to mark a knife line across the full width of the board, and then create the second knifewall. Because even the width of the knife cut can alter the size of the final recess, always position your knife and square so that the knife runs on the waste side of your square.

TOP TIP: *When marking the width of the recess from the second board, angle your knife and reach very slightly underneath the edge (and I mean very slightly!) to create a housing recess that is perhaps less than 1⁄64 undersize. This ensures a snug fit; it takes practice but it's something you develop as you gain increased confidence.*

2. Use a ¾" chisel to remove the waste wood between the two knifewalls. Work from both sides of the board toward the center, or the unsupported fibers will tear on the visible edges of the wood. Take care to level your chisel, or you will dig too deeply in the mid-section of the housing dado. Also, don't cut too deeply—pare down to just above the gauge line.
3. Level the bottom of the housing dado using the hand router.

Many people think the depth of a housing dado is one-third the thickness of the material, but the depth of most housing dado joints is generally no greater than ½". Generally housing dadoes are rarely more than ¼"-⅜" deep.

The Dovetail Joint

The dovetail joint relies on two pieces of wood interlocking at the corner to form the joint. The two parts to the joint are the tail piece, and the pin piece. Developing a well-made dovetail joint relies on accuracy in layout and workmanship.

Examples of early craftsmanship show that craftsmen generally used two angles in making dovetails; For soft-grained woods such as pine and spruce, they used a steeper angle of 1:6, while for harder, more dense-grained woods like cherry, walnut and oak, they used a shallower pitch of 1:8. Though these were accepted angles, most of the pieces I have worked on made by craftsmen of old have proved highly variable. Finer works completed in hardwoods were definitely shallower, whereas less refined pieces made from pine had the steeper angle. The theory behind this is that soft-grained woods compress more under pressure and need steeper angles to resist the pressure. Today, we use a 1:7 angle for making dovetails. This reflects the standardized angle now accepted in most joinery and furniture making, derived by combining the shallow and steep angles.

Instead of creating two pieces measured and cut separately to interlock, we use one as a template for the other. That way, they will always fit snugly. Take time to think through each stage as you work and enjoy the making process. Keep your tools sharp and remember to judge the compressibility of the wood. Laying out begins with a sharp, long-pointed pencil so that your lines are ultra-thin. For this dovetail joint, use two pieces of wood ⅝" x 2" x 8" long.

Method

Start with the tails:

1. Take the tail piece and, using a pencil, mark the shoulder line using the thickness of the pin piece as a guide for judging the distance this mark should be from the end of the piece. Make only a small mark.
2. Use the square to continue this shoulder line across the face, this guarantees your line is dead square. Square the line onto all four faces.
3. In the same manner, repeat the procedure for the pin piece.
4. Now make two marks ⅜" in from each edge onto the corner.
5. Square these marks across the end of the tail piece.
6. Use your sliding bevel set at a 1-in-7 pitch, register it against the end and use the pencil to continue these marks down to the shoulder line to outline the shape of the dovetail. (If you are unsure how to set your sliding bevel to a 1-in-7 pitch, refer to page 108 in this chapter, where I also show you how to make a very useful dovetail template.)
7. Use the tenon saw to cut the angles of the dovetail piece. Start your cut with the tail piece low in the vice, and with your saw blade on the waste side of the line. Begin with light, vertical saw strokes across the end grain to establish a very shallow groove and then alter the angle of your saw blade to carefully follow the angled dovetail lines. Keep your saw level and stop just before the shoulder line. Your pencil lines should always be visible after the completion of your cuts.
8. You must now cut the shoulders on each side of the angled saw cuts that create the dovetail. To do this, form a knife line on the three sides of each shoulder, transferring the shoulder lines as usual. (See page 93 of this chapter for the full procedure of transferring shoulder lines.)

Flush the second piece with your fingertips and make a mark.

Square the lines with the pencil and square.

Mark ⅜" from each side on the corner edge.

Square the lines onto the end.

Use the sliding bevel to mark the dovetail angles.

The layout looks like this.

Cut down the lines with the dovetail saw.

Cut close to the lines on the waste side.

Establish the knifewall with the knife and square.

Define the knifewall with the chisel.

Saw down the shoulder line to the angled cut.

TECHNICAL POINTER: *When using shoulder lines and knifewalls to make dovetails, do not continue the knife cuts all the way across every surface. Only use the knife to mark across the waste. If you use your knife to cut all the way across parts of the joint that are visible, it will leave unsightly knife marks.*

9. Create the knifewalls with your chisel, along your shoulder lines either side of your sawn dovetail shape.
10. With the tenon saw, remove the waste corners as defined by the knifewall up to the angled dovetail cuts, taking care not to cut into the sides of the dovetail.
11. Clean up the shoulders with a sharp chisel, holding the tail piece in the vise.

Make the pins:

1. Clamp the second piece of wood, the tail piece, in the vise, level with your plane lying on its side. This supports the opposite end of the tail piece and keeps it steady as you mark around the dovetail with the pencil.
2. Line up the shoulders of the tail piece and with a sharp pencil, mark around the dovetail onto the end of the second piece, the pin piece.

TECHNICAL POINTER: *When you use a soft-grained wood such as white pine, it's best to use a sharp pencil rather than a knife to define the tail recess cut lines because the knife mark disappears in the soft wood fibers of the end-grain. For harder, dense grained wood, a knife works perfectly.*

3. Using the square, or the square side of the dovetail template, square the lines on the outside face of the pin piece, down to the shoulder line.
4. With the pin piece clamped vertically in the vise, saw across the marked end grain, down to the depth line, taking care to cut on the waste side. Again, make certain that you follow the pencil lines exactly and that your lines are still just visible after the cut.
5. Using the knife, cut a shoulder line between the saw cuts. Do this on both faces of the pin piece to create the knifewall needed to cut a perfect shoulder line square across from outside face to inside face.

Level the tail piece and hold it steady.

Mark around the dovetail with a sharp pencil.

Make sure the lines are fine and exact.

Square the lines down onto the face.

Cut down the lines on the waste side.

Use the knife and square to define the shoulder.

A small knife nick ensures accurate transfer.

Define the opposite shoulder between the cuts.

Further define the knifewall using the chisel.

Work from both sides towards the middle.

Remove the waste and if necessary trim the recess.

Carefully press the tail into the recess.

The finished joint looks crisp and neat. After trimming and planing, all the surfaces will be flush.

REMEMBER: *To transfer the knife line to the opposite face, make a small nick with the knife directly on the corner. Then transfer the nick to the opposite back face corner, again using a small knife nick.* *(chapter 6 page 93)*

6. Using the chisel and knifewall method, gradually deepen the shoulder lines, working from both faces of the piece, until they meet somewhere in the middle. Work carefully to minimize any tear-out within the shoulders of the cut. Clean up the recess with a sharp chisel.
7. Press the dovetail piece into the tail recess of the pin piece, carefully taking care not to use excessive force on the joint and being prepared to trim off any excesses hindering its closure.

Mortise and tenon

In its basic form, the mortise and tenon joint creates either an 'L' corner or a 'T' intersection. The method for cutting both joint variations is basically the same.

Precise layout is central to a well-fitting joint, but its success is guaranteed only if you cut exactly to the layout lines made with the knife and the mortise gauge. Be prepared to check your progress as you chop, saw and shave the components to shape, constantly making fine adjustments of direction, pressure and angle, as you use the tools...

Start with two pieces of softwood, pine, fir or spruce will work well, 1¼" x 2" x 10" long. Avoid any knots at this stage. You'll find plenty of knots where you don't want them on future projects. After a quick check on the corners with a square, make your face and face-edge marks as usual.

Though you can cut either the tenon or mortise first, I prefer to cut the mortise hole first so that I can cut the tenon to fit. This is because the mortise hole is governed by the width of the chisel and in general is never altered.

Chopping the mortise

Mortise holes must be accurate if they are to hold the tenon. My favorite method takes advantage of the natural properties of the wood, as well as the mechanical application of the bevel of the chisel, to drive and separate the fibers and allow them to be cut and removed from the mortise. Using this method, a 1½" deep, ½" wide and 4" through mortise in oak, cherry or walnut takes me about four minutes to chop out neatly and accurately.

1. Somewhere near the center of one of the pieces, square two lines 2" apart (the thickness of the second piece of wood) across one wide face of the piece using the square and pencil. Next, square these lines onto both narrow faces. These lines mark the width of your mortise hole.
2. Set your mortise gauge to the ½" chisel you will use to cut the mortise, and then set the stock ⅜" in from the pin as shown.

TECHNICAL POINTER: *It's very important that the mortise gauge pins are set at the very points of the pins and not the base of the pins, which would create an oversized mortise hole. The points of the pins should be tight against the sides of the chisel. Then the gauge is set.*

3. Run your mortise gauge lines in between the two pencil lines on the narrow face, registering the stock of the gauge against the face marked with the face-edge mark. Repeat this on the opposite narrow face, again making certain to run the stock of your gauge against the face marked with the face-edge mark.

TECHNICAL POINTER: *When using the gauge, make certain that the gauge isn't misdirected by following awkward grain. This usually happens when too much pressure is applied to the gauge, forcing the pins down into the fibers. It's not necessary to apply a lot of pressure, but it is important to apply controlled pressure and guidance. Pressing lightly and keeping the stock firmly against the wood will give two accurate, fine lines. Light, controlled but firm is the rule when using all gauges.*

Square the lines for the mortise hole onto each face.

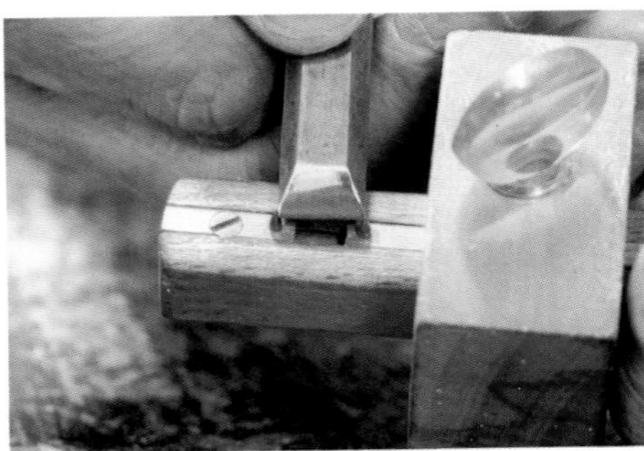

Set the mortise gauge to the ½" chisel.

Measure ⅜" from the stock of the gauge.

Score the parallel lines for the mortise hole.

Use the knife between the gauge lines.

Further define the knifewall with the ½" chisel.

Chop the mortise hole…

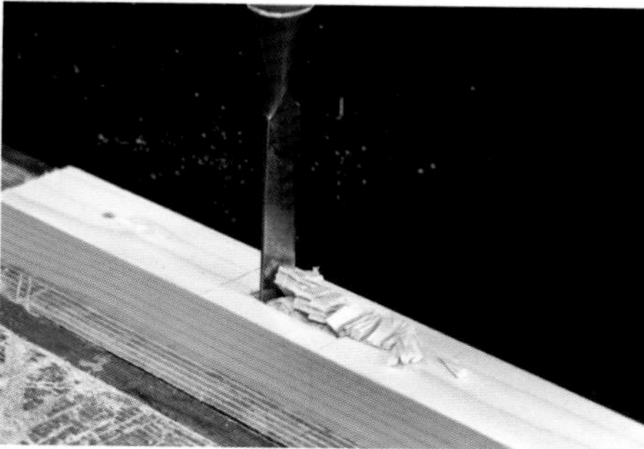
…from one side of the mortise to the other.

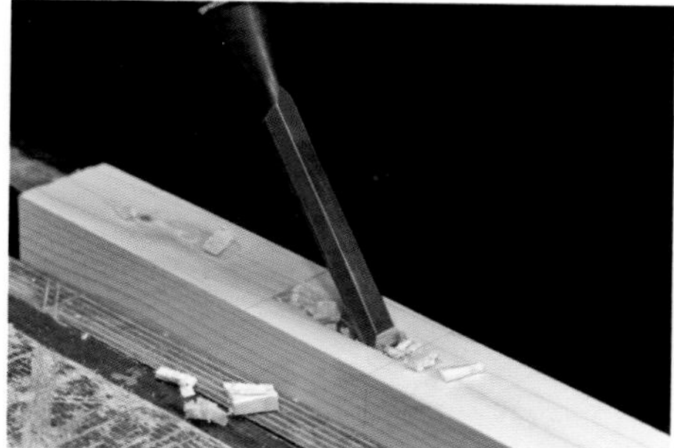
Reverse the chisel and work from the other end…

…until halfway down and to an even depth.

TECHNICAL POINTER: *Don't clean up the fibers on the inside walls of the mortise hole because this widens the hole's width, which should always be governed directly by the width of the chisel. A few protruding fibers are of little consequence and can be removed later if necessary.*

4. The gauge lines now define the mortise between the pencil shoulder lines. Now, take your knife and form shoulder lines at each end of the mortise. Transfer the shoulder lines to the other side of the mortise. Next, form the knifewalls with the same ½" chisel you'll use to cut the mortise.
5. With the knifewall in place, begin the process of incrementally making a series of cuts working away from the knifewall. At this stage the chisel is held vertically and the bevel is orientated in the direction of travel. With every ⅛" step, drive the chisel in ⅛" deeper than the last cut. In this way, you'll quickly reach a depth of at least halfway through the mortise.
6. As you reach a point about $\frac{1}{16}$ shy of the knife line, reverse the chisel and hold it so that the bevel is perpendicular. This will allow you to lever out the waste using the bevel as a fulcrum. Starting about ⅓ of the way back, with the bevel facing the direction of travel, chop out the remainder of the mortise on the first side.
7. The last $\frac{1}{16}$ is removed by chopping down on the knife line with the bevel facing the mortise hole. This can be done in incrementally steeper cuts, avoiding any pressure on the wood fibers on the non-waste side of the knife line.
8. Once you have cut halfway through, begin chopping from the opposite side using the same sequence. This way you won't damage the unsupported fibers by cutting all the way through from one side only.

Cutting the tenon

The most critical aspect of cutting your tenon is not to cut so far down that you lose the gauge lines. Provided you have set the tips of the points to the exact width of the chisel you will be using to chop the mortise—and you do not alter this setting—the tenon will be the exact width of the hole and will fit perfectly.

1. Square a line 2" from the end of the tenon piece onto each of the four faces. This guides your permanent marks with the mortise gauge.
2. With the shoulder line marked, use the same mortise gauge to trace the cheeks of the tenon, and also use the same pin and distance setting. Clamping the tenon piece in the vise will give you better control. Score two parallel lines onto the two narrow faces and onto the end of the tenon piece by running the stock of the gauge along the wide face of the wood. Remember to press lightly with the pins but firmly against the wood with the stock.
3. Using a sharp knife and square, cut the knifewalls across the three sides of the shoulder on both sides of the tenon. This defines the exact shoulder lines of the tenon.
4. Use the 1" chisel at a slight angle to further define the knifewalls and form the step down needed to guide subsequent cuts with the tenon or dovetail saw. This will be the shoulder of the tenon.

Use your fingertips to establish the shoulder line.

Square the line onto each face with the square.

Use the mortise gauge to score the tenon lines.

Define the exact shoulder line with the knife.

Develop the shoulder line with the 1" chisel.

Cut the shoulders with the tenon saw first…

…then the cheeks. Cut on the waste side only.

The finished mortise and tenon joint.

5. Cut the shoulders of the tenon with the tenon saw, using the knifewall to guide your cut square across and down into the shoulder.
6. Saw down the cheeks of the tenon, taking care to cut on the waste side of the gauge lines. Carefully follow the gauge lines but don't cut into the cheeks of the tenon, which will make the tenon loose and unusable. You can also use a 1" wide chisel to cut, split and pare the waste from the tenon cheeks.
7. With both cheeks cut, offer one corner of the tenon into the hole to see whether it enters with slight but firm pressure. Then offer the opposite corner to see if that's the same. Usually it is, and the tenon needs no trimming, in which case press firmly and carefully until the joint goes fully together. If the tenon feels overly tight as it enters the mortise, take it out and look for any bruising on the tenon cheeks. These shiny spots must be pared down with the chisel, working on both sides of the tenon, if required. Work carefully to minimize any tear-out within the shoulders of the cut. Clean up the shoulder with a sharp chisel.
8. Hold the tenon in the vice, if it seems easier, and firmly ease the mortise down until it seats fully against the shoulders of the tenon.

TECHNICAL POINTER: *If there are gaps at the shoulder lines, you may need to pare down the inside of the shoulders to remove any waste preventing full closure. Do this in a vise and be careful not to cut any of the knifewall. If there is a gap on only one side, you have not transferred the shoulder line correctly.*

Making a dovetail template

There are dozens of different dovetail templates you can buy or make, but this one has served me well since my apprenticeship began in 1965. It's simple to make and to use, and if done accurately will last a lifetime. The pattern originates with craftsmen of old, some of whom trained me. Its most useful quality is not so much the dovetail angles but the built-in square, which we use continuously throughout dovetailing procedures.

Before you start, here's how you set your sliding bevel to a 1-in-7 pitch:

1. Square a pencil line onto the face of the board.
2. Intersect this line at 7" from the edge.
3. Make a second mark 1" away from the line on the corner along the edge of the board.
4. Connect the two points to establish the 1-in-7 pitch for the angle you need for your dovetails.
5. Now set your sliding bevel to the 1-in-7 pitch and lock it off. You are ready to make your template, or simply mark out your dovetails using the sliding bevel. Press the dovetail piece into the tail recess of the pin piece, carefully taking care not to use excessive force on the joint and being prepared to trim off any excesses hindering its closure.

When you layout and cut your template, remember to work with care. The quality of your template will be reflected in all your dovetails.

The dovetail template.

Square a line from one edge.

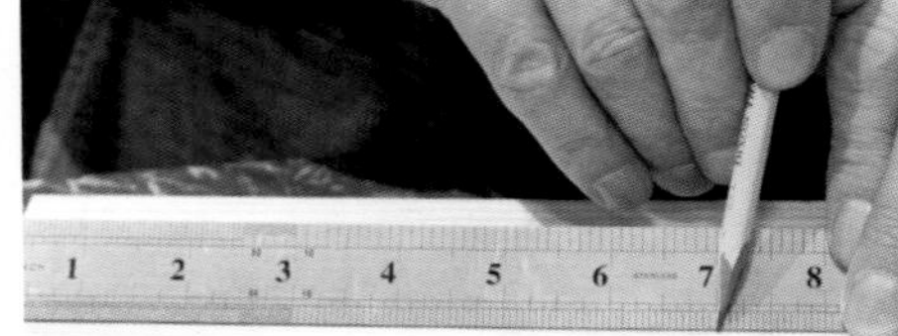

Measure up from the end 7".

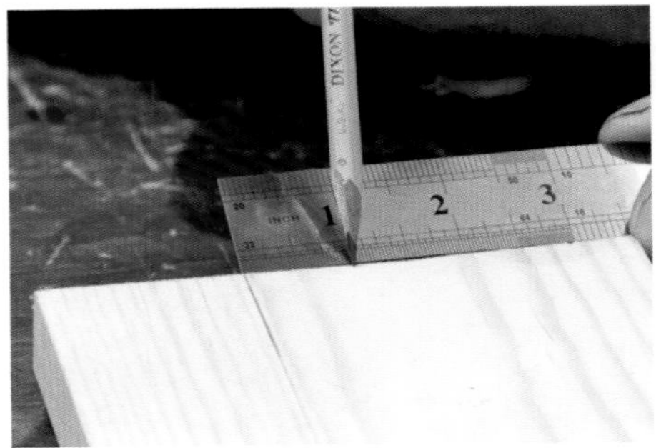

Make a second mark 1" from the square line.

Connect the two points.

Set the sliding bevel to the angle.

Mark all the shoulder lines onto the blank.

Score the parallel lines with the mortise gauge.

Establish all shoulder lines with the knife.

First cut the shoulders and then the cheeks.

A blank ⅞" x 1¼" x 4" makes a convenient size. Of course, any wood will work, but denser grained woods last well and retain their shape and edges better. Work carefully when laying out and cutting the shoulders of your template, because inaccuracies will always be reflected in the dovetails you make. To establish the angles for the dovetails on your template, use the sliding bevel you have just set. Firstly, lay out the lines on your template with the pencil, square and sliding bevel. These lines will guide the mortise gauge when you run the parallel lines for the cheeks of the gauge.

1. Onto one edge, measure 1½" from each end and draw two shoulder lines. Take one shoulder line square all the way round. When you take the second line across the faces, use the sliding bevel at a 1-in-7 pitch, then join the lines on the opposite edge. These lines define the central stock of the template as shown in the photo on the opposite page.
2. With the pencil lines outlined onto your workpiece, set a mortise gauge to ⅜" between points, in the same way you would to lay out a tenon. Use firm lateral pressure to run the parallel lines onto your blank, ¼" from its outside face. You can also set the single pin of a regular marking gauge to ¼" and run the gauge lines from both sides of your blank to establish the ⅜" tongue.
3. With all the gauge lines in place, use the knife to define both the angled and square crosscut lines, transfer shoulder lines as usual and create your knifewalls. Remember to make all cuts on the waste side of the line.
4. Use your tenon saw to crosscut both the angled and square shoulders of the template. Cut down to the depth lines, taking care not to go beyond your gauge marks. Take your time to cut accurately.
5. With the shoulders sawn, you can now saw along the grain to form the tongues, as you would for cutting tenons. Take care to cut closely to the line along the whole length.
6. Clean up the faces of the template with a sharp 1" chisel.

This template will enable you to progress quickly through any future dovetail layout work. I have made dozens of them and they never break or wear out.

Conclusion

The use of the joints you have just made spans millennia. Even in their most basic forms, these joints open up a vast range of opportunities for you to create everything from bookshelves, boxes, and greenhouses to garden gates and tables to chairs. You are now ready to progress by using your skills to create a series of jointed projects as you follow the course.

Start to think through where you can use these joints for future projects and consider the parts and how they relate to your aspirations. I find great value in looking beyond the visible surfaces of furniture pieces and buildings to imagine the joints hidden within. Museums, craft centers and craft shows will inspire you as you examine the joinery and furniture work of past and present artisans. Your awareness of craftsmanship will increase, and as this permeates your consciousness, it may start to change your perspective on what we consider worthwhile knowledge.

7 Making the Shaker box

Cultural influences on design

The Shaker style of furniture was developed in colonial and early post-colonial America. The Shakers were known for their pure and chaste lives. Being devoted to their community, they were admired for the high standards of their craftwork. Though the Shaker community has ceased to exist as a functioning religious church, the legacy of their early labors continues as a recognized style in woodworking.

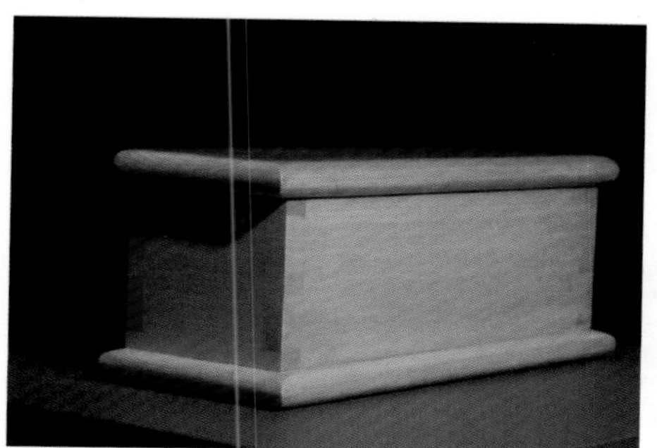

The Shaker tradition and style continues.

Characterizing design elements of simplicity, functionality and beauty, the Shaker candle box is an ideal project to develop skills in box making. Adapted from an original Shaker design, I developed this project to strengthen the skills you learned in the first part of this course, particularly dovetailing. Though this box is a small piece it follows the same principles we use for making larger items such as drawers, toolboxes, blanket chests, and much more. This concept is scalable according to the demands of our projects.

The dovetailed joint and roundover detail.

The dovetailed Shaker candle box

The original Shaker storage box was made from white pine, but you can use any type of wood once you've mastered the skills. This small box will test your layout accuracy and cutting precision.

Remember to work carefully and think through every stage. Where necessary, rehearse steps to see if things 'feel' right for you. Many aspects will be new and you may feel clumsy and awkward because of your lack of experience, but soon your confidence will grow. Begin with sharp tools and be prepared to stop mid-cut if a tool feels dull or the wood looks bruised or ragged when cut.

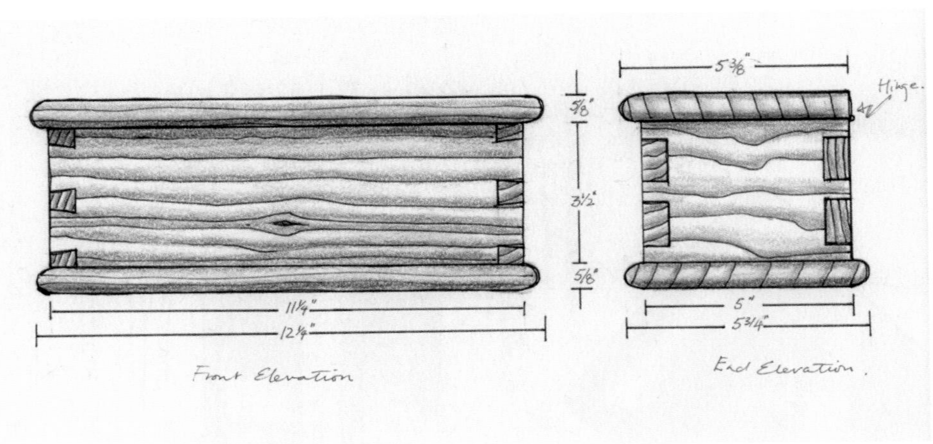

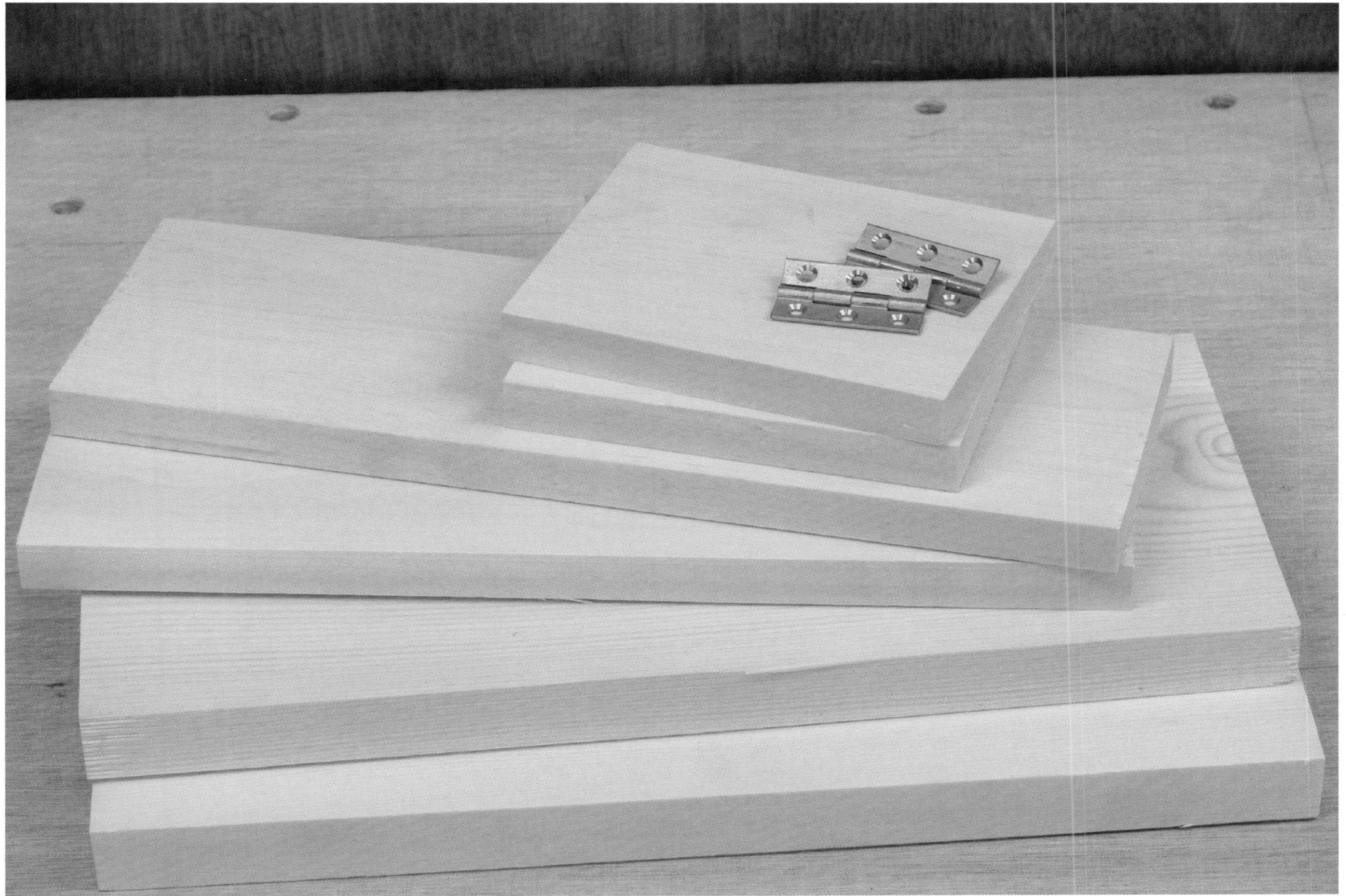

These are the prepared parts for making the box.

Before you start

You need to make sure you are fully conversant with two critical processes, transferring shoulder lines (Chapter 6 Page 93) and creating knifewalls (Chapter 6 page 94).

Before starting, I make pencil notes on my pieces such as top, bottom, left end and right end. This prevents confusion later. I choose the grain of each piece and compare it to related pieces to make sure that they complement one another.

Choose pine as free from defects as possible. Surface planer marks and saw marks from machines can be planed and sanded smooth at various stages of the project: Before, during or after assembly. With your wood prepared and cut to finished sizes, you are ready to begin.

TECHNICAL POINTER: *When you choose your wood, see if you can fit the lengths required in between the knots, so that as you cut pieces to length, you leave the knots out. There may be interesting grain and decorative knots that you like the look of, but make sure these are included through your choice, not just because you forgot to check.*

Materials list:

TOP / BOTTOM: 2 @ 5/8" x 5¾" x 12"

SHORT ENDS: 2 @ ½" x 3½" x 5"

LONG SIDES: 2 @ ½" x 3½" x 11¼"

Joining the box sides

1. Having chosen your outside faces, stand all of your pieces on edge in the exact configuration you want them in the finished box, to ensure they complement each another. Make marks on each corner so you can easily match them after cutting each joint: A to A, B to B and so on.
2. Instead of measuring your distance from the end of the wood, simply place one of the other pieces flush with the end and mark the distance with a sharp-pointed pencil. Do this to each end of all four pieces and use the square and pencil to square a line onto the adjacent faces. These lines represent the shoulder lines of the tail and pin recesses.

TOP TIP: *You may want to make other notes to record your decisions too, such as 'front piece', 'top', 'side' and so on. Mark the best face of each piece with the face mark and one straight edge with the face-edge mark—and stick to them throughout.*

Arrange the pieces according to grain color and grain configuration.

Use your fingertips to establish the shoulder lines.

Do this to every piece and every outside face.

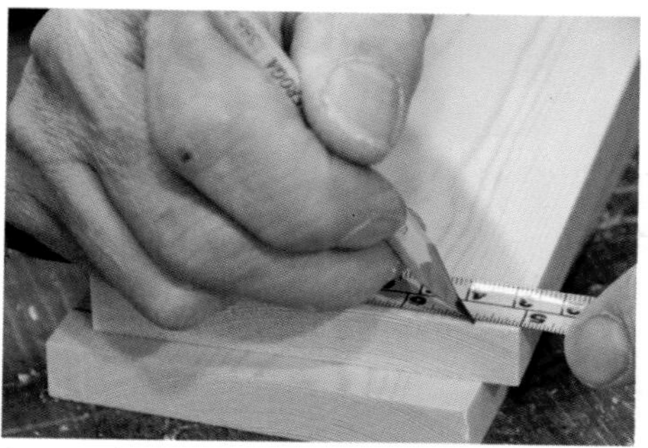
Lay out the dovetail points directly on the corner.

Square the lines across the end.

Use the template or sliding bevel for the angles.

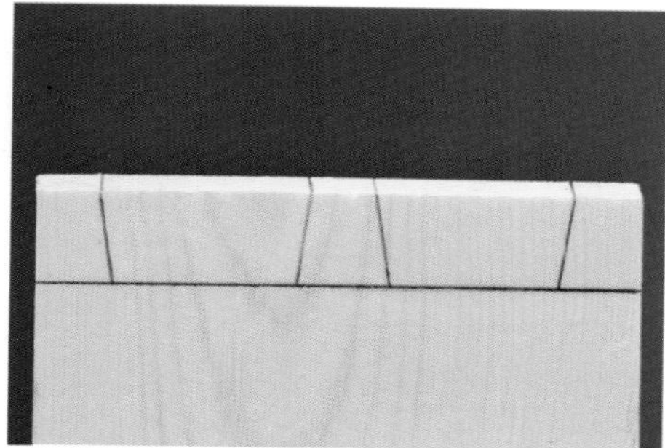
Layout will look like this.

Cut to the lines on the waste side and down to just above the shoulder line.

Cut your two tails first:

1. I prefer the tails of dovetails to be cut on the long pieces. The dovetails start ⅜" in from the top and bottom edges and the middle one is centered between. It's easiest if you measure the 1¾" for the center and then mark $^{3}/_{16}$" on either side of this centerline. Make your marks directly on the end corner and not on the depth (shoulder) line, as this would make the dovetails smaller. Using the square or the dovetail template, square the lines across the ends of each of the long pieces, and then, using the angled shoulders of the template, do the same for the splayed dovetail lines on the face of the front and back pieces.

TECHNICAL POINTER:
Remember to always cut on the waste side of the line—the part you are going to throw away. I usually cut all the dovetails on the four ends first, before marrying the front and back to the end pieces, rather than completing the individual joints one at a time. I then complete each joint to each corner in turn so that I can focus better on cutting the full joint in sequence.

2. Use your tenon saw to cut down the sides of the dovetail layout lines just shy of the shoulder line, taking care to cut on the waste sides of the lines. Press firmly forward, but take care to suspend and feed the saw teeth into the wood. The weight of your hand and the saw itself should be all you need to make these exact cuts. Make every effort to cut precisely parallel to the line.

3. Change the orientation of the workpiece in the vise and start cutting the shoulders. The knife and square ensure perfectly square and defined shoulders, providing the knife is extremely sharp.
4. Using the knife and square, cut through the cross-grain fibers on either side of the dovetails and continue the cut onto both edges, and repeat this on either side of the workpiece.
5. Now use the chisel to create a knifewall on the outside edges of the tail piece, then use your tenon saw to cut down and remove the corner.
6. Switching between vertical and angled horizontal chisel cuts, work through the center pin recess from both sides, until they meet in the middle.

TECHNICAL POINTER:
We continue angling our cuts towards the knifewall (shoulder line) and leave the outer corner intact so that the waste stock is fully supported until the final breakthrough cut is completed. Otherwise the end grain fibers inside the pin or tail recess will tear.

Use the knife and square to cut the knifewall…

…between the tails and on the outer edges.

Further define the knifewall with the chisel.

Cut down the shoulder lines with the dovetail saw.

Chisel into the knifewall to establish the recess.

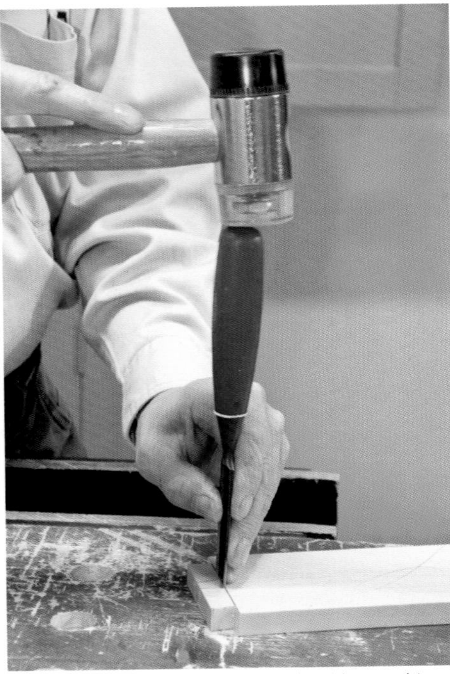
Use vertical cuts to deepen the shoulder, working from both faces equally.

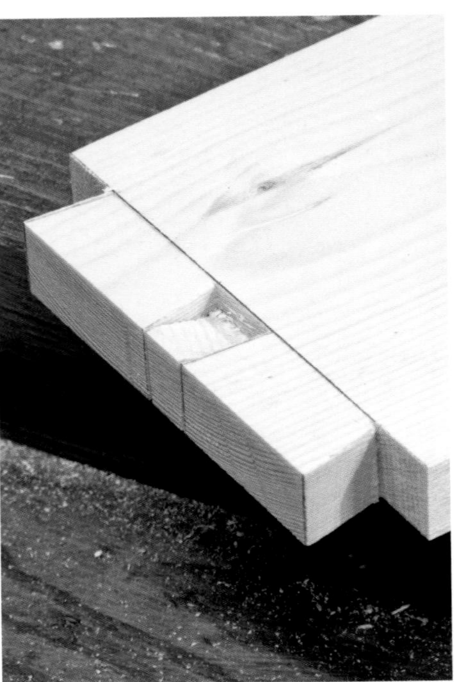
Angle the cut leaving the rim of the waste stock to prevent end-grain tearing inside the recess.

Anchor the pin piece in the vise and use the plane as a platform for the tail piece.

Use a sharp pencil to trace around the dovetails.

Square the lines down on the outside face.

Mark the pins from the tails

TOP TIP: *The shorter pin piece may be held in the vise and registered to the same height as your plane lying on its side. This provides a firm support platform as you mark around the tails.*

1. Transfer your newly cut tails to the end of the pin piece and use a sharp pencil to mark directly and deeply into the inside corners of the dovetails. The sharp pencil ensures the accuracy of these marks, which will reflect in your final dovetails.
2. Square the lines down onto the outside face only. You won't be able to see the other side, so there's little value in marking both sides of the piece.

TOP TIP: *Most common soft-grained woods such as pine are light in color, and so we generally use a sharply pointed pencil to mark around the dovetails. Knife cuts usually don't show very well because the grain closes back when the knife is removed or compresses so easily it looks like a gap around the finished dovetail. On hard, dense-grained woods, the knife mark works well.*

3. Now take a pencil and clearly mark the waste sections with an 'X': in this case, that's the inside of the tail recesses. Take care to cut on the waste side of the line, so your lines will be seen on the pins when the cuts are finished. Don't go beyond the depth line, as any overcuts will show in the finished box.

TECHNICAL POINTER: *When you create the shoulder line on the wider shoulders of the tail recesses, it's important that the two recesses line up perfectly, both from side to side and from outside face to inside face. Any discrepancy will result in gaps along the joint so transfer the shoulder lines with care.*

4. The next step is to define the shoulders of the tail recesses very accurately with knifewalls on both sides of the workpiece. To do this, start by forming the two knifewalls on the first side, using your knife and square. Your 'X' marks will show you which parts are waste and which parts are the pins.
5. Transfer the shoulder lines to the other side of the workpiece and form the other two knifewalls.

TOP TIP: *If you break out and splinter beyond your knifewall, you have either gone in carelessly with your chisel, or you have not mastered that crucial final pass with the knife. The last pass should be precise but deep. A shallow final pass will make it more difficult to get a clean shoulder.*

6. Deepen the knifewalls, alternating between vertical and angled chisel cuts. Work from both faces of the workpiece, until your cuts meet somewhere in the middle.
7. Now repeat these steps to create joints on all corners of your box.

Mark the waste wood with an 'X'.

Cut down the lines on the waste side.

See the cuts within the waste areas.

Establish the shoulder lines between the saw cuts.

The small nick transfers the line to the other side.

Further define the knifewall to the tail recesses.

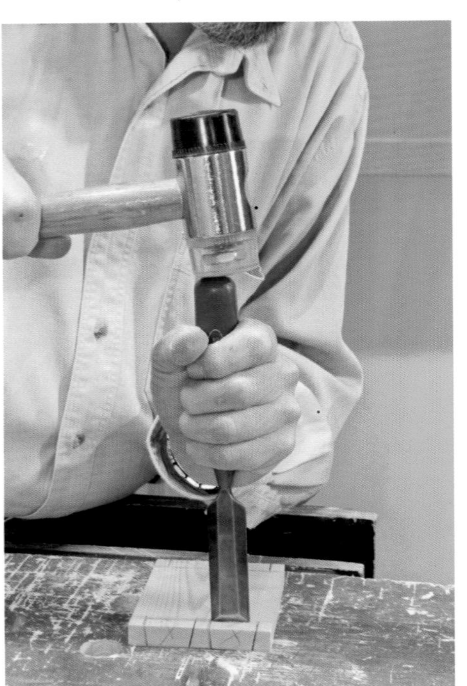
Chop the waste between the pins from both sides.

Press the dovetails carefully into the tail recesses.

Sand the inside faces, avoiding the pins and tails.

Apply glue in the tail recesses, pulling the glue up the pins with a glue stick.

Also glue the tails.

Press the joint together and seat it with a hammer.

Ensure that all the joints are tight.

Box assembly

To prepare the box for gluing, plane and sand the inside faces of the walls. Planing takes skill and confidence. Make sure you've practiced with the plane first and set the iron to take off very fine shavings. Take great care with this because if you plane off too much this will affect the tight fit of your joint. If you are in doubt, simply use sandpaper, making certain not to round over the pins and dovetails as this will show as gaps along the joint. Using a block will prevent this. Sand only in the direction of the grain.

1. Before gluing any project, make sure you know exactly how the project fits together. Gluing up is the point of no return, so it's good practice to rehearse the steps. Gluing one end to the front and back first may make it impossible to glue in the opposite end without forcing the glued joints and causing damage. So, glue up either the front or the back to the two ends first, then glue up the opposite face. It is best to clamp the box in your vise, but you can also use clamps as long as you use scraps of wood to cushion the jaws, otherwise, you will bruise the box walls when pressure is applied.
2. With the box clamped, either in the vise or using clamps, check it's square by measuring diagonally from inside corner to inside corner in each direction. If the two measurements are unequal, loosen the vise slightly and use your mallet to tap the longer corner slightly until both diagonals are the same. If you are using clamps simply slacken them off a fraction and do likewise. This really works. Now set the project aside to dry.

TOP TIP: *It is always a good practice to leave any glued-up assembly to set and dry overnight.*

3. After the glue has dried, plane the outside faces until they are level. If the pins or tails protrude more than 1⁄32", pare down the excess with the corner of a sharp 3⁄4" chisel, and then plane each outside face.

TOP TIP: *To pare down any slight protrusion of pins or tails, rest the flat face of the chisel on the box, and with one hand on the handle, press the chisel firmly down on the workpiece near the bevel with the fingers or thumb of the other hand. Use a sideways slicing motion to slice the end grain fibers. Never try to cut the fibers on the edge without slowly rotating the cutting edge of the chisel in towards the workpiece as you cut, or you will leave an ugly splintered edge.*

4. Plane the long faces of the box from each end towards the middle, so that the unsupported fibers on the corners don't tear and fracture. It's difficult to plane the short faces in the same way, so use a full-width piece of wood between the edge of the box and the vise jaw and plane into this piece instead.
5. After planing, sand the box using 150- and 220 grit sandpapers.

With a sharp chisel, slice away the excess protrusions.

Work carefully towards the outside face, and then pare from the outside face, back in towards the center.

With the tails and pins now chiseled flush, you must now plane the outside faces.

Plane from each end towards the middle.

A support piece prevents unwanted tearout.

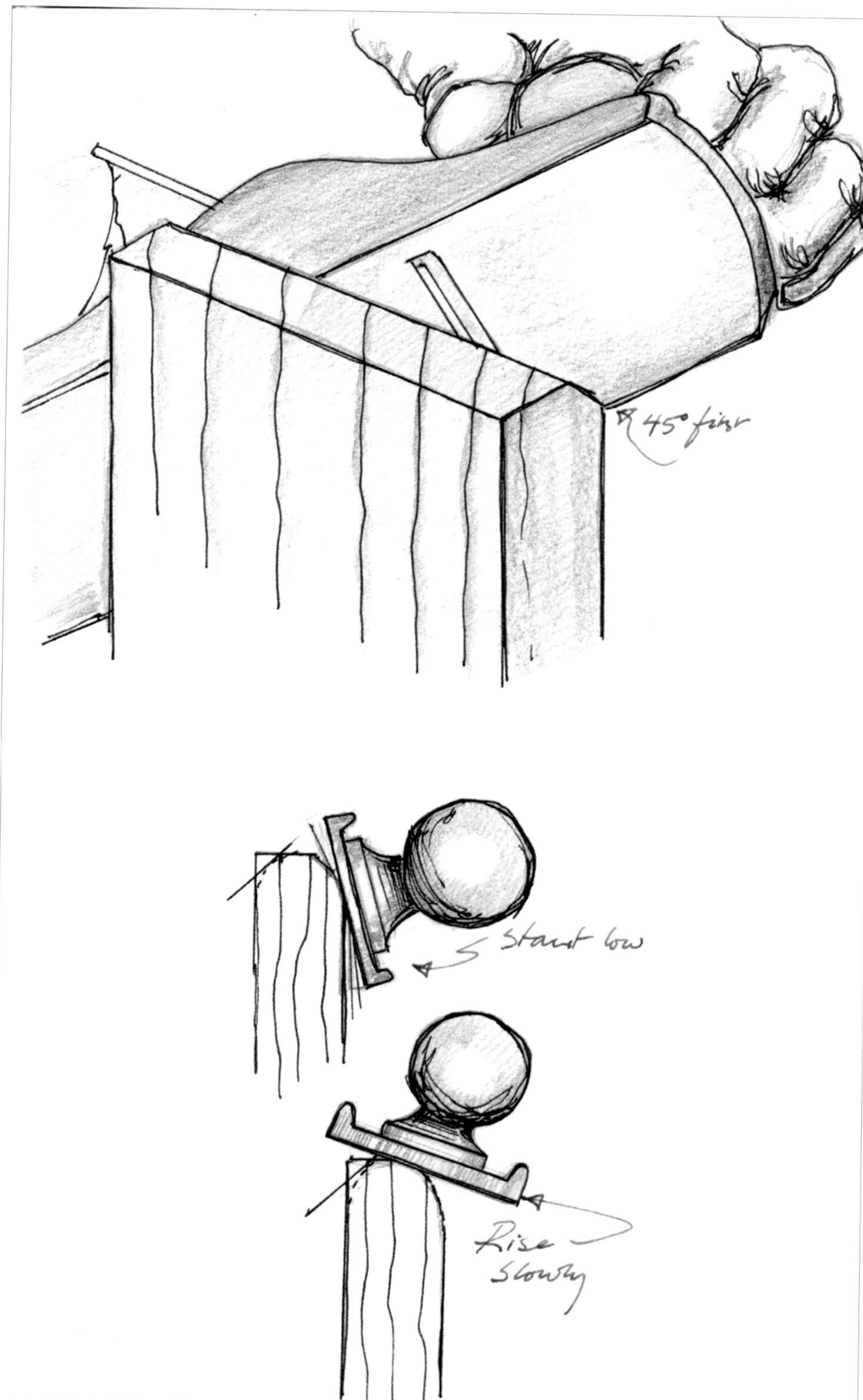

Sequential plane cuts form the rounded edges.

Shaping the lid and base

As an apprentice I rounded the edge of boards for stair treads and windowsills using no more than a number four smoothing plane and sandpaper; hundreds if not thousands of linear feet. It worked well for me then and it will work as well for you now, especially on small projects like the box lid and base you're about to tackle. Using this method eliminates the use of a power router. It's quick and efficient and works on any wood and it's also safe for me and safe for my materials.

Both lid and base are the same size, but the width of the lid will be cut ⅜" narrower than the base. The bottom piece has a ⅜" overhang on all four sides, but the top overhangs only at the front and ends. This is because the back lies flush with the back face of the box to allow the hinges to function freely.

You will shape the half-round profile on the end grain of the top and bottom pieces first, using your smoothing plane to round over the corners. The process is simple enough but will take practice to ensure good results. Practice on a scrap of wood around 5" wide.

1. Secure the bottom piece in the vise with one end uppermost first. Remember that this piece has roundovers on all four edges. Plane the ends first to reduce the risk of tearing the unsupported fibers at the breakout point on the corners. That way, if there is any breakout, planing the long corners will remove any damage. Plane a 45-degree chamfer on the corner along the whole length. Make continuous cuts so that the chamfer remains parallel. Correct any discrepancies by using short plane strokes in any areas as needed. Angling your plane at 45 degrees (compound angle) gives the slicing action necessary to cleanly cut across the end-grain fibers.
2. Once you've created a bevel about ¼" or so wide, change your presentation angle to a much shallower cut. Starting at the bottom, gradually work towards the top with full-length strokes. Alter the angle slightly with each stroke to create a series of small flats less than ⅛" wide. Do the same to the other side.
3. Now, adjust your plane to a very fine setting, and, starting again at the bottom of the roundover, work your way with successive stokes towards the top. Then repeat for the other side.
4. Your roundover should now be fair and even and ready for sanding with 150 grit followed by 220 grit. Repeat this process at the opposite end and then for the two long edges. Finally, repeat this procedure for the lid piece, but this time you need only roundover one of the long edges.

Begin rounding the end first at 45 degrees.

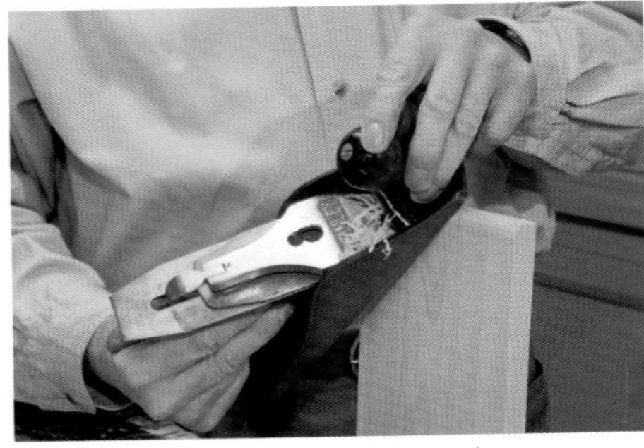

Alter the angles as you round the end.

Further refine the roundover by sanding.

Roundover the long edges.

The bottom piece has all four edges rounded over.

Only one long edge is rounded on the box lid.

Plane the box rim with the smoothing plane.

Make small reference marks in the inside corners.

Run a bead of glue along the bottom rim.

Place the box onto the bottom piece carefully.

Apply clamps to express any glue and leave to dry.

Plane the box rim and glue up

It's usual for the box rim top and bottom to need some leveling. Test the base and lid against the box to see if they rock. If so, look for any high spots and remove them with the hand plane. To do this, place the heel of your plane on the opposite side wall of the box to the edge which you will be planing. This way, as you plane, you can keep the edge face flat. When both lid and base close up nicely, you are ready to glue on the base.

1. Sand the bottom board and place the box on the base, an equal distance to the edges all around. Mark the inside corners with small pencil marks to help you locate the box properly as you glue up.
2. Apply a thin bead of glue to the bottom rim of the box and carefully align the box to the inside corner marks made in step 2. You may find it easier to first secure the two components together in the vise, check the positioning, and then apply the clamps to the opposite ends. Now remove the clamped box and apply further clamps to opposite sides, making sure you apply even pressure all the way around. Leave it to dry overnight.

Setting the hinges

Many woodworkers look for face fix hinges because they are intimidated by setting recessed hinges. The following method will always yield good results if you take the time to lay out your hinges and work with sharp tools. Don't underestimate slight discrepancies, because they always translate into unsightly gaps and cause lids and doors to be misaligned.

1. Before laying out for your hinges you must trim your box lid down by ⅜". Measure ⅜" from the back edge and make a small mark. Now use your finger as a guide and continue this line along the full length of the back edge. Use your handsaw and cut slightly away from your line and use the plane to smooth the edge and also bring you all the way down to the line.
2. Measure 1½" from the end of the box, not the lid. Using a pencil, mark the outside position of the hinges across the face of both the back of the box and the lid. Mark an 'X' to both box and lid to show which side of the line the hinges will be positioned.
3. Mark the length of the recess first, using the hinge upside down so that its knuckle acts as a square against the back edge of the box lid. This will help guide your knife as you cut the knifewall at each end of the hinge, and along its edge.
4. Set your marking gauge to the thickness of the hinge flap and score a depth line between the knifewalls marked from the hinge.
5. Make a series of cross-grain cuts with your ½" chisel, bevel down, across the recess area. Then remove the fractured waste by paring with the same chisel.

Mark a line ⅜" from the back edge of the box lid.

Cut the waste on the waste side of the line.

Remove the saw marks with the smoothing plane.

Measure 1½" from the end of the box, not the lid.

Mark an 'X' on both lid and box for hinge position.

Lightly mark the hinge position with the knife.

Set the gauge to the thickness of the hinge flap.

Further define the knifewall.

Small chisel cuts weaken the fibers.

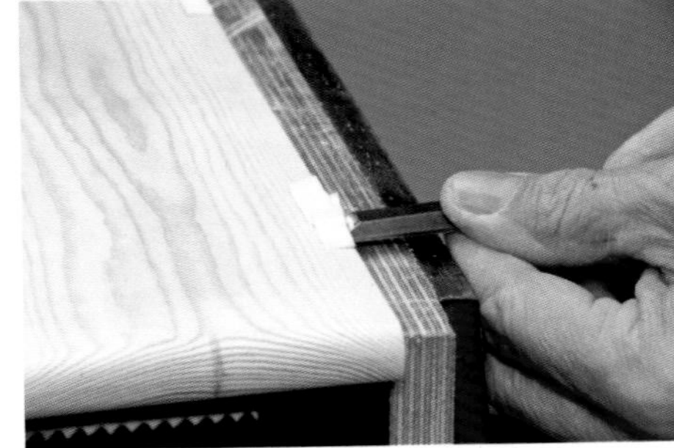

Remove the waste by paring with a ½" chisel.

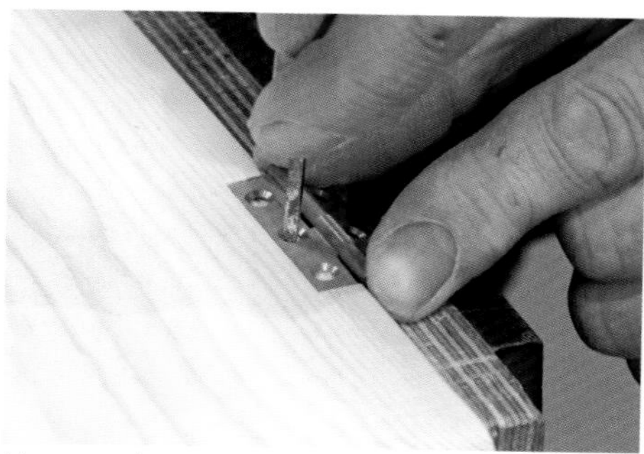
Use an awl to ream starter holes and screw the hinges into the box lid recesses.

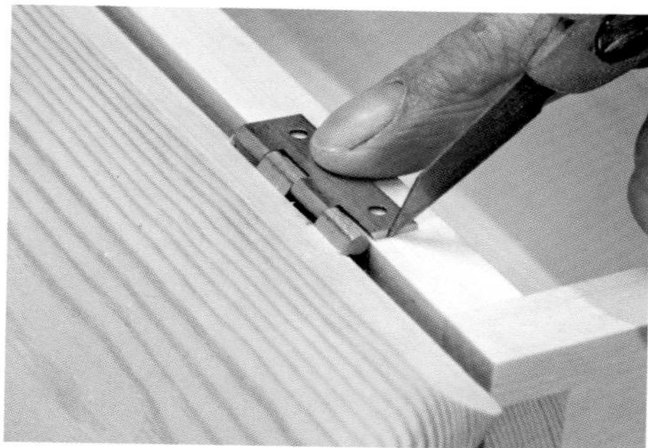
Trace the position of the hinges on the box rim and recess as before.

Make the start holes and screw the lid to the box.

Align the hinge screws for a well-finished look.

The box is now ready for a protective finish.

TOP TIP: *With the hinge fitting snugly, take an awl and ream a small hole towards the back of the holes in the hinge. This ensures that as the screws are put in, the countersunk heads tighten the hinge towards the back of the recess.*

6. With the hinges screwed to the box lid, turn the lid over and rest the hinges (with an equal overhang on both sides), with the hinge flaps flat on top of the back rim of the box. Now use your knife to define the position of the hinges and a marking gauge, set as before, to scribe between the lines for the depth of the hinge flap. Use the hinges to guide your knife along the length of the hinge, giving you the cut line needed to make the recess. Remove the waste wood as before.
7. Finally, screw the hinged lid to the box.

TOP TIP: *Small things make the difference to fine work. Align the slotted screw heads along the length of the hinge.*

Your finished box should be stored in its final resting place for a few weeks before you do anything else. If you have made it in your outside workshop, take it indoors to a drier environment. If the lid cups slightly, unscrew it, plane it flat and even up the roundovers. At this point, sand your box lightly and apply a coat of shellac, varnish or paint to complete your project. Clear shellac is a great sealer and is easy to apply. If you wish to use dark colored shellac, apply it quickly and confidently, wearing disposable gloves and don't be tempted to go over the same part twice.

A typical box, just completed by one of my students. This will look great with a few more coats of shellac

Conclusion

You have just entered the wonderful world of box making. Shaker artisans knew the value of mastering the common dovetail joint because they used it so extensively on a wide range of projects. Mastering the skills takes practice, but soon perfect dovetails will be coming straight from your saw. Make more of these boxes until you are completely confident. They'll be good training for your apprentice piece—traditionally, your own toolbox.

8 Making a four-shelf wall unit

This project covers the construction methods for building display shelves and bookcases—two important areas of woodworking and furniture making. I've used two joints in the project to show how the strength of one will compensate for the weakness of the other. Often, bookshelves have the inherent weakness of having only housing dado joints to rely on for lateral stability. Generally, adding a panelled back will give them the rigidity required to resist lateral pressure. In this project, we use tenoned cross-rails to add this rigidity and I'll show you how to add a shaped arch to the rails to create a more elegant look.

The skills you will learn can be adapted to many different areas of woodworking. Scaling this project up and down by doubling or halving the measurements will give you a full-sized bookcase or a small spice rack. You may want to change the spacing to accommodate large or small books, or remove a shelf.

I have chosen pine as a suitable wood for learning on, but there are many others you could choose. To develop your finishing skills, we'll explore four finishing options: paint, clear shellac, stain or varnish.

We will be developing two types of joint in this project: the mortise and tenon and the housing dado joint.

Preparing your work

With your pieces cut to the finished sizes, use the smoothing plane to remove any machine marks and surface defects. Remember, planing the surfaces to an ultra-smooth finish takes skill and practice with the hand plane. If you have not yet gained a working knowledge of bench planes, go to the sharpening section and learn how to set up and troubleshoot your hand plane in chapter 14 pages 231 to 255.

Examine the pieces and look at the grain for color, grain configuration and texture, which will help you decide on their ideal position. Arrange the pieces on the bench in their relative positions to see how the pieces work together and how they complement one another—a critical step often overlooked even by experienced artisans. Make notes such as: top left, top right, mid shelf and so on to signify how you want to arrange the pieces in your project.

Start with the sides:

1. Place the two side pieces with the insides facing each other and back edges uppermost. Flush the back edges and clamp them in the vise. Lay out the positions of the stopped housing dadoes in the back edges of the side pieces, referring to the drawing for the measurements. These are the housing dadoes that will hold the shelves. Use the square and pencil to place these initial lines so you can make permanent gauge and knife lines within the joint area.
2. Square the lines onto the inside faces and, with a marking gauge set to ⅞", score the distance line from the front edges onto the inside faces of both side pieces.

Notes from my sketchbook.

Lay out the position of the shelves on the back edge of the two side pieces.

Square the lines onto the inside faces.

Set the marking gauge to ⅞" and score the lines.

Follow the patterns for making a housing dado.

Carefully deepen the knifewall with the 1" chisel.

The square guarantees the exact knifewall line.

Use the knife to reach tight into the corner to establish the exact position of the second knifewall.

TOP TIP: *At this stage, don't be concerned with the top and bottom pieces, I'll show you how to accurately mark and join these once you have the first trial assembly complete.*

3. Set your marking gauge to ¼" and mark the depth on the back edge.
4. With guidelines in place, use the knife and the square to establish the first knifewall on the inside faces of your pieces. You need to remember two things here: Firstly, you are cutting a stopped housing dado joint, so the knifewall must stop at the ⅞" gauge line you made in step 2. Secondly, cut only one knifewall to each of the housing dadoes at this stage. You will cut the second knifewalls only when the corresponding shelves can be used to establish the precise width of each housing.
5. With the mallet and 1" chisel, make perpendicular cuts along the full length of the knifewall to deepen the wall of the housing. Take care not to strike too hard or this will compress the wood fibers and move the knifewall. This is especially true in soft-fibered woods like pine.
6. Alternating between perpendicular and angled horizontal cuts, work down the knifewall, stopping slightly above the depth line.
7. Once all six housing dadoes are cut to the required depth on one side only, you can then mark the other knifewalls. This is the crucial step that is 'make or break' for the accuracy of your joints. For precision, use the corresponding shelves to mark the next knifewall lines. Place the first board end against the corresponding knifewall and, with your layout knife, make a small cut tight into the corner to establish the exact position of the knifewall line. There is no room for error here, otherwise gaps will appear and the finished joint will be loose.
8. Now register your knife and square with the nick you have just made. Then, using the square to guide the knife, make a careful knife line. Establish your knifewall and follow the usual method to deepen the knifewall down to the full depth of the housing dado.

9. Use a ¾" chisel to remove the waste wood taking care not to cut too deeply. When you're slightly above the line—no more than ¹⁄₁₆" —you can use the hand router to trim down to the depth line and level the bottom of the housing dado. Square up the front corner of the housing dado with the chisel.

Repeat this procedure for all the remaining housing dado joints. This will complete all the housing dadoes to the side pieces. If you own the video on making this project, check out the methods and techniques that make this process fast and accurate.

The second knifewall follows the same pattern...

...alternating between vertical and horizontal cuts.

Remove the bulk of the waste with the ¾" chisel, cutting with the bevel up.

Trim the inside corners neatly with the same chisel.

Use the hand router to guarantee the exact depth.

Cross cutting to length follows exact knifewalls.

The saw lines up with the knifewall perfectly.

Establish the step with a small knife mark…

Trim to the knifewall lines with the plane.

…square across the front edge with the knife…

…and onto the adjacent faces.

Notch the corner with the tenon saw.

Trim as needed with the chisel.

The finished notch looks like this.

Making the shelves

With the housing dadoes complete, crosscut the shelves to length. Follow the same patterns for all cross-grain cutting by creating a knifewall first. This knifewall goes all the way around the board so the fibers don't tear beyond the knife cuts. Cut carefully up to the knife-line and use the smoothing plane to level any protrusions as necessary.

> **TECHNICAL POINTER:** *Always use a well-sharpened, well-set hand plane for end grain planing. Take very fine shavings and work carefully. Keep the workpiece low in the vise to reduce vibration and be very sensitive to the results as you take each pass with your plane. Don't plane right to the farthest edge or the unsupported fibers will break and fracture on the outer edge. Stop short and turn the workpiece round in the vise to prevent this.*

1. Fit each shelf into the corresponding housing dado in its correct orientation and slide it towards the front, giving the back edge a gentle tap to make sure it seats fully. Make a small knife mark on the front edge of the shelf to mark the exact depth of the step down at each end.
2. After removing the shelf, transfer the knife line around the shoulder defining the notch you are about to cut out. Use your marking gauge set at ⅞", and mark a light gauge line to define the other three shoulder lines.
3. Further define the knifewall with the 1" chisel, on the front edge only. It's not necessary on the other faces.
4. Cross-cut the shoulder with your tenon saw down to the ⅞" gauge line and finally use the saw to cut along the gauge line to remove the corner. Repeat the process for all the other shelves. Make sure to trim any sawing discrepancies with the chisel as protrusions will hold off the shoulders.

First trial assembly

Assemble the side pieces and the shelves and carefully clamp all the unit parts together to make certain the joints are fully seated. This step enables you to take exact measurements for the distance between the housing dadoes in your top and bottom pieces directly from this first trial assembly.

Making the top and bottom pieces

1. The top and bottom pieces are ⅞" wider than the side pieces, and the housing dadoes stop ⅞" from the front edge. This allows the full width of the side pieces to slot in, with the top and bottom pieces protruding by the same distance.
2. The absolute reference for the first knifewalls is taken from the inside measurement between the side pieces, directly adjacent to the shelf. Measure the top piece from the top shelf and the bottom piece from the bottom shelf by centering the piece on the assembled frame and using the knife to make the knife marks on the inside corners.
3. When you have these distance marks (knife marks), lay out the joints with a gauge and pencil, just as you did for the side pieces. Establish these first, inside knifewalls in the usual manner.
4. Individually offer the joints to the corresponding ends of the side pieces, marking the second knifewall positions with an equal amount of care and precision as before. Cut and finish the housing dadoes as before, and check for fit.

Dry-assemble the shelves and clamp together…

…and use the knife to transfer the exact distance.

Again, follow the steps for cutting housing dadoes.

Mark directly in the corner with the knife.

Chisel the second knifewall.

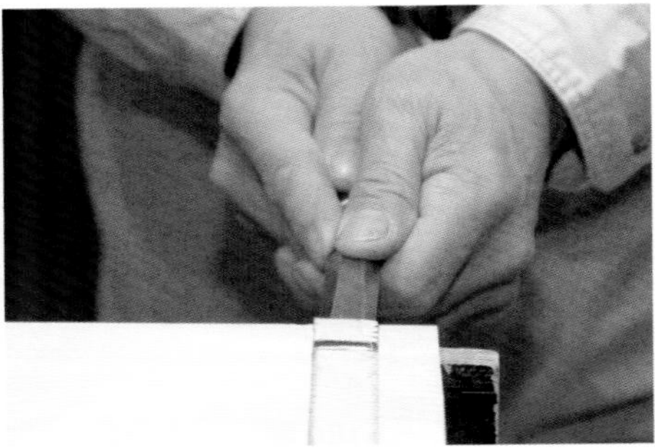

Remove the waste.

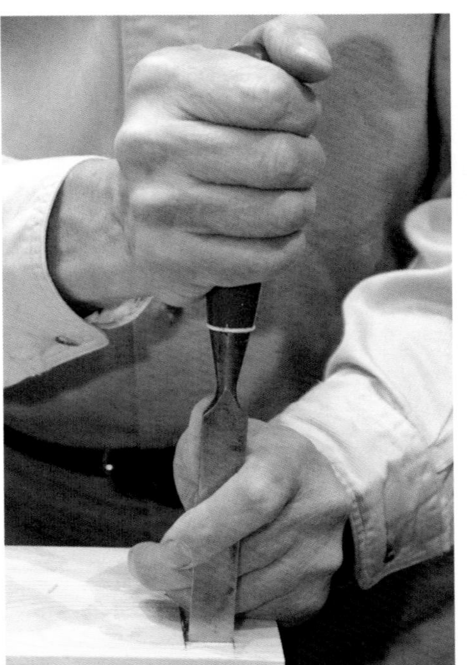

Trim the inside corners.

Level the bottom with the hand router.

Laying out the cross-rails.

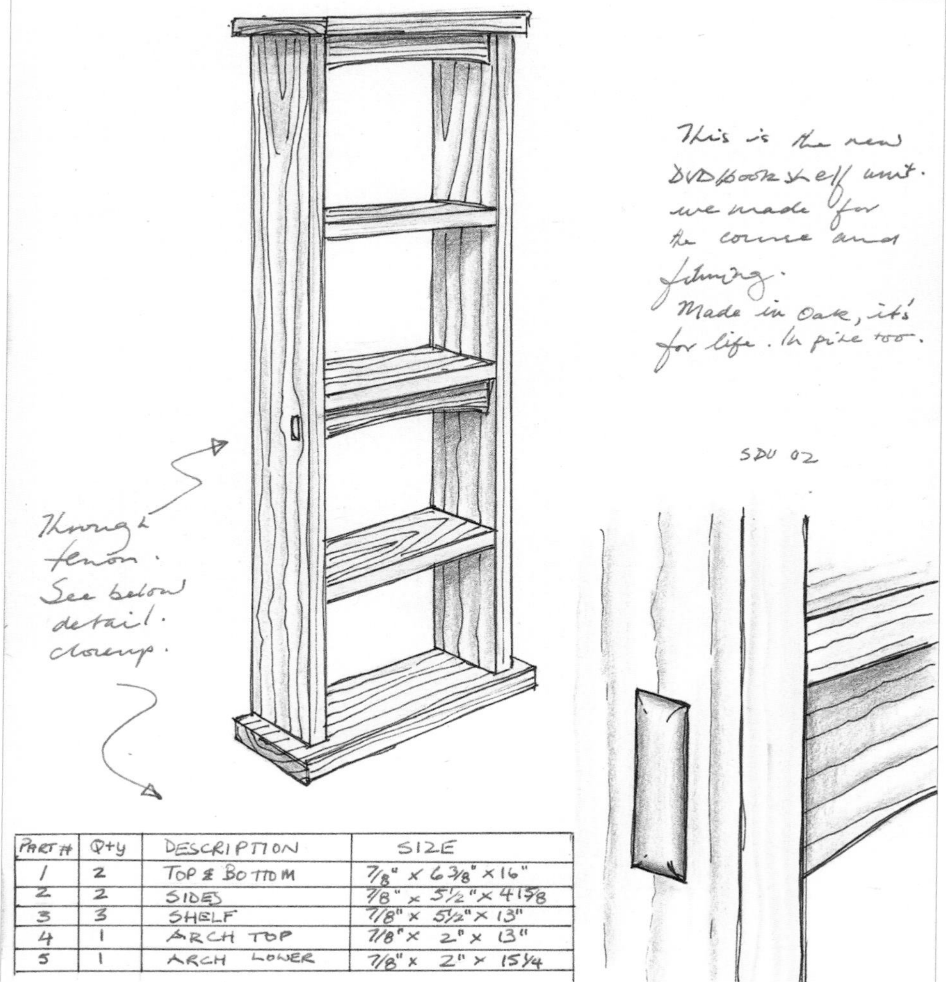
This is the new DVD/bookshelf unit. we made for the course and filming.
Made in Oak, it's for life. In pine too.
SDU 02
Through tenon. See below detail. closeup.

PART #	Q+y	DESCRIPTION	SIZE
1	2	TOP & BOTTOM	7/8" x 6 3/8" x 16"
2	2	SIDES	7/8" x 5½" x 41 5/8
3	3	SHELF	7/8" x 5½" x 13"
4	1	ARCH TOP	7/8" x 2" x 13"
5	1	ARCH LOWER	7/8" x 2" x 15¼

Cutting list from my journal.

Your second trial assembly

Now assemble and clamp the entire shelf unit ensuring that all the housing dadoes fit correctly. You will be using this assembled frame to take measurements for the arched cross-rails, so any adjustment to your joints should be made at this time. Typical adjustments may include trimming out the waste in the end corners of the stopped dadoes, cleaning up the dado joints with more care, or carefully planing very fine shavings from any shelf or side piece which is too tight. For the next stage, the whole unit needs to be fully assembled and clamped in place after any adjustments you have made.

Cross-rails and mortises

The concealed joint used for the top cross-rail comprises a blind mortise and a stub tenon. The lower cross-rail uses a through mortise and tenon joint, with the tenon ends protruding through the side pieces. I will show you a practical and attractive way to make these through tenons a feature that adds a finishing touch.

The cross-rails you are about to cut and fit have three main purposes. Firstly, the through-mortise and cross-rail provides a solid and permanent support to undergird the shelves. Secondly, this through cross-rail prevents the sides from moving outwards. Thirdly, the shoulders cut on both cross-rail tenons provide lateral stability. Sideways force would otherwise strain and rack the housing dado joints, transforming the square frame into a trapezium and shortening the life of the bookcase considerably.

With the clamps still in place, offer the top cross-rail to the underside of the top shelf and using a sharp pencil, mark the width of the rail onto the two side pieces. Repeat this for the middle cross-rail.

Mark the top mortises using the top cross-rail.

Use the mortise gauge to score the mortise lines.

Again, mark the lower mortises using the cross-rail.

Set the pins to the chisel you will use to cut the mortise holes.

> *"the shoulders cut on both cross-rail tenons provide lateral stability"*

Blind mortise holes

1. Separate the parts and mark the position of the top mortises on the inside faces only, using the mortise gauge set to a ½" chisel, with the first (moveable) pin set to ⅞". This is also the same setting for the lower cross-rail mortise.
2. Create a knifewall across the grain to the two extremes of the mortise width using the knife and square.
3. Chop the mortise to ¼" deep, and clean up the corners of the mortise holes.

Chop the mortise with the ½" chisel…

…stop when ¼" deep.

The top mortises look like this.

Through-mortise holes

1. Now you can focus on chopping the through-mortise for the lower crossrail. Mark out the mortise as you did for the top cross-rail, only this time transfer the knife lines to the outside faces of the side pieces; this also includes the line of the underside of the shelf. By doing this, the mortise may be cut from both sides and the shoulder lines will match perfectly.
2. You can now score the parallel lines of the mortise with the mortise gauge you used for the top cross-rail.
3. Cut the knifewall with the square and knife to the exact width of the middle cross-rail piece, which is 2".
4. Cut the mortise hole with the ½" chisel, working from both inside and outside faces of the side piece until they meet in the middle. Then repeat to the opposite side piece.

Mark the mortise hole lines with the gauge.

Mark the knifewall on the inside face...

...transfer the knifewall using a small nick...

...and onto the outside face.

Further define the knifewall with the chisel.

Chop the mortise, cutting from both faces.

Cut up to the line, but don't lever on the knifewall!

Complete the mortise from the inside face, but take care not to burst through to outside face.

With the mortise cut through, pull the chisel back and forth in the mortise hole to remove any fibers.

Mark the shoulder lines from the assembled unit.

Use the square and knife to establish the knifewall shoulder line.

Make an incised chisel cut into the knifewall.

Cut the shoulder with the tenon saw.

Cut down the tenon to the shoulder.

Making the tenons

The tenons have only one shoulder to the front face of the cross-rail, the other back face is left untouched. This type of tenon is commonly known as a 'barefaced' tenon.

The distance between shoulder lines of the tenons corresponds exactly to the distance between the side pieces when assembled, so eyeball for center and mark this distance directly to both the top and middle cross-rail pieces, using the knife to mark the exact positions of the shoulders.

Note: The top rail needs to be ½" longer than the measurement between the side pieces, as the stub tenons are ¼" long on each end.

1. Create the knifewall across the front face of your top crossrail.
2. For making tenons we use a marking gauge set to a ½" chisel to mark the thickness of the tenon, registering the stock against the back 'bare' face of the tenon.
3. Clamp the rail in the vise and chisel into the shoulder line on the waste side of the line, deepening the knifewall.
4. Cross-cut the shoulder line with the tenon saw down to the gauge line.
5. Saw down the gauge line to develop the face of the tenon and trim as necessary. You may also choose to split the tenon face with a chisel, which is perfectly acceptable provided the grain run is suitable.
6. Repeat with the opposite end and try the tenons into their relevant mortise holes.

TECHNICAL POINTER:
Remember that the distance between the side pieces can vary depending on which point you take your measurement from. Make sure that when you are marking the shoulder positions of the tenons, you mark them from near to the final position in the piece.

7. Now repeat the whole procedure for the middle cross-rail tenons, which are longer because they pass through and protrude ⅜" past the outside faces of the side pieces.

8. Fit the tenons to their appropriate mortise holes, making sure they seat fully with no gaps at the shoulders.

TOP TIP: *The end of the stub tenon may hit the bottom of the blind mortise, and prevent the shoulder from fully seating. If it does 'bottom out', either trim the stub tenon, or deepen the blind mortise further.*

Cross cut the knifewall shoulder line.

Mark the front face of the tenon with the gauge.

Chisel in to the knifewall.

Saw or split the tenon and trim to an even surface.

The stub- and through-tenons look like this.

Dry-assemble the shelf unit to check the joints seat well with no gaps.

Mark the tenon lightly for the round over detail.

The marked through tenon.

9. Dry-assemble all components to ensure that all the parts correspond and there are no gaps and no adjustments are necessary.
10. Now mark around the protruding tenons, using the outside edge of the mortise holes as a guide. Mark all the way round lightly with a sharp pencil and then take the unit apart, making sure all corresponding joints are marked clearly on the back edges of all parts.

TOP TIP: *Trial assembly always takes care, particularly when mortise and tenon joints are involved. Wherever possible, I always hold the tenon member firmly in the vise and ease the mortise part onto it with a very slight rocking motion. Also worth mentioning is the use of packers underneath the shelf unit to prevent the protruding tenon from sustaining damage and causing the unit to rock.*

Shaping the arched cross-rails

Even if I am only making one piece, I generally find it best to make a template for shaped parts. Sometimes a part needs replacing or replicating. The arches are centered onto both arched pieces between the shoulders of the tenons. The actual radius is 24", but you can freehand the arc using your arm or forearm as a beam to sketch the desired shape, or scale up the pattern on page 320.

The stop-cut method

1. Instead of using the bandsaw, or even a bow or coping saw, make a series of saw cuts across the grain, stopping 1⁄16" or so above the line. We call these saw cuts stop-cuts because they stop the wood from splitting beyond the cut.

Templates ensure accuracy, but it's also good to practice freehand arches to establish initial shapes.

Sawn stop-cuts work well for forming arches.

Keep the saw cuts about 1" or less apart.

Chop away the waste wood, working from the high point down into the low area...

...working from each end...

...and meeting somewhere in the center.

Even out any undulation with the spokeshave.

2. Use a 1" chisel and, with the bevel facing downwards and using your chisel hammer, chisel from the high points at the end, down and towards the center at the low point. Watch constantly for the run of the grain to ensure you're not running below the stop-cuts. Work first from one end and stop in the middle, then cut from the opposite end, again towards the center, always working from the higher points downwards towards the lower points.
3. With the bulk of the waste removed and with your chisel still held bevel down, carefully pare off any uneven steps, working close to the line but not quite touching it. You can then use your spokeshave (flat-bottomed) to finish shaving any uneven undulations down to the line.

Shaping the tenon ends

The protruding tenon ends add an interesting aesthetic detail, but they should also be shaped to complete the dovetail and prevent any corner fibers from breaking.

> **TECHNICAL POINTER:** *To make sure that you don't round over the ends of these tenons too much, don't forget to offer them into the mortise making sure they are fully seated and make a light pencil mark on all four sides of the tenon to indicate how much it protrudes. This will help you to make sure that you only round the part of the tenon that protrudes.*

The round over on the wide faces is formed in the same way as the round over on the Shaker box lid. We use a series of incrementally finer passes with the plane to form the shape. It's important to round over these wide faces before the narrow faces, otherwise corners can fracture and repair is difficult.

We now round over the tenon end.

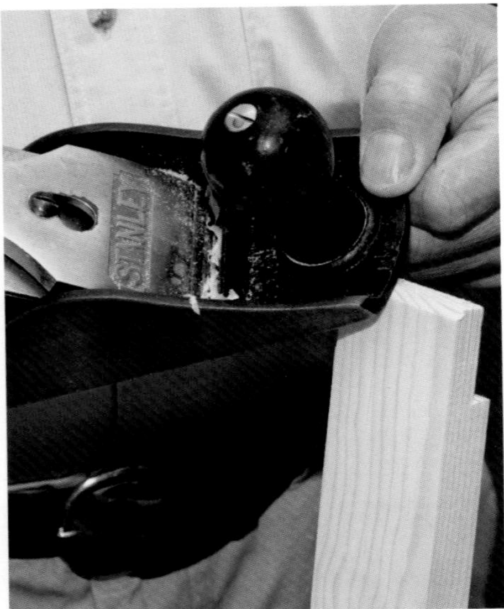

Use the plane the same way you made the box lid.

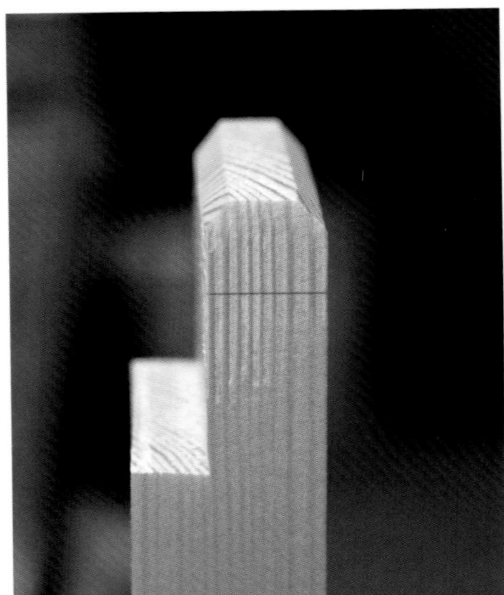

Chamfer first…

…followed by rounding over the broad faces.

Angling the plane gives best results.

The end becomes more rounded with finer cuts.

Keep the first cut at a low angle…

…the next one slightly higher.

The sequential steps to rounding the narrow faces comprise a series of separate cuts with a wide chisel.

Finish all the round overs with the flat file using arching strokes.

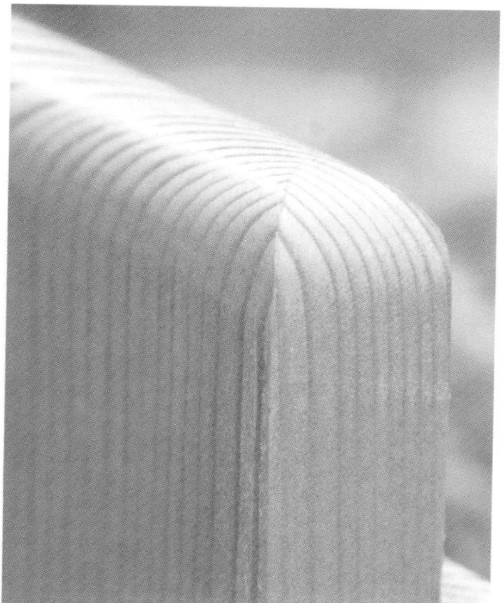

The final tenon end looks crisp on the corners and round overs.

1. To round the narrow ends of the tenon we use a definite sequential method using a 1" chisel. You can do this by placing the chisel as low as possible on the outside of your pencil line, and giving the back of the chisel handle a short bump with the heel of your hand. This quickly takes off the waste, while giving you complete control.
2. Then move the chisel ⅛" nearer to the end, raising the chisel elevation further and repeat this procedure until the bulk of the waste is removed and then use the file for final shaping.
3. File the edges in careful sweeping strokes in one direction only. The file will give a clean and polished finish, as shown in the photo. Sand the arched pieces to 220 grit.

Assembling the unit

Sand all faces to 220 grit and remove any hard corners before final assembly. Again, rehearse the gluing-up procedure beforehand and set your clamps to the right distances to save time. Make sure you cushion your wood from direct contact with the metal clamp heads during gluing using small scraps of wood. Glue the components in the following sequence:

1. Starting with the two cross-rails and center shelf, glue these into one of the side pieces.
2. Then slot in the remaining intermediate shelves before adding the opposite side piece.
3. The top and bottom go on next. Seating the housing dadoes on the sides will hold the shelf unit together while you reach for the clamps.
4. With all the parts assembled, apply the clamps and check that the whole assembled unit is square by measuring from corner to corner.

Mark tested joints with letters or numbers.

Glue shelves and cross-rails to one side piece first…

…making sure all the components fully seat.

Add the opposite side piece.

Use clamps with protective pads on each joint.

Use clamps back and front to equalize the pressure within all of the joints.

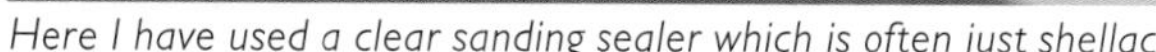
Here I have used a clear sanding sealer which is often just shellac.

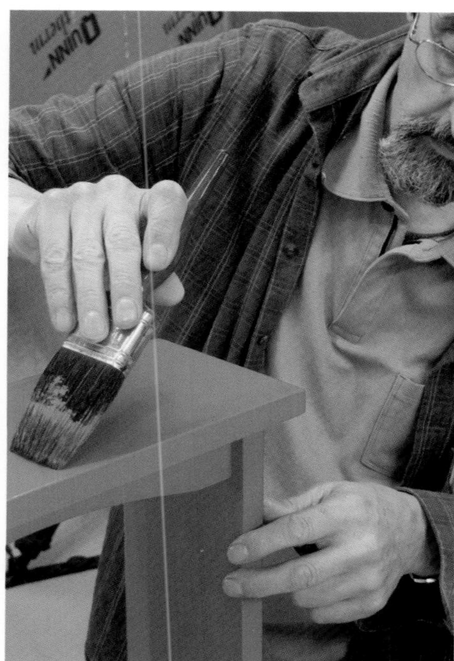
Paint can look lovely as well.

Finishing the job

The clamps can be removed the following day. Any visible glue around the joints should be carefully sliced off with a sharp chisel. Any glue on a visible face, can be pared off and sanded with the grain to remove all traces. It may be barely visible at this stage, but when you apply any finish other than high opacity paint, it will be very visible.

This shelf looks good with a clear protective coat of water-based varnish, a rich shellac, or a quality matt or eggshell paint.

Applying a finish that looks good primarily depends on four factors:

THE OPACITY OF THE FINISH: A strong color on a light background is going to create streaks more readily than a lighter shade of the same product. If you are using a clear finish, this eliminates this problem. Paints generally cover evenly, but translucent finishes such as colored stains, shellac and varnish are more prone to blotching and streaking and so require successive coats to 'fill' the grain to an even look.

THE DRYING TIME: A water based varnish will give you more time to get an even coat than with say shellac. Shellac, being based on alcohol, needs to be applied very quickly and evenly, there is no going back to dab it a moment later as this 'pulls' or drags the previous coat.

SURFACE TENSION: Oil based paints and some varnishes have a self leveling characteristic that evens out a coat within moments of application. The solvents (white spirit or water) allow the finish to even out across the surface due to surface tension.

TECHNIQUE: This is an area that could justify a book in its own right. It is not my intention here to furnish you with any depth or breadth of teaching at this stage, as you will learn all this later on in the course. I suggest you follow the manufacturer's recommendations for any finishing product you may choose. If you are not confident about the application, practice on some scrap first and examine the results. If you are in doubt, go for a clear finish of shellac or water based varnish. You can progress to darker shades as you get used to working quickly and evenly.

As I said, this rudimentary information is just a basic guide to get you started.

Conclusion

This project has demanded precise cutting, absolute squareness, exact depths and accurate knifewalls which will have improved your artisan skills. Although striving for high levels of workmanship is a constant struggle, they are within your reach. Now that you understand the joint making process, and how the weakness of one type may be bolstered by the strength of another, you may consider designing projects to reinforce your new skills. You can scale this basic pattern up or down, and develop alternative designs. Only through practice will you develop accuracy and sensitivity in your work. You'll also be learning more about your tools and how to tackle the wood grain from different angles. You are now entering the realms of becoming a new-genre artisan.

9 Making a chairside table

Tables come in every shape and size and are very much a part of our everyday lives. I've made every type of table from conference tables to desks, lamp tables and sofa tables, but the unique quality that unites them all is one most people will never see. Just about every table ever made relies on a single joint type—the mortise and tenon. By making this chairside table, you'll learn the skills for making virtually any kind of table, regardless of size, and you'll scarcely need to even alter the size of the joint. This project walks you through the step-by-step process of making heirloom quality tables. Tables are one of the most commonly bought furniture pieces and solid oak ensures the heirloom quality continues.

Notes from my woodworking journal.

Structural Design

The table relies on only nine pieces of wood to form the main frame and a glued up top. The construction isn't complicated, but it does follow a structured procedure that guarantees good results.

What you will need:

For this project, you will need most of your general equipment.

For the joinery, you will need the ten or so tools from your joinery set, and a few shaping tools.

Make sure your sharpening equipment is near to hand and all your tools are sharpened up before you start.

Materials list:

TOP: 1 @ ⅞" x 15" x 15" (You may need to glue two pieces together. In fact, the top will be more stable if you do).

APRON RAILS: 4 @ ⅞" x 4" x 12¼"

LEGS: 4 @ 1⅝" x 1⅝" x 24"

Turnbuttons: 3 @ ⅞" x 1¼" x 3½" (This will make 6 turnbuttons)

This mortise alignment guide is simple to make and really works!

You only require two pieces of wood.

Line it up and flush the edges when you glue it.

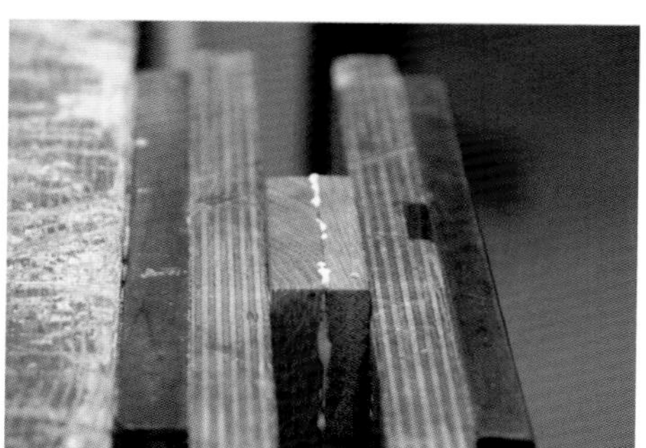
Leave it clamped in the vise until fully dry.

Planning Ahead

As with any project that uses glued-up boards to form wider panels, you may want to prepare the top in advance by planing the edges, gluing and clamping it together as shown later in this chapter.

The mortise alignment guide

Chopping mortises is a simple task, but there is one aspect that is particularly important. In order to achieve perfect results every time, the mortise must be square to the mortise face. I developed the mortise alignment guide so that my students could cut perfectly aligned mortise holes every time. I recommend that you use the guide to align your chisel perpendicular as you chop deeper into the mortises. After a short time you will develop the ability to cut accurate mortise holes both square and fully aligned without the aid. I recommend that you use the guide until you develop the skill to work accurately and with confidence.

1. Cut a piece of wood that is 3½" wide, 3½" long, and about ½" thick.
2. Now take a second piece of wood the same length as the first but only 1½" wide. The thickness of this second piece is the same as the distance that you want the mortise to be from the edge, ⅜". Notice that this narrower piece is placed with the grain counter to the main piece. This orientation reduces the wear on the guide and strengthens the assembly.
3. Now glue the second piece to the first with three edges of the second piece flush to the edges of the first.

When you cut your mortise holes you can now clamp this guide in the vise with the piece as shown to ensure a perfectly aligned mortise every time. This guide will work for cutting any mortise hole regardless of how wide but only if it is the same distance from the outside face. For a longer wearing guide you can glue a piece of laminate onto the surface that the chisel registers against, but you must account for the extra thickness of the laminate.

Preparing the legs

To prepare the four legs, begin by lightly planing each face of the leg, to remove surface defects and machine marks. I first consider the grain color and structure and match them as pairs so that they complement one another. Next, place them all together in the arrangement you have chosen. By marking them in this position, you'll keep the same configuration as you work on the mortise and tenon joinery.

At this point I would also choose the outer faces of my apron pieces, to again choose complementary grain configuration, color and so on. I generally choose darker or closer grain features for the lower half of the aprons and mark the tops of each piece with a 'T'.

Surface planing the legs removes machine marks.

I place the aprons, looking for best color and grain.

Stand the legs on end and choose them carefully.

I mark the leg ends at the top systematically.

Measure down 4" from the top of the legs.

Square a line across all four legs.

Make a second line 1" from the top of the leg.

Set the mortise gauge pins to the ³⁄₈" chisel.

It's quick to use the ³⁄₈" chisel to set the stock.

Mark the mortise lines from the outside of the leg.

The layout looks like this, with both mortises positioned on the inside faces of the leg.

Making the mortise holes

1. With the legs marked as shown, focus on laying out the mortise joints at the top of each leg. Lay all four legs on the bench with the inside faces up. These are the faces into which you will chop the mortise holes. Measure down 4" from the top of the leg and square the line across the faces of all four legs together.
2. From the top of the leg, measure down 1" and square a second line, across all four legs.
3. Square these lines onto the adjacent inside faces of the legs.
4. Set the two pins of the mortise gauge to the ³⁄₈" chisel you will actually use to chop the mortises, and set the stock ³⁄₈" from the first pin, as shown.

TECHNICAL POINTER: *It is vital that you always set your mortise gauge with the chisel you intend to use for cutting your mortise. This is especially important when setting the mortise gauge for marking your tenons. If you are using a chisel which is not exactly ³⁄₈", if it is 10mm for example, then you must set your gauge using this chisel so that your mortise and tenon will be perfectly matched using the standard of your chisel whether that is 10mm, ³⁄₈" or whatever other size you are using.*

5. You are now ready to chop the mortises. To ensure the walls of the mortise run parallel to the outside faces, use the mortise guide to keep the chisel perfectly aligned and parallel to the outside face of the leg as you deepen the mortise (for details on how to make and use the mortise guide see page 153 of this chapter). This mortise hole is a non-through mortise, and as such it's difficult to know with certainty that the mortise is running parallel to that outside face, but this is vital for well-fitting shoulders and a perfect joint.

6. If you have chosen to use a guide, clamp this into the vise with the leg, as shown. Using the ⅜" chisel, begin chopping the mortise as we practiced in chapter 6 page 104. Work from one side of the mortise to the other, keeping the chisel perpendicular as you work your way across the mortise area, reversing the direction of the chisel cut to equal out the mortise depth. Keep the chisel tight up against the guide so that the chisel aligns exactly. Be very conscious of your depth, both mortises in each leg are 1⅛" deep from both inside faces and will meet to form a corner inside the leg. Work neatly and progressively, taking care not to strike too hard and burst out the outside face. Also take care not to cut too deeply. You will be only ⅜" from the outside face when you reach the bottom of the mortise hole.

The mortise guide guarantees perfect mortises.

Deepen the mortise with each cut.

Position yourself directly above the mortise hole.

Align the chisel edge with the jig with each chop.

The last vertical cut is directly on the line.

Clean out any waste from the mortise hole.

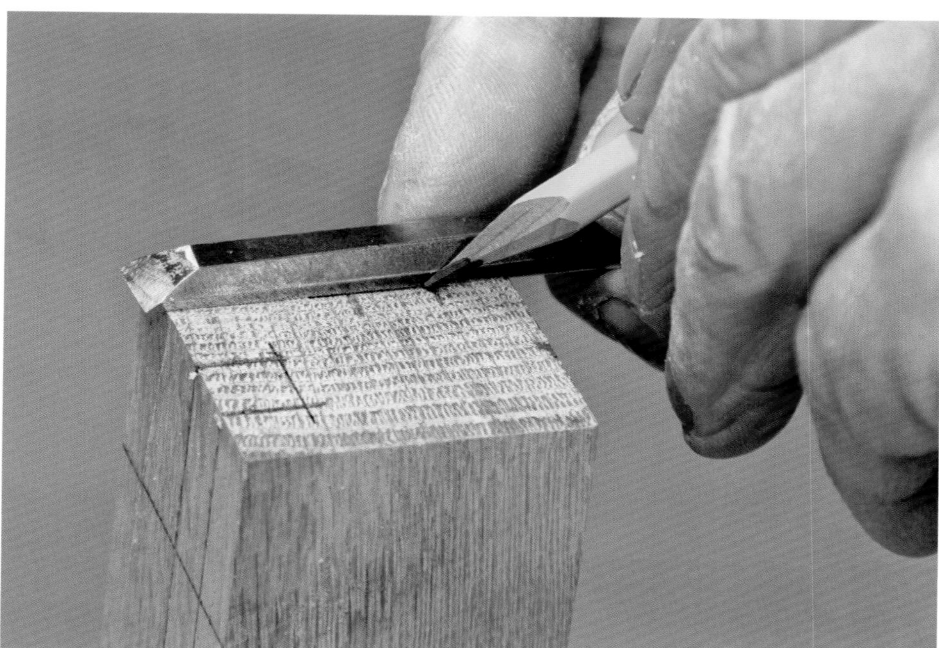
It's quick to use the chisel to mark the depth of the mortise haunch area.

7. To cut the haunch area at the top of the legs, use the tenon saw to cut the cheeks and then split and pare out the center section with the chisel from the end.
8. Repeat this procedure on the other inside face of all four legs.

Align the tenon saw to cut the haunch recess…

…on both sides.

Chisel out the waste wood.

The haunch looks like this.

Making the tenons on the aprons

1. Surface plane both wide faces of the apron pieces with the smoothing plane. Choose the position of each apron by considering color and grain configuration. Look for consistency on all four outside faces.
2. To ensure distances between the tenon shoulders is exactly the same on all four apron pieces, clamp them together in the vise and measure 1⅛" from each end. Square the lines across these edges using the knife. These lines show the position of the shoulder lines for the tenons.
3. Square the knifewall onto the remaining faces of the apron pieces and at both ends. These will be the shoulder lines for the tenons.
4. The pin settings on the mortise gauge, remain the same distance, but the distance between the gauge stock and the first, moveable pin is now ¼" from the stock. This centers the tenon in the apron.
5. Run the mortise gauge lines onto the ends and the adjacent edges of all four apron pieces.
6. Use the 1" chisel to further define the knifewall.
7. Cut the shoulders with the tenon saw.

Make a mark 1⅛" from the ends of the aprons.

Use the knife and square to ensure exact cut lines.

Create the knifewall around all four faces.

The ⅜" pin setting is now ¼" from the stock.

Further define the knifewall to the shoulder line.

Use the tenon saw to cut the tenon shoulders.

Now cut the tenon cheeks with the tenon saw.

Splitting tenons is fast when the grain is straight.

A hand router ensures an accurate tenon face.

Mark the mortise width onto the tenon.

Check that the split follows straight lines.

Pare the tenon cheeks to final depth with a chisel.

Test the tenon in it's corresponding mortise

Use the ⅜" chisel to mark the haunch cut line.

8. To cut the cheeks, alternate between methods. The most common method is to use the tenon saw, but this is also the slowest. Splitting with a wide chisel from the end is the fastest, but this depends on straight wood grain. Cross-grain paring with a 1" chisel is both safe and fast, even with contrary grain. I prefer this method, which works in any wood type.

TOP TIP: *If you want to split off the waste with a chisel, always take off the minimum amount first to check the grain isn't splitting into the non-waste wood towards the tenon.*

TECHNICAL POINTER: *We use gauge lines to determine the final depth of the cut. So avoid cutting below the lines made with the mortise gauge. We generally fit the tenon to the mortise hole rather than the mortise to the tenon.*

9. Fit each tenon to each mortise hole and number or mark them accordingly. Offer each of the corners into the mortise at an angle to see if they pass fully inside and down to the shoulder. If they do, cut the haunch to the tenon.
10. To define and cut the tenon haunch, place the tenon inside the mortise hole and mark the width of the mortise hole directly onto the tenon. The depth of the haunch is ⅜", so use your ⅜" chisel against the shoulder to mark this depth with a pencil.

11. Remove the corner section with the saw, but this time, instead of cutting on the waste sides of the lines, cut to the non-waste sides. This creates an extra reduction in the haunch part of the tenon allowing the tenon shoulders to close tight without the haunch bottoming out.

Now try your tenon fully in the mortise to check that the shoulders seat and that the tenon isn't overly tight. A tenon that's too fat will split the leg at the top. It should however be a snug fit.

> **TOP TIP:** *To make sure the tenon does not split the leg, clamp the leg in the vise so that the jaws constrain the mortise on both sides.*

12. If the tenon seats well, miter the end of the tenon. Reach through the adjacent mortise with your knife and mark the inside face of the tenon directly at the wall of the mortise hole. Then withdraw the tenon and square the line across the width.

13. Use the combination square to mark the 45-degree line on the end of the tenon.

14. With the tenon saw, cut the miter, again cutting on the non-waste side of the line so that the miter falls a kerf-width short of the internal corner of the mortise hole.

15. Repeating this procedure on all of the joints, work on two opposite sides first and then unite these opposites with the adjoining aprons. Take care with each joint and aim for a good friction fit.

It's quicker by hand than machine.

Test fit the tenon and shoulders.

Layout lines help guide the saw cut.

Cut on the non-waste side to shorten the tenon.

Take care here! This area is fragile and can split.

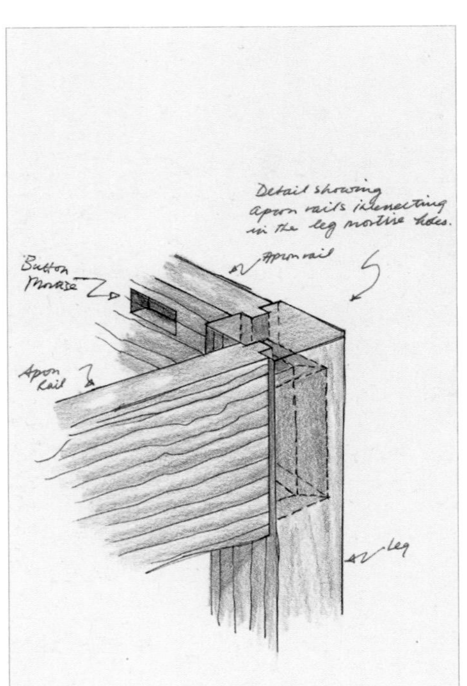

My journal drawing shows the inside of the joint.

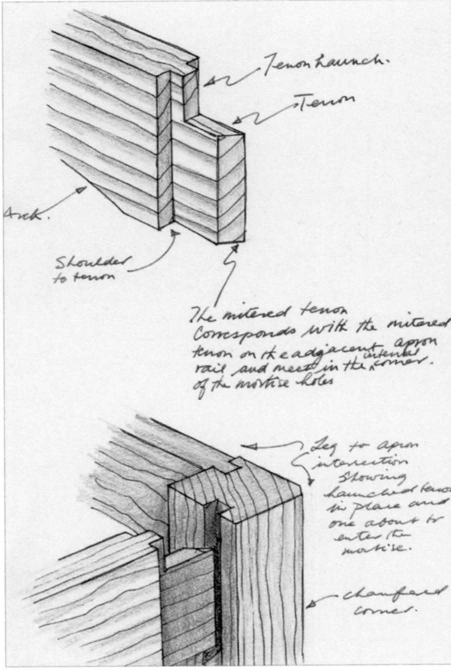

I use drawings to pre-plan a jointed assembly. I plan out complex pieces with detailed drawings.

I love to see completed joints on the bench ready for assembly.

Clamping up a dry fit serves as a rehearsal for the glue up as well as an essential test for the joints.

Trial assembly

With all the joints fitted and tested, clamp two opposite sides and add the cross-rails to connect all the components together. Clamp these also.

TECHNICAL POINTER: *Until you fit the adjacent aprons and clamp them up, you won't know if every shoulder will seat perfectly with no gaps.*

Turnbutton mortises

With the joinery completed, you are now ready to set out and cut shallow mortises on the inside faces of the aprons. These mortises will receive the turnbuttons that hold the tabletop permanently to the table later. Turnbuttons are the stepped blocks of wood that hold the top down while allowing the tabletop to expand and contract throughout the life of the table.

1. While the table is together, roughly mark the positions of the turnbutton mortises so you know where they will be positioned; you don't want mortise holes on the outside faces of your aprons. Also, the aprons have two mortises on two opposite aprons and one mortise in the center of the adjoining aprons.
2. While the table is still assembled, roughly mark the arches to each apron, ensuring the arches get cut on the bottom edge of the aprons and not the top.
3. Disassemble the table leg frame. Focus first on laying out and cutting the mortises. For the aprons with two mortises, begin each mortise 1½" from the shoulder of the apron and ½" down from the top. All the mortise holes are ½" x 1½" long. The mortises in the other two aprons will be in the center of the aprons, ½" down from the top.
4. Set the mortise gauge to a ½" chisel and ½" from the stock of the gauge to the first pin. Score the parallel mortise lines between the distance marks.
5. Clamping the aprons to the bench top, use the same technique learned earlier in the course, when making the bookcase, to mortise the holes using the ½" chisel to a depth of ⅜". Don't mortise too deeply. It's easy to burst all the way through to the outside face.

Freehanding an arch helps ensure you cut the arch on the right edge later.

These mortises should be quick and easy.

Set a gauge for the guidelines…

…and run the lines as shown.

Follow the patterns for chopping mortises.

It's best to chop mortises on the solid bench top.

Templates ensure a consistent shape.

The vise is the third hand for holding the work.

Stop-cuts finish just above the line.

Remember! Bevel down for convex cuts.

Work from high to low from each end.

Pare away unevenness, still with the bevel down.

Spokeshave an even arch.

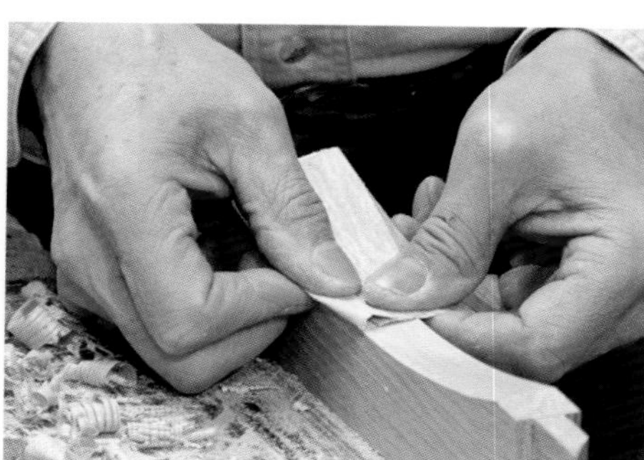
Sand to remove any unevenness.

Cutting the arches

Now create the arches for the aprons. Not only do these arches lighten the appearance of the piece, they also give it grace and style. The radius we use is 16". You'll find it easier to make a single template on one of the arches and then use this arch to transfer the same shape to the other aprons. You might also want to make a permanent pattern if you plan on making more tables with this arch pattern. There is a half scale pattern for this on page 320. I prefer to use shallow rather than deep arches on shorter aprons like these.

1. Trace the shape onto just the outside face of each of the apron pieces. It's not necessary to mark this onto both sides.
2. Securing the piece in the vise frees both hands for sawing and shaping. Saw down across the apron at approximately 1" intervals, to just slightly above your line, to make a series of stop-cuts.
3. Working from the high point at each end of the arch, cut down into the bottom from either end using the 1" chisel, bevel down, to chop and pare the waste wood, close to just above the line.
4. With the arch shaped close to the line, use the spokeshave to refine the arch down to the line. Set the spokeshave to a fairly shallow setting and remove any obvious high or uneven areas first. Again, work from both high points to the bottom of the arch, and feather out the close of your cut at the bottom by lifting the heel of the spokeshave at the end of the stroke... As your arch becomes more uniform, adjust the iron to take off finer shavings until it looks smooth and even.
5. With the arches completed, sand them and set them aside while you shape the legs.

Shaping the legs

For many years, I have used an optical illusion that makes table legs look as though they curve outwards slightly. This flair works well as an aesthetic touch and it's fairly simple to replicate as you can mark out all of the curves from a template.

I make a plywood template because the shape needs to be consistent on eight faces. Either enlarge the half scale pattern on page 320 or follow these instructions:

On a narrow strip of plywood, ¼" thick, 1¾" by 23⅛", run a line on one edge about ¼" from the corner, most of the way down the leg, but then, when you are 4" from the end, curve it towards the edge, stopping 1" from the end. On the opposite edge cut a curve, starting 7½" up from the bottom of the leg and sweep it down to a depth of ½" at the end.

1. Place this template with the front toe (bottom) against the front outside corner edge of the leg, and the back edge against the opposite edge. Now draw along both sides of the template. Flip the template over and repeat the process for the adjacent outside face of the leg. We call this type of chamfer, where the chamfer feathers back to a square edge, a stopped chamfer.
2. On the underside of the leg, on the end, make marks 1" in from each outside face. These marks are guidelines for the inside sweep that curves downward towards the outside of the leg.

Using a template ensures consistent shaping detail.

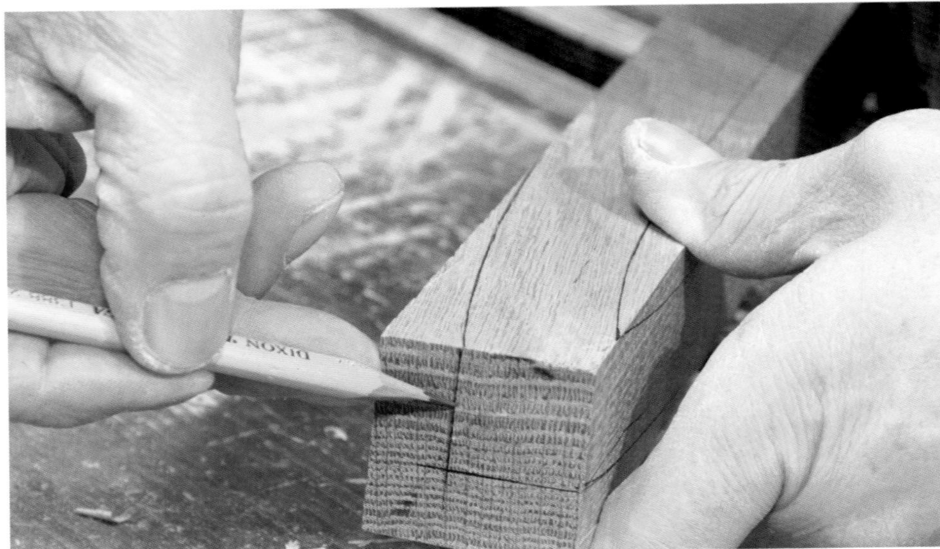

Transfer the curve lines onto the bottom of the leg.

We mark for the uplift also.

The spokeshave removes masses of stock first...

...and the plane trues up undulations.

Take care to make the transition point as even as possible: No dips!

The leg is too wide for a single-pass chisel cut...

The smoothing plane works very well for refinement

A light pass with the plane creates a clean surface to the outside faces.

3. Create a stopped chamfer on the outside corner using the spokeshave and plane. You can also use a wide bevel-down chisel to begin the stopped chamfer, and then continue with the plane. Make the sweep from the bottom of the leg long and gradual to add graceful lines to the shape.
4. Use the 1" chisel to shape and pare the outside curve, starting at the low point on the leg, with the chiseling angle as low as possible, working towards the bottom of the leg. You will need to remove waste with successive sweeps, working down gradually until you reach the line. Do this to both inside faces.
5. Use the plane and / or the spokeshave for refining the chisel work.

6. Now use the spokeshave to chamfer the inside corner. Here, you'll want to create a long sweep, starting about 10" up from the bottom of the leg and widening gradually to about ½" at the bottom.
7. Do the same to the adjacent corners, further refining the flare. Shorten the length of the sweep, this time by starting 8" up from the bottom of the leg, widening gradually to about ⅜" at the bottom.

Square off three diagonals to mark the leg end…

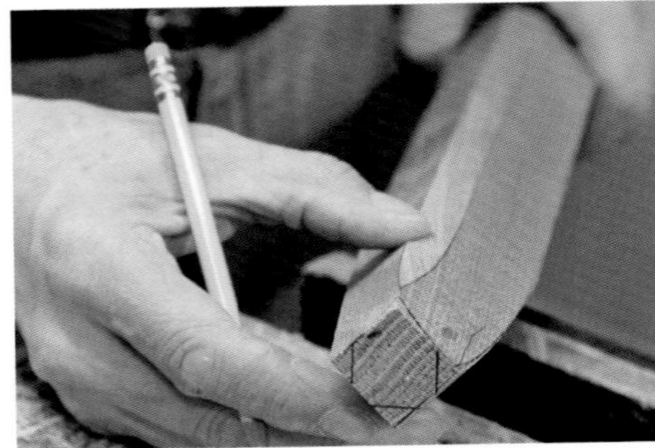

…like this. Do not remove the stopped chamfer.

Sweep a curve up on each side of the diagonals.

Chamfer down to your line with a spokeshave.

With the sweeping chamfers complete, your leg should look like this.

Use a 1" chisel to chamfer the bottom of every leg.

Make sure the leg is held securely.

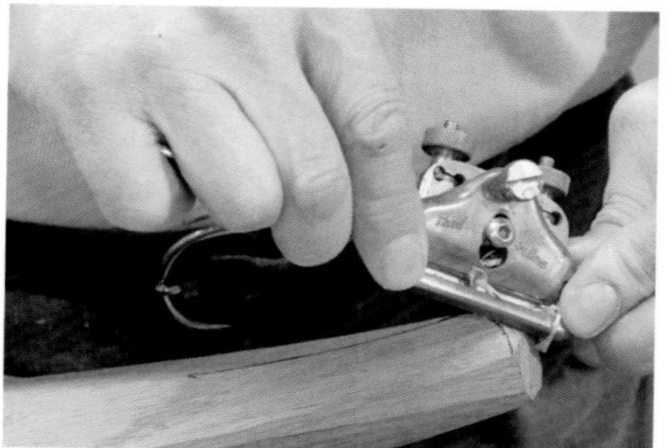

Always work towards the end of the leg.

File towards the end of the leg.

This is an attractive detail that make the table appear to 'float' slightly off the floor. It also has the important function of preventing the end grain from splintering out if the table is scraped along a hard floor.

8. The final part of shaping is to create a chamfer on the bottom of each leg. Use a 1" chisel to remove the bulk of the waste, then file a sweeping stroke to both round and smooth the foot, as shown.
9. With all of the legs shaped, all that remains is to sand the parts to 220 grit.

Making the tabletop

If you read the earlier note on planning ahead, you'll have glued-up the tabletop the day before you started the rest of your project. This allows the glue to fully cure and set to maximum strength.

The tabletop can be made from more than one piece; in fact, this is often better than using a single, wide board. The pieces should be flat and without any distortions. Even if the stock is machined, still hand plane it to remove any marks and to true up the surfaces of the wood.

1. With the main faces planed, focus on composing the pieces for their final appearance. Cut your boards to ⅛" over the length needed so that you can plane the edges flush after glue-up. Look for differing colors and grains and arrange them for their most complementary positioning. You can now identify them with a 'V' across the jointed edges, as shown. This way you will know exactly which position to place them in as you plane and true the adjoining edges.
2. To plane these edges, it's usually easier to true two adjoining edges together, at the same time. Place them upper face to upper face and line up the edges flush with each other. Then clamp them in the vise with the edges to be trued uppermost.
3. Having first aligned the iron of the plane accurately, set a very fine depth of cut and, starting from the middle, work in short successive strokes on either side of the center, working outwards by increasing the length of each stroke. Remove shavings from the center with each stroke until no more shavings emerge. Next, lengthen your strokes until you take one continuous stroke from one end to the other. The edge should now be straight.

   Because the boards are clamped face to face in the vice, any out-of-square discrepancy is compensated for by the opposing angles on each board. This will mean that when brought together, the jointed boards will create a truly flat surface.

Look for grain match, color and texture.

After selection and placement, mark with a 'V'.

Edge joint both adjacent edges at the same time.

TECHNICAL POINTER: *You should aim to minimize any discrepancy to no more than one or two degrees. Too much of an angle will result in the joint slipping when you come to glue and clamp the pieces together.*

Use a zig zag method for even gluing.

Clamp and check for slippage.

Always remove excess glue from joint lines with a dry cloth.

4. Arrange two clamps and set the boards between them. Now glue the long edges. Apply the glue to one edge in a zigzag pattern and bring the edges together with a sliding motion, rubbing the joints to disperse the glue evenly along the full length of the joint. Remove any excess glue. Apply pressure to the clamps carefully so that the glue is expressed evenly. Check for any slippage between the boards. Wait a few seconds to allow the glue to fully express, and then tighten the clamps further. Again, wipe off the excess glue with a cloth and then add a third opposing clamp as shown.

TOP TIP: *It's best to remove any glue build-up around a joint area because it slows down the drying process inside the joint. Another reason we remove any excess is that hardened glue can damage the cutting edge of the plane and scraper.*

Surfacing the tabletop

1. When planing the tabletop I find it best to begin by turning the end-grain edges, followed by the long-grain edges. This way, any breakout can be removed along with the main surface planing. When planing the end grain edges, work in from each corner towards the middle. Don't take a full sweep all the way to the edge farthest from you, or you will splinter off the unsupported fibers. Use a very finely set plane iron and lift up the heel of the plane when you are halfway across the end-grain. You can take a full pass with your plane when you plane the long grain edges.
2. Now focus on surface planing the main top, working only in the direction that the grain runs and tackling any high areas first. Use your plane to check for high points by tilting it and resting it on one edge of the plane's sole, looking for any light between the corner and the surface of the tabletop.
3. Once the high spots are planed down, use the smoothing plane to plane along the grain. Move from one side, working with the grain. Move across the surface with each successive forward stroke; take long even strokes with a shallow-set plane, taking care not to plane against the grain.

TOP TIP: *Run some pencil lines over the top, take a few swipes with the plane, and you can easily see the high spots as the pencil lines are shaved off. Repeat as necessary.*

If I plane past here, I risk breaking out the unsupported fibers at the out-plane edge of the board.

High areas must be removed first.

Remove the high spots by planing across the grain first, then back off the iron and go with the grain.

To ensure I achieve an even chamfer on all edges, I count the same number of strokes each time.

Scraping with a sharp scraper always gives good results.

Remove sharp corners with fine, even chisel cuts.

TOP TIP: *If the surface grain is in any way difficult to plane, use a No.80 cabinet scraper, working from each end towards the middle, always finishing the final strokes with the grain.*

4. Remove the sharpness from the corners by taking three or four strokes with the smoothing plane. Count the number of swipes you make and use the same number on all the corners so that they look the same.
5. On the corners, use a sharp chisel or flat file to make a small radius to soften the hard edges.
6. Finally, sand all of the surface faces and edges, and sand any sharp corners to form a slight round over. This prevents the sharp corner from fracturing.

Gluing up the leg frames

This is always a critical time and now, you'll know we always rehearse the steps before applying any glue. Set the clamps to the correct distance and slip wooden pads between the clamp jaws to make sure that they don't damage the surfaces of the legs.

1. Glue-up opposite sides first so you don't strain the other joints. Glue one end and insert the first tenon into its corresponding mortise hole. Repeat at the other end and then clamp the legs to the first apron. Keep the clamps parallel to the top edge of the apron and centered in the width of the apron.

> **TOP TIP:** *Using the correct amount of glue takes experience but soon you will be better able to judge the right amount. If a large amount of glue is forced out of the joint when you put it together then you are applying too much. This is better however than 'starving' the joint, which means applying so little glue that it is absorbed leaving very little holding the joint together. If you are unsure then err on the side of using too much glue rather than too little and as you gain experience you get a feel for how much is correct.*

2. Repeat with the opposite side.

Think through the glue prep stage thoroughly.

Make sure the joints are tested and numbered

A bead of glue on the mortise rim aids insertion.

Spread the glue evenly

Keep the clamps parallel to the run of the apron.

Work quickly but carefully, following the procedure you have rehearsed...

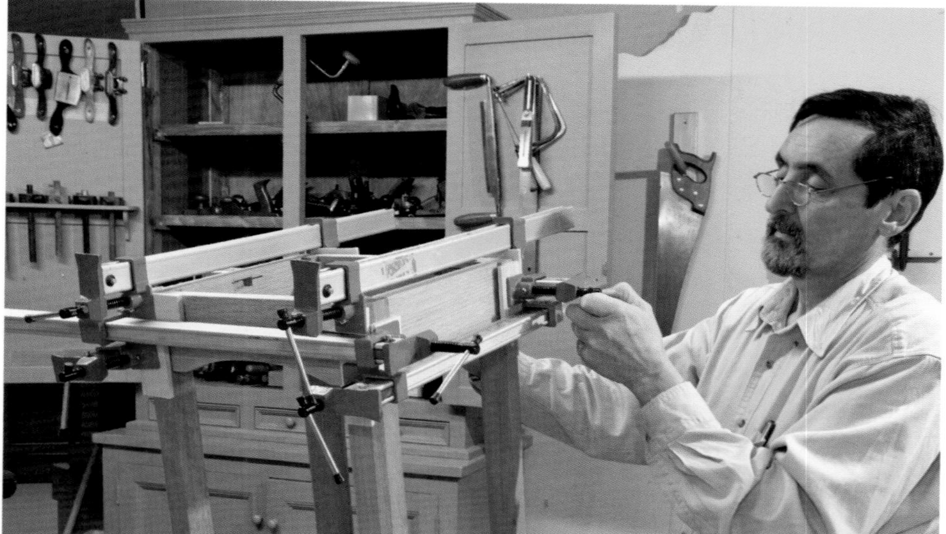
Think through the clamping procedure, setting the clamps to the approximate spacing beforehand.

Finally, check for squareness by measuring from corner to corner.

3. To glue the remaining aprons, lay the first leg assembly on the bench with the mortise holes uppermost. Glue one end of the tenon and insert it into the correct mortise hole. Press the apron fully into the hole so that the shoulder seats as tightly as possible. Repeat with the opposite apron and then glue the opposite end of the aprons before fitting the opposite side of the table.
4. Applying the clamps to this side is a little trickier. Because the other clamps are already in place, there's not enough room to position the clamps near the center of the rails. For this reason, use two clamps for each rail, placing one above and a second below the adjacent clamp. Equalize the pressure on each of the clamps so that the shoulders close fully and evenly.
5. After checking that the assembled frame is square by successive corner to corner measurements, set the leg assembly aside until the glue is dry, usually overnight.

Making the turnbuttons

Turnbuttons are used for securing the tabletop. They can be made quickly and easily. I will show you how you can cut two turnbuttons out of one blank very quickly.

Make a mark on the face 2" from the end and square these lines down part way onto the sides as shown. Repeat this from the opposite side and make sure that you measure from the opposite end.

Use a marking gauge set to slightly (around $\frac{1}{16}$") over $\frac{1}{2}$" and mark a gauge line between the pencil lines on the sides. Do this from both sides and on both edges.

Saw down to the depth line on both sides.

Place one end slightly elevated on another piece of wood so that the center part is not supported. Now hit it with the hammer to separate the two sides.

Trim to the lines as necessary.

Drill a $\frac{3}{16}$" hole in the center of the turnbutton and countersink it.

Turnbuttons are quick and easy to make.

One gauge setting works the same distance from both faces.

Cut down to the second line from both sides.

Tap and snap!

Chisel any unevenness.

Find the center.

Center the table on the tabletop.

Drill and countersink.

Mark the position on the inside corners.

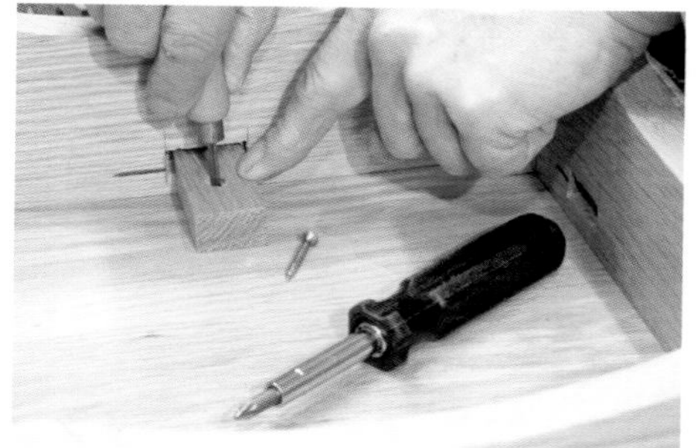
Screw the turnbuttons in place.

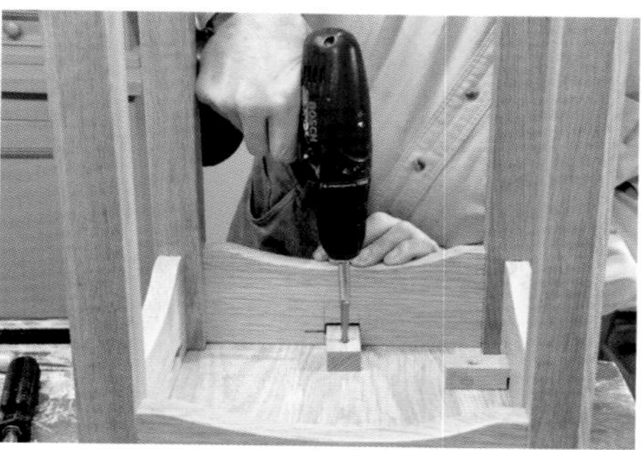
Use a drilldriver if preferred.

The tabletop secured.

Attaching the Tabletop

- Lay the upturned tabletop on a padded bench and place the leg assembly onto the tabletop.
- Use a tape measure to equidistance the leg frame on the underside of the tabletop to center it. Mark this position on the inside corners with a pencil. These marks will help fix the position as you screw the turnbuttons to the tabletop.
- Use 1½" woodscrews to secure each turnbutton, first by using an awl to start the hole.

Applying the finish

I usually use shellac for this table. It's a durable finish with only one main fault: Shellac is dissolved by spirit alcohol. If this is an issue then you may want to use an alternative finish. Water-based varnish works well and is alcohol proof.

1. I usually wear disposable latex gloves to apply the shellac as it stains the skin and leaves a sticky residue. Always work quickly and evenly when applying shellac.
2. With the first coat applied and dry, which is usually after about 20-30 minutes, use 220 grit sandpaper to sand off any grain raised by this first coat.
3. It usually takes three to four coats to fill the grain so that the sheen from the finish is even, with no flat spots but these successive coats must be applied quickly. After the final coat, rub every surface with 0000 (extra-fine) steel wool.
4. To finish, apply a coat of dark paste wax. This darker color fills the grain and gives a pleasing contrast, which enhances the final appearance.

Sanding at last!

Apply finish only when sanding is done.

I applied three coats of clear shellac…

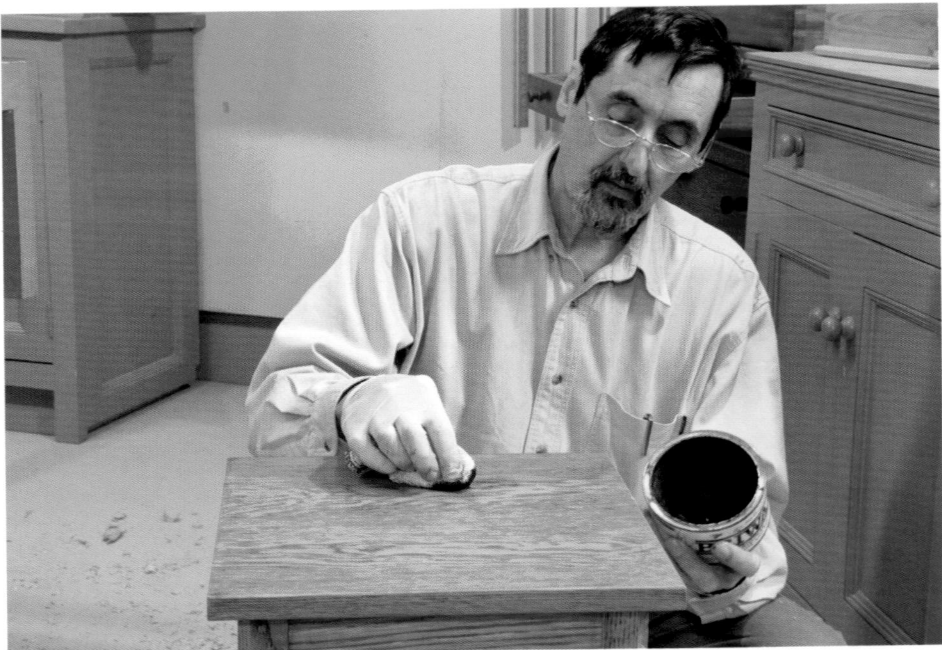

…followed by a colored wax.

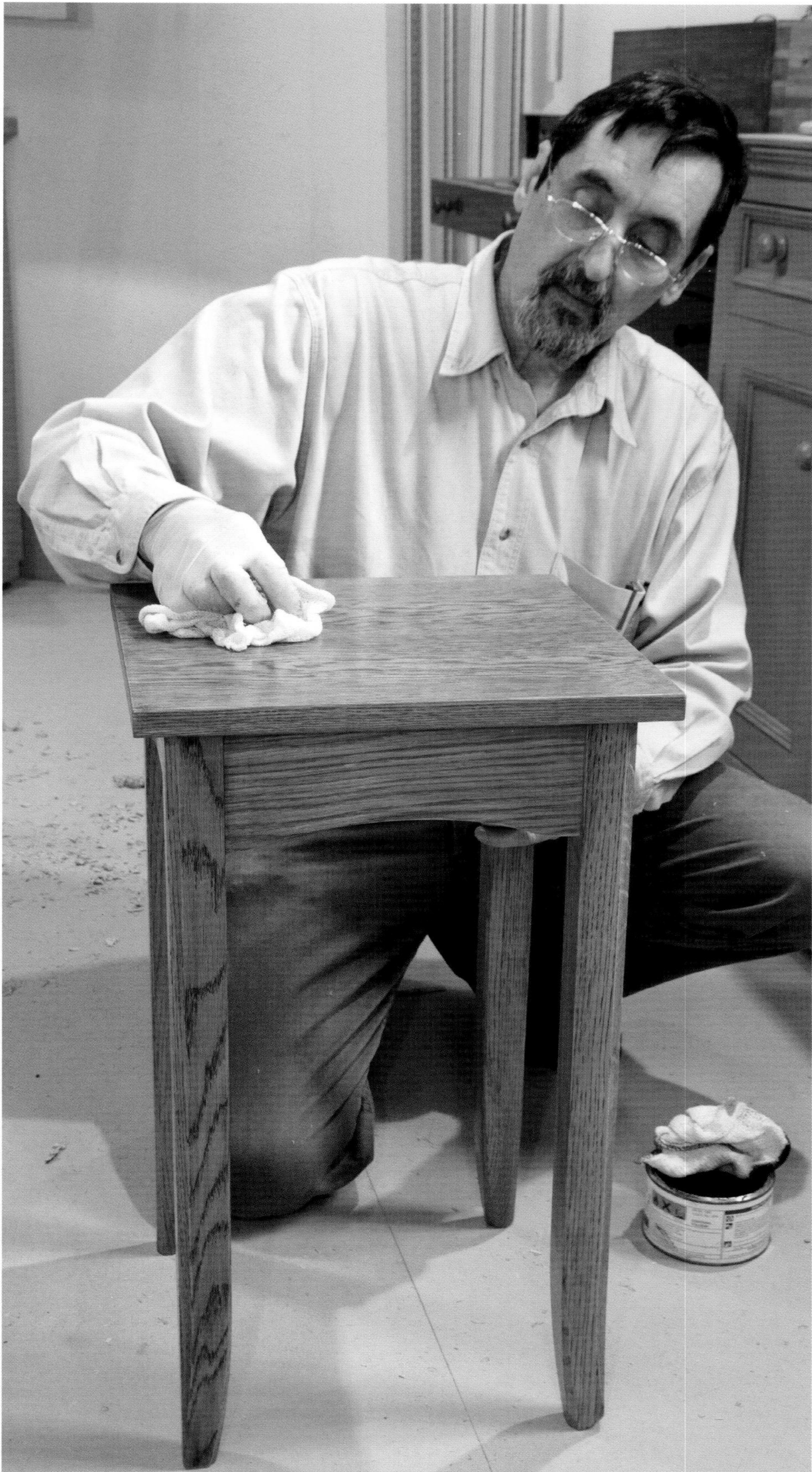
The finished table.

Conclusion

I first designed this table to stand alongside one of my oak rocking chairs. The original had the classic Shaker-style tapered leg. Although I liked the simplicity, it lacked the graceful lines I wanted. By working through this exercise, you'll have seen how some simple shaping skills can add a touch of flair.

Mastering the mortise and tenon joints and using the techniques described in this project have paved the way for making just about any table imaginable. I suggest you repeat these methods and create a coffee table or a second matching table, to hone your skills further.

10 Making your traditional European workbench

Since machines have generally replaced many hand tool methods for working wood, a full working, craftsman's workbench is a scarcity in modern woodworking shops. In fact, the vise anchored to the bench is the third hand which no true hand tool enthusiast can work without. The bench and vise become a single unit—the epicentre of an artisan workshop.

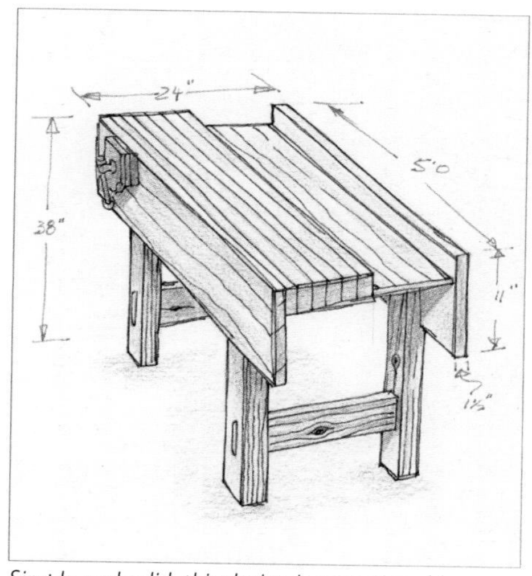

Simple and solid, this design is centuries old.

Serious woodworking begins with a sturdy workbench (along with an equally substantial vise), so I've included making one as part of this course. It's an inspiring piece to make and launches you into a serious project early on in your woodworking development. Without these two pieces of equipment to grip and support the wood, hand tools are only half as effective. It's at the bench we layout our projects and arrange the components, make measurements and prepare our wood using planes, handsaws and other tools. A vise must be anchored and immovable; the basic workbench provides a place and a way to use it most effectively.

Workbenches should always be as simple as possible. What many often call 'European benches'—with complex work-holding systems, multi-angle vise jaws and houndstooth dovetails—are difficult and expensive to build and cumbersome to use. However the simplest design of all the European workbenches pre-dates this complexity, and served joiners and furniture makers across Britain for centuries. This bench will handle the work of even the most demanding woodworker and furniture maker.

Choose the right wood

"Be careful when choosing your wood that it's dried well and not too badly distorted"

Though you may prefer a solid hardwood workbench with denser grain, a spruce or pine bench works equally well and costs a fraction as much without compromising the build quality. In fact softwood benches, will last more than a lifetime.

Be careful when choosing your wood that it's dried well and not too badly distorted. You can use just about any of the softwoods available from your local lumberyard: Spruce, fir, pine or indeed any alternative. However, because you will be working the wood with hand tools, take extra care as you pick your wood.

Look for solid, straight-grained pine with mid- to small-sized tight knots and check for all the usual twist, splitting and bends associated with lower grades of lumber. Joinery-grade softwood has a darker, closer grain than the light, fast growing pale timber used for house framing and general construction.

Design

The design of this bench uses the strength of traditional mortise and tenon joints to give built-in solidity and resistance to pressure in any direction. The 'H' frame legs have incredible strength and rigidity and when housed into the thick aprons, a structure is created that resists lateral shaking. The laminated benchtop is glued to the front apron, forming an 'L' shaped section where the strength is based on engineering principles. Follow the steps carefully and you will have a good workbench after just a weekend's steady work that will last for a lifetime. I never hesitate to recommend using laminated tops and aprons. They stay flatter, resist distortion, and have increased strength with less flex than a solid single piece.

Hand tool woodworking relies heavily on the use of the vise, so most work is concentrated in a relatively small area immediately around the vise. I am right-handed, so I like my hand tools on my right hand side and the right side of my vise. The main work surface area is 12" wide and 60" long, which is easily large enough for all of my work. I also prefer a well to hold my tools, so that they don't roll off to the floor.

This bench measures 24" deep x 60" long x 38" high, but if you are taller or shorter you may want to devise a height which best suits you. Also, if you prefer a longer or wider bench size, you can adapt the size without changing all of the component sizes (dimensions).

Allow an extra inch or so when you cut to length.

Spread the glue evenly.

Tighten the clamps until the glue squeezes out.

Take off any excess glue.

Shown here is the clamped benchtop. You can laminate the aprons in the same way by simply changing the orientation of the 3" x 2" timber.

Lamination

To prepare my stock for laminating, I cut all the wood to 1" longer than I need and surface plane all of the meeting faces for the laminated sections with my smoothing plane. This removes any surface defects or planer marks left by the machine. It's also an ideal opportunity to practice your planing skills using the smoothing plane, but take only fine shavings. You should only need to smooth, not straighten.

The laminated pieces of the benchtop should make up a section 10½" wide. Therefore, using 3" deep x1½" thick stock, you will need seven lengths. It's best to leave the stock 1" longer and trim the laminated top to length after the glue sets, slicing ½" off each end with a good sharp panel saw. That way, it's easier to get a uniform, square-cut end grain surface suitable for planing once the bench is assembled. After gluing up the pieces and clamping them as shown, leave them until the glue dries.

The bench relies on the wide aprons for lateral stability during heavy planing. Whether you use single-piece aprons or laminated stock, the joinery is the same. If you are going to laminate stock (which is my preference here), you must glue up and clamp the sections sufficient to make two aprons 11" wide by 1½" thick. I usually glue up both aprons in the same set of clamps to save clamps. I leave a dry joint between the two apron sections, so that when I take off the clamps I have two separate apron panels.

Materials list:

BENCHTOP:	1 @ 2¾" x 10½" x 60"
APRON:	2 @ 1½" x 11" x 60"
LEG:	4 @ 2¾" x 3½" x 34¼"
TOP RAIL:	2 @ 1½" x 3½" x 22"
BOTTOM RAIL:	2 @ 1½" x 3½" x 23"
BEARER:	2 @ 1" x 2¾" x 21"
WELL BOARD:	1 @ ¾" x 12" x 60"
QUADRANT:	2 @ ¾" x ¾" x 60"
WELL SUPPORT:	2 @ ¾" x 1¾" x 60"

Making the leg frames

The legs are made from 3" x 4" stock, so after the process of surface planing the pieces, before and after laminating, they will have final dimensions of around 2¾" x 3¾". You can laminate smaller sections or use solid stock if available. The sizes given are ideal for adding bottom-weight and enough bulk to accommodate a substantial ½" tenon. The cross-rails have wide shoulders to prevent any distortion of the leg frames. These design elements are essential to ensure the long and useful life of the bench.

With all of the components for the frames cut to the sizes given, we are ready to lay out and cut the mortise and tenon joints. We'll begin first with the mortises in the legs.

Mortising

1. Lay out your mortise holes according to the drawing. Firstly, measure up from the bottom of the leg and square the line onto each face.
2. Now place the cross-rail exactly on this line. Mark the position of the second parallel line that indicates the exact width of the mortise hole. Again, square the line onto each face.
3. For the top mortise hole, place the cross-rail flush with the top of the leg. Mark the distance with a pencil and square the line all the way round the leg. Then measure down 1" from the top of the leg (the thickness of the blade of most combination squares is usually 1" wide) and square the line all the way around the leg.
4. Set your mortise gauge to the ½" chisel you are going to use to chop the mortise hole. The mortise holes are centered in the legs and marked onto both of the opposite narrow faces.
5. Use a knifewall to define the width of the mortise holes using the knife and square.

Lay out according to the drawing.

Take the measurement from your top rail.

Mark the haunch onto the end grain with the same mortise gauge setting as all the mortises.

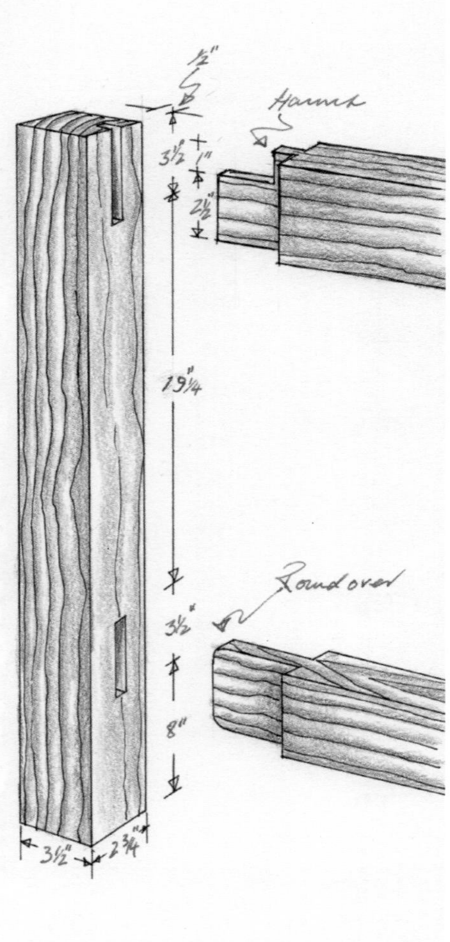

Layout to these measurements.

Chop out the mortises in the usual way.

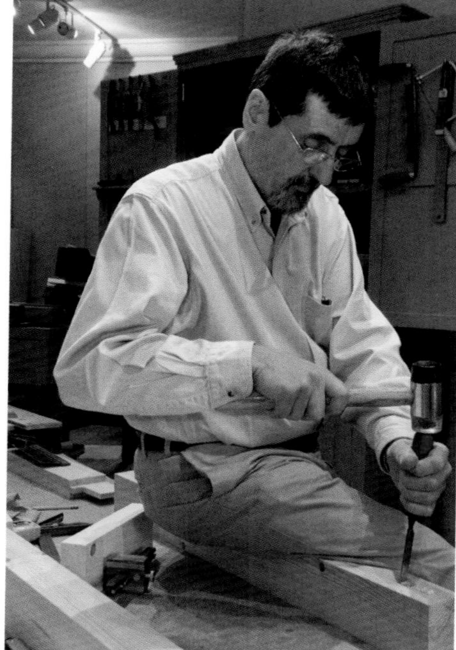
I found that this held the leg still while I chopped.

Top mortise before cutting haunch.

Saw in line with the mortise walls.

The finished haunch.

6. Use a regular ½" bevel-edged chisel to chop the mortise holes, working from each outside face, down into the mortise, chopping towards the middle of the leg. This prevents any unsupported fibers from splitting on the outside faces of the legs. It also guarantees that your mortise holes will be parallel to the outside faces, which prevents the possibility of creating a twist in the frame.

TOP TIP: *In general, I do not clean up the inside cheeks of the mortise holes by paring with the chisel. This can lead to inconsistent width between the mortise hole walls, which then results in poor glue surfaces. I simply chop and leave any fuzzy surfaces there, and do any trimming when I fit the tenon.*

Haunches

A haunch helps to ensure integrity at the corner placement of a mortise and tenon joint, so this is a good place to practice this simple feature:

1. Mark the extension of the mortise hole ½" down from the face at the top of the leg, as shown.
2. Saw down these cheeks to the ½" depth line.
3. Chisel out the waste.

Making the tenons

I lay out my tenons using the same procedure every time. It's an established pattern for most tenon cutting. There are two commonly used variations on the tenon that will be helpful in your future projects. Firstly, the lower cross-rail tenon joint, uses the standard through-tenon with some extra decorative features. The other, the top rail joint, uses a haunched tenon to form the mortise and tenon, at the top of the legs, which is often used at the corners of frame joints, in projects such as tables.

The drawings on page 182 show the differences between the tenons. Although the tenons are slightly different, they are all cut according to the following sequence:

1. Use the square and pencil to lay out the tenons to the ends of each cross-rail. Notice that the rails are different lengths: The top rails are shorter than the bottom rails. This is because the bottom rails have extended tenons that protrude past the outside faces of the legs.
2. Use the same pin setting in the mortise gauge that you used for laying out the mortise holes, but move the stock of the gauge, so that the mortise is centered in the rail as shown. Make the parallel lines. Take care to stop at your pencil lines. Work with the stock registered against the same face so that they are exactly opposite. That way, any inaccuracies in the gauge setting or thickness of the rails will not compromise the gauge lines.
3. With the gauge lines marked, use a knife and square to establish the exact cut lines for the shoulder line cuts, 15" apart. You might find it helpful to clamp both top and bottom rails in the vise and then square these lines across both pieces at the same time, allowing for the differences in the lengths. Clamping ensures that the shoulder lines are exactly the same distance apart, **15"** in this case, so the finished frame will be parallel.

Make all eight tenons the same, and then trim and haunch the tenons for the top cross-rails.

Mark the position of all the shoulder lines together.

Set your gauge pins exactly to your chisel.

Score the tenon line with the gauge.

Start the tenon with your knife cuts, three passes !

Use the chisel to create the first knifewall.

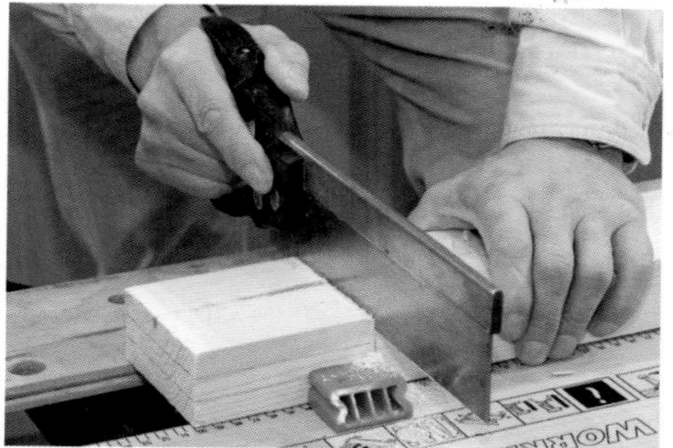

Cut the shoulders, just down to your gauge lines.

Start the tenon carefully on the end grain.

Drop the heel of the saw gradually, following the end grain slot, but don't quite touch the gauge line.

4. Further define the knifewall on each of the shoulder lines with a 1" chisel. This forms a slight step down that will guide the tenon saw.
5. With the tenon saw, cut down to the gauge lines at each shoulder, taking care not to cut below the line, which will make the tenon weaker. There are three practical ways of cutting tenons. The first method is to saw down the cheeks of the tenon with the tenon saw. The second method is cross face paring the tenon face with a wide chisel. The third method is to split the grain from the end of the tenon. This last technique depends on having straight grain in the wood to split accurately. Take this opportunity to practice all three methods and see which you prefer.
6. Sawing the cheeks means you must cut on the waste side of the gauge lines. This is the side you will throw away. Use your thumb to guide the saw in the usual manner and slide the saw teeth directly up against the line, so that you can see the gauge line on the tenon throughout the cut.
7. Having sawn along the top edge for a few strokes, drop your hand with successive strokes so that you're sawing along the face of the tenon. This will mean your saw is now angled upwards and cutting corner to corner. Once you're down to the shoulder, continue cutting, but focus the fore part of the saw on the opposite side of the cut, so that the cut is now guided by the previous angled cut. The cuts you just made will further guide your saw and keep you on track until you reach the shoulder line square across and the cheek waste falls away.

There are two alternative methods to saw-cut tenons:

CROSS-GRAIN PARING—You can grip the 1" chisel with both hands and, with short, decisive two-handed stabbing actions, chisel cross-grain removing thin slivers in a similar fashion to paring. You can view this technique on the DVD also.

SPLITTING—Splitting seems a little unpredictable, but the risk is greatly reduced if you read the surface grain and avoid any wild or varied grain and knots. Don't split directly on the line; instead, split away from the gauge lines a little. That way you can see which direction, if any, the grain is splitting. If it splits away from the gauge line, you can drive your chisel with impunity. If it splits toward your gauge line, revert to sawing or cross-grain paring methods. Splitting, when done correctly, is by far the fastest method for cutting tenons.

Take care not to lose your gauge lines too early. These are your only reference lines, and the best way to keep every face of the tenons parallel to the outside faces. Use a larger hand router to surface trim or plane the faces of the tenons.

"Splitting seems a little unpredictable, but the risk is greatly reduced if you read the surface grain"

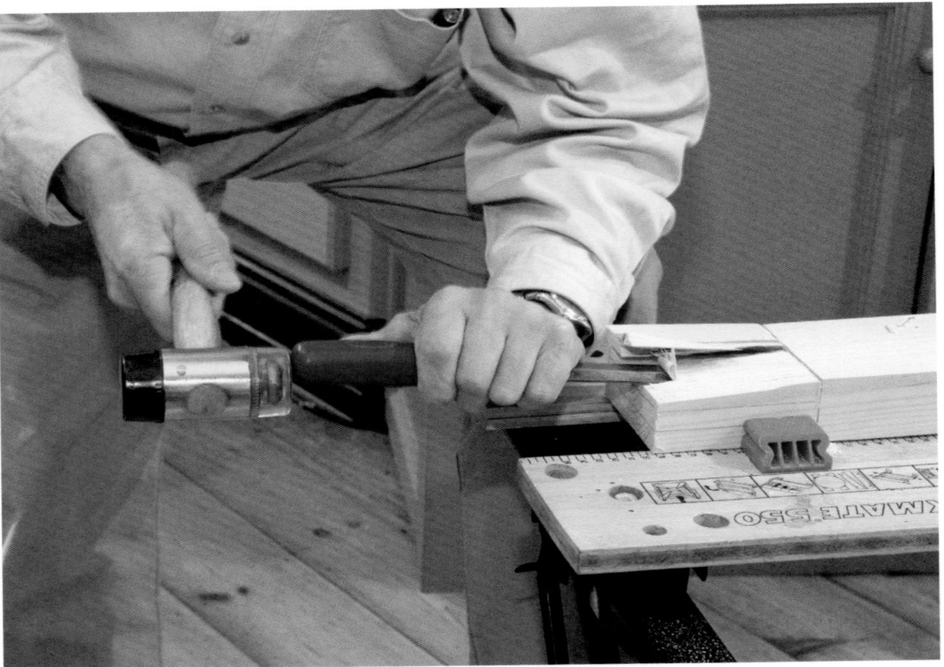

This grain is splitting towards the outside of the tenon, so I can continue down to my line.

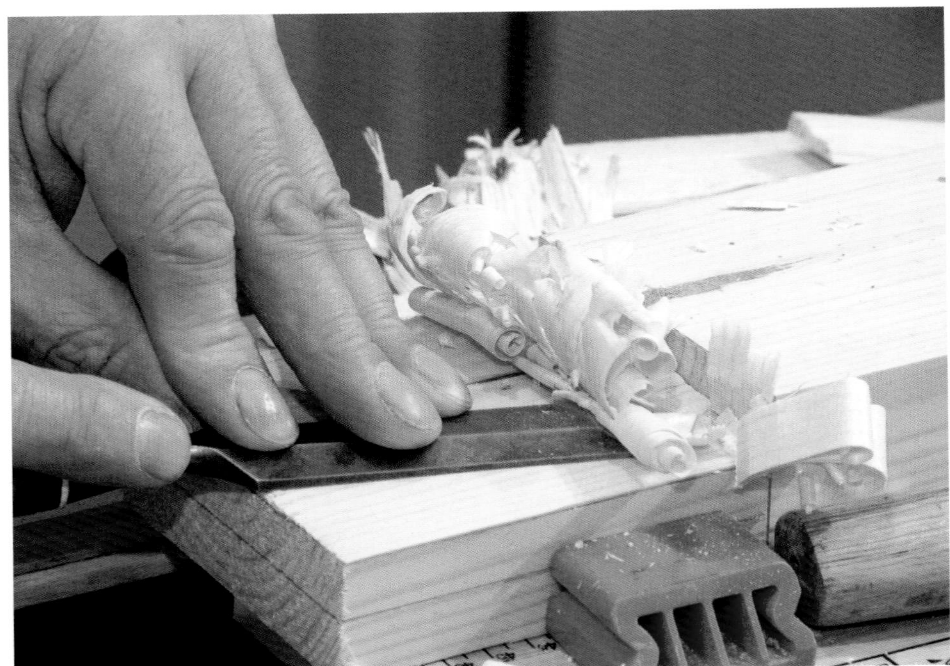

After splitting the waste off, I use the same chisel to pare down to my line, but only just down to it, never below.

The tenons should be a close, friction fit. Hold the tenoned rail in the vise and remove the leg with a gentle side to side motion whilst lifting.

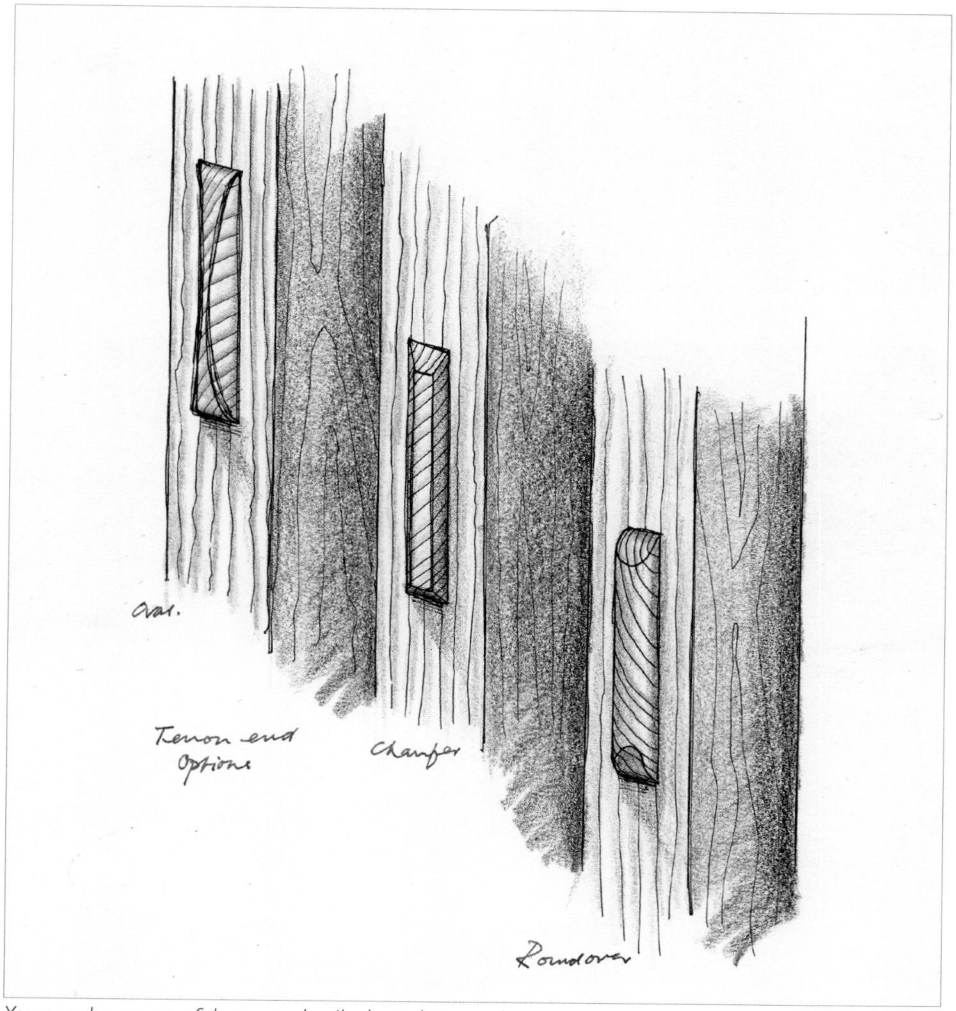

Fitting the bottom cross-rail tenons

I prefer to fit each tenon into its mortise hole and mark them accordingly. That way, I know that I have tried it fully and it seats well. I begin by offering the tenon to the hole at an angle to see if it goes in. If it does, I try the opposite corner. If necessary, I remove thin shavings and keep offering the tenon to the hole until it goes down to the shoulder with gentle but firm pressure on both cheeks.

The bottom rail tenons protrude ½". Rather than leave them square, I like to add a more decorative finish like the roundover or chamfers shown. The methods are very similar. I use a plane to round over the wide faces, and a chisel for the short ones. The actual techniques can be seen more clearly on the DVDs.

You can choose one of the tenon details shown here, or design your own

Forming a roundover

1. With your rail firmly secured in the vise, plane a consistent 45-degree chamfer onto the corner using a sharp smoothing plane. The flat you create should be about 3⁄16" wide.
2. Drop or increase the angle to plane a second and third angle along each of the hard corners.
3. By setting a shallower setting on the plane and working from bottom to top, take a series of strokes, working up with each subsequent stroke until the plane is flat and reaches the top.
4. Repeat the above for the opposite long edge.
5. With the rail placed lengthways in the vise, place a 1" chisel on the tenon at a shallow angle. Pop the chisel to make the first cut. Then make a series of successive cuts, increasing the angle with each cut. This creates a series of mini flats ready for further refining.
6. Use a large, flat file to further refine all of these roundovers and create a crisp, clean finish to the tenon.

Start the roundover with a ¼" chamfer on the tenon end. Drop the plane lower and take incremental cuts.

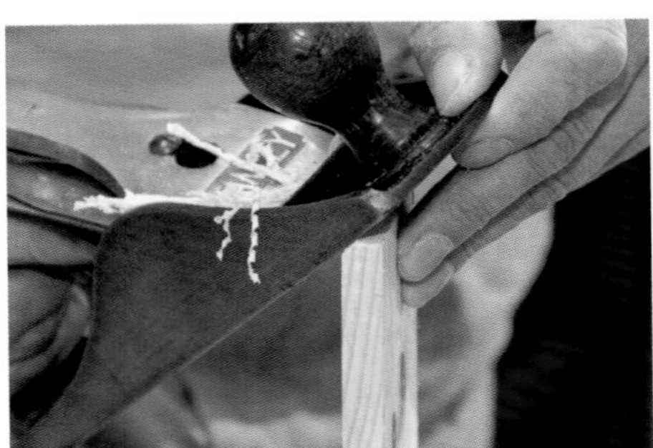

See page 144 for the detailed sequence.

Pop the corners off with a chisel.

Use the mill file to smooth and polish the roundover.

This is the tenon detail after assembly.

Use your ⅜" chisel as a guide.

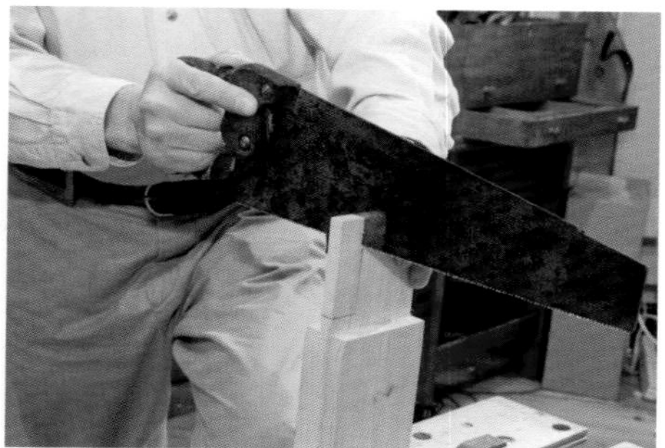
Rip the tenon on the waste side of the line.

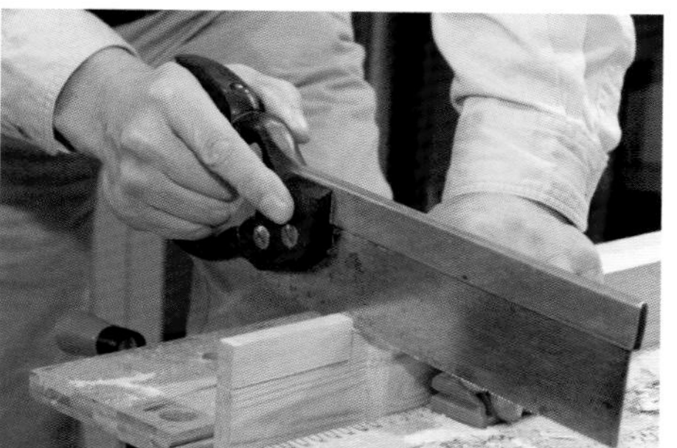
Cross cut on the non-waste side of the line.

The finished haunched tenon, ready to clean up and glue.

Step 5: Chamfer the bottom corners of each leg.

Ease all the long edges with a 45 degree chamfer.

Cutting haunched tenons

With the top rail tenons cut, they must now have the haunches cut to fit into the narrower opening of the mortise.

1. Place the ½" chisel against the shoulder of the tenon and mark the ½" line onto the cheek. Place the end of the tenon next to the mortise, in the position it will fit into the mortise hole, so that you can mark the exact tenon width.
2. Cut down the ½" line to the width line, but this time cut on the opposite side of the line rather than the waste side. That way the haunch will be a saw thickness from the bottom of the haunch mortise. This ensures that the haunch doesn't in any way hinder the shoulders of the tenon from fully seating.
3. Before you glue up, test each joint to ensure the joints remain uncompromised.
4. With all of the joints tested and a dry fit of the whole frame together, sand all surfaces and make sure the joints are marked to ensure they go into the right mortise holes.
5. Chamfer the bottom corners of each leg with the plane to reduce the risk of splitting the unsupported fibers at the corners of the leg where the leg meets the floor. This is standard procedure for all table, desk and bench legs.
6. Now glue up the frames, but rehearse the sequence beforehand to make sure you're familiar with the best way to proceed.

Gluing up—my rules

Gluing up is the critical point of no return. Make sure you:

1. Rehearse thoroughly beforehand.
2. Have protective pads for clamps sized and readily accessible.
3. Adjust the clamps to the correct distance allowing for any protective pads.
4. Don't answer the phone once gluing up begins.
5. Let nothing else distract you at all.
6. Have an assembly hammer and block at the ready.
7. Glue up all the components in sequence.
8. Move deliberately, because glue can 'freeze' a joint in a split second before fully seating. Do not hesitate in using the assembly hammer at any point. If you've dry fitted beforehand, there should be no reason for the joint not to go together. If the joint does seize, apply greater clamp pressure and hammer the joint area at the same time. This has never failed me yet.
9. Apply additional clamps as necessary to make sure any joint shoulders are fully seated.
10. Apply consistent pressure to all clamps.
11. Check the work is square by measuring from corner to corner before leaving it to dry. If the measurements are equal then the frame is square. If not, adjusting the clamps is a technique that often works well, but remember that it's usually poor positioning of clamps that causes the problem in the first place.
12. Allow overnight drying to ensure the glue sets properly.

Zig zag the glue as per usual.

Spread evenly, on both sides, avoid the roundover.

Glue up the haunched tenons.

Do not hesitate to use a hammer and block.

Check all the joints are seated and the assembly is square.

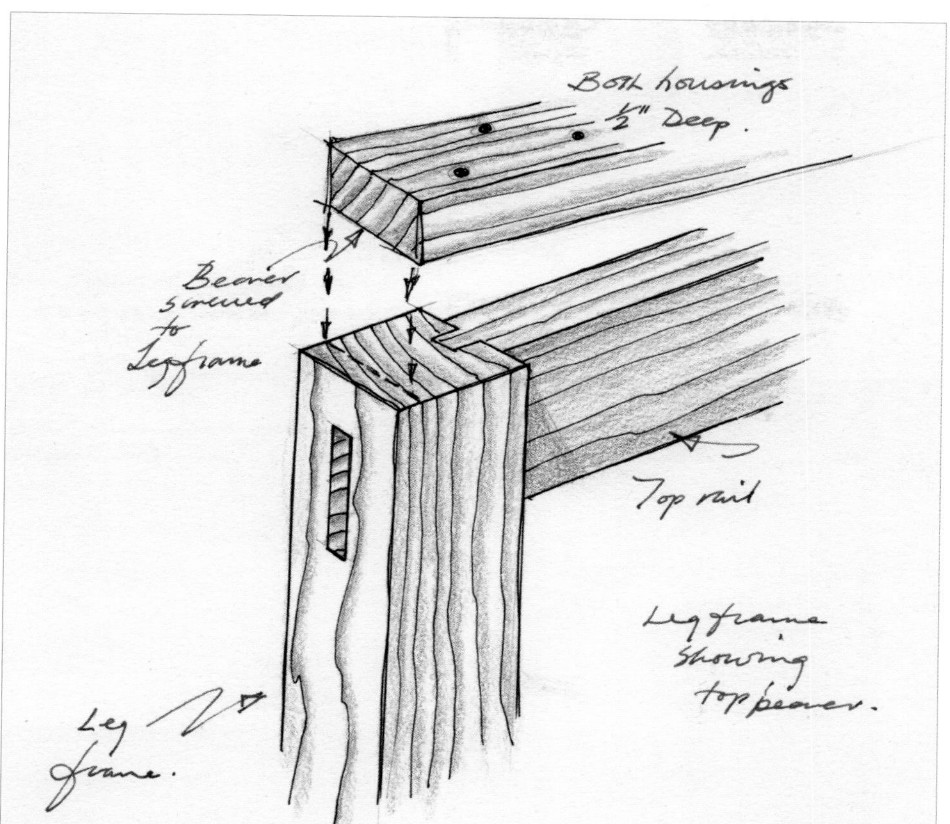

This drawing shows the detail of fitting the bearers.

Adding the bearers

The bearers offer a simple way of fixing the benchtop and well to the leg 'H' frames. This is simply a question of gluing and screwing the 1" x 2¾" bearer into the top rail and legs of the frame with 2½" woodscrews. Pre-bore ³⁄₁₆" holes in the bearer first to avoid splitting the wood. The bearers are 1" shorter than the 'H' frame width and are fixed centered on the leg frame; ½" from each side.

With the bearers in place, bore the ³⁄₁₆" holes you will need to screw through the bearer into the underside of the bench top and well.

This is the structural arrangement of the main parts of the bench.

Main parts of the workbench

1. Bench top
2. Front apron
3. Back apron
4. Leg frame
5. Well board
6. Quadrant molding
7. Bearer
8. Leg
9. Top cross-rail
10. Lower cross-rail

Making the apron housings

With laminated aprons, we must first surface plane the boards to an even finish ready for joint layout and sanding. The aprons must also be parallel, so plane one of the edges straight before planing the second edge perfectly parallel to it.

The housings enclose the legs at the top, where we unite the benchtop and legs. This critical point creates the long-lasting rigidity and stability needed for a strong bench. One thing we do not want in a bench is any movement during planing, sawing or chiseling operations once the bench is finished. This joint guarantees no such movement will occur. We've combined the joint with glue and screws for added security and strength.

1. Having prepared the wood by planing, lay out the housings 42" apart using the square and pencil only. The distance from the top edge of the aprons is the thickness of the benchtop plus 1¹⁄₁₆", which allows for the thickness of the bearer and for planing flush after the benchtop is added later.
2. Set the gauge to ½" and score lines between the walls of the housing.
3. Knifewalls guarantee exactness. Use the knife and square to create the first knifewall only on each of the housings.
4. Further define the knifewall with a wide chisel along the whole length.
5. Make perpendicular cuts with the 1" chisel and mallet.

Measure down the thickness of the top plus 1¹⁄₁₆".

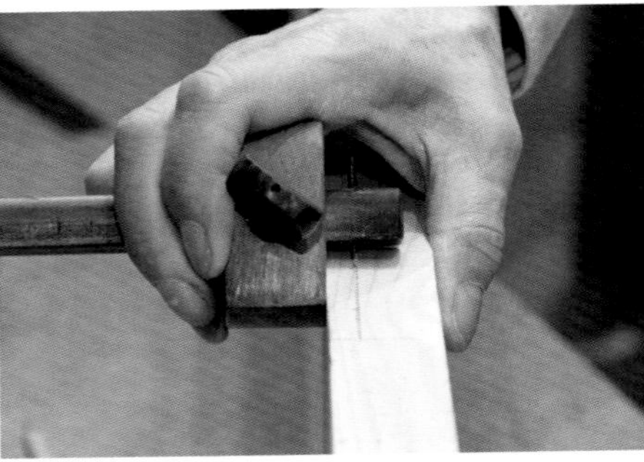

Mark the depth of the housing dado with the gauge.

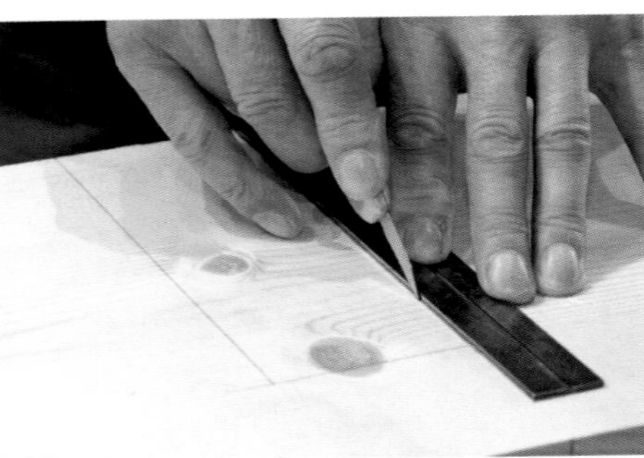

Make sure that your knife line is square to the edge.

Create the knifewall.

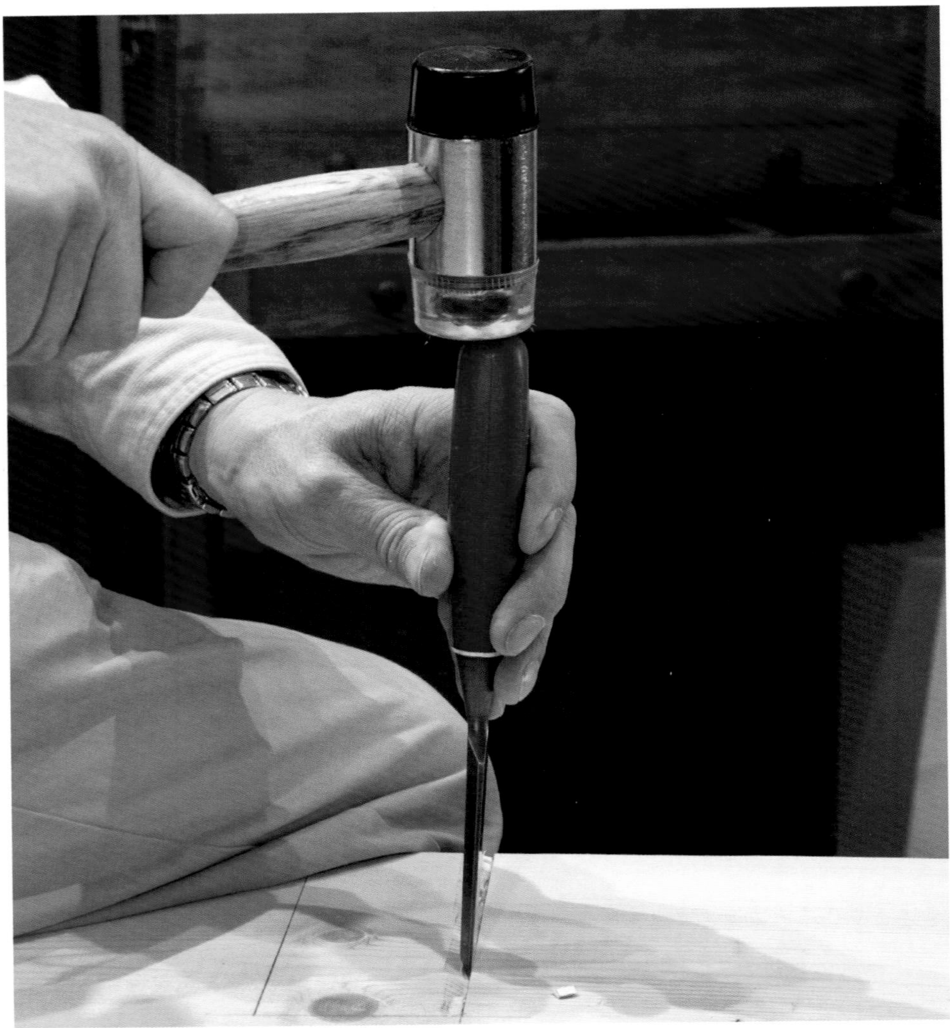

Further define this with vertical chisel cuts.

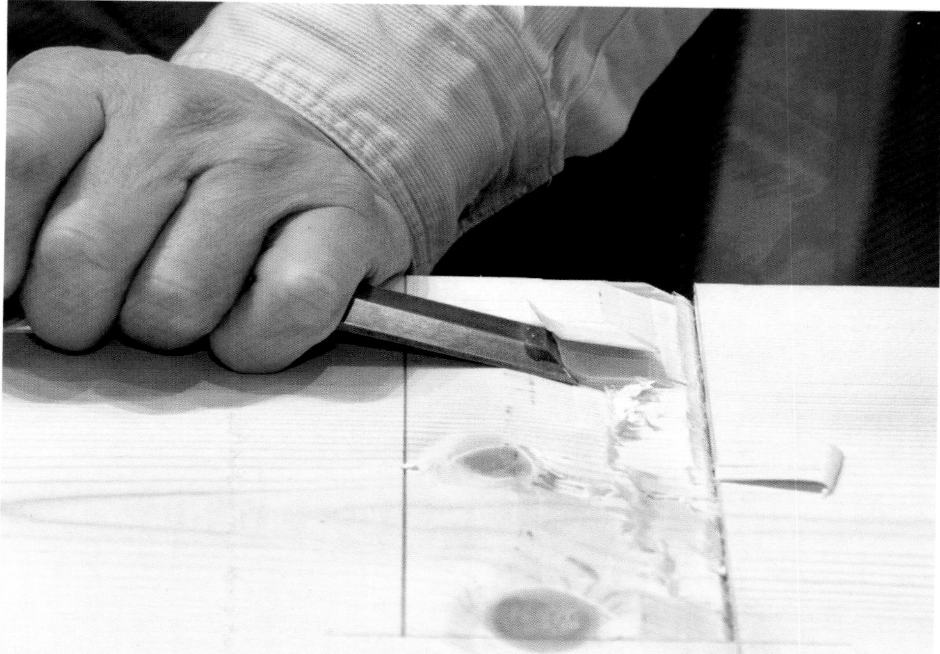

Although it is on a large scale this is still just a standard housing dado.

Use the corresponding leg to mark the width.

Clean out most of the waste with the 1" chisel.

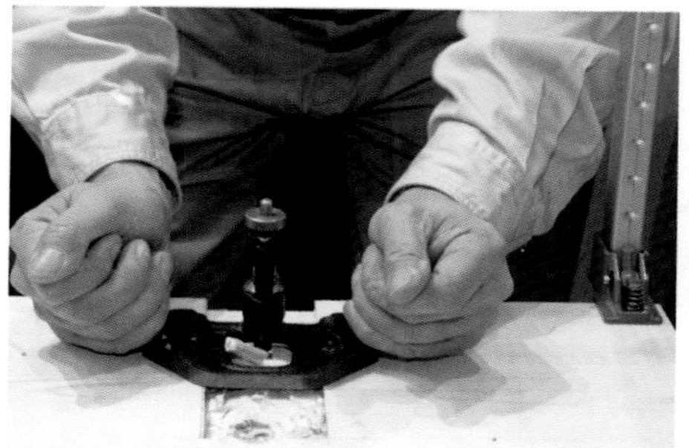

A router ensures that the depth is even.

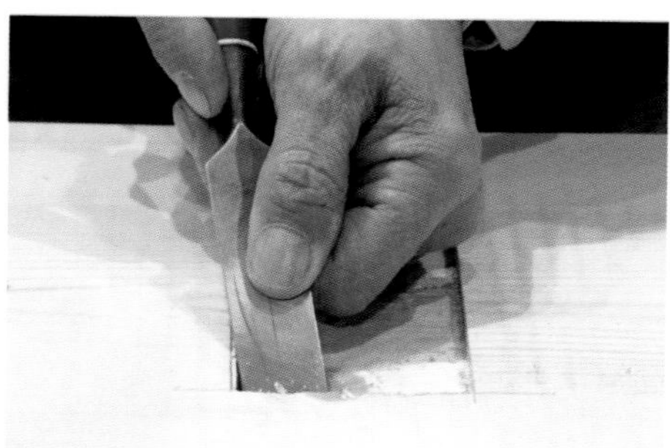

Clean up the front corner.

After drilling the holes countersink them as shown.

6. Follow with angled cuts toward the knifewall and repeat until you are down to just slightly above the depth line—about $\frac{1}{32}$".
7. By placing the leg into its housing, you can mark the dead width of the leg with your knife.
8. Use the square and knife to create the second, parallel knifewall.
9. Follow the same procedure to get the second knifewall down to just above the depth gauge line.
10. To guarantee the depth of the housing across the entire recess, use a hand router set to the gauge line.
11. Dry fit the leg 'H' frame to each housing, making certain of a good, unhindered fit.
12. Drill three $\frac{3}{16}$" diameter holes through the apron housings. Put the holes on a steeply angled line, so that none of the holes align in a single line of grain and countersink the same.

Fixing the aprons to the 'H' leg frames

With two people, this procedure is easier. If you are on your own use any folding portable workbench to support one leg frame while fixing the other frame at the opposite end of the apron. Make certain that the leg frame is fully seated into the housing. Apply plenty of glue and screw through the apron into the leg frame. Now repeat with the second frame at the opposite end.

Stand the frames up and onto the legs. Apply glue to the housings of the second apron and screw it to the leg frames, again making certain the leg frames fully seat into their housings.

Zig zag the glue into the stopped housing dadoes.

Fix the apron with screws, through the pre-drilled aprons.

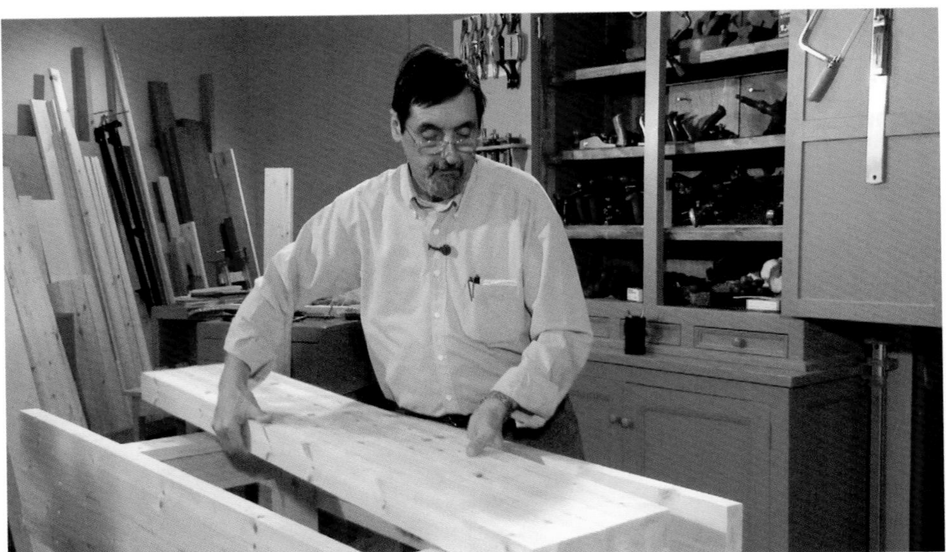

Before you fit the benchtop, plane the underside flat.

Plane out any twist from the underside.

You can glue the benchtop to the front apron…

…and then clamp up and screw them together.

Fix the top to the bearers from underneath.

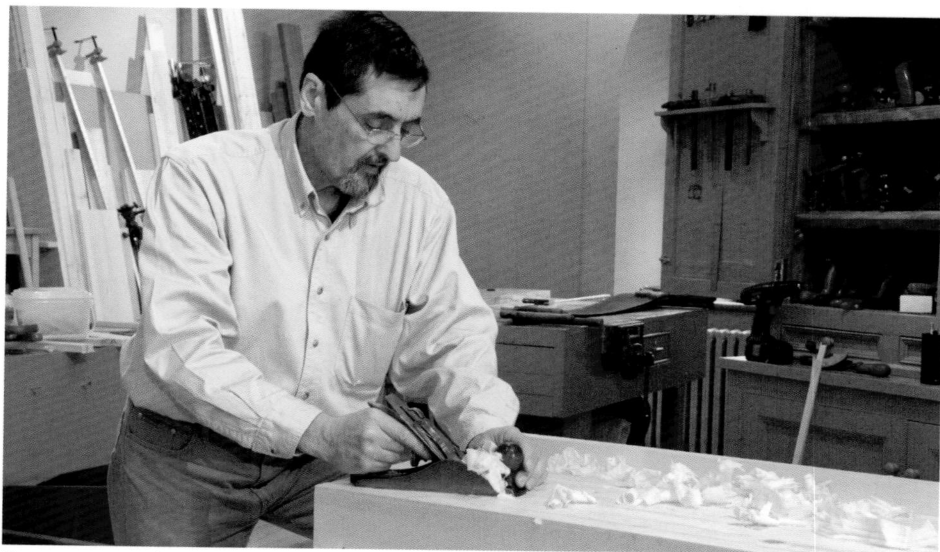
You may want to leave it overnight for the glue to set, before surface planing the top.

Adding the benchtop

Preparing the benchtop is simply a question of planing the surfaces and sighting the edges for straightness. We also plane the edges to true them and make sure they are parallel. That done, we must check the benchtop isn't twisted, by sighting the underside face. In the unlikely event that it is, we must plane out any twist before fixing it to the apron and 'H' frames. I do this by turning the benchtop upside down and laying it across the bearers. It's not necessary to plane the final top surface at this point, it's easier to do this after it is fixed to the apron and the leg frames.

1. Check the meeting edge of the benchtop to the apron and make sure it fits well. The edge of the benchtop may need planing to close any gaps.
2. With the benchtop planed to match the apron, run a zigzag of glue along the meeting edge of the benchtop and clamp it all along the edge. I screw through the apron into the edge of the benchtop.
3. From the underside of the benchtop, screw through the leg frame bearers into the benchtop with 2" screws and wait for the glue to set.
4. Surface plane the benchtop until it's perfectly flat.

"We must check the benchtop isn't twisted, by sighting the underside face"

Fixing the well board

1. To support the well board, add lengths of 1"x2" pine to the inside of the back apron as well as the underside edge of the benchtop, in between the leg frames.
2. The well board is oversized in width. It must first be fitted. Fit one edge to either the benchtop or apron by dropping it into the opening at an angle and checking to see how the edge fits. Mark it and plane it ready for fitting to the adjacent piece.
3. With the edge fitted, measure the width and cut the board down to rough, slightly oversized width and then plane the final fit into the opening.
4. Screw the well board in place from the underside.
5. Trim both ends of the benchtop, aprons and well board, taking care to cut them dead square. Finish the endgrain with a very sharp, finely set smoothing plane.

Glue the batten to the underside of the benchtop.

Screw it in place.

Screw a batten to the rear apron.

Fix the well board to the bearers.

Trim the well board, benchtop and aprons to length.

Glue and pin the quadrant in place, but do not fix it to the well board. This allows for shrinkage and expansion

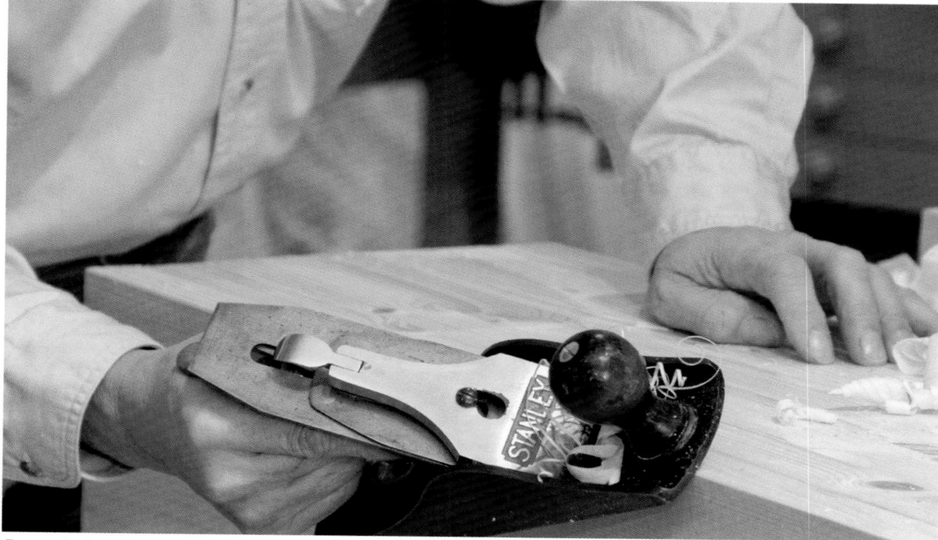

Ease all the edges evenly.

6. Nail two pieces of ¾" quadrant molding into the apron on the back and the benchtop at the front, but not to the well board. This allows the well board to expand and contract freely. Use 1" finish nails.
7. Ease all the corners with a chamfer. Count the number of passes you take with the plane to make sure all the edges look the same.

Fitting the vise

Though the bench is central to the workshop itself, it's the vise that places it at the core of handwork. The vise is the extra hand we rely on for gripping and holding the wood during so many woodworking tasks.

Fitting the vise is straightforward, though heavy and awkward. As I am right-handed, I find it convenient for all my tools to be front-and-right as I face my vise. It makes sense therefore that on most benches the primary vise is at the left corner of the bench when facing the bench. I also like the addition of a tail vise to my bench. That way, with a series of bench dogs, I can clamp my panel work securely to the benchtop. For everyday use this is less essential, because I find it just as convenient to clamp my work to the bench or add a bench dog to push against. Still, it is useful to have.

I find the best position for the vise is directly next to the bench leg. That way, when I use the mallet to chop mortises in the vise, there is plenty of support and no bounce or flex.

1. Place the vise nearby so that you can take measurements directly from it as you layout the vise opening. You'll need to cut out a shape that closely follows the profile of the parallel sliding bars and machine thread. To begin, measure directly onto the apron, starting with the line that shows the position of the inside of the leg of the 'H' frame. It does not need to be an exact fit. In fact, on quick-release vises there are moving parts that sometimes need space for the mechanism to operate properly. However, too large a gap may cause weaknesses in this critical point where the apron needs the strength to brace the leg frame.
2. With the opening marked out, bore a couple of large holes to allow entry with a pad or stab saw. Use a 1" chisel on the long grain sections that need splitting and paring down.

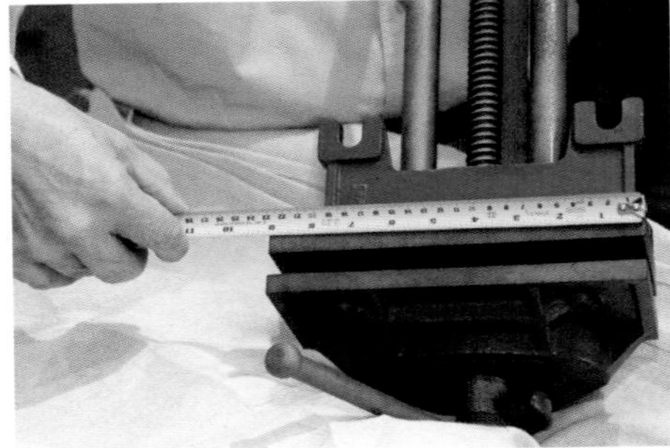

Measure the width.

Make the marks for the vise opening based on the vise itself.

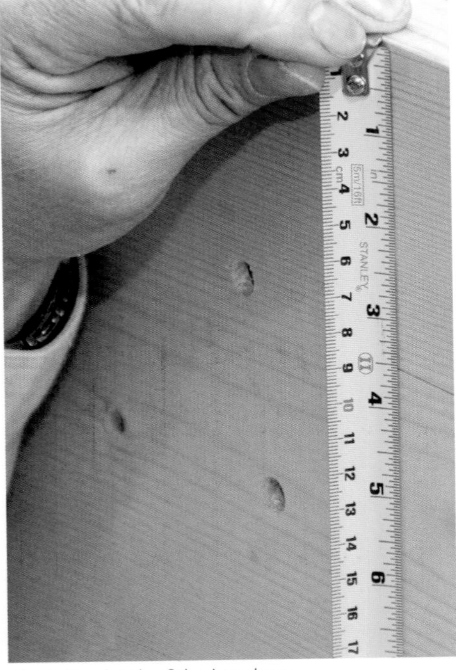

Mark the depth of the benchtop.

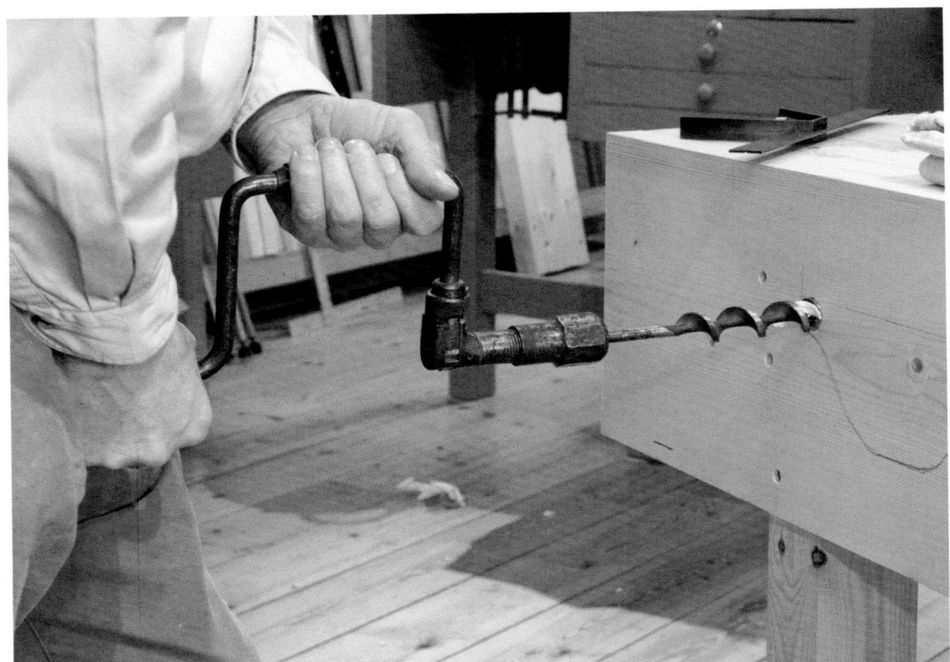

Bore through the corners after marking the shape of the opening required.

A sharp padsaw will quickly remove the waste.

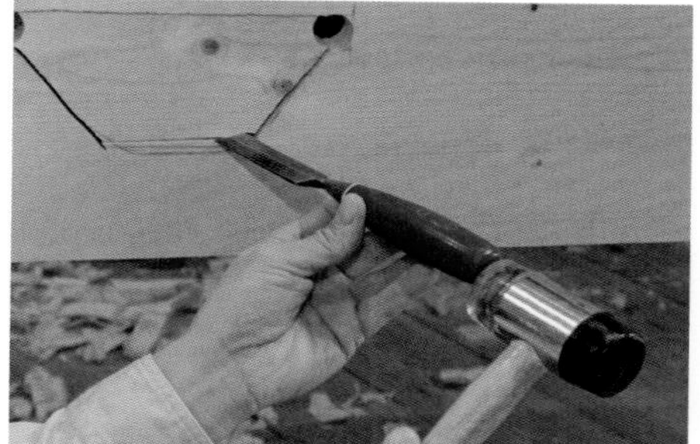

After cutting three sides, the waste will split easily.

This is what the opening should look like.

Take care, the vise is quite heavy.

When it fits well, bolt it to the benchtop.

3. The top of the metal vise jaws need to finish 1⁄16" below the surface of the benchtop so that the plane won't catch the vise when you are planing. Depending on the vise you purchase, you may need to pack between the underside of the benchtop and the top of the 'L' of the vise. Plywood will work well. Once you have the right packing, nail it to the underside of the bench but remember that you will be boring pilot holes for any coach bolts used to anchor the vise.
4. With the opening cut and the vise fitted with packing, you can now anchor the vise to the benchtop with heavy coach screws. It's best to bore pilot holes that take the main body of the screws while allowing the threads to fasten fully into the wall of the hole. This minimizes any risk of splitting the benchtop.

Fitting vise jaws

The vise must be fitted with jaws made of wood or plywood. These jaws cushion the wood being worked and also set a protective barrier to prevent damage to your tools. Any ⅞" thick hardwood will work, but I choose woods like oak or maple. I also like to use a good grade of ¾" plywood for added strength and resilience. These wood linings should sit about $1/16$" above the vise mechanism and bars and slightly above the benchtop. Once fitted, they can be planed flush with the benchtop when the jaws are fully tightened. They can be up to an inch wider than the jaws, but no more. If they are too wide, they will be less supported by the vise jaws and may bend under any applied pressure. Most vises have screw holes, so you can screw the jaws through these: Into the benchtop for the rear jaw, and through the vise jaw and into the wooden jaw for the front jaw.

Screw right through into the apron.

Use shorter screws so the points of the thread do not emerge from the jaws.

Your newly finished bench.

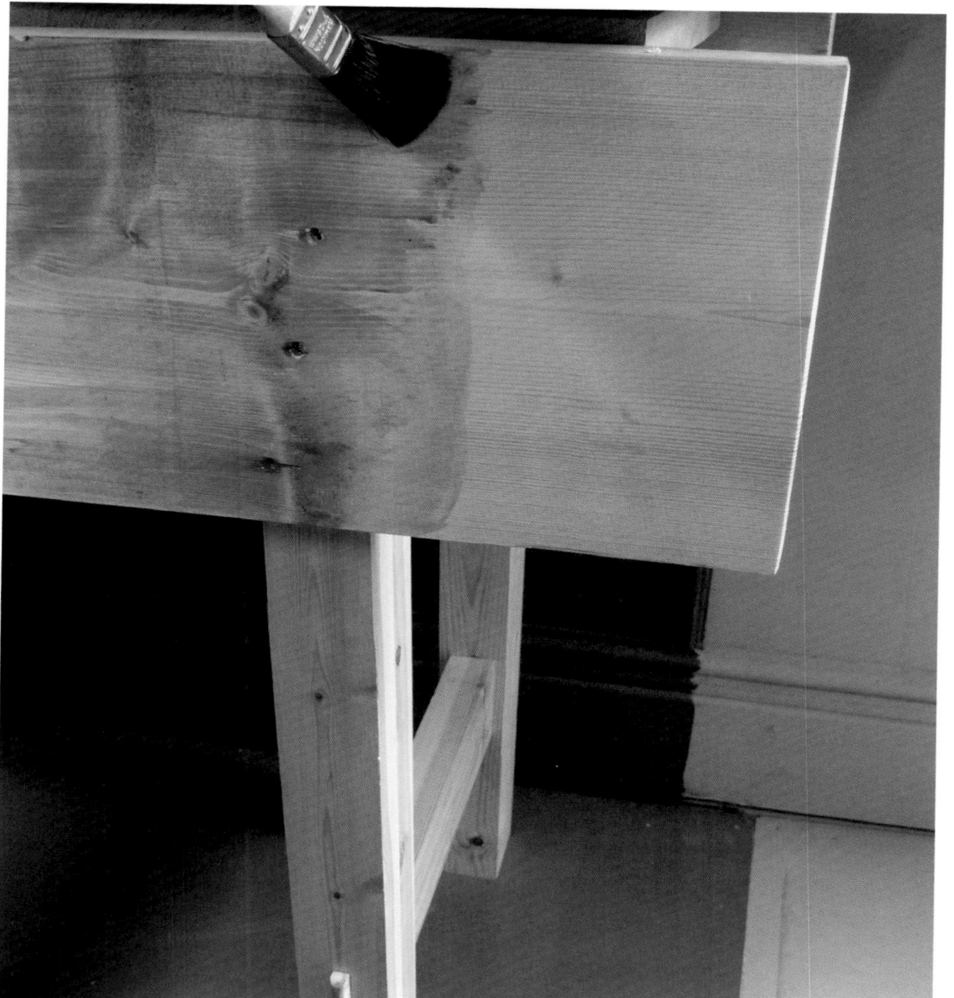

You can apply a colored or clear sealer or stain.

Applying a protective finish

Almost any finish will work for a bench, but I like waterborne stain varnish finishes because they last well, are easy to apply and dry within an hour or so. Two coats will usually suffice. You could also use two or three coats of Danish oil, which also works well but takes longer to dry. Sand the bench first with 150 grit abrasive paper.

Customizing your bench

After you have been using the bench for a while you may want to further customize it by adding an additional bench dogging system, like the one made by Veritas, or a tail vise with holes along the bench top to hold long pieces such as panels. You could also add a drawer or cupboard to store tools and equipment. This will add extra weight to help hold the bench in place.

Conclusion

You have just completed a workbench designed to withstand the rigors of heavy woodworking, and give you the stability you need for either the most intricate of precise inlay work or heavy joint making, planing and sawing. It's an investment of time and resources that starts to quickly repay your efforts the moment your bench is finished and every day it's used thereafter.

Drawers will easily fit into both ends...

...or into the middle of the apron.

This is a home made dog that fits into the vise.

I have wooden pegs that hold the work across the bench.

In this chapter, I will show you how to become totally self sufficient with every tool that requires sharpening and routine maintenance. The few tools and related pieces of equipment fit into a shoebox, and most will last for many years before you need to replace them. This kit, will sharpen, service and maintain the four categories of tools that require sharpening:

EDGE TOOLS: Including every plane type, spokeshaves, chisels, gouges, knives, axes, and most carving tools.

SAWS: Ripcut saws, crosscut saws, tenon or back saws.

SCRAPERS: Both hand held card scrapers and cast-iron cabinet scrapers.

AUGERS: All sizes are sharpened using the same method.

11 Sharpening hand tools

Of all the tasks every woodworker must master, sharpening is the single most important. Sadly, sharpening skills once commonly practiced by all woodworkers have become shrouded in mystery and misinformation. Today, I find perhaps only one in several thousand woodworkers understands even the basic principles of sharpening saws, scrapers, planes and edge tools with most instruction provided by tool manufacturers and salespeople and no longer by skilled artisans. This chapter aims to challenge and reverse that trend.

"I will show you how to become totally self sufficient..."

As an apprentice in the 1950s, I saw a trend begin to emerge where joiners started to send out their saws to 'specialist' saw doctors. This trend grew in popularity leading to the gradual but increasing reluctance of craftsmen to maintain and sharpen even their own saws. In my later days with the joinery firm, young apprentices no longer received the essential discipline of saw sharpening, and indeed sharpening many of the other hand tools used in woodworking also diminished. This trend, combined with a heavy reliance on machinery for even the most simple tasks, has led to the present day dilemma: people like to work with razor sharp tools but today few know how to create and maintain a good cutting edge.

The good news is you can learn to sharpen any type of tool in just a few hours. The methods and procedures that follow in this section will both de-industrialize the process and totally revolutionize the way you perceive hand tools. I have demonstrated these same sharpening techniques to experienced craftsmen, who were often surprised by their own conclusion: Realizing they had never used really sharp tools before, the most frequent response, across the full range of abilities and experience, was amazement at the time saved by establishing simple hand sharpening methods and techniques.

12 Sharpening edge tools

Apart from knives and axes, edge tools have a sharp edge formed between a large flat face and a short bevel. The aim in the edge tool sharpening process is to refine this edge by removing steel from the bevel using successively finer sharpening media. We measure the fineness of the particle size by referring to a 'grit size' or 'grade'. To get some idea of the scale of the particles, compare coarse 40 grit sandpaper with say, a sheet of 400 grit sandpaper, which seems fairly smooth in comparison. Emery paper is available in finer grades, and 1200 grit is silky smooth and would produce a well-refined edge. However, for your tools to perform to a level which will enable you to achieve fine levels of work, you need to learn how to maintain and sharpen them to a standard adhered to by master artisans through the ages. I will show you a three-stage process that will enable you to sharpen to around 15,000 grit quickly and easily.

"I want you to be able to look at any edge tool, in any condition, and know exactly what is needed to make it cut efficiently."

My method, which I've taught to thousands of students for over twenty years, gives you immediate sharpening capability and a sense of complete control. By providing all the energy yourself, you'll take off exactly the right amount of steel to get to the pristine cutting edge you need. I have drawn up a flowchart and I suggest that you become familiar with each process and the order of those processes. I have also provided an explanation of every part of it that should answer your questions on my methods and reasoning. I want you to be able to look at any edge tool, in any condition, and know exactly what is needed to make it cut efficiently.

Edge Tool Sharpening Flow Chart

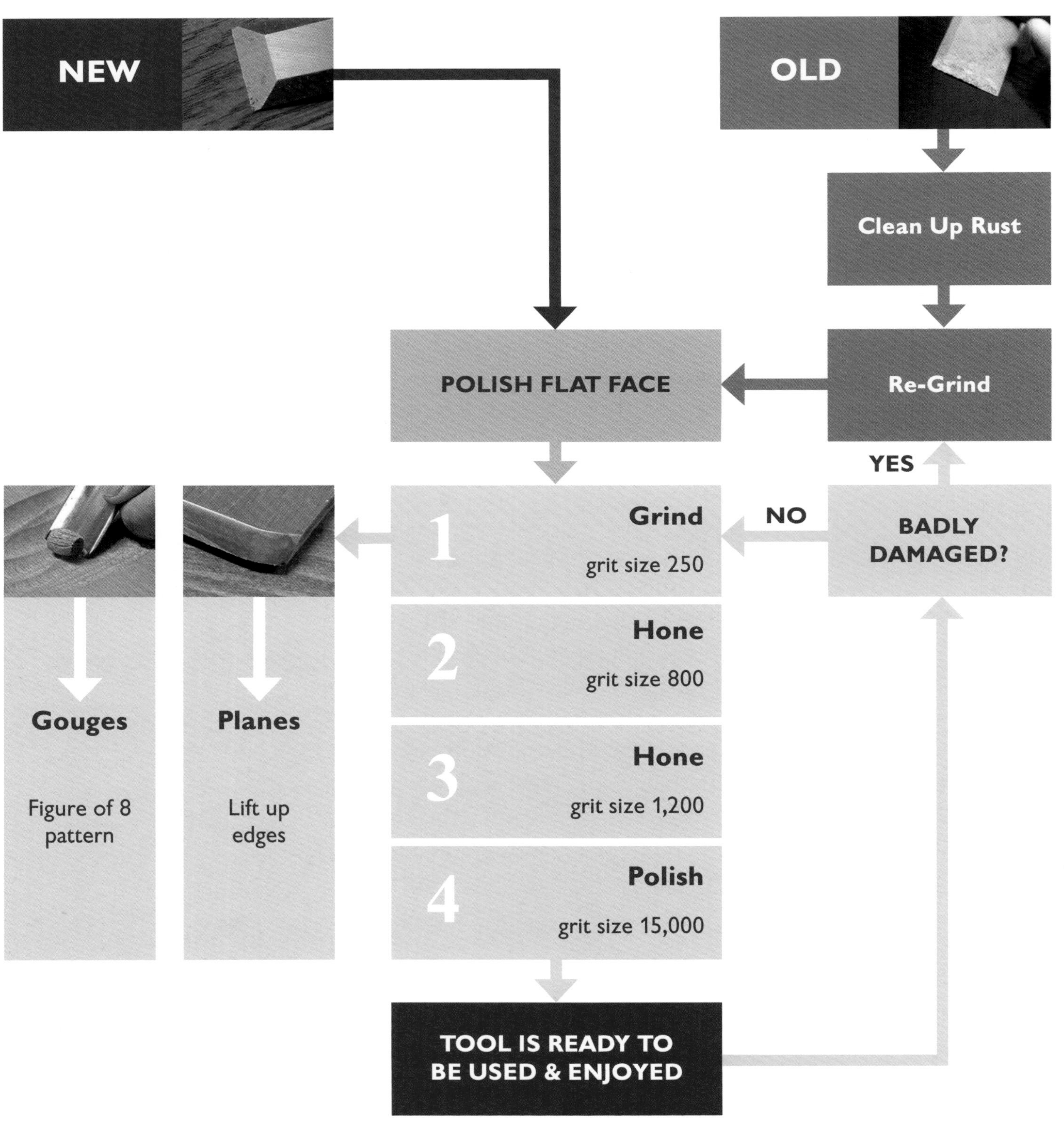

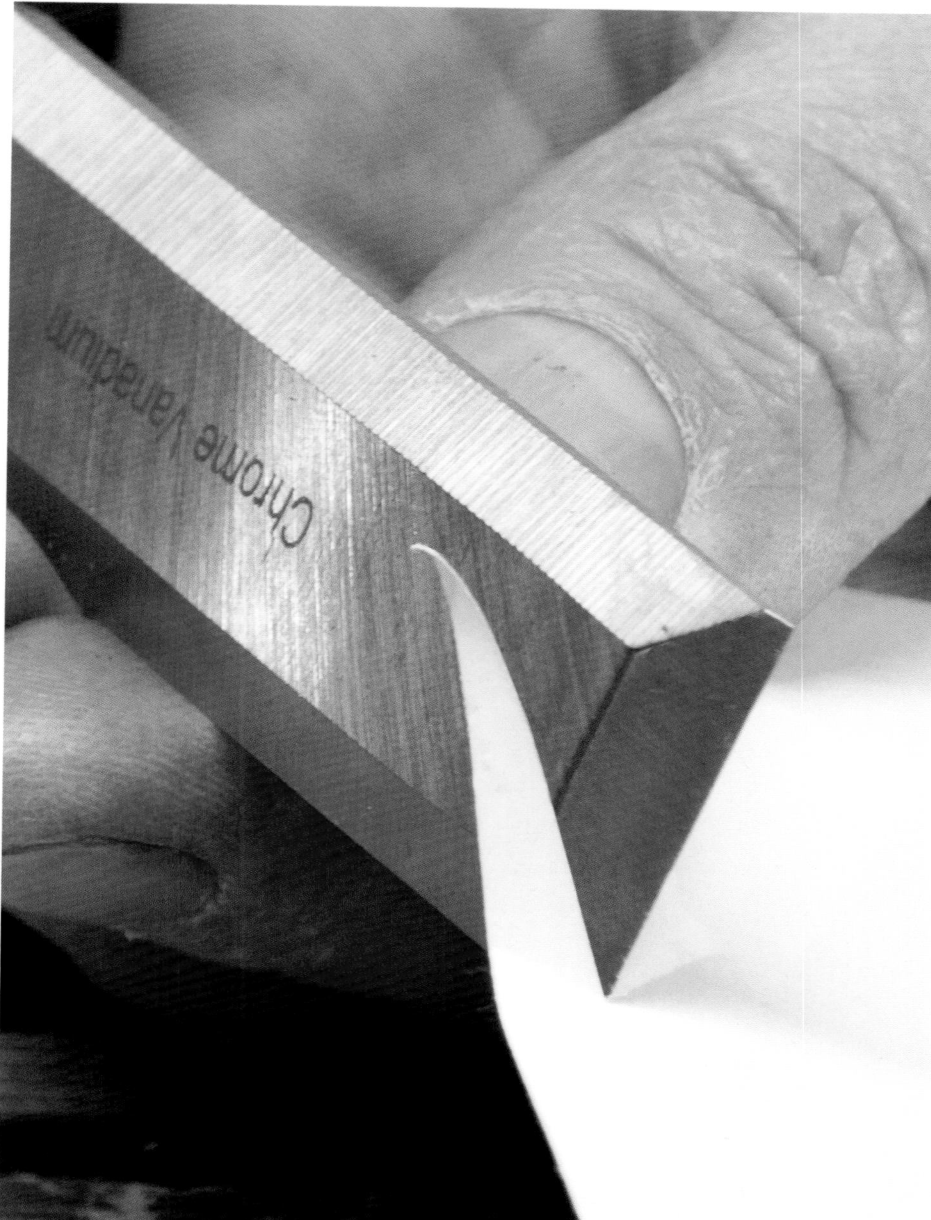

Sharp tools make your work more accurate and clean.

A flat face that is not polished cannot result in a sharp edge.

The entire cutting edge should be polished like a mirror.

Polish the flat face

With any chisel or plane iron, polishing the flat face is the first, immediate step in creating a refined edge. It's of minimal consequence honing and polishing the bevel to a mirror polish, if the flat face is not polished to an equal level. Grinding marks left by the industrial grinders and abrasive discs used in the production process must be removed, so too rust pitting often present in old tools, unless they have been particularly well cared for. The flat face must be restored to a flawless condition to achieve a good cutting edge.

Most woodworkers concentrate on the bevel only, but the flat face must be polished to the same level, otherwise the edge will only be as sharp as the less polished of these two faces. This is the first step with any edge tool where the flat face is not mirror polished. In the case of a gouge both the bevel and the inside face are curved, but the same principles of refinement still apply.

Getting steel to a highly polished level can only be accomplished through incremental levels of abrading—and no level should be skipped, or you will be left with clearly visible scratches that, though polished, will not accomplish the highly refined edge you need. Simply hone and polish the flat face, working through the grades of abrasive, finally polishing up on the leather strop block. Take care to keep the flat face dead flat when using the strop, as any roundover near the cutting edge will mean starting again from scratch. Take your time and really take care.

It may take twenty minutes or more to flatten and polish the flat face of an edge tool, but in reality you won't have to repeat the process very often if you take good care of your tools.

Most people believe the actual bevel and flat face wear down, but really it's only the actual cutting edge itself, where these two faces meet, that crumbles and wears. Hold an edge tool to the light and any rounded edge automatically reflects the light, which shows as a white line. A sharp edge cannot reflect light.

Method—three steps to sharpness

Though the edge-tool group is fairly expansive, they are all sharpened using the same principles. They require a little practice, a modest amount of strength and some disciplined control to achieve and maintain consistent results.

I use diamond coated steel plates as my chosen abrasive, and I refer to them as 'stones', 'diamond plates', or just 'plates'. I prefer to use diamonds and I explain why on page 225 of this chapter.

My three steps are:

- GRINDING
- HONING
- POLISHING

Initially I grind the bevel on a coarse grinding diamond plate and then hone on two finer diamond plates, before final polishing on a 'strop', charged with abrasive compound. It is this critical last step that is most often neglected. All stages rely on the same reductive process of abrasion. Developing manual sharpening skills takes practice but lasts a lifetime. That said, for anyone who has difficulty in keeping the cutting edge of the tool placed accurately, I do recommend purchasing a simple honing guide. This can be a good stepping-stone to help maintain the right angle and develop the necessary 'feel' for sharpening.

TOP TIP: *The board I use to make my sharpening plates more organized is ¾" thick by 11" by 12". The plates are set into recesses about ⅛" deep. You can customize the size to suit your preference. I used solid wood, but plywood works well too. The recesses need not be perfectly accurate as you can use silicone to set the plates into the recess and fill any gaps and cushion the edges of the stones when housed.*

I sharpen across my diamond plates in order.

Make sure and remove all the machine marks from the bevel before polishing.

When you have an even burr across the whole width you know that you have ground enough.

This is a magnified view of a burr which shows the folded edge of the steel.

Grinding

Grinding should remove just enough steel to form a clean, new edge. With the bevel against the stone, and the tool held at about 30 degrees, I apply a combination of light pressure and forward motion. I hold the blade with my left hand and the handle with my right hand. This is reversed if you are left-hand dominant. I always grind first on the coarse diamond plate. This is my maintenance program and I never stray from it. Otherwise there's a tendency to keep lifting the tool on the finer sharpening plate, which ultimately creates a progressively steeper angle than intended. I feel for the bevel angle and use the full length and width of the plate. I keep the tool in constant contact with the plate the whole time I'm moving over the abrasive. I examine my work periodically to make sure I'm being consistent over the whole bevel and that I'm working evenly from side to side, correcting any bias by varying finger and hand pressure as needed. Using the coarse stone (250 grit) creates a small burr folded over the edge and onto the flat face. The most critical step during grinding is to grind until you create a fine but even burr over the entire width of the tool's edge.

An even, full width burr guarantees you have removed enough steel to create a truly sharp cutting edge as you progress to the honing stage. The plates I use are ideal at 3" by 8". A 2" by 8" plate will work too, but you might find it too narrow for the wider plane blades.

TOP TIP: *I use a proprietary window cleaner in a squirt bottle to prevent the diamond plates from surface clogging with steel particles. You can also use light oil if you prefer. Just plain water, or slightly soapy water, works well too.*

Honing in two stages

Honing refers to the same abrasive process as grinding, but the grit size is much finer. I use the same technique as for grinding, and again I use diamond sharpening plates. My honing starts on a fine 800 grit plate, before progressing to a superfine level of 1200 grit. It's important to go through these stages, otherwise you end up polishing across the scratches left from the coarse grinding without actually taking them out.

Most woodworking instruction suggests flipping the tool over at this point and abrading on the flat face, but as your flat face should already be polished, there is no need for this at this stage, just tackle the flat face as a separate process. See page 207 of this chapter.

After grinding the goal is to remove the coarse grinding marks by honing.

Most of the burr will usually break off when you are honing.

Here you can see only fine scratch marks. This edge is ready for polishing.

Take care to only pull the edge across the strop. Never push it into the leather.

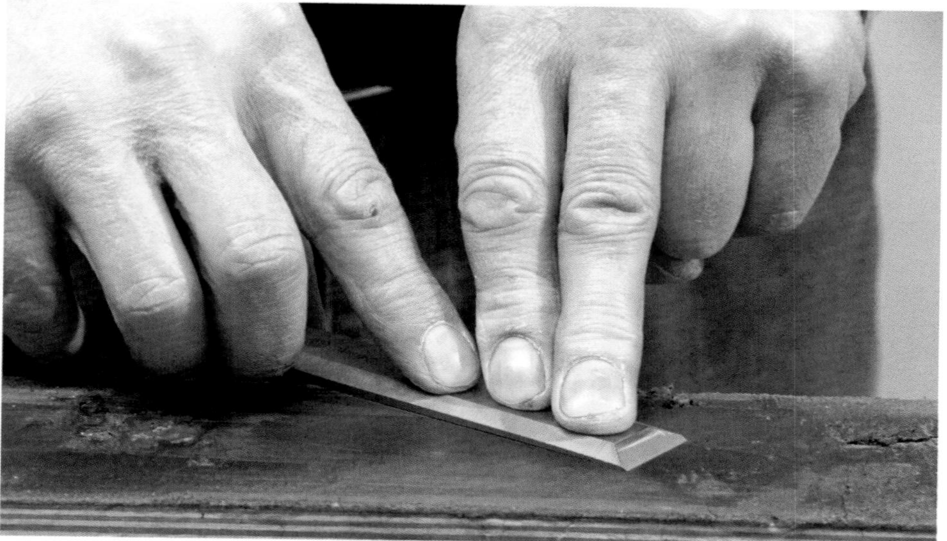

Finally remove any remaining burr by stropping the back face.

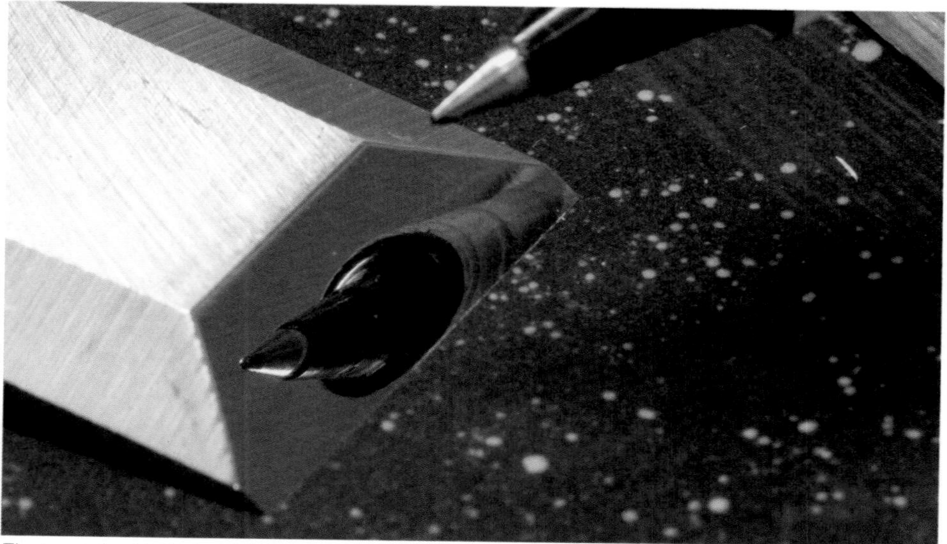

The bevel should also be polished to a mirror finish.

Polishing

Polishing removes any scratches from the surface of the bevel. I refine the bevel to a mirror finish using a polishing compound in a wax block on my leather strop. The grit size of the compound is around 15,000. I usually start with the bevel and (being careful never to lift it up past around 30 degrees) draw the edge back quickly over the leather strop, always in the same direction, around 20 to 30 times, depending on the width of the tool. With the bevel now polished, the last step is to flip over the cutting iron or chisel. Now carefully draw the tool back a few times, keeping it absolutely flat on the strop, so as not to round this critically flat face while easing off the ultrafine burr.

Sharpening is a discipline, a routine that must be built into your daily woodworking routine. This method works particularly well as a quick, regular edge maintenance program. I would expect all of my students to regularly visit the sharpening station in my shop throughout their working day. I make it a habit never to put a dull tool away, that way, I begin each work day with sharp tools and I never have to wonder if a chisel will chop or pare effectively. My three diamond plates and the strop remain close to hand when I'm working, usually fixed in the vise of a nearby bench.

"I prefer to save time and just sharpen by hand"

My question is this: with such a quiet, fast and reliable method of sharpening, why would anyone want to use a machine? Sure, if you have the time you can make some machines work reasonably well, but I prefer to save time and just sharpen by hand. If you adopt this method, you'll need to invest a modest sum, but the result will be that it will take only a minute or so to sharpen your tools to this level of perfection every time and diamond stones will last you a lifetime.

Honing guides—freehand sharpening

For almost forty years I have sharpened cutting bevels on my chisels and plane irons, with consistent success, by hand and with no guide. In my formative years as an apprentice, however, the results were not so successful. Some of my narrower chisels inevitably ended up as skew chisels; not what I wanted or needed. That's the same for most of my students who, though they try hard, cannot often get consistent results. Being perfectly square is not always that critical, but eventually, if left uncorrected, the skew gets increasingly worse and the chisel will be useless for most aspects of woodworking. The problem becomes exaggerated in planes simply because of the increased width of the iron, where eventually the lateral adjustment lever cannot correct the skewed edge.

There are many aids to help woodworkers get the correct angle on their edge tools and they work well for this purpose. Set-up time using these guides, however well made, interrupts the flow of work. Even so, I use them to correct severe defects as an initial guide when the students' practice chisels are badly out of alignment and the bevel is grossly misshapen. Once the bevel is re-established I can begin sharpening freehand again. So, I recommend using guides to correct discrepancies, change bevel angles and as a step to establishing real skills.

This is how I hold a chisel to sharpen it.

The Draper guide in use. It grinds a flat bevel but will get your chisels sharp, and at the right angle.

My overhead guide

The conventional guide is the simplest of all guides and works really well. The overhead guide shown here is one I developed myself and is simple to make and to use. I like it because it allows me to establish the convex bevel I prefer on my chisels, plane irons and spokeshaves, something all other guides deny me. This guide is made from any piece of wood and is simply clamped to the tool being sharpened. The position of the guide remains the same for every level of sharpening on the abrasive plates or stones. It can also be used on the strops too.

My guide design allows you to shape the bevel but keeps it square.

This is a very simple guide.

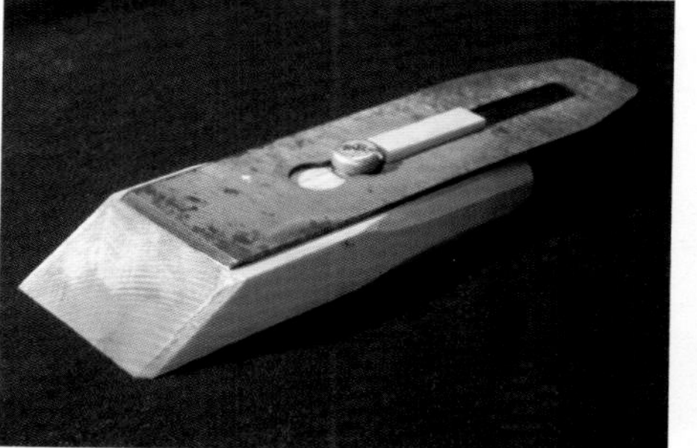

You can adapt this guide to be used for plane blades.

It also allows you to round the corners of the blade which is critical when sharpening plane blades.

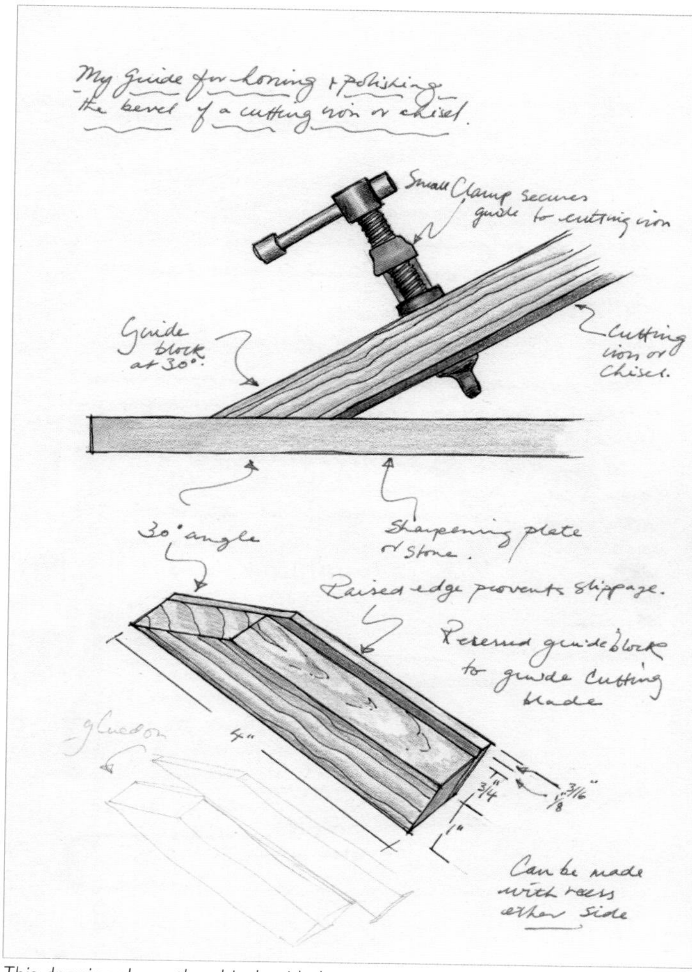

This drawing shows the chisel guide I use.

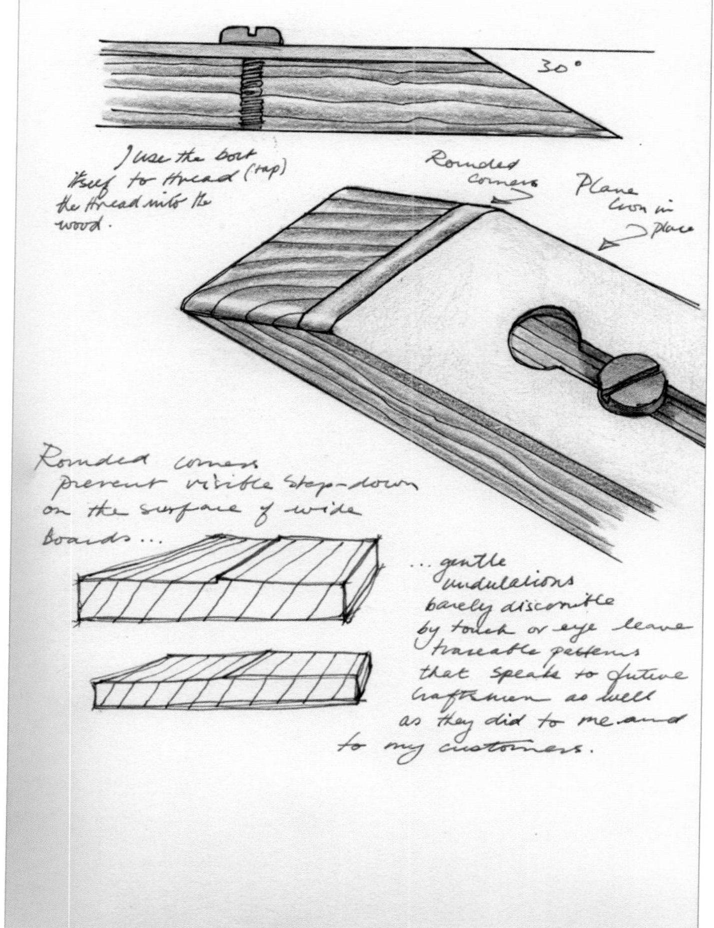

These are the drawings for my plane iron sharpening guide.

New tools are often NOT ready for use

It seems logical that new tools should arrive sharp and ready to use straight from the box, but in my half century of working wood I've never seen it happen. Most makers do establish the ground bevel and refine it to a certain level. In most cases the tools will actually cut, but the levels fall far short of the refinement we need for good results. The flowchart gives you the clear steps required to prepare a new tool for first time use. You will notice that I strongly recommend that you mirror polish the flat face of all new edge tools—see page 207 in this chapter.

The sharpening process will soon become second nature. That said, you must master certain techniques and understand the basic physics of what you are trying to accomplish by refining the cutting edge. Most woodworkers are bemused by the process and experience untold frustration simply because there is so much misinformation available. But with some guidance the practice becomes so intuitive that sharpening a chisel or plane iron takes no longer than a minute or two at most.

This brand new chisel (lower) is not ready for use. It needs sharpening to look like the one above

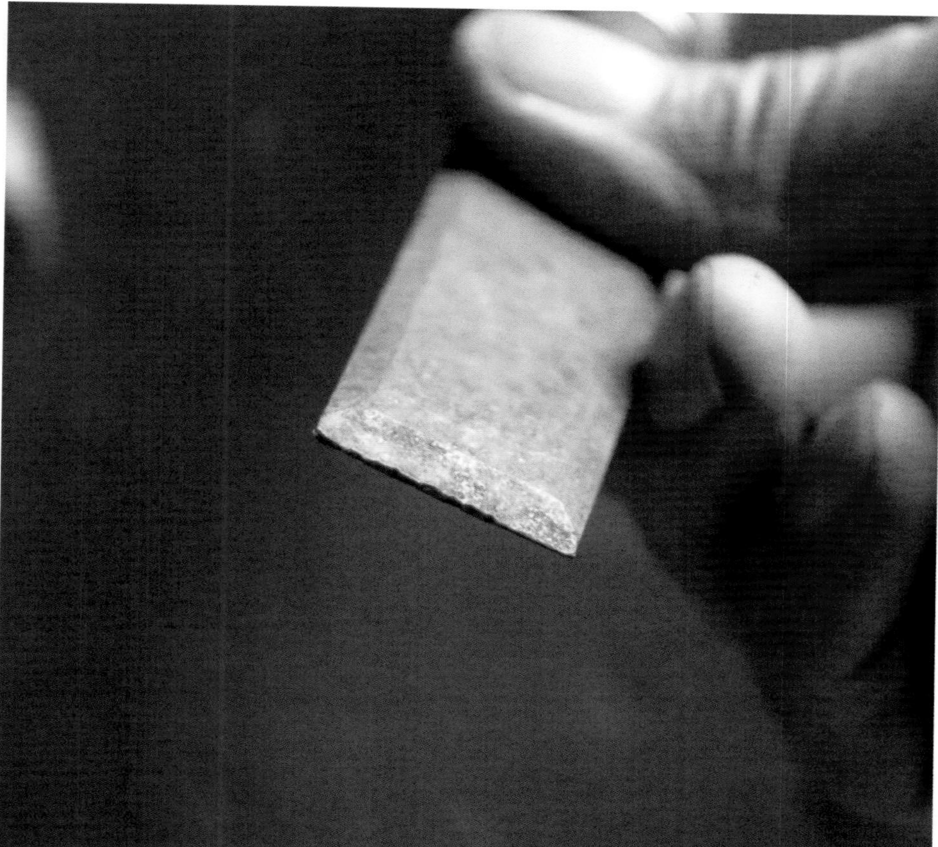
An ugly rusty and misused chisel

The cutting edge will need grinding clear of all the deformation resulting from misuse and neglect.

Remedial steps for old or damaged tools

The secondhand tool market is thriving thanks to car boot sales, flea markets, garage sales and eBay. Many older tools were made from excellent materials, so even heavy surface rust can be concealing a good chisel or plane. Personally, I look for well-known makers like the older Spear & Jackson, Record, Marples, Stanley and several others. Remedial work should be minimal and normally focuses on removing surface rust and contaminants such as paint, and then grinding the steel clear of any rounded edges, dings or nicks.

Old tools

Today, many newly manufactured tools are made of a poorer quality materials than those made in the past, primarily because many manufacturers cut corners to increase profit and reduce the price of the finished product.
It's easy to be impressed by refined adjustment mechanisms, which a true artisan can recreate manually with some basic techniques such as hammer-tap-adjustments. It's also true that older planes benefit from a well-worn open throat and slack in the threaded adjustment wheels. So you shouldn't dismiss well-worn older models as good,

practical choices for your plane range.

Restoring edge tools

1. Remove all rust, surface grease and oil using abrasive paper, wire brushes, steel wool and solvent cleaners where necessary. Depending on the degree of rust, begin with the appropriate grit of abrasive paper. For heavy rust use coarse 150 grit first and then move through 180 and 220 grit until all rust is removed.

2. Despite obvious concerns surrounding the use of mechanical grinders, they do serve a useful purpose. Sometimes with old, new or damaged tools, the flat face is not flat, but has a slight roundover, to the corner areas of the cutting edge. In this case, a grinder will soon bring the cutting tool back into a condition where you can start the processes of polishing and refining the flat face and sharpening.

A good clean up of the whole tool is the place to start.

A grinder, although not essential, is a useful addition to any workshop.

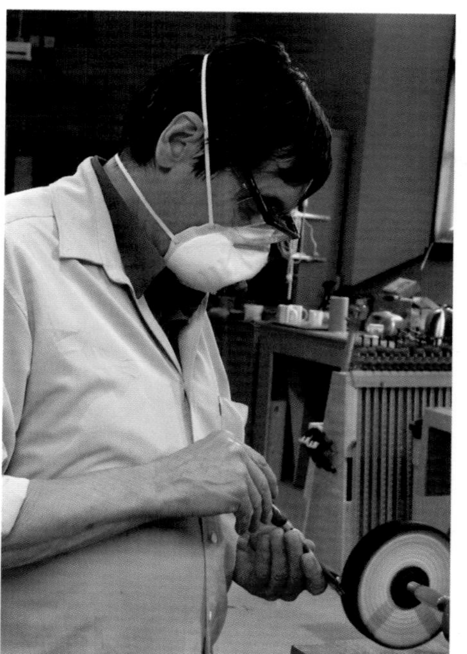
Always take care when using a mechanical grinder.

Heat builds up very quickly.

You will burn the edge if you are not extremely careful.

Safety with bench grinders

Often the remedial steps can be accomplished more quickly and consistently using a mechanical bench grinder like the one shown here. All machines have their own inherent dangers and though bench grinders seem fairly innocuous at first, they have several risk factors that can create hazardous situations. Please take all recommended guidelines provided by the manufacturers.

Guards and guides

Because many tools have awkward shapes, it's tempting to remove tool guides and protective guards to get better access to the wheel. Don't. The machine's bite can grab and throw small edge tools back in the face, body or hands of the user. Always wear a face shield and goggles as standard and also be especially conscious of others working around you.

Guides built into the body of the machine assist to provide consistent angles to register the piece against. Their safety value far outweighs any awkwardness.

Dust masks

The dust and debris from grinding wheels is a serious health hazard, so use an appropriate dust mask for every grinding operation.

Buffing wheels

Sometimes we use cotton, sisal and fabric mops and wheels, charged with buffing compound to polish awkward shapes and surfaces. These abrasive compounds and waxes can be harmful when breathed in, so again always use a dust mask. Always wear a face shield and goggles because the fabric can grab the tool and flip it back at the user. This is especially true with small component parts and cutters.

Sparks and heat

Grinding wheels quickly generate heat, which travels gradually along the steel and becomes too hot to hold. In extreme conditions it can even start a fire, so make sure that the work area is free from materials such as wire wool, wood shavings, sawdust or any flammable material and liquids.

DON'T USE BELT SANDERS FOR GRINDING STEEL. *Many people think belt sanders work well for removing steel to grind the bevel, but there are serious risks involved. One is that they are not intended for sharpening steel and have no guide to support the tool being sharpened. Also, because they are not intended for grinding metal any spark can ignite the fine dust inside the machine and/or dust bag. The draft created then fans the spark and the dust smolders for hours before igniting.*

The right angle

To sharpen any edge tool, we generally create an edge formed by two intersecting faces. While one face is nearly always flat, the bevel may be flat, hollow ground (concave) or intentionally curved to form a convex surface. The angle created by these faces determines the amount of resistance we feel when we push the tool into the wood. The steeper the angle, the more resistance there is and the more effort it takes to make a cut. In theory, any angle can be sharpened below 90 degrees and greater than zero, but the most practical angle is somewhere between 25 and 30 degrees. Obviously, the lower the angle of the tool's cutting edge the less resistance there is, but when the angle is too shallow, the edge is weak and non-viable.

The angle at which we sharpen has less to do with sharpness than it does resistance and strength. The reason a shallow-angled cutting edge fractures is because carbon steel becomes brittle when hardened. We use this characteristic to make cutting tools that can resist wear. If steel, or any other metal for that matter, is too soft, it will not hold an edge that will cut for very long. Heating steel and quenching it by plunging it in oil or water alters the steel's structure and makes it hard and brittle. A cutting edge treated this way lasts many times longer than it would if it was left untreated, but in this state the steel is too hard for repeated sharpening. A process of heat treatment must then be used to alter tool steel by what is commonly called tempering. This process makes the steel somewhat softer but also tougher, and means it can be more readily abraded or filed. Even so, shallow-angled bevels can still break easily because they are still somewhat brittle, and when the steel is so thin it breaks to create a jagged edge. When edge tools such as chisels are too hard, they frequently fracture along the cutting edge with only minimal lateral pressure.

The angle at which we sharpen has less to do with sharpness than it does with resistance and strength.

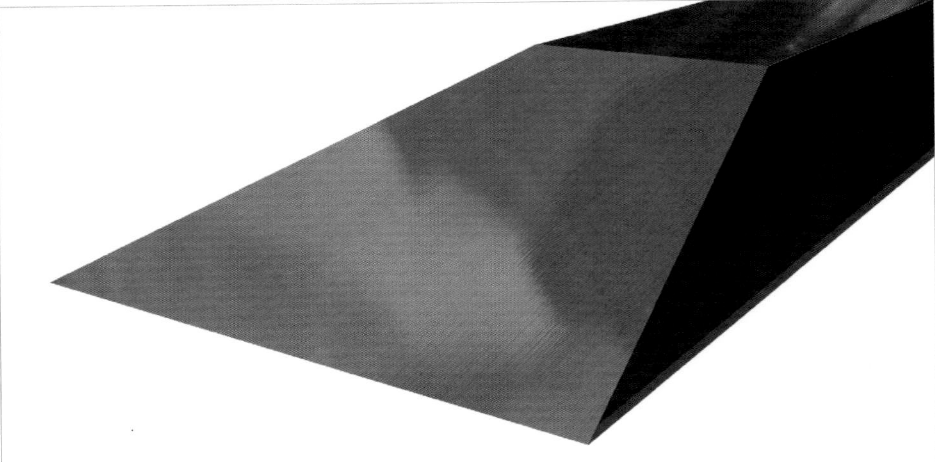

This shallow angle will give a fragile edge.

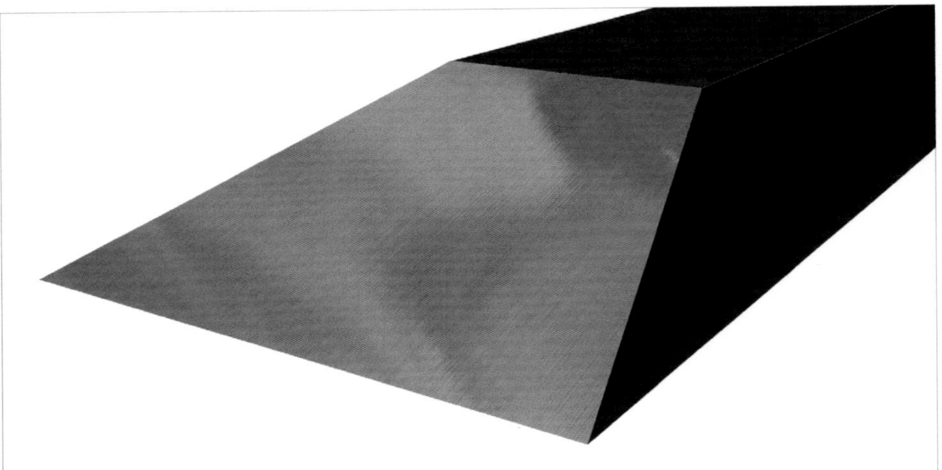

This 30 degree angle is about right.

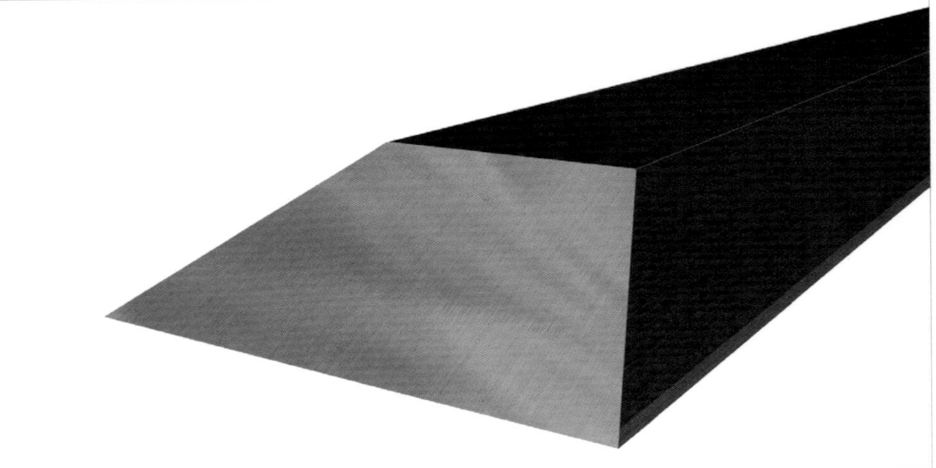

A steep angle will be strong but requires a lot more effort to make cuts due to the greater resistance.

Though this shallow angle gives the least resistance in the cut, it also fractures more easily along the cutting edge with the slightest of pressures.

This steep angle of 40 degrees has great strength but so too resistance. Not too practical for most woodworking tasks.

30 degrees gives optimum flexibility and good sharp cutting-edge retention.

Shallow angles—paring chisels

Many activities with edge tools use a technique called 'paring'. This means using the chisel in a slicing motion and applying only hand pressure to the chisel. We can generally use a shallower angle on the bevel to develop a less resistant cutting edge.

Steep angles—mortise chisels

Some tasks need the high impact of a heavy mallet. For this heavy work, we could create a secondary bevel to strengthen the steel at this critical area surrounding the cutting edge. Alternatively, we could use heavier duty mortise chisels, where the whole bevel is sharpened at the steeper pitch. Generally, in furniture making, I use only bevel edged chisels for almost all my work. A timber framer however, making large mortises in oak, would need the edge strength of a steep angled mortise chisel. This larger profile allows heavy leverage in deeper mortise holes.

Steel reacts differently to being sharpened depending on how it is hardened.

Steels used for hand tools

The key characteristic for steel used in hand woodworking tools is their toughness—their ability to resist fracture under normal use.

Depending on the alloy used, some steels resist edge fold, but will instead fracture along the cutting edge; those that resist fracturing may fold more readily. O1 steel cutting irons are generally preferred because they take a sharper edge than their tougher counterparts made from A2 steel. Sharpening O1 steel is easier than sharpening A2 steel, so even though the wear resistance factor is higher, greater effort is needed to re-establish a cutting edge. (Note: 'O' designates oil-cooled steel and 'A' denotes air-cooled steel).

The cutting efficiency of woodworking tools can be reduced in one of two ways. They can be damaged by contact with another hard object such as a nail or tool, or they can be blunted by normal use. Under a high magnification lens, we would see two indicators of normal use of a very sharp edge:

Plastic deformation, where the concentrated force deforms the sharp edge and forms a rounded 'nose'. Even very hard steel can bend and fold under pressure.

Micro-fracturing of the crystal structure. Tool steel, being an alloy of pure iron, carbon, iron carbide and other alloying metals (tungsten, chromium, nickel and manganese), has a complex crystal structure, where individual crystalline grains fracture off the cutting edge. This occurs when the internal stress created by deformation is greater than the bond strength at the grain boundaries.

In both cases, the result is that the cutting edge starts to tear the wood and bruise fibers rather than shaving them, or compresses and distorts them instead of severing them cleanly.

Many modern grinding wheels only measure 6" across unlike this old 18" wheel.

Shape

Though there are many ways to grind the bevel, most woodworkers choose one of two methods to maintain the sharp cutting edge they need.

-The first method involves some form of mechanical grinding to reform the bevel. They then refine it further with a secondary-bevel (or micro-bevel) to strengthen the edge.
-The second method is called the single-bevel method, in which we grind and hone the bevel to form a continuous polished surface.

I would like to compare these two approaches by looking at the historic development of grinding systems.

In previous centuries, craftsmen didn't generally enter the scientific realms of trying to understand micron sizes or specific abrasive material types by analysis. They simply made an 18" stone wheel, housed it on a handled spindle, built a wooden water bath beneath the spindle and ground the bevels of their tools. From there they refined the edge on bench stones and strops in the same way we do today.

The post-war decade brought many developments to sharpening, but primarily, the mass production of electric motors allowed the 6" electric grinding wheel to be adopted en masse. This small diameter abrasive wheel created the famed hollow-ground bevel. This concave bevel was incapable of supporting a viable cutting edge. It had to be strengthened by a second bevel we now call a micro- or secondary-bevel (see the drawings overleaf showing the results of flat, convex and concave (hollow) grinding).

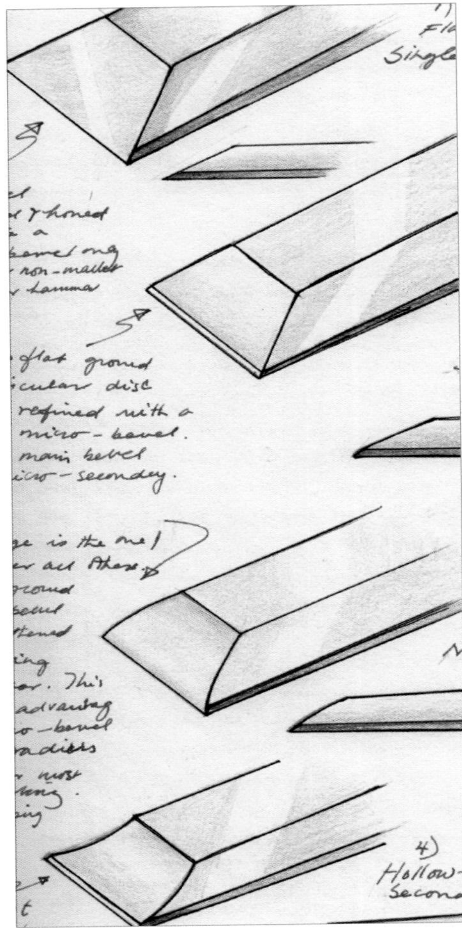

The convex bevel created has a proven strength and versatility.

We always have to grind away steel to create the fresh edge we need, and the quickest way seems to be with an abrasive wheel, disc or belt. The grindstone at best will only tackle the first stage, that of grinding, which can be easily accomplished using a coarse diamond plate. In reality, it's comparatively slow if you include the time spent setting up the jig. Add to that the risks of overheating and burning the steel, grinding off more steel than is necessary and the increased risk of personal injury, and you'll understand my quest for something simpler, more efficient and safer.

The issue of what shape of bevel works best has been discussed in woodworking circles for years. It is never going to determine whether or not you can work to high standards, but it is worth a brief discussion.

Convex, flat or concave?

Though many if not most craftspeople today still use conventional grinding wheels, other systems are now available, such as horizontal rotary grindstones or wheels. These mechanical grinders have built-in adjustability, so any angle can be ground with a flat bevel instead of hollow. The flat bevel is an improvement on the concave shape described above, but it does have its limitations, as we shall see.

Regardless of vertical or horizontal grinding, an article written several decades ago recommended micro-bevel sharpening as a standard procedure for all woodworkers. The problem for practical woodworking is that a different bevel shape, a convex curve, is very useful for cuts such as hollowing and bevel-down cuts. This is because the heel of the convex curve falls away in a continuous but gradual curve, allowing the chisel to naturally follow the concave surface of the scallop. The actual cutting bevel is the same angle in both cases, but with the micro-bevel there is only a flat or hollow bevel to ride the wood if the chisel is being used bevel-down. This type of cutting action is a very common practice used by woodworkers for a wide range of woodworking tasks. Furthermore, a single convex curve surpasses the strength of the cutting edge created by the micro-bevel method—there is more strength and rigidity due to the support offered by the shape.

When I sharpen edge tools by hand, the natural back and forth motion creates a slightly convex shape on the bevel. I am always conscious that when I draw the chisel back, I never lift up higher than 30 degrees. As I push the bevel across the sharpening plate, I drop down by no more than 5 degrees. This is a natural part of sharpening for me that I don't even need to think about. The convex bevel created has a proven strength and versatility.

Sharpening Abrasives

In theory, you could sharpen up a tool on any abrasive material that is harder than steel, and historically, all manner of natural stones have been used. Man made abrasives have been introduced recently (in the past hundred years), such as silicon carbide, alumina and synthetic diamonds, which all have very significant industrial applications. These materials are vitrified (fired in a kiln to bond together), sintered (a similar process), bonded to paper or bonded to a substrate by electro-plating. In all the processes, a finely graded powder of very hard particles is processed to create solid, useful abrasives in many shapes and sizes.

Many stones used for sharpening are natural stones.

Stones

There are many different types of natural bench stones, with a wide range of names including whetstones, water stones, Japanese stones, oil stones, Washita stones, Arkansas stones, Charnwood oilstones, slate stones, turkey stones, Belgian blue stones, diamond stones (or plates), ceramic stones, Norton stones, India stones, honing stones and many more.

Many of these share the same quality, functionality and even material. The different varieties have often been reconstituted from natural substances and then high-fired to produce a consistent internal structure of refined grits.

Whichever you choose, a good sharpening stone must be consistent throughout the length, width and depth, otherwise coarseness levels vary too much and create a mixed cutting quality in the abrasive and the tool. Sharpening stones can be cut from naturally occurring rock, or manufactured as man-made stones from substances such as carborundum and aluminum oxide (corundum). Most synthetic stones at least equal natural stones in their abrading capabilities and are considerably cheaper to buy. Some manufacturers produce double-sided stones, coarse on one side and fine on the other. Norton Abrasives, a large industrial abrasives manufacturer, produces a wide range of stones in varying grits from very coarse to superfine, both oil and water stones.

Carbide Paper

Paper abrasives must be fully supported on a dead flat surface. You can buy a granite floor tile ⅜" thick from any flooring company. Check its flatness with a steel straight edge before you buy. You can also use thick float or plate glass. If you also buy a range of carbide paper from 250 through to 1200 grit, you can work through the grades, and flatten and polish just about everything you need to. With a light mist of water on the back, the paper sticks to the granite and you can flatten your chisels and plane irons as quickly as you can with diamond stones. The paper wears down quickly and will need replacing depending on the work to be done, but it works well. It is cheap in the short term and can be used as a temporary alternative to diamonds (you can also restore and sharpen the bevels) just as we did with the grinding and honing stages of abrading on the diamond plates.

Carbide paper.

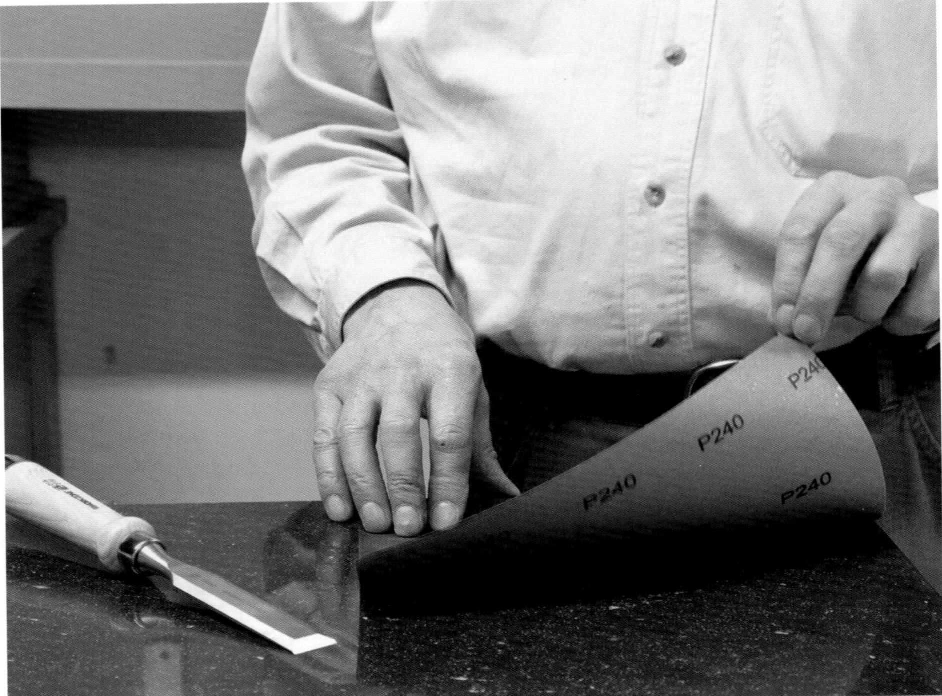

If using a paper abrasive it must be used on a perfectly flat surface.

I keep my diamond plates set in this board.

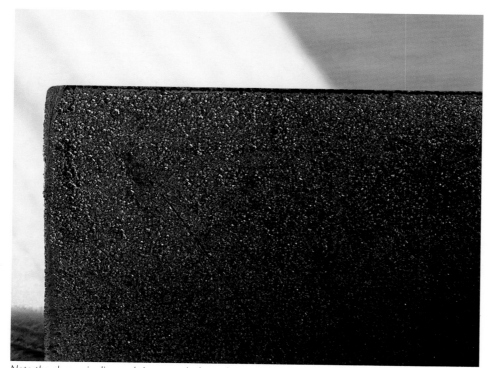

Note the change in diamond size towards the end.

TOP TIP: *If you are choosing diamond plates as your sharpening system, do not be tempted to save money by buying cheap diamond plates. Closely examine the edges and corners of the plates, looking for any inconsistencies in the size of the diamonds at the edges. In the photo, you can see what a cheap diamond plate looks like. Avoid this, the coarse edges will leave deep scratches in any edge tool you are attempting to refine.*

Diamond plates

Diamond plates are electro-plated and surface-coated with diamond particles attached with nickel alloy. The alloy allows the industrial-grade diamond particles to emerge from the nickel holding the particulate permanently to the surface of the plate. More reputable manufacturers guarantee that the plates will stay flat to within 1/1000", an important factor for woodworkers.

"Diamond plates are the system I recommend and use daily"

I've used diamond sharpening plates for more than a decade at the woodworking school with many students using them throughout each day. They are the system I use daily and without reserve recommend. They suit my particular needs perfectly for four key reasons: They cut steel fast, require minimal maintenance, last a long time and stay perfectly flat. That said, not all diamond stones are created equal and there are many cheap substitutes of poorer quality. Diamond plates come in several grades, and though they are not graded by standard US or UK grading systems, the coarse grit approximates a 250 grit stone, the fine grit 800 grit, and superfine 1200 grit. I use the coarse 250 grit for grinding, the fine grit for refining the bevel and removing the marks left by the coarse plate, and superfine 1200 grit for final honing before further polishing on leather strops.

13 Sharpening gouges

Gouges are the largest group of carving tools. Their sizes vary to correspond to the range of widths and radii necessary for carvers to produce their work. The curvature or shape of the gouge is referred to as the 'sweep'. This ranges incrementally from the shallow No 1—which is almost straight—to the tightly curved No 9, as do the widths, from $\frac{3}{16}$" to 1½".

"This method works well and produces the surgically sharp and shaped edge needed for excellent results."

Most woodcarvers, however, rely on only a handful for their everyday work, and woodworkers and furniture makers often use the same gouge for everything from spoon and bowl carving to shaping seat scallops. Because of the complex range of gouges, most woodcarvers use a specially-shaped sharpening stone called a slipstone to remove the burr on the inside of the curved edge after grinding and honing the bevel. Again, because of the wide range of curves and widths, slipstones come in several different sizes. Their radii correspond to the various curves of gouges and they are also sharpened for specific areas on a particular project.

I developed the following method for sharpening gouges to eliminate the need for a slipstone and to simplify the whole process by establishing a system of non-mechanical grinding. This method works well and produces the surgically sharp and shaped edge needed for excellent results. It's simple, fast, efficient and inexpensive.

Though you can use abrasive paper to sharpen and shape the bevel of any gouge, I generally find it quicker and more effective to use the same diamond plates I use for sharpening all of my other edge tools. The effect of using these abrasive plates is the same, but the technique is somewhat different.

Sharpening and shaping the bevel

Sharpening the bevel is a little different to sharpening straight-edged tools like chisels. This is because of the curved cutting edge and slightly convex bevel. There are two ways to establish the main bevel and refine it prior to honing and polishing:

Figure-of-eight method

Holding the gouge in similar fashion to chisels, orient the gouge corner on the sharpening plate as shown. Roll the gouge as you move it forward and backward in a figure-of-eight motion. You must see each of these motions as a continuous figure-of-eight motion. As with regular chisel edge sharpening, we must be conscious that the bevel is curved. The whole of the bevel must receive an equal amount of abrading to maintain the convex bevel and expose the cutting edge on the closing strokes. We must flex the wrist to create this fluid figure-of-eight motion, keeping the bevel in constant and even contact with the surface of the diamond plate. We work through the three levels of abrading on the plates before we hone and polish the convex bevel being careful to only pull not push the gouge on the strop.

Rolling method

Another method is to hold the gouge bevel down on the sharpening plate. Rotate the bevel as you move the gouge forward and backward along the length of the plate. As you hone, drop the angle of the gouge with each successive stroke slightly to create and maintain the shape of the convex bevel.

Using either of the above methods gradually develops the critical burr we need inside the concave of the curved edge, which must eventually be removed.

If you use the figure-of-eight method make sure you hone the entire edge.

Rotate the gouge slowly, following the arc of the cutting edge, as you move back and forth.

Take small cuts when cutting the channel.

Make the final channel as even as possible.

Define both ends using the gouge you are going to sharpen.

Plane down to the radius marks on either end.

This strop works best if the leather is stretched tight.

You can use the same leather for both sides.

Making a gouge strop

We must now further hone and polish the curved bevel. To do this, make a shaped strop from a piece of scrap wood. This strop will incorporate both a concave channel and convex edge in the same piece. The wood should be the width of the chisel or slightly wider, so for a 1" gouge use a piece of wood 1⅛" by around 2" x 10" long.

Secure the wood in the vise, narrow (1⅛") edge up. At one end, place the gouge you just ground and honed, and strike it to make a curve to the end corner. The gouging does not have to be crisp and clean—in fact, it is unlikely to be so until you complete the honing and polishing process. The gouge will be sharp enough to make the strop and can be further refined after the honing is finished. Using both hands, you can now work backwards from that opening cut to remove a fairly even channel along the full length.

To create the curve on the opposite edge, use the gouge to define the profile on the edge at both ends. Use the smoothing plane to further develop the profile along the full length. Sand the profiles and even out the hollow as necessary.

You can now use abrasive paper in varying grits to further refine the bevel if necessary. Alternatively, charge a piece of leather with buffing compound and, anchoring the leather and profiled wood in the vise, draw the bevel of the gouge along the channel until fully polished. Take care to trail the cutting edge so as not to gouge the strop leather.

Turn the strop and block over and repeat for the inside of the curve, until the burr is removed and the edge is fully sharpened.

This method also enables you to cut similar profiles to the exact shape of other gouges. The whole process of sharpening gouges can be accomplished using only this strop and abrasive papers.

Conclusion

As you get used to the fluid action required to produce a consistent, sharp cutting edge, the process will become quick and easy. Persevere with this and the results will improve as you develop skill and confidence.

14 Adjusting your bench plane and spokeshave

The cast steel hand planes and spokeshaves we use today have simple adjustment mechanisms that make them incredibly versatile. Hand planes are indispensable in preparing stock, shaping wood, jointing the edges of boards prior to joining them, and smoothing the surface of wood. A spokeshave is the first tool that I give to children when teaching them woodworking, not as a plaything, but as the first item in a potential craftsman's toolbox. A spokeshave can round, sculpt, flatten, smooth and shape wood whether it is convex, concave, round, square or replete with ornate curves. The full value of the versatility of these tools can only be fully realized if they are in prime functional condition, ultra sharp and well adjusted. In this chapter, I will cover some basic restoration methods and the fundamentals of adjustment.

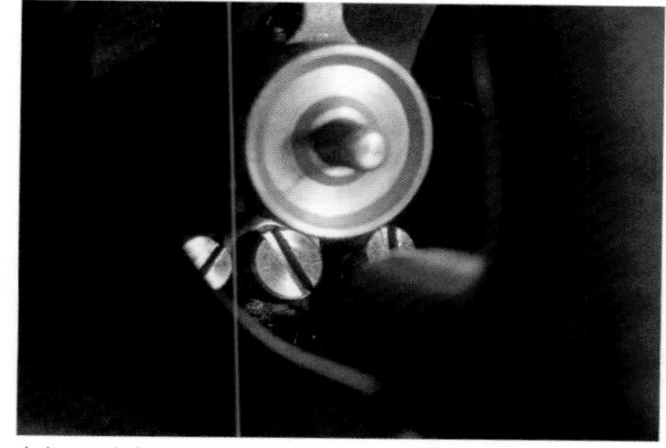

Adjustability makes this plane efficient to use.

This is an area that I have always been passionate about, as many woodworkers don't seem to appreciate the significance of these hand tools in today's workshop. The hand plane can accomplish tasks that no other tool or machine can, but this is often overlooked. If either the hand plane or the spokeshave is dull or badly adjusted their use can become frustrating and unproductive, leading to a dismissive and skeptical view of their viability. In contrast, I have known few people who have not experienced a sense of awe as they use, for the first time, a well adjusted and ultra sharp hand plane.

Even the best new planes will need adjusting and sharpening. The soles on lower quality or older planes usually need flattening too, to remove hollows, high spots and sometimes a slight twist in the casting. Small adjustments make a big difference to how your plane works, so practice first on a spare piece of wood. A badly set plane could irreparably damage your project. Sharpening the cutting iron differs only slightly from chisels so most of this section will focus on the adjustment of both the hand plane and the spokeshave.

The dimensions of bench planes

The two most popular bench plane sizes are the No. 4 and No. 4½ smoothing planes. In these two planes the main difference is the width of the plane body, and therefore the width of the cutting irons which measure at 2" and 2⅜" respectively. The plane lengths are the same at around 9½". Both planes work well, but I find the No. 4½ works more effectively because the extra weight and width provide better balance. This is a personal preference, so choose a plane that suits you.

A second plane I find very useful is the No. 5½ jackplane that I've included in the general equipment list. Widely used across a range of projects, it's 14" long, and this longer sole is highly effective for straightening stock such as table legs, door stiles and tabletops. Between the smoothing plane and the jackplane, you will be able to tackle all the woodworking projects in this course that require smoothing and flattening.

Smoothing planes are manufactured in a variety of lengths and widths but use the same adjustment mechanisms. Regardless of which length you use, the adjustments and methods of sharpening require the same basic treatment.

Apart from the dimensions, there is a difference in the design of metal-cast planes that divide the tools into two categories. There are two main patented designs, the Bailey-pattern and the Bed Rock-pattern. The most noticeable difference between these two designs is the configuration and adjustment of the cast block of iron commonly called the frog. While it is important to take note of this difference, it makes only minimal difference to the way that the plane works.

This is my Stanley No. 4½.

The Stanley No.5 has a longer sole.

The Bailey pattern frog. *The Bed Rock pattern frog.*

Exploded drawing of a Bailey pattern plane.

Parts of the Bailey pattern plane

1. Lever cap retaining screw
2. Lever cap
3. Back iron
4. Cutting iron
5. Lateral adjustment lever
6. Frog
7. Depth adjustment wheel
8. Sole casting
9. Fore knob
10. Rear handle

Preparing your bench plane—five steps

I wish everyone had access to the hands-on training I received from the craftsmen that I worked under as an apprentice forty-five years ago. I remember the disappointment I felt when I pulled my new plane from its box only to find that it felt nothing like the old Stanley I'd been borrowing. George Mycock laughed at my forlorn look and snatched the plane from me. The next hour would equip me for life, in the use of that and any other plane that has ever crossed my path.

Plane preparation is usually a once-in-a-lifetime event for each plane and will take only an hour or two. Once you've corrected the more serious flaws in the plane assembly and castings, you will probably need only minor maintenance from then on.

Only the finest planes, which often cost between $100-$300, will need no remedial work before use, other than sharpening and rounding the cutting iron edges. Regardless of the condition of your plane it is always worth checking each of the following points to make sure that the plane is in excellent working order, but only make changes where you obviously need to.

Clean up before you tune up

Make a close inspection of the entire plane, flipping the plane over and looking at each part to make certain nothing is missing and to get a general feel for how the plane has been assembled and how it has been cared for. Cheaper planes are often coated with thick varnish that must be removed. This surface coating causes the plane to drag on the wood as you plane. Apply suitable varnish stripper with a brush or rag and use '000' grade steel wool to dissolve and remove the coating before you begin any other adjustments.

Remove the lever cap and the cap iron/cutting iron assembly by pulling the lever upwards and away from the cutting iron assembly. Clean the plane all over by removing any oil, grease and dirt with a solvent or degreaser and a small, brass wire brush or toothbrush. This can be a dirty job on old and rusted planes, so wear protective rubber gloves and eye protection, and dispose of any rags in an environmentally appropriate manner.

Truing the plane's sole

Once you have cleaned up every part of your plane, rebuild it and restore the whole cutting iron assembly into the plane body. Withdraw the cutting iron slightly so it does not protrude past the sole and clamp the lever cap back as normal. This applies the usual amount of tension to the assembly and will actually flex the sole back into its normal operating shape. This is important when truing the sole as, without this tension, the casting warps slightly out of shape. Offer the plane to the light with a straight edge along the sole, to see whether any light appears between the straight edge and the sole. If there is no light, you have a flat sole. If the light appears at either or both ends, the sole is round and must be lapped (flattened) in the belly area. If light appears in between the two ends, the sole is hollow and again must be lapped to reduce the high points.

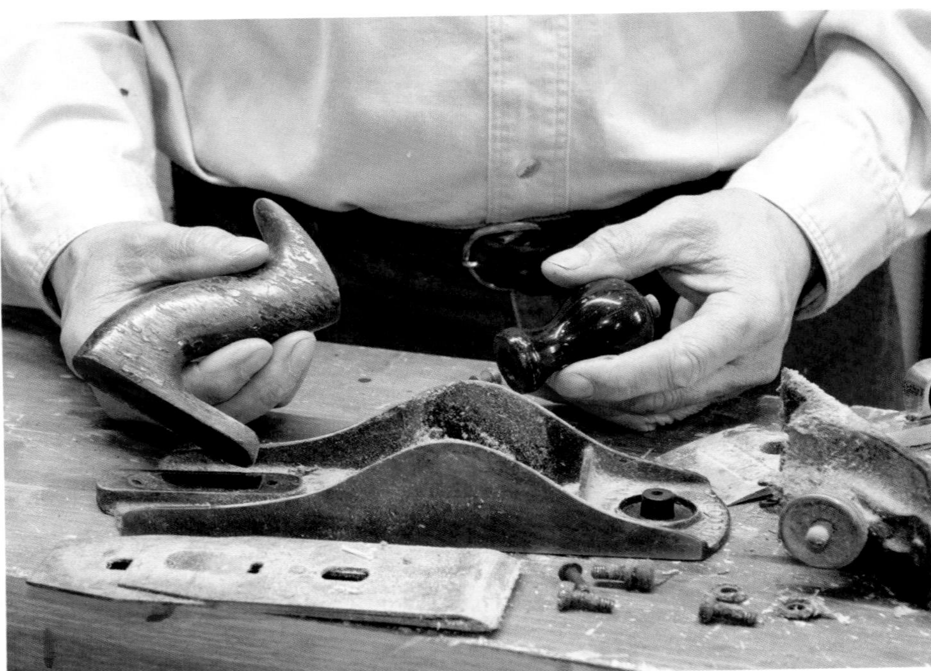

Strip the entire assembly down and clean up all the pieces individually.

Check the sole for flatness.

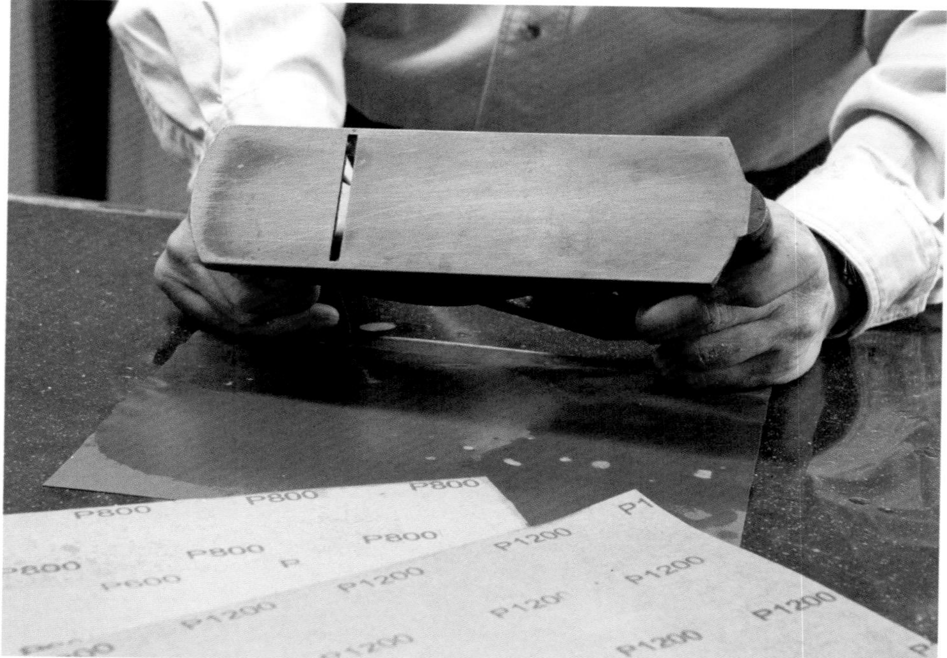

When you start to lap the sole, you will see the light and dark areas indicating the high and low spots.

You can lap on diamond plates or carbide paper.

A twisted sole will never result in anything but a twisted surface and so a plane's sole must be perfectly true. There is no point checking the sole of the plane with a straight edge that is not straight. Use either a straight edge from a trusted brand or one tested against a trusted flat surface.

I lap my plane soles on my coarse diamond sharpening plate, which is accurate to within one thousandth of an inch. If you don't have one of these, you can take your straight edge to Home Depot or B&Q and test one of their granite floor tiles until you find a flat one. Also, any piece of thick, float glass will work too. Then, buy some emery abrasive sheets, with water-resistant backing, the kind used for car body repairs, and use this to lap the sole of your plane. Begin with 150 grit and work through ever-finer grits to 350 grit. A light coat of low-tack adhesive will hold the paper temporarily, or just use water. Some modern plane makers like Clifton, Lie Nielsen, Juma and Veritas, need no corrective procedures. Rub the whole of the sole of the plane across the abrasive surface, taking care not to rock the plane, and examine the face of the sole periodically. Any shiny spots are high spots that need lowering by repeatedly rubbing the plane in a forward and backward motion over the abrasive. With the high spots removed, you can now further polish the face of the sole by changing the abrasive paper to finer grits or using finer diamond plates. Polishing the surface reduces the amount of friction on the sole when you use the plane.

The plane handle

For smooth, accurate and consistent planing, the plane handle and fore knob must be rock solid. Because we use the plane handle to guide the plane with each stroke, a loose handle makes fine control and adjustment difficult. Old planes often have shrinkage and wear between the bottom of the handle and the sole of the plane, and the screw-threaded rod that holds the handle reaches the end of its thread. If this happens, remove the handle and flatten its underside so that it seats well, and then replace the handle onto the plane. You can effectively extend the length of the handle by gluing a thin strip of hardwood to the underside of the handle, but it's quicker and easier to file off some of the threaded rod until it fully tightens the handle. Placing a washer or two under the handle screw is another option. You can also use the last two methods to fix the fore knob if it's loose too. You may not be able to glue a wooden packing piece under the knob because of the shape of the casting.

True up the underside of the rear handle on 180-grit sandpaper, on a flat surface.

You can plane the underside instead.

Filing the threaded rod to shorten it.

Easing the edges of the sole

Even old planes often feel angular and sharp to the touch. Once, in a car boot sale (flea market) I picked up an old Stanley No. 4½. It felt familiar as I traced my hands from lever cap to toe. I closed my eyes and thought it was mine for a moment, but then remembered I was in the UK for only a few weeks; my own plane was in the US. I bought the plane for £15 and gave it to one of my sons.

Sharp edges and corners can be eased with a single-cut mill file and further rounded with abrasive paper. It takes only a few minutes to file away any sharpness, but the results last for a lifetime. I take off everything that's sharp to the touch until the plane feels comfortable, focusing especially on the sole corners. The semicircular heel extension at the back end of the plane is usually angular and sharp and level with the plane's sole. In planing adjacent surfaces the heel catches and tears, especially on box rims and window sashes, and the damage is often irreparable. For this reason, file off the

Ease any rough edges on the casting.

File the radius of the heel, this will leave marks as you land or lift the plane off your workpiece.

Use the usual process to sharpen up the iron but include the important extra steps shown on pages 240 and 241 of this chapter.

"It takes only a few minutes to file away any sharpness, but the results last for a lifetime"

corner following the radius of the heel, and go further round, so that there is no further possibility of gouging to occur.

With the main sole done, remove the frog from the sole and look for any irregularities that might prevent the underside of the frog casting from full contact with the sole. File them also. This is a critical area because anything less than a solid connection will allow the cutting iron assembly to vibrate as you plane a surface, resulting in chatter marks. Even though the frog is set within the sole sides and is fully covered by the cutting iron assembly, your hands will come into contact with it when you sharpen and reset the iron in the sole, so work its outer edges with the file. Again, it is worth the effort; it takes only a minute and lasts a lifetime. You may also want to soften any edges of the cutting iron and back iron, to remove any burrs from manufacturing.

Sharpen up the cutting iron

SAFETY NOTE: *Planes and Spokeshaves are inherently safe tools to use as the cutting iron barely protrudes from the sole under normal conditions. I do recommend that you feel for the amount of protrusion of the cutting iron. However, bear in mind that the cutting iron is or should be extremely sharp and well refined. To feel for the protrusion of this sharp blade, brush a finger or thumb lightly at 90 degrees to the cutting edge, never in the same direction or along the length of the sharp cutting edge.*

A sharp cutting iron is the key element to successful planing. The iron is sharpened in the same way that we sharpen other edge tools, with the extra important step of establishing a slight round-over to the outside corners. The sharpening process is fully explained on pages 206 to 211 of chapter 12

Tuning up your bench plane—four steps

Modern cast-metal planes give us instant, simple and accurate adjustments to within thousandths of an inch. Instead of relying on tapping the plane body and cutting iron with a hammer, which is the technique used for adjusting wooden bodied and infill planes with wedged cutting irons, we now have total fingertip control. The engineered design of metal cast planes allows us to fine tune a plane with instant accessibility to maximize its performance. Once some basic set up has been carried out, the most frequent micro adjustments will soon be mastered by repetition and increased awareness of the workings of your plane.

Once set up correctly, you will have the confidence to get the most out of your plane.

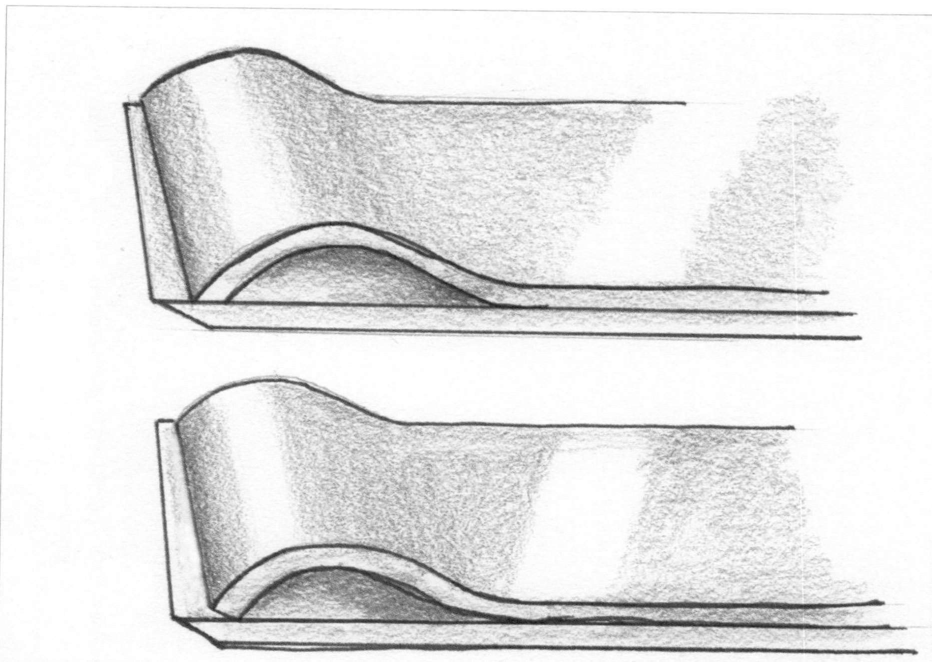
The top drawing shows the back iron in full contact with the cutting iron. The lower drawing shows a gap.

This problem clogs the throat.

Lap the back iron to ensure intimate contact with the cutting iron.

Polish the curved front part of the back iron.

The cutting iron assembly

With the cutting iron dead flat and well sharpened, we can now focus on problems surrounding the area around the back-iron ('cap iron' or 'chip breaker'). Woodworkers often overlook the role the back iron plays in the performance of the cutting iron. The spring clamping force between these two opposing parts is what gives vibration-free planing. The back-iron is most often formed from a 1⁄16" thick plate of steel, bent in such a way that pressure is applied to the cutting iron directly behind the cutting edge.

The cap iron must seat against the flat face of the cutting iron with precision, i.e. no gap along the leading edge, otherwise the newly-cut shavings jam between the assembled parts and this then jams subsequent shavings in the throat of the plane.

If there is any gap along the leading edge, detach the cutting iron from the back-iron. Lay the front edge of the back iron against the face of the coarse sharpening plate or bench stone. The sharpening stones must be perfectly flat with no hollow and no round. Rub it back and forth until the edge is straight and flat, as shown. I find it best to undercut the back edge a little so that the two parts—the cutting iron and the back-iron—have room to flex and bend without opening up that leading edge. Visually check to locate any gap along the leading edge of the back-iron, directly behind where it fits against the cutting edge of the cutting iron. When the underside of the back-iron is shiny across the full width and length of the narrow face, it should unite perfectly with the cutting iron.

It is also advisable to polish the curved front part of the back-iron on the strop. This part deflects the shavings upwards, so polishing helps the shavings pass through the throat of the plane more freely.

The back-iron and cutting iron assembly is held together with a single setscrew that passes through the cutting iron and into the back-iron.

Rounding and shaping the cutting iron corners

In general, because the sole of the plane presents the cutting iron to the surface of the wood at a slightly lower level than the sole itself, planing any surface wider than the width of the cutting iron creates a discernible step-down in the wood's surface equal to the depth of cut. This problem is more apparent on wider surfaces.

No matter how skilled you are, it's not possible to consistently plane a wide board from one side to the other in the hope that each stroke will leave an even surface. Craftsmen of old established a pattern for rounding the corners of the iron so that planing left a feathered edge after each plane stroke. With a little practice, any undulations become barely discernible.

All new plane irons come with flat bevels ground straight across the full width. The same is true of most secondhand planes, too. Once you have initially rounded the corners, it becomes a part of every subsequent sharpening as a routine maintenance practice.

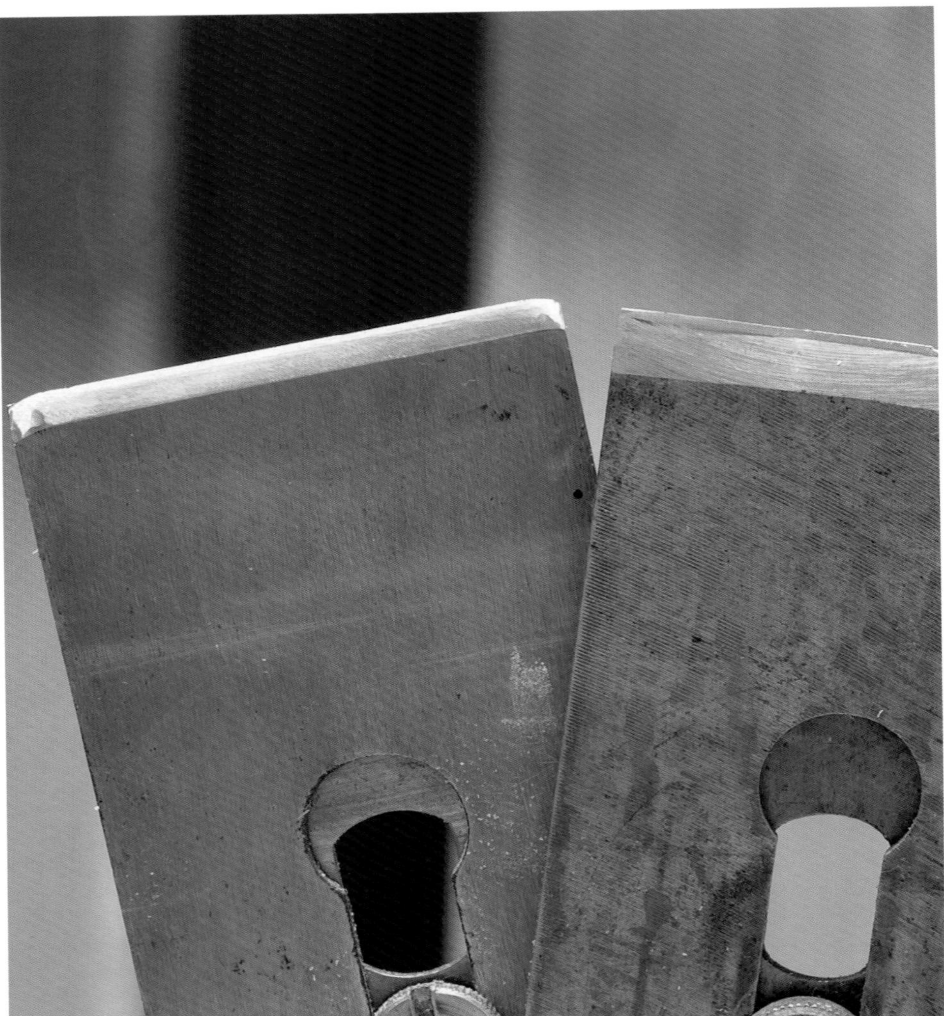

The cutting iron on the right has been rounded over correctly.

Grind, hone and polish, including the gradual lift at the edges.

This is the general shape you are aiming for before you polish up on the strop.

Assemble the cutting iron and back iron.

The hole in the cutting iron facilitates rapid assembly.

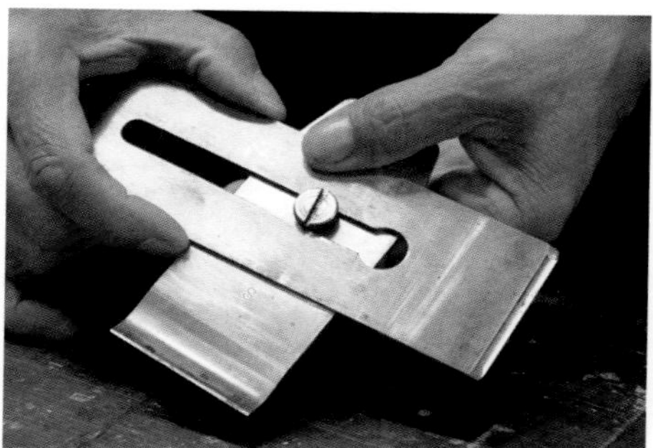

Slide the setscrew down the iron.

Carefully rotate the parts until they are aligned.

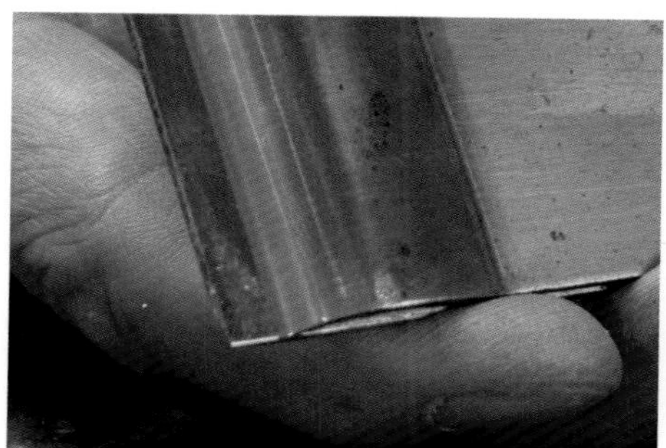

Advance the cutting iron.

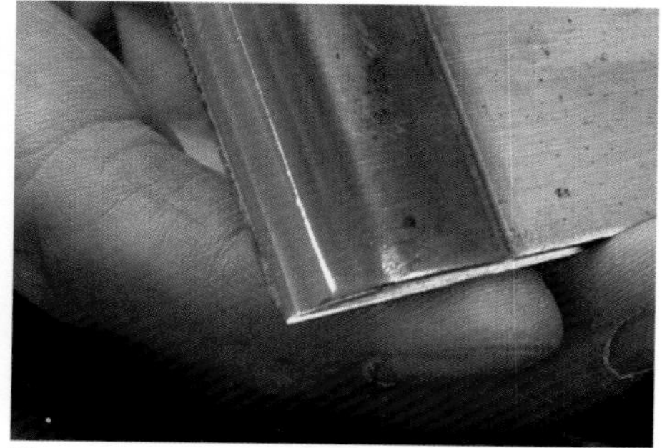

The protrusion should be around 1⁄32".

To create these rounded corners on your plane iron, follow the normal sharpening process as described on page 208 of chapter 12. However, at every stage of the grinding, honing and polishing process, you must include this extra step:

- After working on the main bevel, gradually lift up the outer edge of both sides of the iron with each successive stroke, in turn, to about 3⁄16" above the sharpening plate, as you work the cutting iron over the abrasive surface. This will form a slight roundover and will soften the sharp, angular corner edge.
- Subsequent levels of honing and polishing follow the same procedure, so that the curved outer edges and the bevel are a continuous polished edge.

To prepare the cutting iron assembly, place the cutting iron, bevel uppermost across the inside face of the back iron so that the back iron setscrew passes through the enlarged keyhole section of the elongated slot of the cutting iron. Turn the assembly over so that the back-iron is fully visible. Carefully swivel the cutting iron so that the newly sharpened cutting edge passes beyond the edge of the back-iron. Slide the back-iron towards the cutting edge and stop when the front edge of the back-iron is about 1⁄32" from the cutting edge. Use your fingertips to align the sides of the two irons and tighten the setscrew, taking care not to allow either of the two irons to move or separate. You can now assemble the plane iron in the body of the plane and set the iron to the sole.

Understanding the cutting iron and frog assembly

There are three critical variables in the setup of the cutting iron. Understanding the effect of these variables on the performance of your plane is crucial to effective and appropriate adjustment.

- The distance between the cutting edge and the back iron. (Note: This also affects the throat opening as the back iron can 'choke' the plane if it is advanced too far forward without compensating by moving the frog back a fraction.)
- The distance between the cutting iron assembly and the fore part of the plane sole, otherwise known as the 'throat'.
- The alignment of the cutting iron to the sole of the plane.

All these adjustments center around the frog, and so, depending upon the nature of your work, you may make some adjustments more frequently than others.

The main body of most smoothing planes has two cast-metal parts. These parts are known as the sole and the frog and they are held together with two setscrews or rivets depending on the plane types. All of the adjustments of the plane center on the frog. This is the hub of the plane body and holds the lateral adjustment lever mechanism that lines up the blade's cutting edge to the sole. It also contains the adjustment wheel that pivots the yoke up and down, delivering the depth setting of the cutting iron. Under the depth adjustment wheel is a machine screw which moves the frog forwards or backwards to close or open the throat. Generally speaking, once you find an agreeable setting, the frog remains unchanged for everyday furniture making and general woodworking.

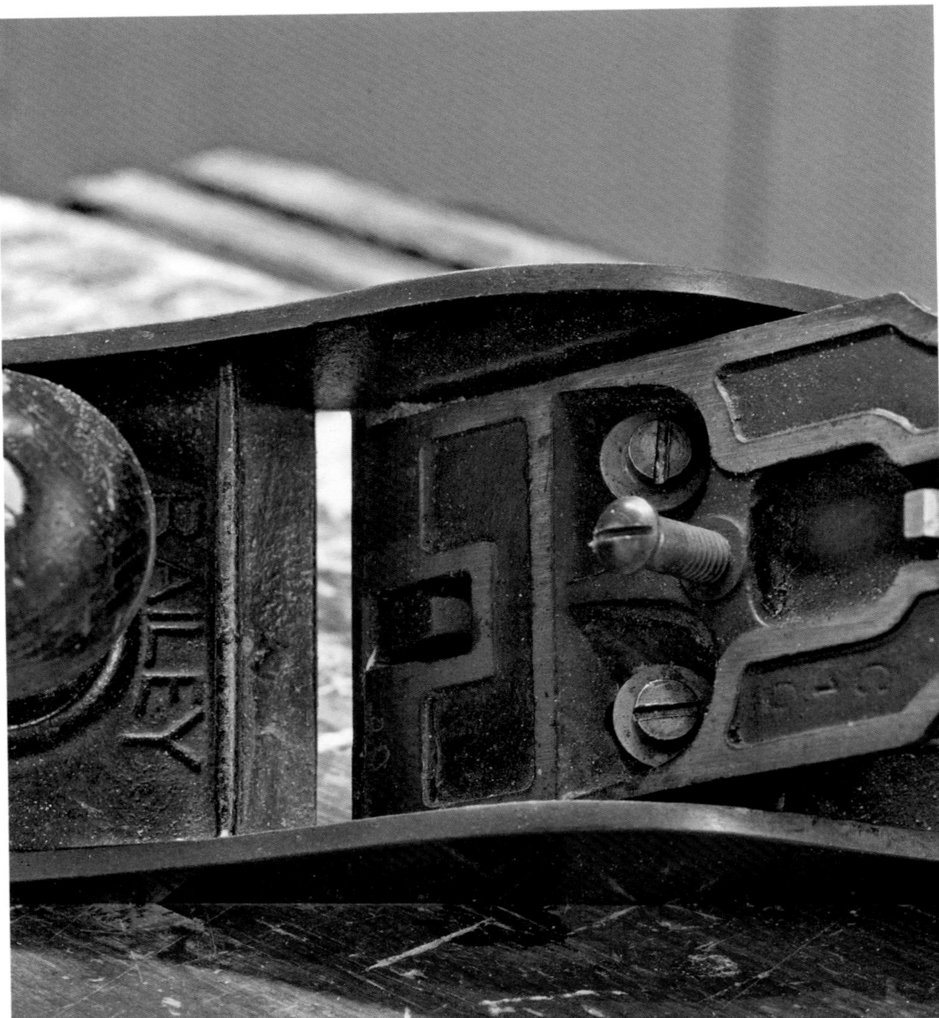

The frog retaining screws on this Bailey pattern plane must be slackened before the frog may be adjusted.

This screw adjusts the frog position.

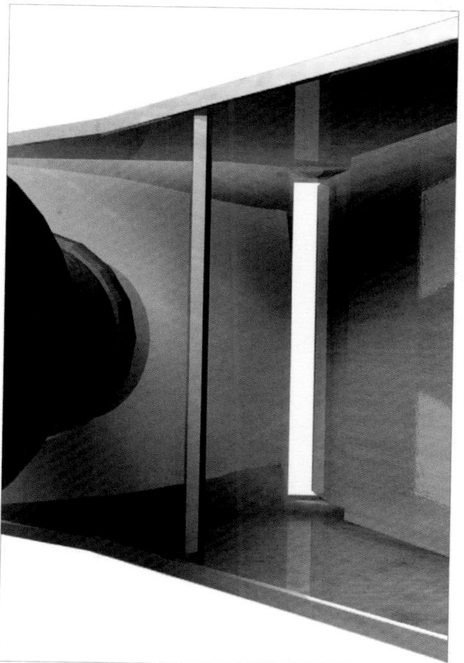

The throat may need to be quite open.

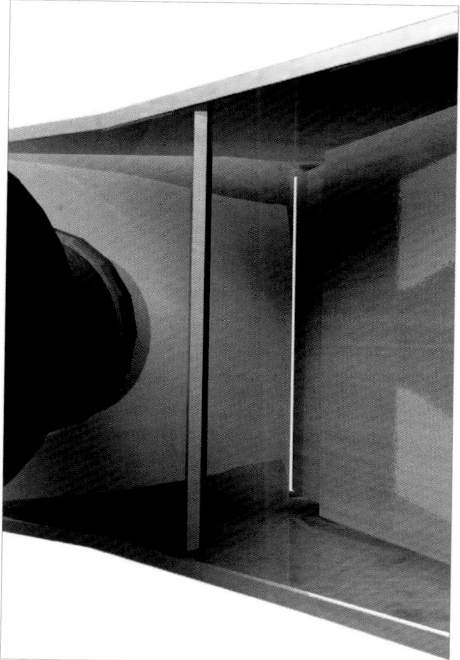

The throat may also be closed to a minimum.

When would I adjust the distance between the back iron and the cutting edge or move the frog?

The distance from the cutting edge of the cutting iron to the leading edge of the back-iron is generally about 1⁄32", but this can be more or less depending on the amount of wood you want to remove with each stroke. This can also determine how wide you want the opening of the throat to be. Many variables determine these adjustments, including the amount of moisture in the wood, the type of wood, its density, hardness, grain structure and more.

I'll give you three examples of scenarios where different adjustments are required. This will help you to understand the principles, allowing you to make your own decisions.

CARPENTRY WORK: Sometimes a carpenter fitting an outside door with damp wood fibers needs a more open throat to prevent the shavings from expanding and clogging. To take off a lot of wood, he must set the back-iron further than normal from the cutting edge. If any board has rough surface fibers and I am trying to remove high spots, I use the same formula. When the surface is less rough and taking thick shaving is no longer necessary, I revert to the normal setting of 1⁄32" and close the throat to about 1⁄16".

FINE WORK: However, for finer work, I move the back-iron nearer to the cutting edge and adjust the frog; with the cutting iron assembly in place—but with the frog screws backed off slightly—I close the throat opening a little by advancing the frog toward the front of the plane with the adjustment screw. When set at my required distance, I remove the assembly and tighten the frog retaining screws. This adjustment is for a Bailey-pattern plane and differs slightly for a Bed Rock-pattern. On a Bed Rock-pattern plane the entire adjustment can be made with the plane fully assembled.

VERY FINE WORK: When I work on really fine work and need to take super thin shavings, I set the cutting iron distance so there's barely any discrepancy between the cutting iron and the back-iron. I move the frog in the same way as before, stopping and tightening the frog when I have a very narrow gap, barely more than the thickness of a piece of paper. This allows you to take shavings which are just thousandths of an inch thick. The throat opening is not essential for producing thin shavings, but the purpose of the narrow opening is to prevent the shavings from rising too far ahead of the cutting iron; the front sole keeps the shaving compressed and allows only the most minute rise before the cutting edge cuts the wood. This is especially useful with difficult grain that is hard to plane.

Aligning the cutting iron to the sole

For a whole host of different applications, having the cutting iron aligned precisely to the sole is an absolute necessity. This is the second most frequent adjustment to be mastered, after depth adjustment. Only with care and sensitivity will you be able to work to the fine tolerances required for accurate set up of your plane.

The lateral adjustment lever is permanently fixed to the frog casting. It pivots the cutting iron from its center point, aligning the cutting edge of the iron with the flat face of the plane sole. The lever moves to each side in a swiveling motion, levering the cutting iron assembly left and right accordingly. This mechanism helps to compensate for inaccurate sharpening where the blade may be fractionally out of square.

To see how the lever works with the cutting iron assembly, set the lever cap firmly in place and push the lateral adjustment lever from left to right and back again a couple of times. You must do this after first placing the iron assembly into place against the frog. Then set the lateral adjustment lever in the central position over the handle and check to see how the cutting iron lies in relation to the sole. To do this, turn the plane upside down and sight along the surface of the sole from the front end of the plane.

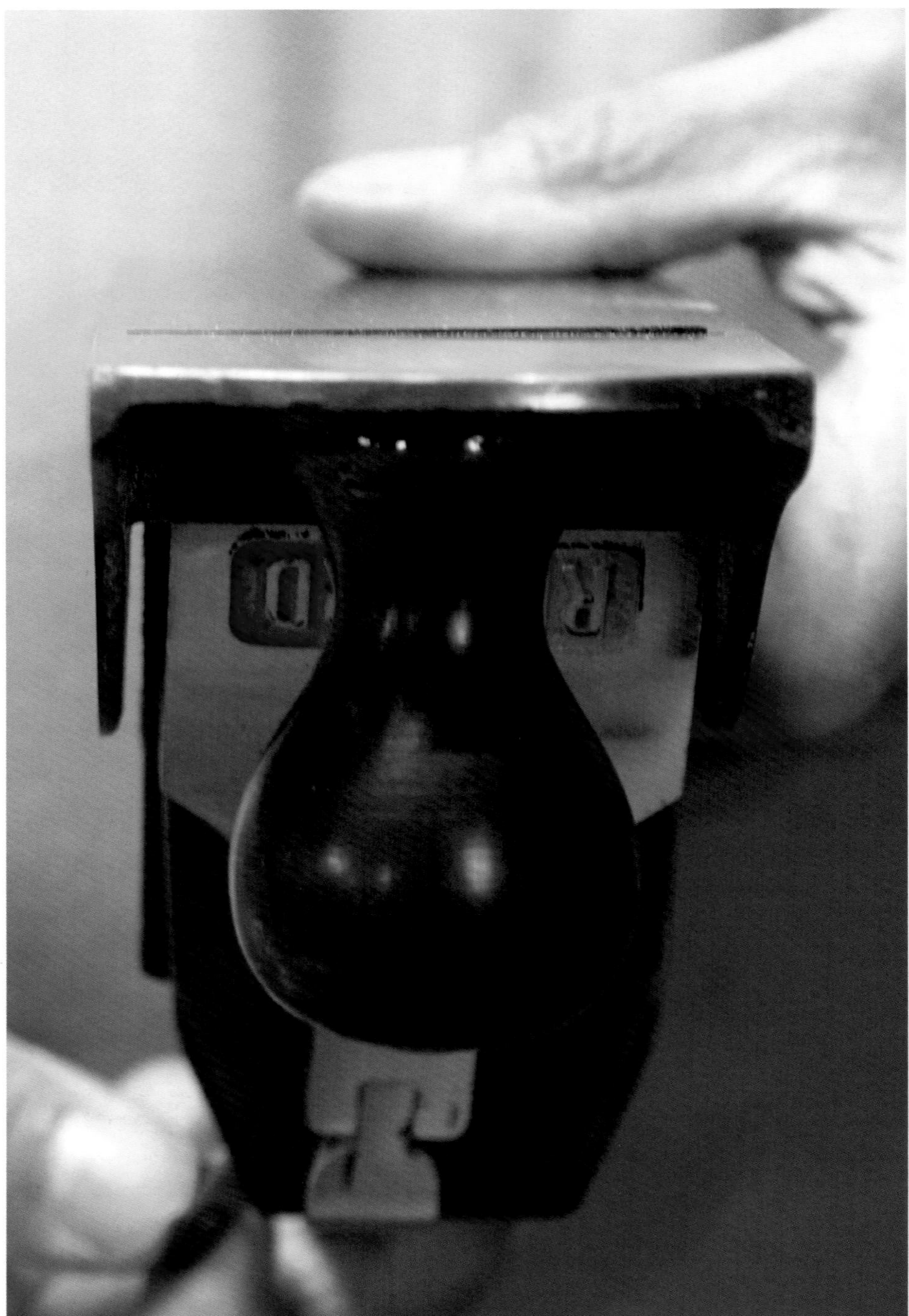

Fully to the left, the iron protrudes on the right. *Fully to the right, the iron protrudes to the left.*

This lever controls all lateral adjustment.

Before you can adjust the alignment, the iron must first be protruding. Adjust the lever as necessary until the iron looks parallel to the sole. This is a first-level sight test. Now, feel the tip of the cutting iron carefully with your fingertips to feel the protrusion. Practice will soon allow you to judge how much the iron protrudes and whether the cutting iron is parallel. Between sight and touch tests you will be close to preparing the plane for the final adjustment on the wood itself. Working with the plane this way will make you sensitive to adjusting the depth of cut.

Procedure for alignment

The aim of the following procedure is to set the cutting iron so that it is perfectly aligned with the sole of the plane.

There are only two adjustments to master: The depth of cut and the alignment of the cutting iron. To reduce the depth of cut, turn the depth adjustment wheel counter clockwise and vice-versa. The alignment lever will need a slight push to the left or right, gripping it with your finger and thumb.

> **TECHNICAL POINTER:** *This is the most important relationship to realize: Although they are independent adjustments, you cannot align the cutting iron accurately without repeatedly reducing the cutting depth to zero and then advancing the iron again to take a very fine shaving. You may be able to get it close, but this method guarantees accuracy, even for the inexperienced.*

The depth of a plane's cut is determined by the amount the cutting iron protrudes beyond the sole of the plane. This depth of cut is controlled by the depth adjustment wheel, located directly behind and connected to the frog of the plane. In general daily use, the depth of cut needs regular readjustment. It's also wise to check the depth of cut after sharpening or frog adjustment.

When you first begin working with hand planes, it's difficult to determine how much adjustment is necessary, but with a little practice you will soon know exactly what to do.

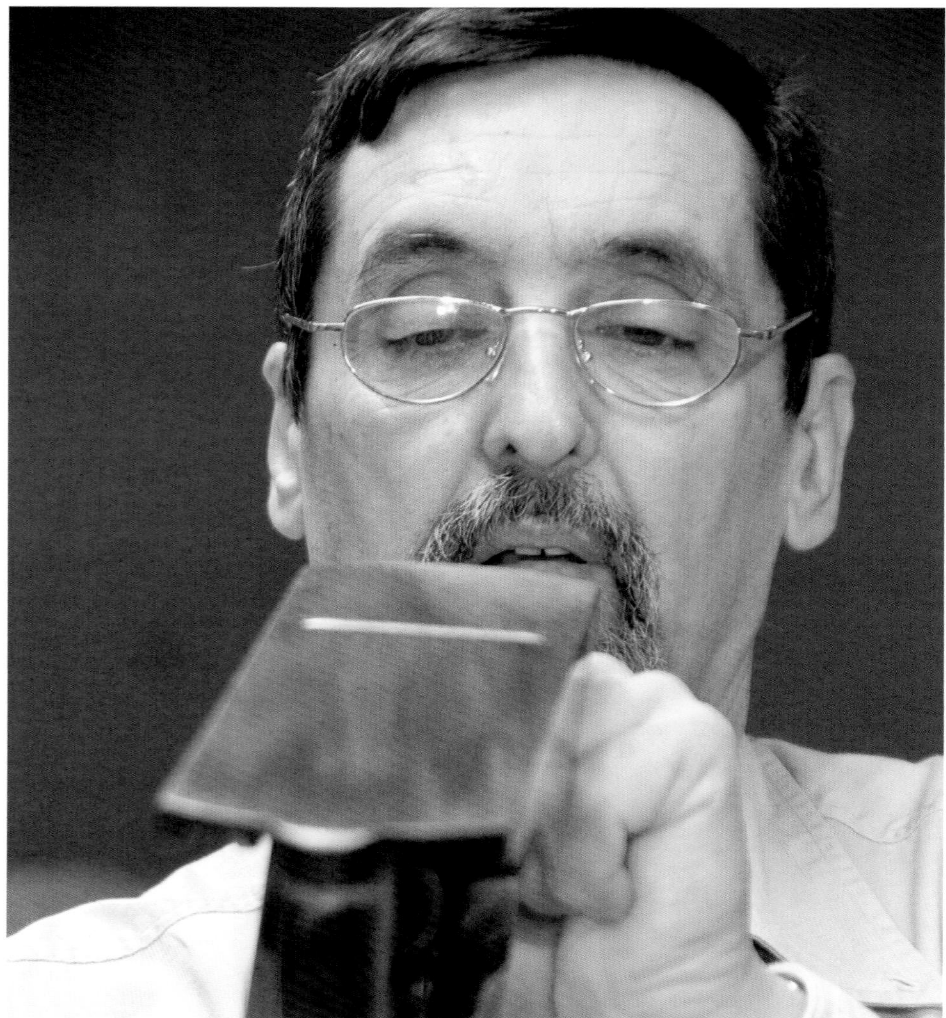

Adjusting by sight and feel is the first step.

All depth settings are controlled by this brass wheel.

The first shaving taken with the right side of the plane is visually wafer thin…

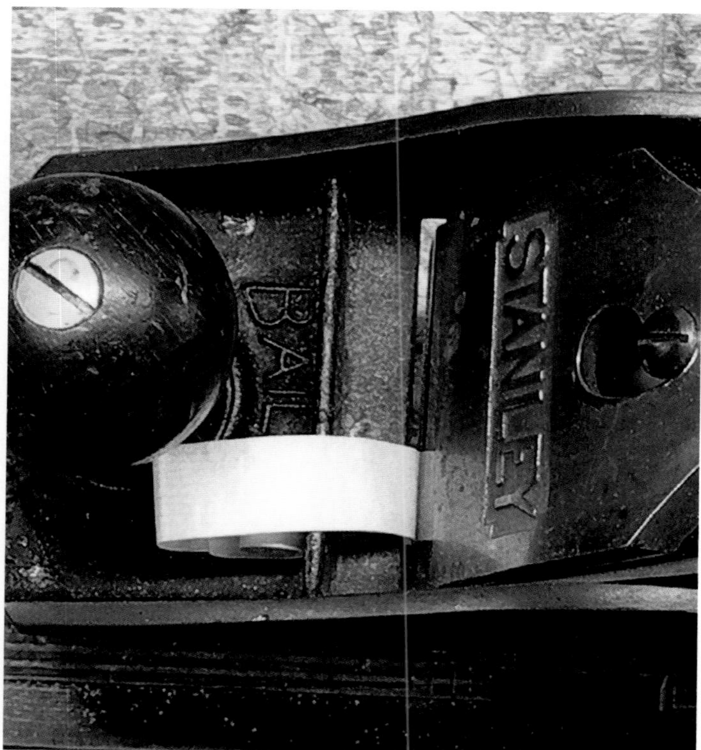

…and many times thicker on the other showing that the cutting iron is out of alignment.

The fingertip test.

A narrow board of say ½" in thickness will allow you to test the thickness of the shavings emerging from the left hand, and then right hand side of the cutting iron alternately. When the iron is set correctly, you should be able to take the finest shavings possible, from both sides of the cutting iron, and on examination, find the shavings to be identical in thickness.

This is an iterative procedure that should take less than a minute.

- To begin setting the depth of the cutting iron, carefully feel for the edge of the cutting iron on the sole of the plane with your fingertips. This is the initial touch test. You should be able to feel whether the tip is flush with the face of the sole or protruding. If you cannot feel it, the iron is set too shallow to produce a shaving. If the iron is protruding, sight down the sole and adjust the alignment so it looks about right.
- Adjust the depth to take a fine shaving and take a shaving from each side of the cutting iron. Listen for the difference in thickness, look at the shavings as they emerge and feel the thickness with your fingers. These three senses will tell you which way to move the lateral adjustment lever, which is always towards the side with the thicker shaving.
- Repeat the process of withdrawing the cutting iron, advancing it to take fine shavings and checking the thickness from both sides of the iron. As you converge on the precise alignment, you will need to make incrementally smaller and more careful adjustments for both depth and alignment.

TOP TIP: *Don't forget to work with the 'backlash'—which occurs whenever you change the direction of rotation, you may have to make a few extra turns of the depth adjustment wheel to take up any slack before the cutting iron assembly will actually move. Some planes have less backlash, others have more. It is definitely not an issue as you'll soon get used to whatever you use frequently, and it does not affect the performance in the slightest.*

Spokeshaves

Few woodworkers see the plane and spokeshave as essentially the same tool. The shaving process is identical in terms of how the cutting iron works. The benefits of smoothing and flattening with the long cast sole of a plane make it indispensable. In contrast, the benefits of the very short sole of a spokeshave include immense flexibility to follow curves, both convex and concave and also the curved radii often used in shaping oval and round roundovers such as chair seats, cutting boards, spoon handles and more. A spokeshave is simply a short-soled version of the plane with side handles. It is really only the length of the sole that defines the different applications of these tools. For this reason, there is much in common in the nature of the setup and performance of a plane and a spokeshave.

A Stanley No. 151 spokeshave.

Adjusting pattern No. 151 spokeshaves

A few different types of woodworking spokeshaves have emerged through the centuries. In recent decades, most woodworkers rely on one main type produced by different companies—the pattern No. 151 spokeshave. Quality varies greatly—as usual, you often get what you pay for. Much of the adjustment of a spokeshave is similar to, but simpler than with a bench plane. When sharpening the spokeshave you may want to skip the additional step of rounding the corners of the cutting iron as doing this is only useful when working on wide surfaces which is a rare task for the spokeshave.

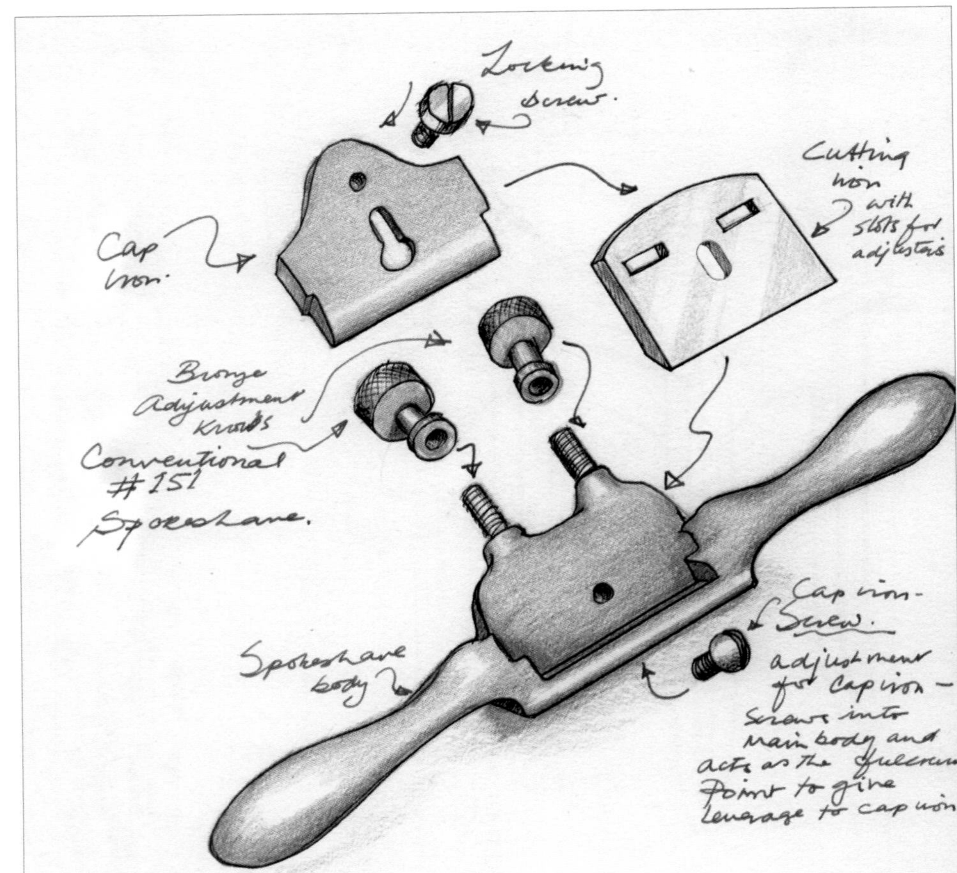

The spokeshave has few moving parts when compared to other planes.

Carefully slide the blade into the throat.

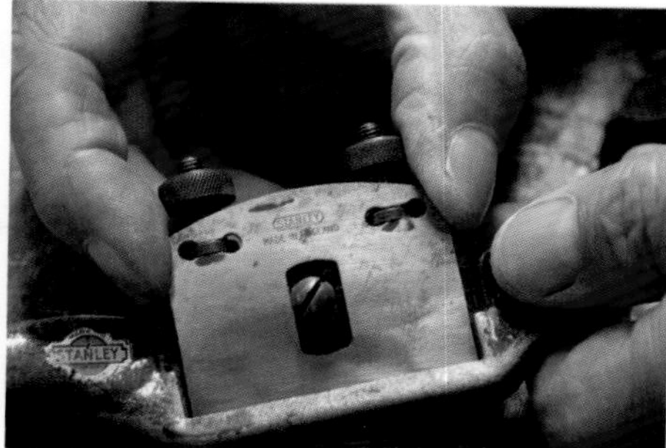
Make sure the blade is fully seated.

Replace the cap iron.

Slide it fully down before tightening.

Feel how the edge is presented in the throat.

Adjust the blade using the knobs.

Installing the cutting iron

1. As with the bench plane, take the spokeshave apart, inspect all the parts ,clean them and remove rust as necessary. To sharpen the cutting iron, use the same method described for edge tools in chapter 12 page 206.
2. With the cutting iron sharpened, replace it in the spokeshave body with the bevel facing down into the throat area of the spokeshave. Make sure that the rims on the two knurled adjustment nuts locate into the slots at the top edge of the cutting iron.
3. Replace the cap iron and tighten the threaded knob until the iron and cap iron are secure.
4. Carefully feel into the throat area for the edge of the cutting iron to see how it relates to the flat face of the sole. You are trying to establish whether the cutting edge is set inside the throat, flush with the sole or protruding through the sole. You are also trying to feel whether the cutting iron is even across the width of the iron with the sole.
5. If it's protruding too much, turn the adjustment knobs counter-clockwise to withdraw the cutting into the sole. You must gauge this with your fingertips or by testing it on a scrap of wood. If it's set inside the throat, you must turn the knobs clockwise and this will advance the iron. Always begin your setting process with the iron withdrawn slightly from the face.
6. With the iron withdrawn, turn the knobs by small amounts until the iron protrudes enough to take a thin shaving from each side of the throat opening. Look at the thicknesses of the shavings to see if they are even. If they are not, turn the relative adjustment knob until you feel they are. Now, withdraw the cutting iron until the shavings are really thin, and test each side again to see if they take shavings that are of consistent thickness. You can now set the depth of cut by turning the adjustment knobs by an equal amount.

Hand planes are capable of planing most woods in most configurations.

Troubleshooting

Hand planes

Even when a hand plane is fully prepared and functioning, problems will occur no matter how experienced the user. In the early stages of learning to plane, planes that don't produce the results we expect soon dampen enthusiasm. Following the steps in this section will help you to solve most common problems and allow you the best chances of success but remember that you cannot gain experience or skill from a book or video, only from practice and consistent use.

Difficult wood.

A badly adjusted plane.

An inexperienced user.

When problems do occur, knowing how to correct them is vitally important. Hand planing difficulties generally occur in one of three main areas:

THE PLANE—Many factors affect the effectiveness of hand planes. Preparing the plane correctly should eliminate many potential problems, enabling you to focus on more routine difficulties that are part of everyday planing.

THE WOOD—As we gain experience, we learn which areas of wood can be planed by 'reading' configurations in the grain's surface. That's not always possible, but it's a first-level step. Knots, crotches, reverse grain and others all present challenges, but with experience we soon learn how best to negotiate the wood and orient and adjust the plane to get good results.

THE USER—Understanding how to adjust the plane is essential and requires total attention and sensitivity. Even a slight jarring as you use the plane will alter the set of the iron. Landing the plane, when you begin a cut, accurately and with confidence takes practice. The follow-through stroke takes full commitment. In other circumstances, a short determined swipe might be required. Total awareness of the wood, the plane adjustment and the required techniques combine to produce predictable and satisfying results.

A NOTE ON CUTTING IRON ANGLE: *Any angle between 25° and 43° will cut just fine. Because the bed angle of the iron on the frog is generally about 45°, and the bevel is housed in the plane with the bevel facing down, it doesn't matter what angle you grind the plane iron to, the presentation of the actual cutting iron to the wood is exactly the same. The difference is not angle presentation at all, but strength of the cutting edge. The shallower the angle, the more fractious and therefore fragile the actual cutting edge retention is. The steeper the angle, the stronger the edge retaining quality of the edge, so there will be a slight compromise to the support of the cutting edge if you choose either of these two extremes. 30° is likely to be the most convenient and optimal angle for support and maintaining the bevel.*

The following Q&A section will help you take logical steps to identifying and resolving plane problems:

Hand plane Questions & Answers

Question 1

Why are plane shavings choking the mouth of my plane?

Answer: Many things can cause this problem and it happens to everyone from time to time. If it's a recurring problem there may be some mechanical fault with the plane or something in the particular area of the grain you are planing.

Possible cause 1: Too much cutting iron protruding through the mouth of the plane.

Solution 1: *Remove the lever cap to free the cutting iron assembly. This will allow you to clean the throat to clear the shavings. Replace the assembly into the plane and reset the plane iron cutting depth and alignment before using.*

Possible cause 2: Difficult grain fibers compressing against the cutting iron assembly and not cutting.

Solution 2a: *Try using a scraper. Some wood fibers and certain grain structures will gather and rise up behind the cutting edge and choke the throat, causing a jam.*

Solution 2b: *Try angling the plane differently or planing in the opposite direction.*

Possible cause 3: The back-iron has a gap at the leading edge, allowing the thin edge of the shaving to pass into the gap and form a jam.

Solution 3: *Rework the leading edge on the underside of the back-iron. Refer to page 239 of this chapter.*

Possible cause 4: Thicker shavings on one side of the plane than the other.

Solution 4: *This might be caused by a misaligned cutting iron assembly. Remove the lever cap to access and remove the clogged shavings, replace the lever cap, then adjust the lateral adjustment lever so that the cutting edge of the cutting iron is parallel with the face of the sole of the plane.*

Question 2

Why am I getting no shavings at all from my plane?

Possible cause 1: Your plane iron is set too shallow.

Solution 1: *Turn the cutting iron adjustment wheel clock-wise until the edge of the cutting iron barely catches the surface of the wood. Advance or withdraw the cutting iron until you have the thickness of shaving you want.*

Possible cause 2: There may be some hollow areas on the board. This means your plane iron isn't making contact with this part of the surface because it is 'suspended' by the higher areas around the hollow.

Solution 2: *Surface plane these high points at either end until the cutting iron reaches the low point in the middle section of the board.*

Possible cause 3: A dull iron. These tend to glide and slide rather than cut and shave.

Solution 3: *Sharpen the plane iron.*

Possible cause 4: The bevel on the cutting iron is too steep. This can cause the heel of the bevel to ride the wood, preventing the cutting edge from contacting the wood.

Solution 4: *Re-establish the ground bevel to 30° and re-sharpen it.*

Possible cause 5: The plane sole is hollow.

Solution 5: *Flatten the surface of the sole by lapping it against abrasive plates, stones or silicon carbide paper until perfectly flat.*

Possible cause 6: The plane sole is round.

Solution 6: *It rarely happens that a convex sole causes difficulty, but the sole can rock and prevent the sole from aligning the cutting edge with the surface to be planed. If this is the case, flatten the sole.*

Question 3

Why does the face or edge of the board come out hollow after hand planing?

Answer: The sole of a plane must be perfectly flat because this is the face that governs the final shape of the surface being planed.

Possible cause 1: The plane sole is convex and so cannot create a straight plane.

Solution 1: *Flatten the sole.*

Possible cause 2: You are not taking full length strokes, and perhaps the cutting iron is protruding too far.

Solution 2: *Withdraw the iron to remove any thinner shavings. Take full-length strokes after adjusting the iron to produce thinner shavings, planing the high ends of the board close to level with the center section.*

Question 4

Why does the face or edge of my board come out convex after planing?

Answer: As for hollow results, remember that the sole of a plane must be perfectly flat, because this is the face that governs the final shape of the surface being planed.

Possible cause 1: The plane sole is convex.

Solution 1: *Flatten the sole of the plane.*

Possible cause 2: The plane iron is dull.

Solution 2: *Sharpen the iron.*

Possible cause 3: You're not planing consistently.

Solution 3: *Practice planing on straight-grained, knot-free wood, periodically checking with the square to make sure you're applying equal pressure everywhere.*

Question 5

Why does the edge of my board end up out of square after planing?

Answer: Inexperience is usually the primary cause and this affects both the planing ability and the adjustment of the plane itself. Practice applying even pressure all over the plane. There are some other possible causes, too.

Possible cause 1: The plane iron is tilted in relation to the sole of the plane. No matter how minimally, each shaving takes more off one side than the other and so the problem increases with each shaving.

Solution 1: *Align the cutting edge of the plane iron parallel to the sole by adjusting the lateral adjustment lever, located behind the top of the cutting iron.*

Possible cause 2: Knots, wiry grain and so on are affecting the cutting efficiency of the plane.

Solution 2: *This can be difficult to deal with sometimes. Try sharpening your plane as normal, but then with immense care, polish the bevel with increasingly lighter strokes on the strop. Finish the bevel off on a clean cotton cloth. Your plane should now deal with the awkward grain, but if you still have trouble, you may need to use a cabinet scraper or even abrasive paper in severe cases.*

Possible cause 3: The back-iron is not aligned properly to the edge of the cutting iron.

Solution 3: *Reset the back-iron to the correct alignment.*

Question 6

Why are my shavings thicker on one side than the other and how do I correct this inconsistency?

Answer: This is not uncommon, even with experienced woodworkers. Resolving the problem doesn't take long, provided you know where to look.

Possible cause 1: The cutting edge might not be lying perfectly parallel to the sole of the plane. If the plane iron is set askew, the plane will take uneven shavings.

Solution 1: *Align the cutting edge parallel to the sole using the lateral adjustment lever. Check by taking shavings from one side of the plane and then the other, and comparing them for thickness.*

Possible cause 2: Uneven hand pressure on the plane handles causes the plane to lean slightly more to one side of the wood than the other.

Solution 2: *Relax your grip and don't be too rigid. Try to correct the tendency by feeling for the pressure you use and centralizing your plane on the wood, especially for narrow edges. Develop sensitivity through practice.*

Possible cause 3: Part of the plane iron is dull.

Solution 3: *Check the cutting edge for sharpness and sharpen the iron as necessary.*

Question 7

Why is the adjustment wheel that sets the depth of my iron stiff and hard to turn?

Answer: This adjustment should turn freely but positively forwards or backwards. New planes tend to be a little stiff to start, but soon break in with use.

Possible cause 1: Dust and debris from shavings and general work often builds up between threads in the screw feed of the adjustment wheel.

Solution 1: *Use penetrating oil to clean the threads on the screw feed and inside adjustment wheel, further lubricating it with light machine oil.*

Possible cause 2: The screw feed or adjustment wheel is damaged.

Solution 2: *Remove and repair or replace the damaged part.*

Possible cause 3: The lever cap is too tight.

Solution 3: *If the lever cap is set correctly, the adjustment wheel should turn easily. Release the lever cap and try turning the wheel forwards and backwards to see if that affects the stiffness. If it turns evenly, you have too much pressure on the iron assembly. Turn the retaining bolt half a turn or so. Reset the lever cap and try again.*

Question 8

Why does my plane leave undulations and other marks that resemble chatter marks after I have finished planing a surface?

Answer: There are many causes for this. Often woodworkers use the generic term 'chatter' to describe such surfacing problems, but chatter is a very specific and unusual phenomenon. Chatter is caused by a series of quick and successive vibrations in the plane's cutting iron due to minute flexes back and forth at the very tip of the cutting edge. Some books advise the use of extra thick cutting irons to prevent chatter occurring. But chatter is not down to the thickness of the blade, it is more about sharpness and decisive action. In most cases, what people call chatter actually isn't chatter at all but stammer, jarring, bouncing, shocking or scudding. Most of the time, practicing your technique is enough to rectify the problem, but there are some other potential issues.

Possible cause 1: The most common cause is having the cutting iron set too deeply, which means the cutting edge protrudes too far through the throat of the plane.

Solution 1: *Check both the depth of the iron setting and the distance from the edge of the back-iron to the cutting edge of the cutting iron. If this distance is too great, the iron cannot be withdrawn enough. This distance should be no greater than 1⁄16" at most.*

Possible cause 2: You're too timid when planing or making some other kind of human error.

Solution 2: *You must gain greater confidence to present the plane to the task and follow through with sufficient force and speed to make a full cut. Any faltering will result in stammer. Practice to gain experience and confidence.*

Possible cause 3: The back-iron is too close or far from the cutting edge.

Solution 3: *Adjust the back-iron setting to suit the wood type, but in any case no farther than 1⁄16" from the cutting iron.*

Possible cause 4: The plane's cutting iron may be assembled upside down (bevel up) to the back-iron, which automatically sends the cutting iron out too far.

Solution 4: *Disassemble the cutting iron assembly and turn the cutting iron around, so that the bevel of the iron faces down towards the throat opening (bevel down).*

Possible cause 5: There is too much flex in the actual cutting iron.

Solution 5: *Occasionally this is because the iron is thin. Practice your technique. Also, make sure the cutting iron and back-iron are the correct type before considering installing a thicker iron.*
I have never found a plane where the cutting iron was too thin.

Possible cause 6: There is insufficient support or pressure between the frog and the lever cap.

Solution 6: *Adjust the frog forwards or backwards so that the whole iron assembly is fully bedded on the frog, and not held off by the mouth of the sole. Remove any high points on the frog casting by filing it or by using a sharpening stone. Tighten the setscrew holding the cutting iron assembly to the frog.*

Troubleshooting No. 151 spokeshaves

Possible cause 7: Shavings are jammed in the throat of the plane between the cutting iron assembly and the fore part of the throat, causing skips and jumps.

Solution 7: *Remove shavings from the throat and check for gaps between the cap iron and cutting iron. If there are gaps, you must hone the under-edge of the cap iron to achieve a closed fit.*

Possible cause 8: The wood grain is too awkward and difficult to plane.

Solution 8: *Some woods just will not plane no matter how good you are or how well your plane is adjusted. In these instances, it's best to use a scraper.*

Possible cause 9: The cutting iron is dull.

Solution 9: *Sharpen the iron.*

Possible cause 10: The cap iron is loose.

Solution 10: *Tighten the connecting setscrew.*

Possible cause 11: There is insufficient pressure on the cutting iron assembly.

Solution 11: *Adjust the setscrew that holds the lever cap, until the lever has just sufficient pressure to lock down.*

As spokeshaves are basically in the same family as planes, with similar adjustments and main parts, the previous section on troubleshooting planes applies well to spokeshaves. There are some variations, but on the whole the same questions and answers apply. The most common problem is choking the spokeshave.

Shavings choke in the mouth of my spokeshave. What causes this and how do I resolve it?

Answer: There's no single cause. Many things can trigger this problem and it happens to everyone from time to time. If it's a recurring problem, there may be some mechanical fault with the spokeshave or something in the particular area of the grain you're working on. Here are some likely causes with suggested solutions.

Possible cause 1: The cutting iron is set too deeply which means that too much of the cutting iron is protruding through the mouth of the spokeshave.

Solution 1: *Remove the cap iron to free the cutting iron and clear the shavings. Replace the cutting iron and follow the procedures for installing the cutting iron and setting the depth of cut and alignment.*

Possible cause 2: Difficult grain fibers are compressing against the cutting iron and will not cut.

Solution 2a: *Try using a scraper. Some wood fibers and certain grain structures will gather behind the cutting edge and choke the throat, causing a jam.*

Solution 2b: *Try angling the spokeshave differently or spokeshaving in the opposite direction.*

Possible cause 3: The cap iron has a gap at the leading edge, letting in shavings and jamming the throat.

Solution 3: *Flatten the underside of the cap iron using abrasive paper and a flat surface to abrade on, or use diamond plates.*

Possible cause 4: A misaligned cutting iron is causing thicker shavings on one side of the spokeshave than the other.

Solution 4: *Remove the lever cap to access the throat and remove any clogged shavings. Then replace the cap iron and adjust the cutting iron with the adjustment nuts, until the cutting edge lies parallel with the face of the sole.*

Possible cause 5: The cutting iron is installed upside down.

Solution 5: *Remove the cap iron to access the throat and remove the clogged shavings. Replace the iron with the bevel facing downwards into the throat of the spokeshave (bevel down).*

15 Sharpening handsaws

In times past, every woodworker sharpened their own saws, but today few craftsmen have learned these simple skills and techniques. You can learn basic saw-sharpening skills in about an hour; practice will take a few hours, and mastery perhaps a few days over a year. Together, we can ensure your saw always slices through wood with ease, and we can start to counter the depressing trend of manufacturing throwaway saws.

From dozens of famed saw makers once synonymous with Sheffield, England, only a few remain. Some companies, despite their long history in traditional saw making, are now tooled up solely to serve industrial processes. Most woodworkers now rely on powered machinery and use disposable handsaws designed to crosscut rather than rip. This is because most woodwork now involves man made sheet materials like plywood, pressed fibreboard and particle board. These materials have multi-directional wood fibres, which means that they can be cut in any direction using crosscutting saws.

Regardless of whether you use machines, handsaws still have a viable place in any woodworking shop. I have used some of my saws for forty-five years. Some I bought secondhand and were made in the late 1800s. I learned to sharpen all my saws as an apprentice but over the years, I have changed my methods and improved my techniques.

Saw sharpening flow chart

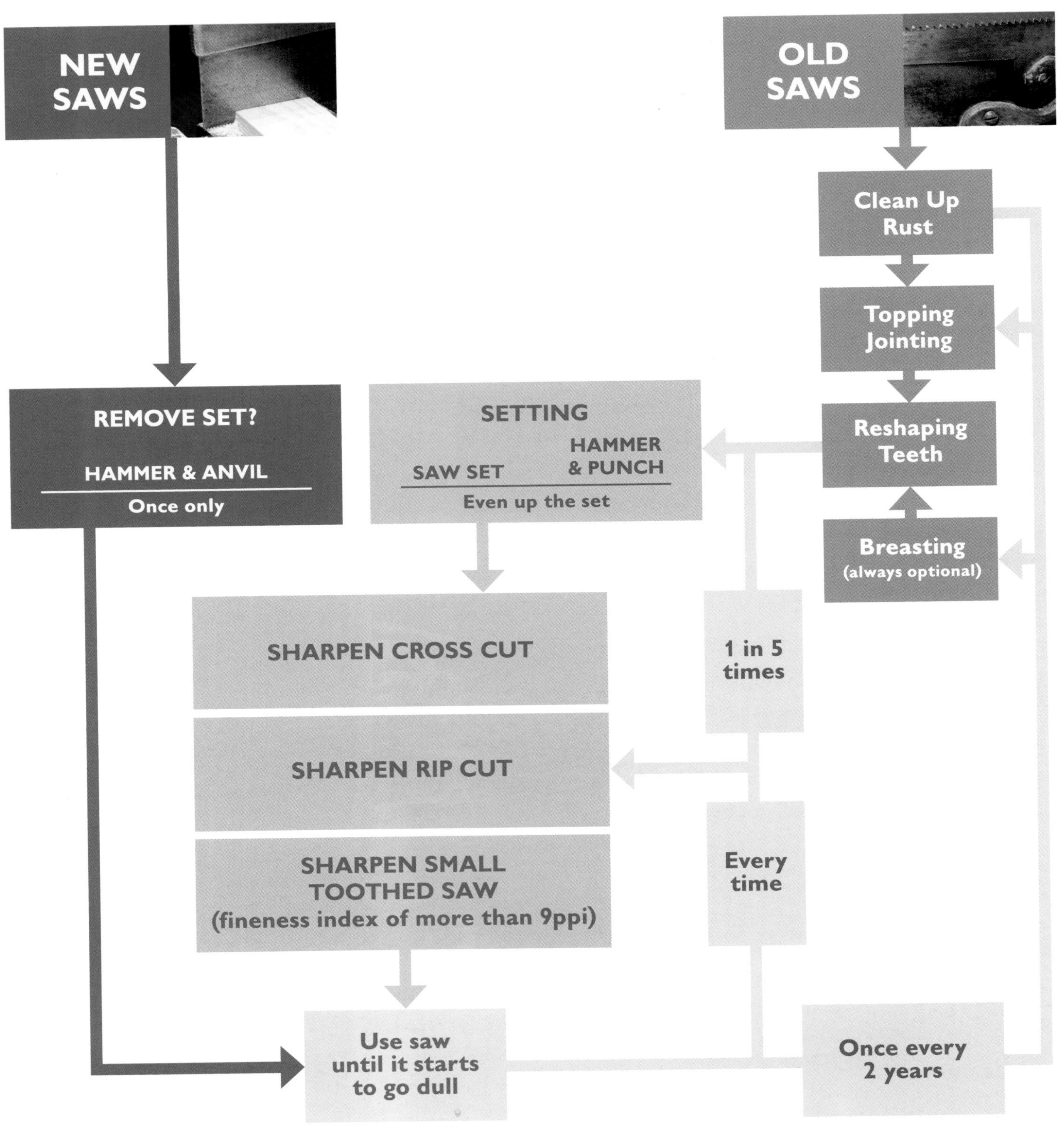
NEW SAWS
OLD SAWS
Clean Up Rust
Topping Jointing
Reshaping Teeth
Breasting (always optional)
REMOVE SET?
HAMMER & ANVIL
Once only
SETTING
SAW SET
HAMMER & PUNCH
Even up the set
SHARPEN CROSS CUT
SHARPEN RIP CUT
SHARPEN SMALL TOOTHED SAW (fineness index of more than 9ppi)
1 in 5 times
Every time
Use saw until it starts to go dull
Once every 2 years

Setting larger teeth is simple with the right tool.

Terminology of saw teeth

Negative or passive rake.

Aggressive rake

Very aggressive rake.

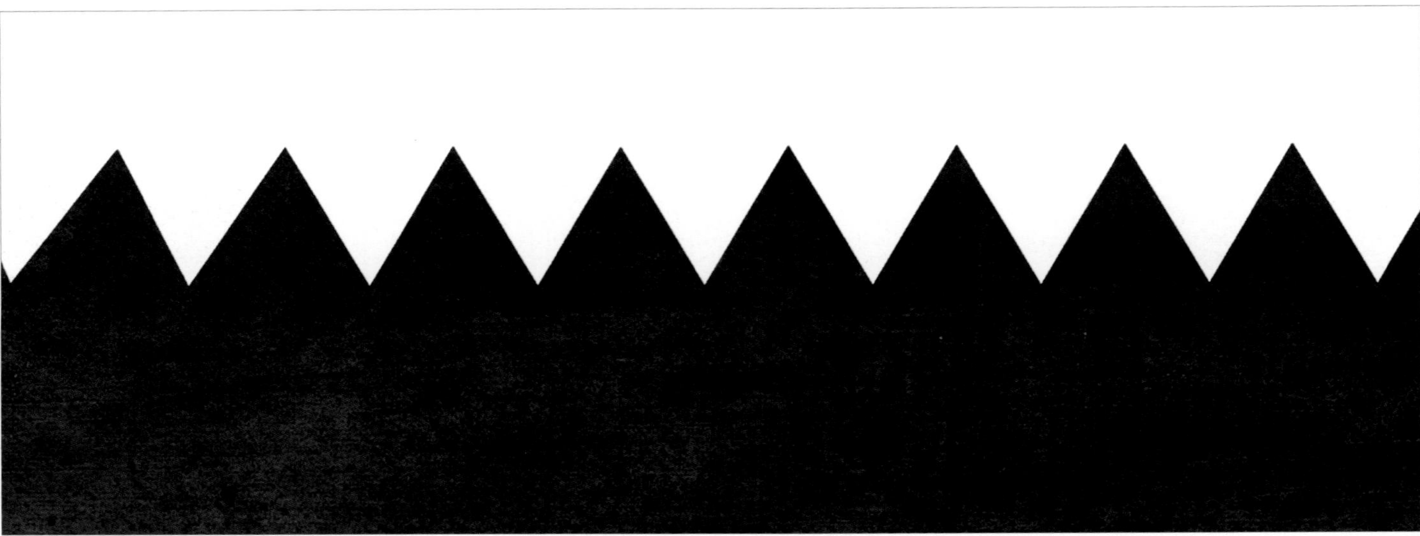

These teeth are sharpened as a passive cut which means that although cutting with it will be easy it is often slow.

Aggressive teeth cut more quickly but take more strength and confidence to use.

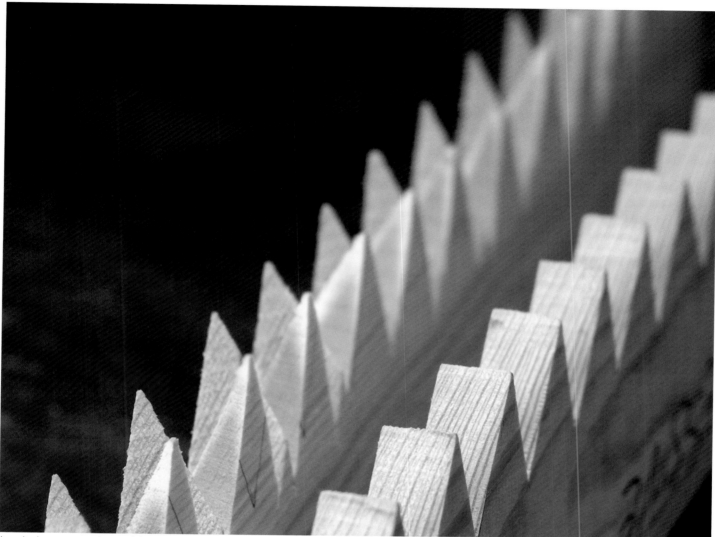

I made these two wooden models to explain to my students the difference between crosscut, fleam teeth (left) and ripcut, chisel pattern teeth (right).

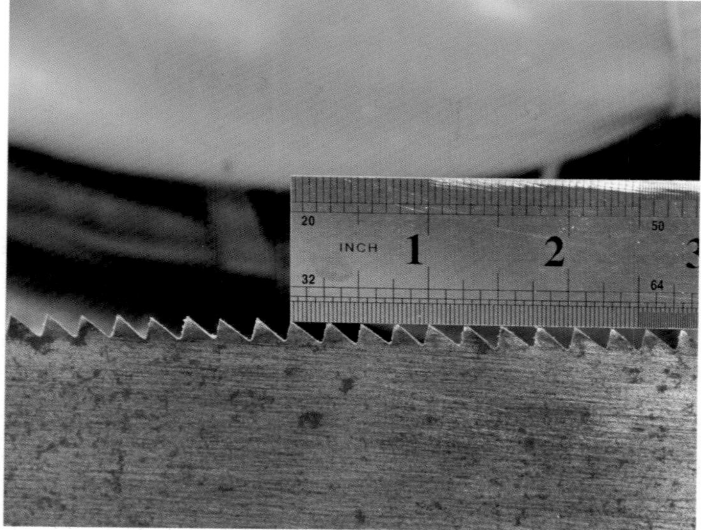

This coarse toothed saw has 5 points per inch (ppi). or 4 teeth per inch (tpi).

This saw is fairly fine at 13 ppi.

Sharpening, Setting and Shaping

Everyday saw maintenance falls into two distinct categories: Sharpening and setting. There's a third process, re-shaping, which is not part of the usual maintenance cycle.

SHARPENING maintains a keen cutting edge on the teeth so that the saw cuts quickly and efficiently.

SETTING bends the teeth of the saw in an alternating pattern out from the plate (blade) to create a kerf—the channel through which the teeth pass into the wood.

RE-SHAPING is only carried out if you're restoring an old or worn saw blade or using a good saw for a different purpose which requires a new tooth configuration. **Re-shaping includes:**

- **CHANGING THE TOOTH SIZE:** In practice, either halving or doubling the fineness of the saw is the easiest size alteration to make. Other than this, the teeth must be completely removed by filing flat and then re-cut from scratch. Nowadays, it's more practical to buy the saw that fits your particular need. Providing the teeth are not induction hardened, a good saw will generally outlast its owner.
- **CHANGING THE CONFIGURATION:** This involves converting a ripcut saw into a crosscut saw or vice-versa.
- **TOPPING OR JOINTING:** Because we use the center section of the saw more than the extremes at the toe and heel, saws generally require more sharpening in the central region. This left uncorrected creates a hollow along the saw and must be corrected by filing the tops of the teeth to a level line, and later tooth filing to restore uniformity to the points.
- **PROGRESSIVE PATTERN CUTTING:** Sometimes, a progressive change in tooth geometry at the front of a particular class of saws can greatly increase their effectiveness. We'll learn more about this later.

Good saws are often a thing of beauty.

Sharpening equipment

Setting saw teeth

All saws have their teeth set to create a kerf. The kerf allows the free passage of the main body of the saw into the cut. Bending each alternate tooth opposite to one another in this way creates a passage slightly wider than the thickness of the saw blade. I am vigilant in getting the right amount of set for a particular saw for a particular job. I like to have the absolute minimum of set possible for fine work, much less than saw manufacturers recommend. For my everyday ripsaw, I use the same criteria because I'm usually ripping down well seasoned dry stock. However, if I'm crosscutting or ripping green or sappy wood, I like to have plenty of set so that the blade can't be bound by the wood fibers in the kerf. As you repeatedly sharpen any saw, you will reach a point where the saw starts to jam on the reverse stroke. This is primarily caused by thousands of minute wood fibers protruding into the saw kerf with each forward thrust of the saw. These fibers then trap the saw blade as the direction is reversed. If you feel resistance on the return stroke, this generally signals the need for setting the saw teeth.

There are two different methods of creating the set; by hammer setting, or using a setting tool. The choice of method is principally governed by tooth size.

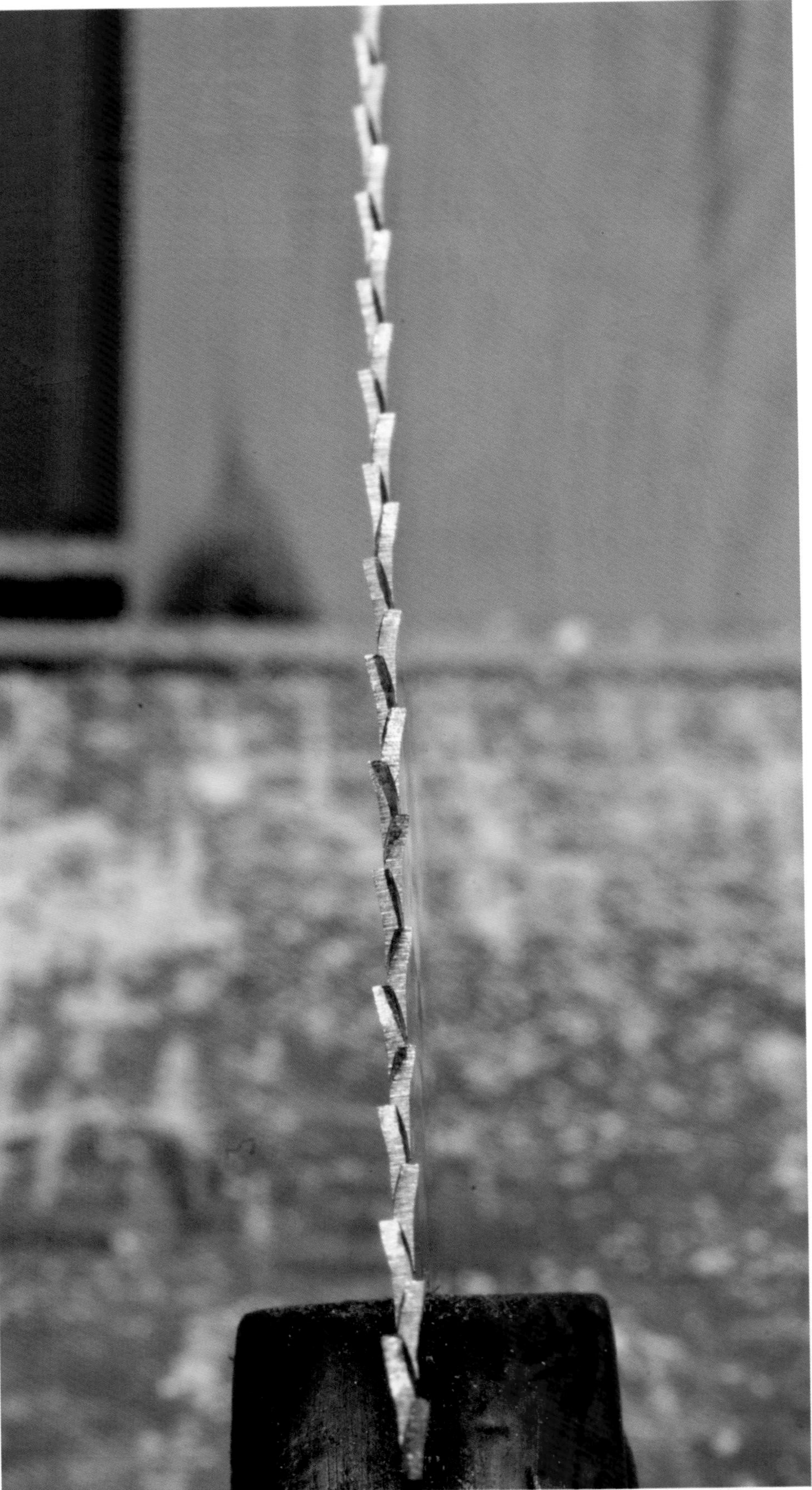

I have put a lot of set on these teeth to leave you in no doubt as to what 'set' means. This saw would cut green lumber with ease.

The teeth sink into the soft pine. I have marked every other tooth with a black line to remind you to skip every other tooth.

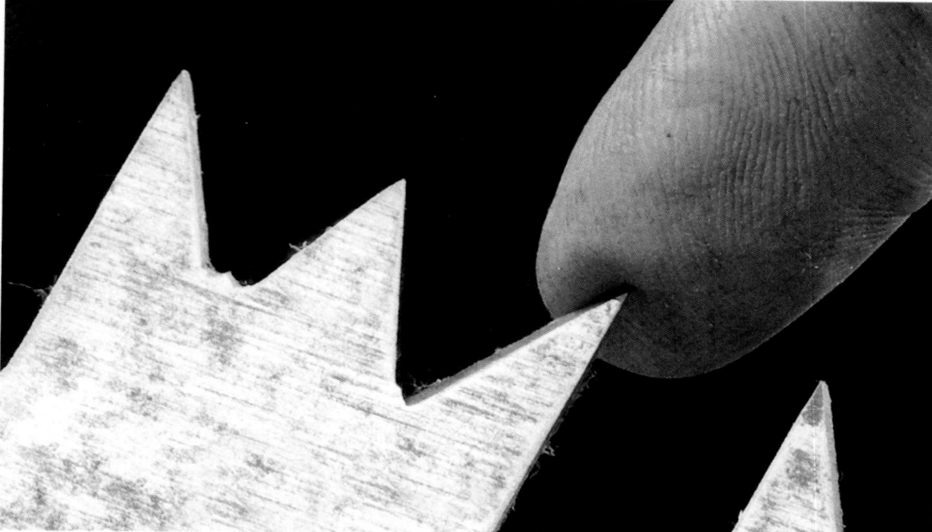

Large teeth can only be set by hammer setting.

Even out the set

Hammer setting

This method is used for setting very coarse saws (those with a fineness index of less than three). These saws are usually set by first laying them on a steel plate with a filed chamfer edge. A hammer is then used to tap every other tooth outwards onto the pre-determined angle of the chamfered plate. After reversing the saw blade, the process is repeated with the other teeth. This method actually works for saws of almost any tooth size, but there are variations in technique for practical reasons.

On smaller saws with teeth finer than 15ppi, I prefer to use a small hammer and a nail punch (nail set). This is my personal preference as it takes only a few minutes to set any tenon saw.

I place the saw on a batten of wood to support the teeth above the bench, compensating for the handle and spine if it's a tenon or dovetail saw. I pack the saw so that it feels firm without any rocking. Again, beginning with the first tooth leaning away from me, I angle my punch against the tooth and tap fairly lightly. I try to maintain the same consistent striking blows all the way along the saw but consistency is not critical at this stage. Next, I flip the saw over and do the same to the opposite teeth.

Even out the set

My next step eradicates any inconsistency. Tighten a second hammer in the vise to use as an anvil. Place the saw teeth on the hammer face and, with quick successive taps, tap all the way along the teeth on one side and then flip the saw over and do the same to the other. There is enough memory in the steel so that as the teeth spring back, the set of the teeth is equalized and consistent.

Using a saw setting tool

For mid-range saws with a fineness index of between 4ppi and 27ppi, a saw set works very effectively. We use a saw set to control the amount each tooth is bent and it guarantees a consistent kerf width.

Saw sets like these will last a craftsman throughout his working life. Squeezing the pistol-grip handle presses a steel plunger against each tooth to bend it against a round steel disc housed in the saw set. The disc, called the anvil, is a small adjustable wheel calibrated with settings corresponding to the ppi. We find the correct setting by counting the number of tooth points that fall within each inch of saw length. For a six-point saw we set the dial wheel to six. They range from 4-12ppi. I have a second saw set that sets teeth from 13-27ppi, but they are not readily available.

I prefer not to use exact dial settings which correspond to the point per inch system because this oversets the teeth excessively. Heavily set teeth take considerably more effort to push into and through the wood. I suggest using a dial setting of twelve for all saws of 9ppi or finer and a dial setting of ten for coarser saws of less than 9ppi. If the wood is wet you may need to set more, but we rarely work with green wood today. Whichever setting you choose, place the saw set on the tooth edge of the saw. For your first experience of saw setting and sharpening, use a saw with larger teeth than a dovetail saw; six to eight teeth would be ideal. You can set the saw by simply holding it freehand. It's of no real advantage to secure the saw for setting unless the saw is large and long.

Push and twist the knurled selector to adjust the dial setting on the anvil.

As you squeeze the pistol grip, the saw is gripped against the anvil and then the plunger bends the tooth.

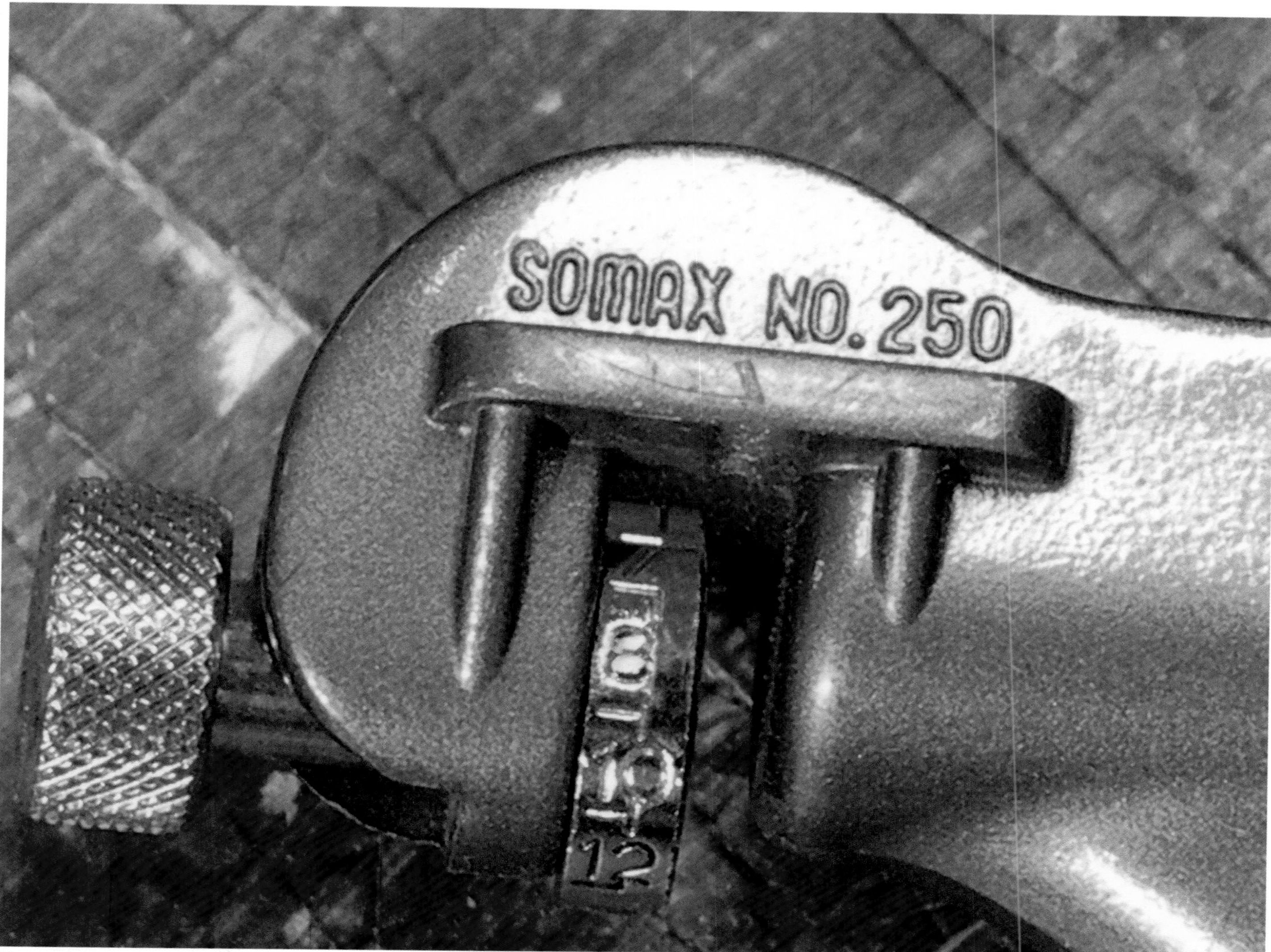

The numbers on the anvil are supposed to correspond to the number of teeth points per inch (ppi). I find this usually gives too much set.

If your saw is new or in good condition, the chances are it is already set, but through continuous use and sharpening, the set requires re-establishing. To set any saw, we begin by determining the direction of the existing set. Look at the teeth to see which way they were originally set (bent) and follow that same direction. You will bend the teeth that are leaning away from you and skip those leaning toward you. If you cannot tell by looking, try feeling the teeth. If you cannot feel any difference, it may be that almost all the set is gone because of successive sharpenings. If so, you must look very carefully at the teeth, as the original set direction will always be discernible, if faintly. Once you have determined which way the teeth are set, place your saw set with the piston plunger centered on the first tooth that leans away from you. Now squeeze the plier handle. You will see the tooth bend as the plunger forces it against the round anvil. Now skip the next tooth, which is the one leaning towards you, and set the next tooth leaning away from you. Continue setting each alternate tooth along the full length of the saw. Now turn the saw around and set the opposite teeth.

TOP TIP: *At which point you set your saw teeth, either before or after sharpening, depends on the condition of the teeth. If the saw is fairly sharp and the teeth need no reshaping, before or after works fine. You don't have to set your saw each time you sharpen, though you can if you want to. When the saw begins to feel slight resistance in the reverse stroke, it's time to set the teeth again.*

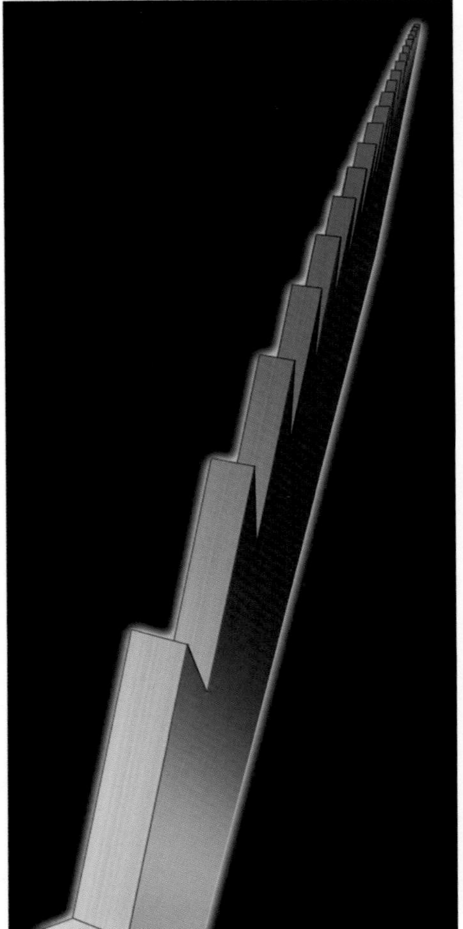
No set–The saw will bind.

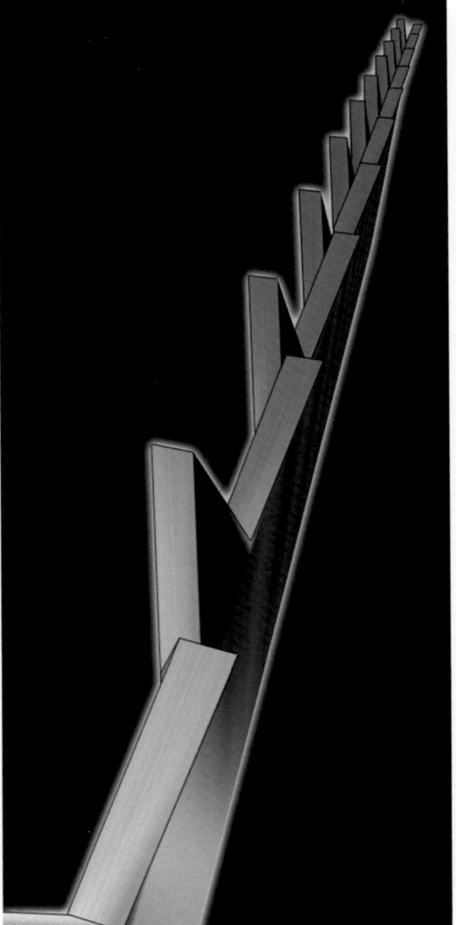
Overset–The kerf is too wide.

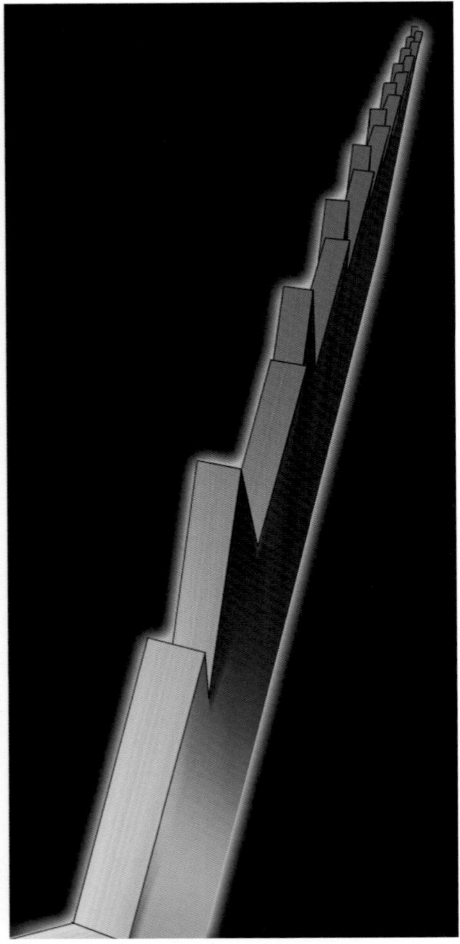
Correct set for a tenon saw.

Overset teeth.

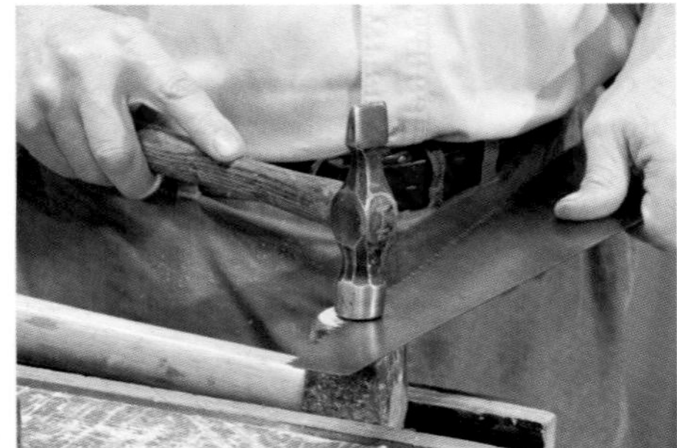
Use a second hammer as a makeshift anvil.

New saws—overset saw teeth

Most European saws are overset by the manufacturers, which makes sawing difficult, inaccurate and rough. If you experience this with a new saw, take the saw blade and lay it flat on a steel hammer face. Then, with a small 10-ounce hammer, gently tap the side of all the teeth, working from one end of the saw to the other. Flip the saw over and do the same to the teeth on the other side. Now the saw should cut smoothly and accurately.

All saw files are triangular. I have a good range to match a range of saws.

Saw files

We sharpen saws using slim triangular files that taper from the point and gradually increase in width toward the handle. This tapered design increases the pressure and cutting power in the triangular space between each tooth and down into the gullet of the saw (the gullet being the lowest point between the teeth). With the one forward stroke, this cuts the front of one tooth and the back of the adjacent one.

Saw files come in different sizes depending on the size of the teeth. The size of the teeth corresponds directly to the number of tooth points within each inch of saw length. The cutting face of the file should always be at least twice the height of the saw tooth. That way, when you rotate the file to a fresh face, you have a full, fresh cutting corner.

All files have small flats at the corners. The small 4" files have smaller flats to allow them to cut into the inner corners of the smaller gullets.

We use the same saw file to cut and file the teeth of cross- and ripcut saws. Again, the saw file size is relative to the size of the saw teeth.

For all dovetail and small-toothed saws, if I'm in the US, I use a Nicholson 6" double extra-slim tapered saw file. In the UK, where smaller saw files are two-ended files with a file at both ends, I use a 4" file, which is actually just over 8" long overall. The US file is usually stamped XX SLIM. The 'X' is used as an abbreviation for 'extra'. The next size up, an extra-slim (X SLIM), works well on saws with a fineness index of 10 points per inch (ppi) or over, regardless of whether it's a backsaw or a handsaw.

Size of saw file	Type of saw	#ppi (fineness index)
6" XX slim taper file	Gent's saw	16-22 per inch
	Dovetail saw	13-15 per inch
	Midsize backsaw	11-14 per inch
7" X slim taper file	Hand, back and tenon saws	8-10 per inch
7" slim taper file	Handsaw	5-7 per inch

"The cutting face of the file should always be at least twice the height of the saw tooth"

Just to recap, these three files will take care of your entire saw sharpening needs. A saw file currently costs around $6.

Setting up for saw sharpening

People often ask how to tell when a saw needs sharpening. Sometimes a saw simply will not cut or is difficult to cut with. You can also examine the points of the teeth. If the tips have shiny white points, the saw must be dull because light cannot reflect off a sharp edge.

"We rely on reflected light to show how much or how little to sharpen the individual teeth"

Sharpening saws requires precise action with each successive stroke across each tooth. I use a tall stool to bring me to the correct height in relation to the saw being held in the vise, and also to steady my upper body as I progress along the saw. Light is helpful too because we rely on reflected light to show how much or how little to sharpen the individual teeth. An anglepoise desk lamp works well for this because you can adjust the light to give the best reflection.

Establishing a good rhythm takes confidence that only comes through practice. Before gaining speed, I find it best to make practice strokes when I begin each saw. This positions my body and synchronizes my arms and hands in relation to the saw. Only increase speed as you gain skill and sensitivity.

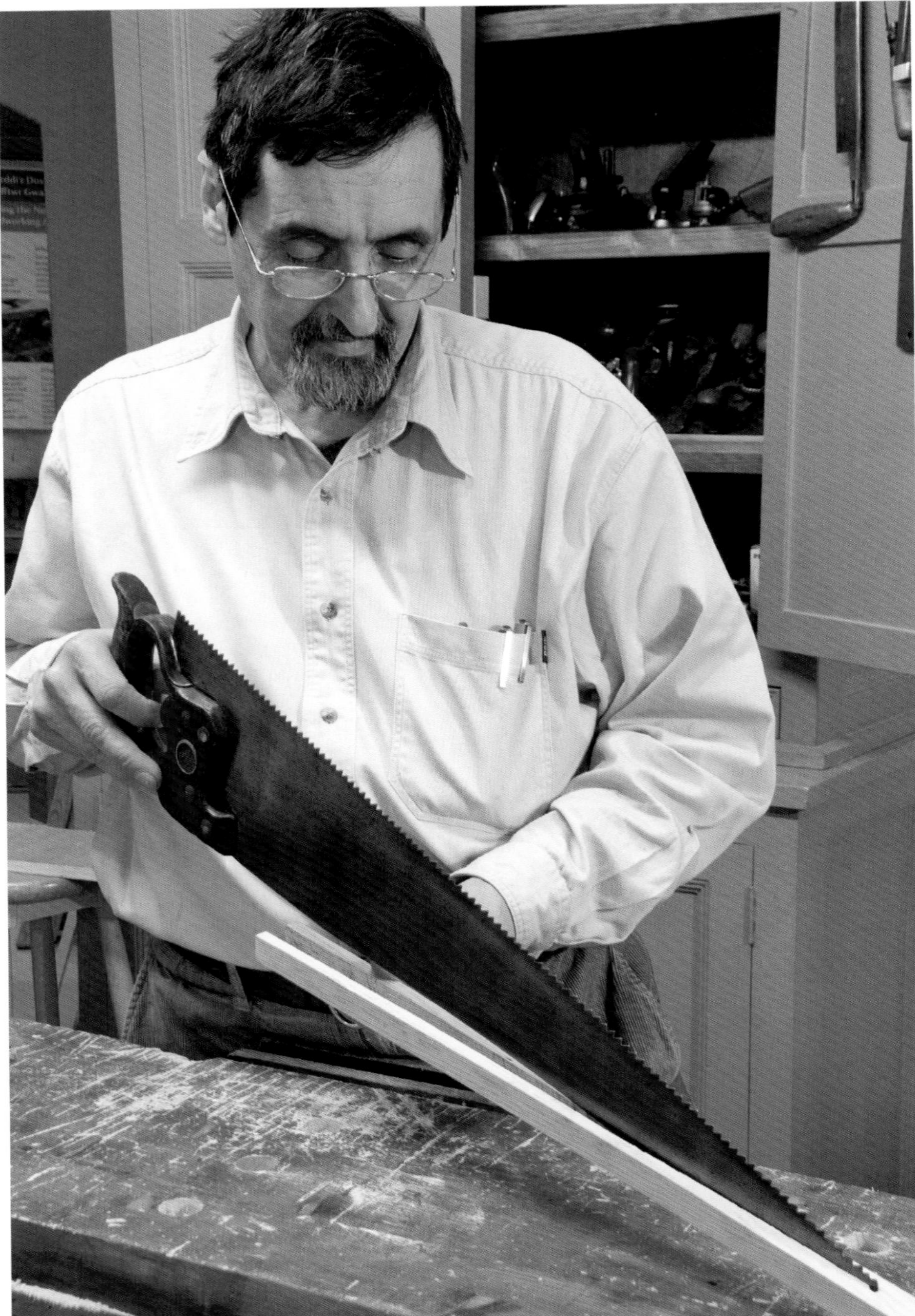

A sawn batten is ideal to hold the saw in the vise.

Make sure that you have no more than ¼" between the gullet and the battens or the saw will vibrate counterproductively.

Use consistent and even strokes on every tooth.

Sharpening a saw: Step-by-step

To sharpen successfully, your saw must be fully supported along either side of the saw teeth in some sort of vise. The clamping force should be close to the teeth to minimize any vibration. You can make a practical saw support from wood. I generally use a piece of 1" thick pine 1½" wide with a saw cut almost down the full length, as shown on the opposite page. It's a simple device that works better than trying to use a pair of battens. This is because it slips over the blade and automatically aligns on each side to clamp in the vise.

TOP TIP: *I don't like to have more than ¼" between the bottom of the gullet and the top of the saw support, or the vibration is counterproductive.*

1. With the saw held firmly, begin at either end by placing the saw file directly in the gullet of the saw. Put the file onto the back of the first tooth that leans away from you, which will automatically place the opposite side of the file on the front of the tooth leaning towards you.
2. When you push the saw file through the gullet, you will be filing the back of one tooth and the front of the adjacent tooth in a single pass.
3. If the saw is in a reasonably sharp condition, one pass may be enough. If not, take one or two more passes, but no more than three at this stage. If the saw needs more sharpening, it's better to complete both sides, taking three strokes per gullet, and then repeat the sharpening along the whole length with one or possibly two further passes but this is only usually necessary for badly neglected saws.

4. Maintain an even pressure throughout each stroke and ensure each file stroke is the same length. This will help to maintain a consistent tooth size and pattern. If you don't, it's easy to over sharpen individual teeth or sections of teeth and distort them.
5. It's also important to ensure you make equal-length passes with consistent pressure. Any variation will again distort the teeth, and you will have high and low teeth. You can usually correct this discrepancy by skipping over the low spots on the teeth in subsequent sharpenings until they all become level again. If, however, you ignore the problem and continue sharpening in the low spots, the saw will deteriorate with subsequent sharpenings.
6. As you did with the saw setting, skip over each alternate tooth until the whole side is completed. For ripcut pattern saws, all the teeth may be sharpened from one side, as the fine burr left by the file is removed on the first use of the saw, and contributes nothing to the sharpness.
7. Turn the saw around and again sharpen the back of the teeth leaning away from you and the front of the teeth leaning towards you. You will automatically be sharpening the unsharpened teeth if you follow this pattern.

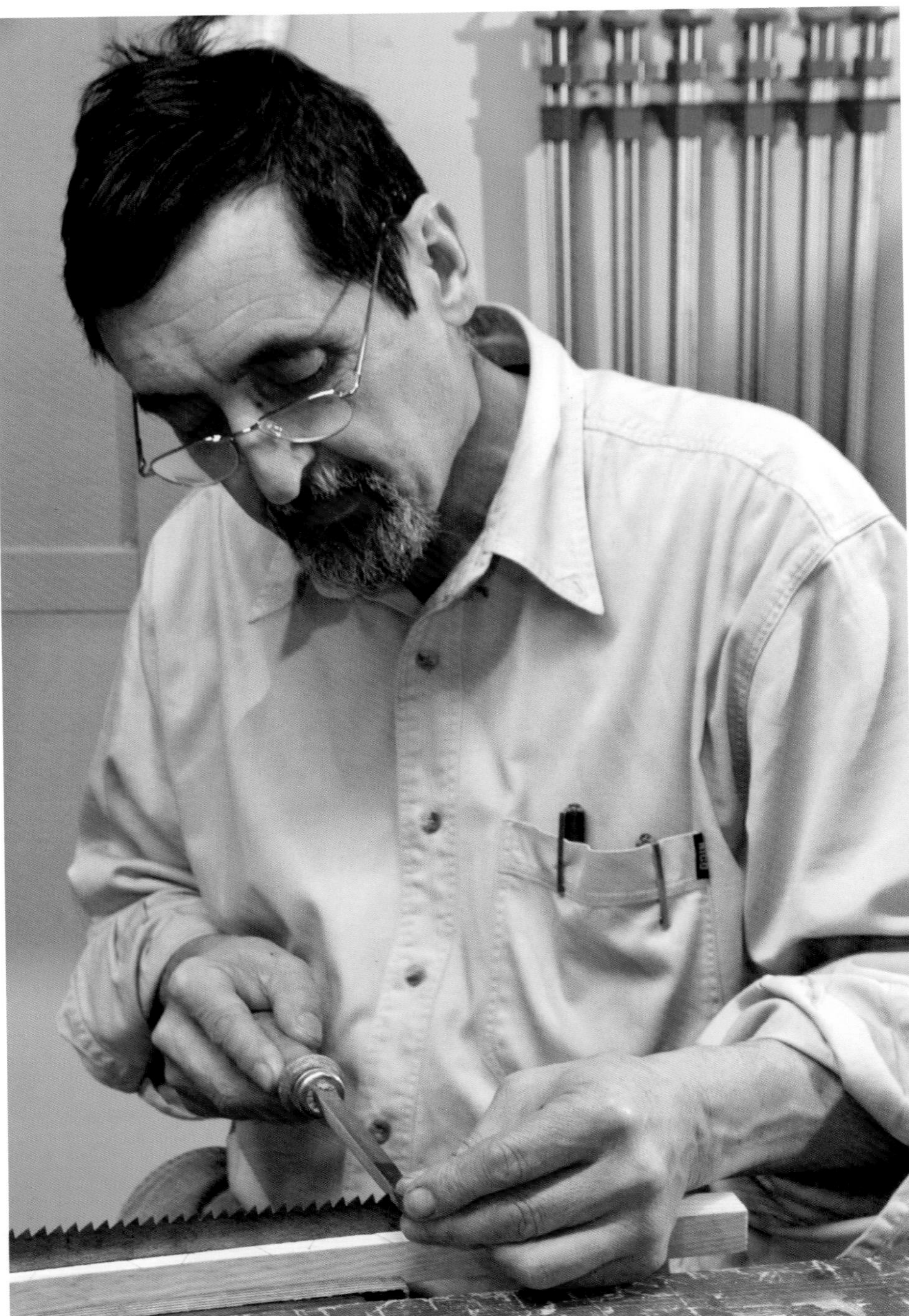

Sit in a comfortable position so you can get into a natural rhythm.

File from only one side if you are sharpening to a ripsaw pattern.

To sharpen a crosscut pattern, you have to skip every other tooth on the first pass, then reverse the saw and repeat.

8. If a saw is relatively new or in good condition, you can use the existing angle of the saw teeth as a guide for the file, otherwise you will have to correct any discrepancy. Most craftsmen who sharpen their own saws do consider how much rake to put on the teeth and vary it according to their own preference.

TECHNICAL POINTER: *The angles given for filing the teeth are shown in the drawings. For every saw type, you will always be filing the back of the tooth leaning away from you, which automatically sharpens the front of the tooth leaning towards you with the same file stroke. The angle of 65 degrees for the fleam-tooth pattern is not critical, but I suggest you follow all the recommended methods in the drawings and pictures to guide you.*

Saws to practice on

Unless you have established some level of skill, it's best to start with a saw that has 6-8ppi. These teeth are big enough not to disappear with a single forward stroke of the file. To gain confidence, buy an inexpensive saw to practice on. Check that the teeth are not induction hardened, which makes the saw disposable and impossible to sharpen with a sawfile. Flea markets are a good, inexpensive source of old saws. Beware, if the saw metal is of poor quality and warped, it may not be repairable. Saws made of better quality steel readily spring back and remain straight after bending with hand pressure. To improve your chances of getting a 'keeper' to practice on, bend the saw and then sight down the top edge to see if it stayed straight.

Follow the steps in this saw sharpening section and sharpen the saw until you develop a rhythm for filing and establishing consistent tooth patterns. You can also try altering the rake of the teeth to develop your skills and refine tooth patterns, testing your efforts to see which you prefer.

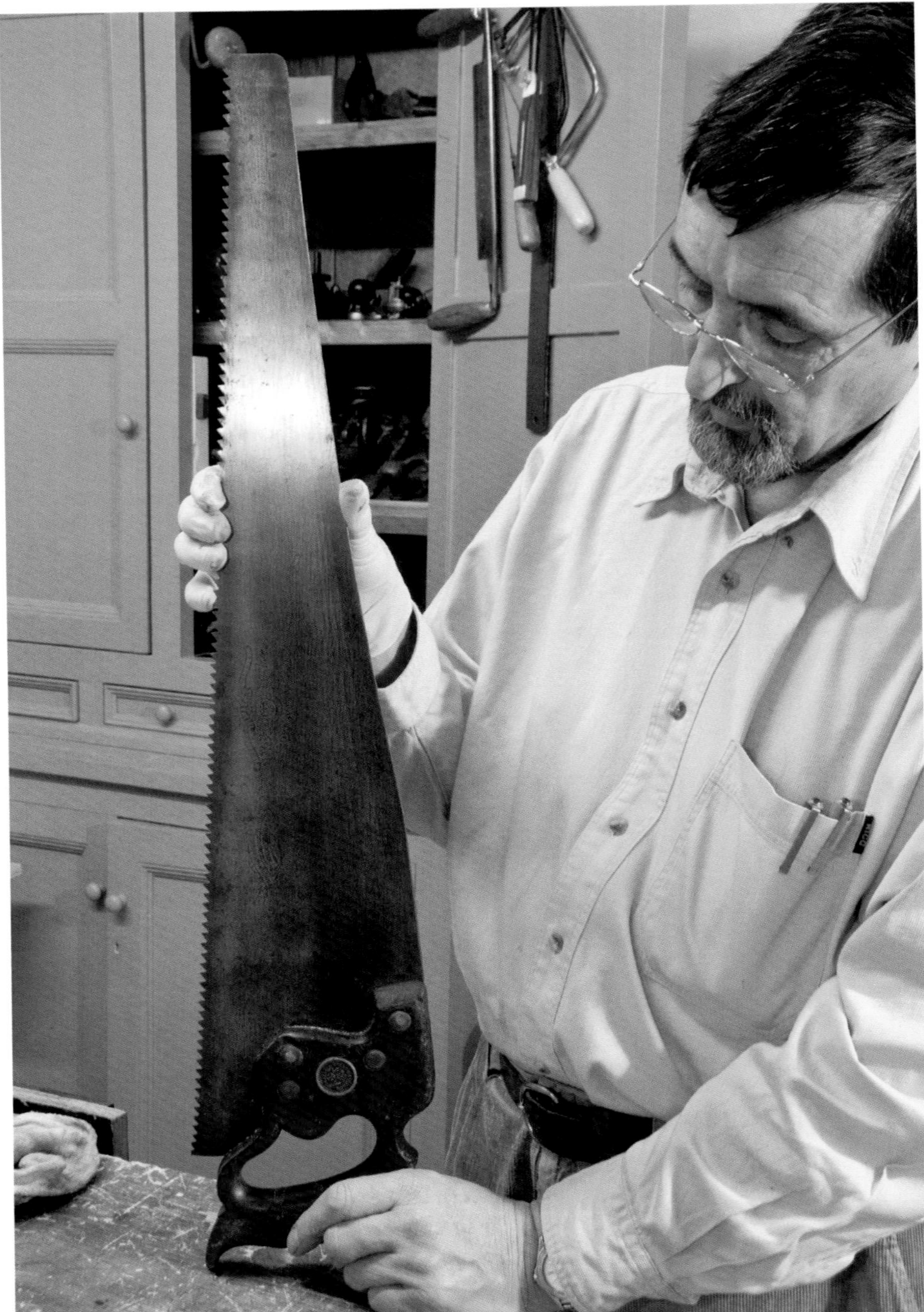

I've just cleaned the rust off this saw. I can now set and sharpen it to a rip pattern.

The number of points per inch is critical.

> *"you need to understand that the fine saw teeth do not slice the fibers like a conventional crosscut saw."*

The relationship between tooth size and sharpening pattern

Wood grain comprises a complex growth system of elongated cells of varying length and diameter. This structure creates the need for two types of saw; one that cuts along these long cells of grain, and one that cuts across them. However, the size of the tooth also has a bearing on the tooth configuration.

Knowing the number of points per inch (ppi) of any saw is critical. Any saw with a fineness index of more than 9 may be sharpened in a ripcut pattern, regardless of the direction of cut. This is not the case with coarser saws below 9ppi.

These coarser saws lend themselves to two very different shapes of saw teeth:

- For ripping wood with or along the grain, saw teeth are shaped like chisels and travel in the same direction as the wood fibers. The sawdust is pushed to the end of the cut with every stroke, presenting the uncut fibers ready for the next pass from the razor-sharp chisel teeth.
- For slicing across the long fibers, i.e. cutting across the grain, the teeth are shaped like small vertical knives coming to diamond shaped points. This is called the crosscut, or fleam-tooth pattern, and is accepted on every continent as the most efficient means of cutting quickly across the grain. Short sections of wood fiber the width of the saw blade are sliced, tumbled and crumpled into the gaps between the teeth, being ejected in a steady stream as the teeth emerge from the deepening slot.

Coarser ripsaws, with a fineness index of less than 9ppi, do not crosscut well at all because the larger teeth snag the fibers. Being unable to slice due to configuration, and unable to shear due to the wider kerf, they simply jam and tear the wood alternately. This snagging worsens if you attempt crosscutting with progressively coarser ripsaws, or if you use more force. Either way, it's not going to work!

When we are dealing with finer toothed saws (9 to 40ppi), it just so happens that a ripcut pattern cuts very effectively across the grain and with the grain. To explain why this works, instead, the fine teeth shear the fibers at each side of the kerf, gathering them into the gullet. On even finer teeth, it's really the only pattern of any value. This has very significant implications to all your saw sharpening, and actually makes the decision making process very simple:

Small teeth (9 to 40ppi): Always sharpen to a ripcut pattern.

Larger teeth (below 9ppi): Simply choose a ripcut pattern for sawing with the grain, or a fleam tooth pattern for crosscutting.

I have a selection of saws, which is more of a luxury than a necessity.

This is my most aggressive ripsaw. I don't think twice about ripping 2" thick stock with this saw.

Ripsaws

Sharpening the teeth of ripsaws is simply a question of filing the teeth square across, with the saw file held consistently at a particular chosen angle, governing the tooth rake. This angle governs the effectiveness of the tooth. If you want a less aggressive cut, one that takes less effort to push the saw into the cut, simply file the leading face of each tooth, the tooth rake, to a more negative rake.

An aggressive rake is created by filing the saw tooth with a perpendicular front angle—90 degrees to the length of the saw. A less aggressive cut, and standard to most manufacturers' ripsaws, is an 8-degree negative rake. A saw configured like this cuts well, and is about right for a general purpose ripsaw.

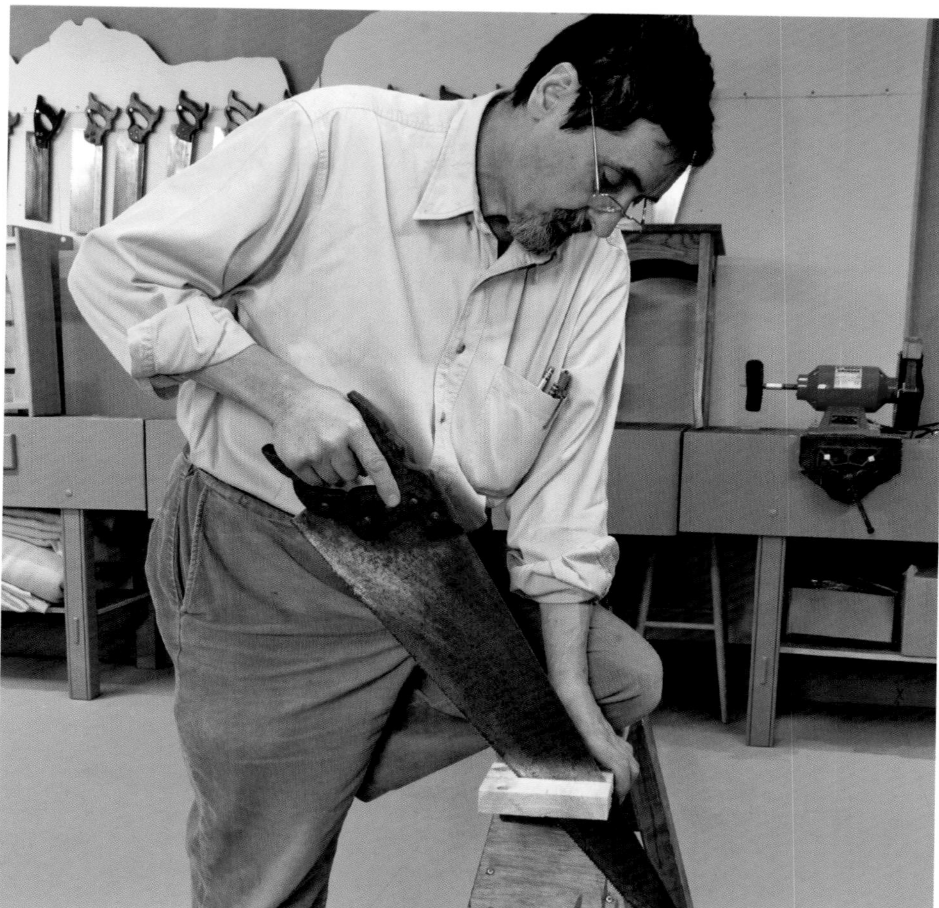

I sharpened this saw for cross cutting. The fleam teeth make short work of any cross cutting required.

Fleam teeth are sharpened at 65 degrees.

> *"We must sharpen crosscut saws to a fleam-tooth pattern"*

Crosscut saws

The crosscut saw has been used ever since the dawn of woodworking. There is one type of dedicated crosscut saw tooth pattern universally accepted as the most efficient and therefore the most dominant. This configuration is known as the fleam-tooth pattern. We use this tooth pattern on coarse crosscut saws for severing trees from their root and boughs and branches from the tree. Typically, a woodsman's saw for this purpose would have coarse teeth of around 1-4ppi.

The same fleam-tooth pattern works well for saws of 4-6ppi, which we use for larger carpentry, framing, crosscutting beams and joists. A size of 8ppi is good for crosscutting thinner panels and boards around ¾" thick.

The tubular cell-growth of a tree means we need teeth with uniquely shaped cutting points that slice crossways through the fibrous strands of grain. Fleam-pattern crosscut saws have diamond-point teeth with a cutting edge along the front and back of each tooth, coming to a pinnacle point. Fleam teeth deliver the beveled edges (as pinnacle points) to the wood in a way that slices two close parallel walls and creates a channel. The saw passes progressively deeper into the cut on both the forward aggressive cut and much less aggressive return strokes. A fleam-pattern crosscut saw requires a little more effort to sharpen than a ripsaw, but the difference in the cutting efficiency on cross-grain fibers is staggering.

The process of sharpening is covered on page 271 of this chapter, but there are some subtle differences for crosscut saws. We sharpen these with the file held level, but instead of passing the file square across and creating chisel teeth, we file at a 65-degree angle.

We file every alternate tooth from one side, working from one end of the saw to the other. Then we turn the saw around and file the opposite teeth at a counter 65 degrees angle. It's this that creates the pinnacle tooth pattern we need for sharpening large crosscut pattern fleam-teeth.

Re-Shaping Saw Teeth

How to vary the rake

The amount of negative rake is reduced as the tooth becomes more aggressive. As with the regular process of sharpening any ripsaw, the file moves square across and level. We change the aggression of a saw tooth pattern by adjusting the orientation of the file in the saw gullet in the following manner:

1. The file becomes an extension of the forefinger, guiding the file in the gullet and then by rotating the wrist either clockwise or counterclockwise slightly, we establish the front pitch of the tooth. This then sets the angle of the file facets in relation to the gullet of the teeth.
2. Rotating the wrist (and file) alters the angle at which the file cuts the front face of one tooth and the back of the adjacent tooth. With ripcut saws, we're only concerned with the front face of the tooth. Pressing the file down in the gullet cuts both the front and back faces of adjacent teeth.

> **TECHNICAL POINTER:** *If a tooth is filed to give it a more aggressive rake, care must be taken not to file the back of the adjacent tooth too heavily, or the adjacent tooth height will be quickly reduced, rendering it unproductive. The result of repeating this error would be a saw that jars in the cut.*

3. By rotating the file even slightly we can lock the hand onto a given pitch and continue sharpening consistently at that pitch. We can easily correct any slippage this way.
4. By keeping one of the file faces almost vertical, we create the aggressive pitch. This is the most aggressive pitch we use in handsaws, including larger tenon saws. We simply rotate the file slightly so that the one wall of the file is now sloping to the 8-degree angle we want.

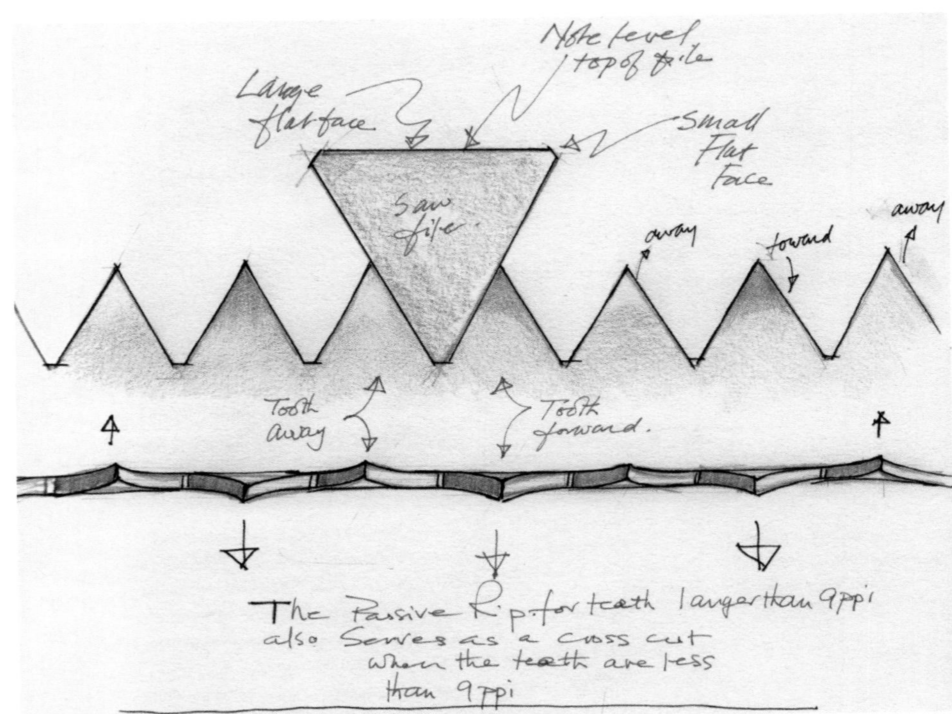

This drawing shows you the symmetry of a passive tooth pattern.

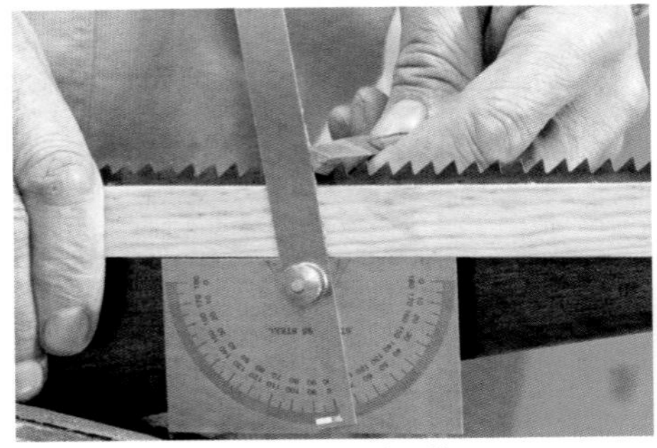

Change the rake by rotating the file…

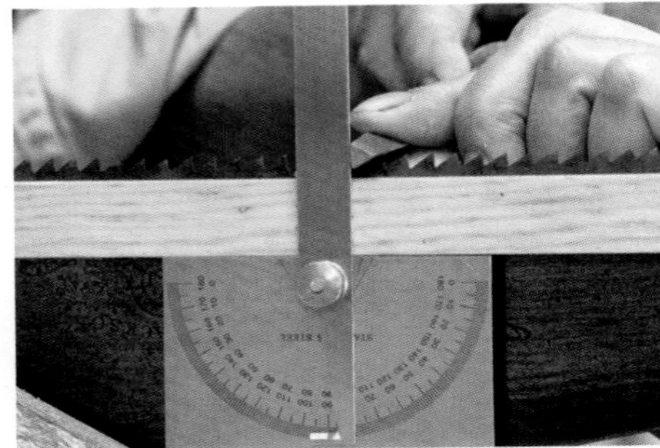

…as shown here.

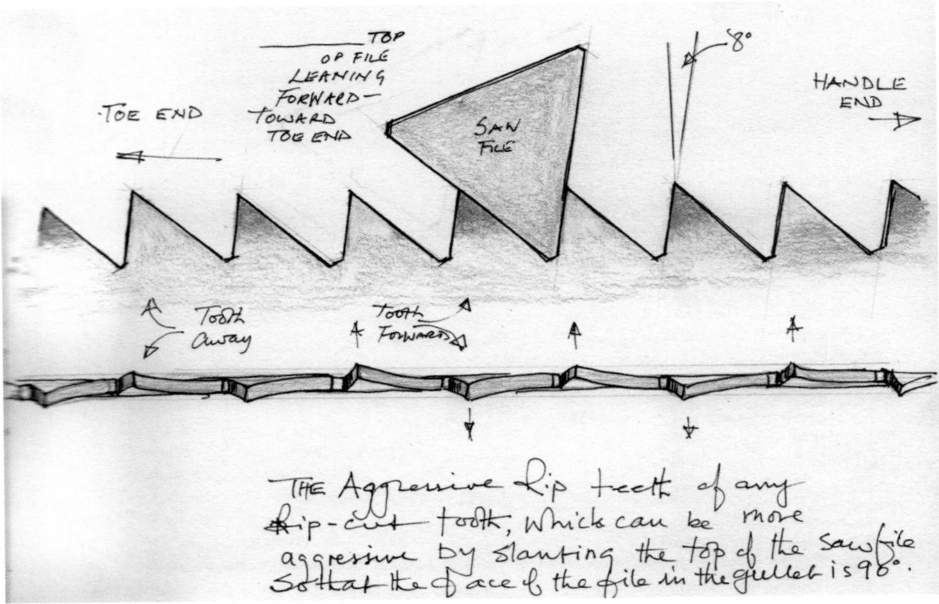

This drawing is from my journal. Notice the gullets are deeper in the top drawing, although the tooth spacing is about the same. The difference is even more visible on page 280.

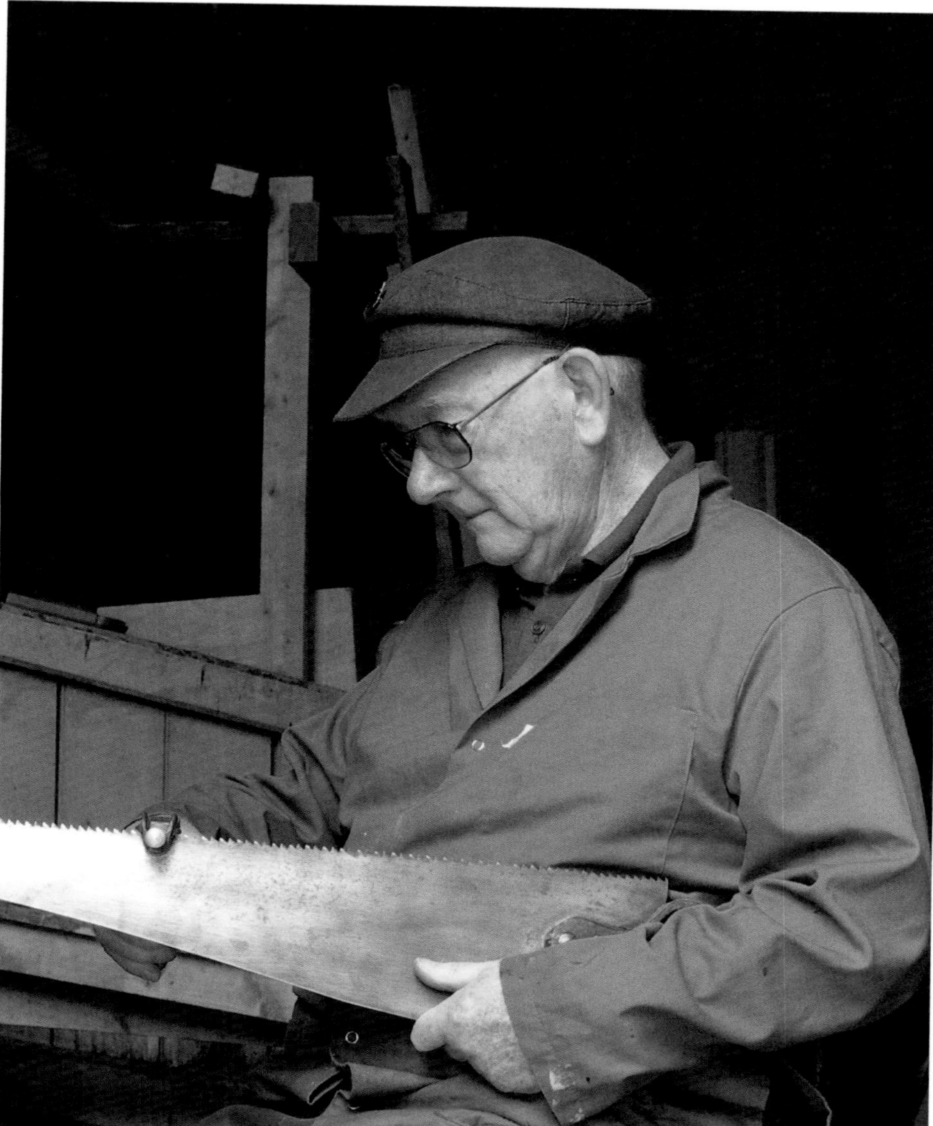

Older craftsmen always set and sharpened their own saws.

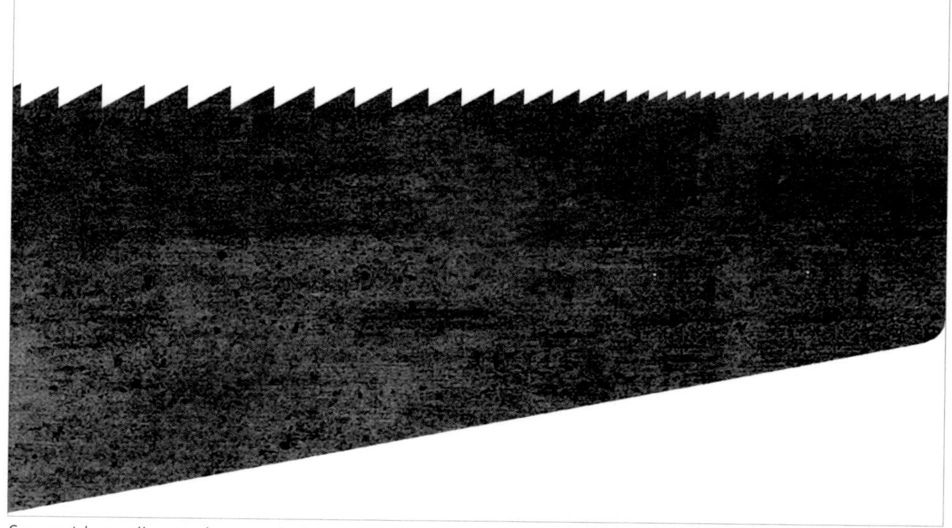

Saws with smaller teeth towards the toe end of the saw are available to buy. They work well but you cannot convert your existing saw into this pattern without a lot of difficulty.

How to cut a progressive pattern

Throughout the centuries, craftsmen and woodsmen have developed methods to improve the ease of starting a saw in the cut. Two distinctly different solutions have emerged over the years. Both use a progressive change in the saw teeth, starting at the toe end and changing progressively into a more standard and regular pattern.

These progressive tooth patterns combine the ease of starting a cut with the efficiency of aggressive sawing. As a rule, I change the configuration of any saw I acquire. The limiting factor for me is a high fineness index of around 16ppi, where the teeth usually start smoothly without snagging, regardless of the configuration.

There are two recognized methods of creating a progressive tooth pattern to a saw.

Progressive change in tooth size

Over the last century, some saw makers introduced a variable tooth size as a pattern for producing and sharpening saws. Progressively increasing the size of the saw teeth—starting with small teeth at the start (toe), gradually increasing the size of each tooth over the first 1-2", and then establishing a regular tooth size along the remaining length—made the saw easy to start and move progressively through the cut.

This pattern works well for sawing, but re-cutting the teeth, general filing, setting and so forth is harder than with conventional pattern saws. You can buy saws with this configuration, but it's not easy to convert your own saw into this type of progressive cut pattern. The existing teeth have to be filed off completely over the section to be altered, leading to an awkward shape to the saw profile and a lot of meticulous and skilled work. A much simpler and more practical way, is to simply change the rake on the fore part of the saw, as described overleaf.

Progressive change in rake

The progressive pattern I teach at The New Legacy School of Woodworking is universally suitable for most saws. For this method, we sharpen the first 1" of teeth at a negative rake of 15 degrees. Then we alter the rake with each tooth over the next 1" by rotating the file incrementally, so that the top face of the file slopes towards the saw tip (toe). Subsequent teeth are sharpened to a more aggressive rake, even to perpendicular (zero negative rake) depending on the general use for the saw. The advantage here is that the number of teeth per inch is not altered and so the operation is very fast. The difference is amazing. This works well for a tenon saw, but for a longer panel saw, sharpen 2" at 15 degrees and then change the rake over the next 2".

Because we are changing the rake progressively, it's best to begin sharpening at the toe end of the saw. Each cut is square across and level from file tip to handle. The procedure is just the same as for the ripsaw sharpening. If you're unfamiliar with changing the rake on the fore part of the saw, a good way to start is by sticking a matchstick or toothpick to one flat face of the saw file. A blob of hot melted glue is a good temporary method, or you could use superglue or tape.

Check the start and finish angle of the matchstick at the start and the end of the progressive section. As long as you work from the toe end and gradually change the angle, you will have a perfectly graduated change in the angle of the leading edges of the teeth.

This method works for saws up to a fineness index of around 16ppi. On really coarse saws, it works just as well and you will be impressed with the results. Changing the rake was commonly used by craftsmen and makes saw starting quick and easy.

"Changing the rake was commonly used by craftsmen and makes saw starting quick and easy."

Note the aggressive teeth gradually become passive towards the toe end of the saw. The most simple method is to gradually deepen the gullets. The tooth points will lower slightly as you progress towards the more passive angle.

When fully supported, you can progress quickly through the wood with an aggressive saw.

I use a much more passive saw for ripping in the vise or the vibration reduces cutting efficiency.

Sharpening your saw for different jobs

Though it's likely that you will purchase one handsaw to start with, realistically it's impractical to change the aggression level of the saw teeth for different jobs. It's obviously best to own an extra saw or two, each dedicated either to more or less aggressive cutting.

I own two ripsaws with different tooth rakes and pick the one best suited to the job in hand. As a good rule of thumb, I choose a very aggressive saw to cut a board where I can saw from above with lots of downward pressure—a 'power-drive' that is uncompromised as far as stability and resistance goes. This works well when a board is too long to go in the vise of the bench, and I must first rip the wood using an overhand method with the board supported on sawhorses. I use my most aggressive ripsaw for this because I can really bear down on the saw and the support board. I can also adjust the angle of the saw's presentation to the wood, from a perpendicular to a low angle, depending on the wood and my preference.

If I am ripcutting a short piece, I can hold it in the bench vise. If I'm working over my head or in some other awkward position, I choose a saw with a less aggressive rake—say 8 degrees. In this case, I need less force and my action is more slow and steady.

Buying new saws can be expensive, but thankfully they are readily available secondhand from different sources. You can usually pick them up for between \$5-\$50 (or £5-£50 in the UK).

Basic saw blade restoration

Most old saws have rusted surfaces. They may also have badly-shaped and dull teeth. If the rust is deeply pitted, you may want to reconsider whether it's worth restoring. The following passages will guide you on sharpening and reshaping the teeth of any saw, but before you begin, remove all rust from the saw. I use abrasive paper. Wet and dry works well. Start with 240 grit and take it progressively to around 600 grit. Finally, apply a wax coat. Any wax works, including clear furniture wax. It doesn't stay on for long. I use a special piece of equipment for applying thin coats of oil—a 4oz tomato can with a folded rag rolled up and tightly coiled to fit into the can. The rag stands ½" above the rim of the can and is subsequently filled with light machine oil.

Re-shaping damaged or worn teeth

Re-shaping teeth eroded through use and neglect is a common task when you buy old saws, but often it's worth the effort. My favorite saws came to me with surface rust and misshapen teeth. If a saw has a large disparity between tooth sizes in adjacent teeth, they must first be shaped until they are of equal size. It may seem daunting at first, but with practice you'll gain confidence and skill and the task is quickly completed.

Make certain before you buy a saw that there are no kinks in it. A bend can be tolerated and even corrected, but I generally avoid bends too. I'm specifically talking about handsaws, not back (tenon type) saws; bends in tenon saws can be straightened.

Carbide paper and soapy water will remove most of the rust with ease.

These teeth are irregular, with some sharper than others. Some restoration is required here.

Keep the file level and take firm, even passes, checking for the glint of light on the flat spots after every pass.

"Start by examining the saw teeth to see if they have been properly maintained"

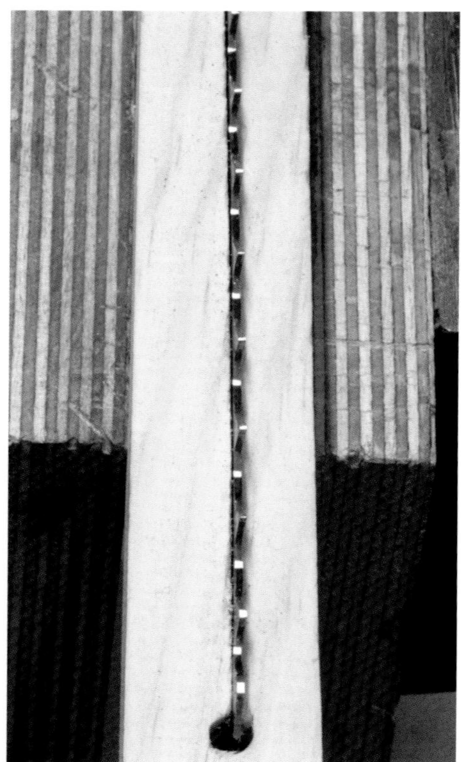

Look at the flat spots, these teeth were very uneven.

Jointing (leveling or topping) the saw

Nothing affects the performance of a saw more than uneven levels in the tooth line. Without correction, the problem only worsens. In general, both well-used and abused saws can develop inconsistent tooth patterns. When this becomes extreme, the saw jars severely in the cut and stops it from cutting, or creates uneven, poorly controlled cutting. To correct this problem you must level the teeth to create either a straight or breasted (convex) cutting line of teeth. We call this process jointing (topping, UK) the teeth.

Start by examining the saw teeth to see if they have been properly maintained. If they have, sight along the teeth from handle to toe to see if the teeth are in an even level line... After several years of sharpening, saw teeth tend to wear more in the mid-section. If it's hollow it must be corrected and filed straight by jointing. This is also true if the sight line undulates. Everyday tooth sharpening will never correct this, but jointing will take care of even the most problematic and un-even teeth.

To joint a saw, take a fine single-cut 10" mill file and level the teeth, filing along the length of the saw on top of the teeth points. Lay your file flat on the teeth and straddle the file with the palm of your dominant hand, using your fingertips on each side of the saw to guide the file evenly along the tops. Place the heel of your other hand on the handle end of the file and, with an even, light pressure, push the file positively along the tops of the teeth from saw heel to toe. Examine the tips of the teeth to ensure they have tiny flats at the top. You may find several teeth without flat tops, or just an occasional tooth. If this happens, repeat the filing until all the teeth have flat spots.

Occasionally, saws lose a tooth. It's not necessary to joint all the teeth of the saw down to salvage a tooth or two. Subsequent sharpening will restore the missing tooth over a period of time. When blocks of teeth are missing, all the teeth must be removed and re-cut into the new edge. Generally, jointing always takes place before any sharpening or shaping, and I only use this procedure when I encounter badly shaped, uneven teeth. The flats of the teeth become the registering line to guide subsequent shaping and sharpening of the teeth. Remove the handle from the file so that it passes unhindered along the teeth. Successive passes may be necessary to level the teeth. Provided the disparity of height is not too great, stop when the first pinpoint of light shines from the lowest tooth (ignore any missing teeth). Remember, jointing takes place before shaping.

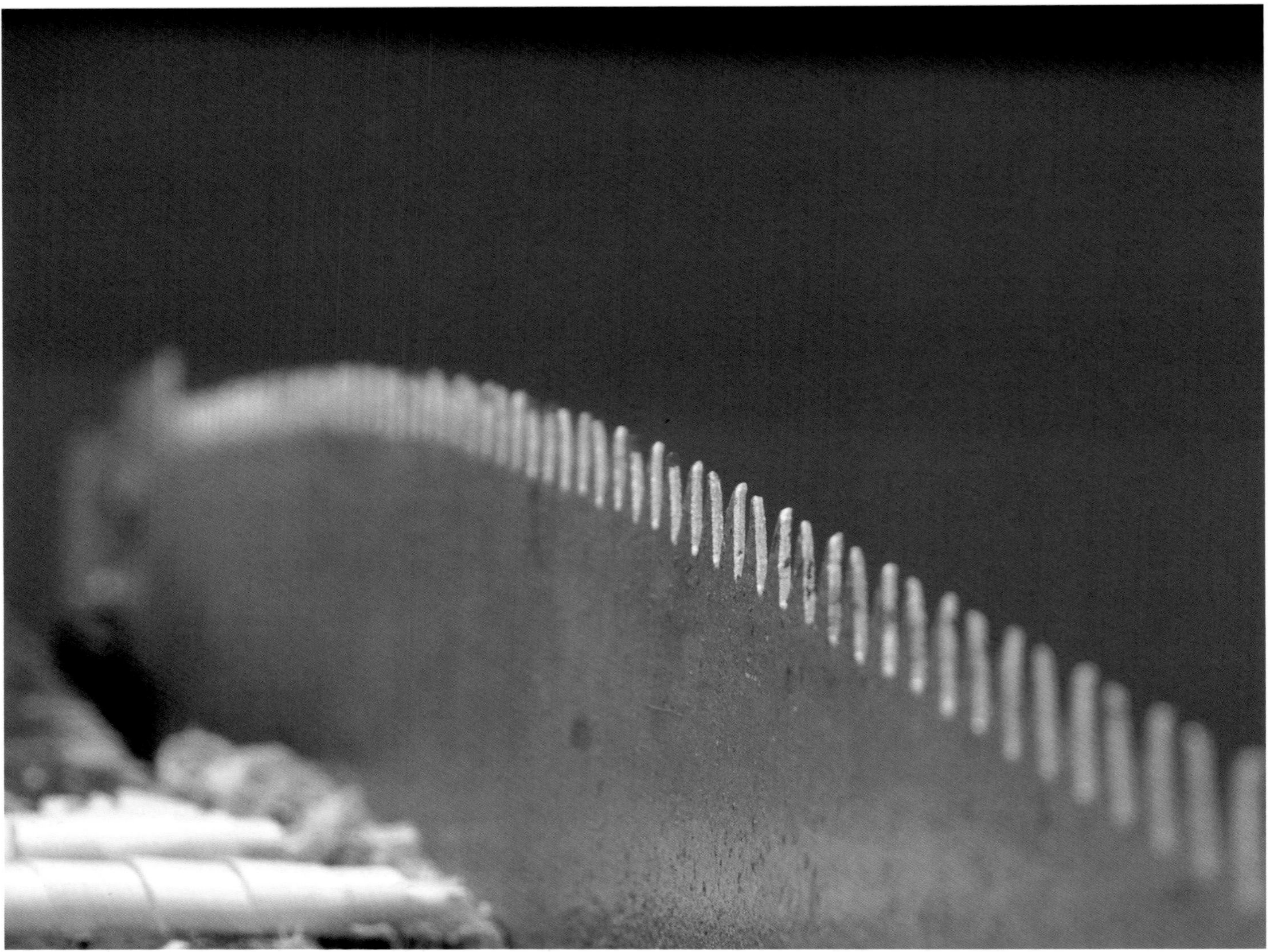

This is a fine example of breasting, shown here on a large toothed ripsaw.

Breasting

Some saws are convex. This can be accidental, but it can also be intentional. Saws are sometimes 'breasted', meaning cut to a slightly convex form along the length of the saw, to give better cutting power. This was once quite usual on long handsaws used for ripping and allowed for a full power-stroke in overhand ripping on the sawhorses. A breasted saw presents the latter, heel teeth of the saw at the right angle of cut and transfers the effort from the arm and shoulder effectively throughout the whole cut. In contrast, a badly hollowed saw blade has a tendency to lift out of the cut, putting more strain on the wrist through attempting to control this counter productive motion. The main application for a breasted shape is for larger saws, where high speed, productive force is of paramount importance.

For most of your saws, a dead straight profile works best, especially for all classes of tenon saws.

The flat spots are your reference point.

Shaping and sharpening after jointing or breasting

After jointing or breasting, the saw teeth will always need some shaping afterwards. This becomes a combined process solving both sharpening and shaping in one process. The most important indicator after filing the tops of the teeth, is the size of the flat spot on the filed tooth point. This flat spot tells you exactly how much steel to file off to form level, even teeth. On very low teeth, there may be no flat spot whatsoever, as the flat file has not touched the top of the tooth.

1. As a general rule, work from one end of the saw, and work on each tooth in turn, never filing more than half of the flat spot off from any one side. This is absolutely critical. At this stage, you are more lowering the gullets, than working on the actual teeth.
2. Make sure you leave the faintest whisker of a flat spot on top of every tooth. This faintly reflective line is similar to a pencil line when you are cutting a dovetail. It is an absolute reference point.
3. Work this way along the whole saw.
4. Once you have completed the first pass, taking care to leave your reference lines at the dead center of the saw tooth, you are ready to form the sharp pinnacles.
5. To do this, start from one end and take a full even pass with your file, as you would normally. To sharpen a fleam tooth crosscut saw, skip every other tooth and reverse the blade for the other teeth. For ripcut saws, sharpen all from one side only. This last step completely removes your reference lines, but gives you a super sharp and dead straight tooth line.

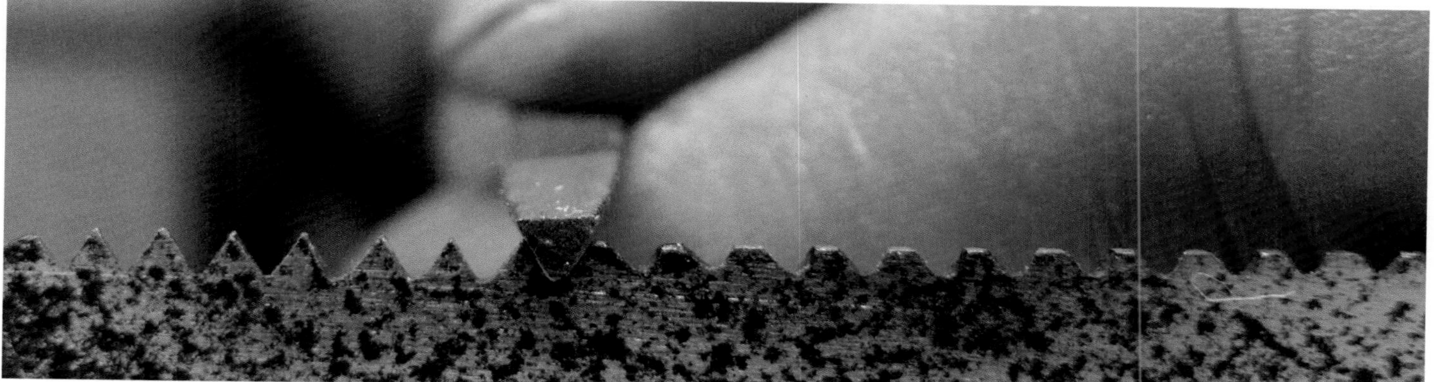

Master these techniques, and you can bring good, old saws, back to life.

Conclusion

These corrective restoration patterns develop skill and understanding so that, as you develop consistency and confidence, your saw restoration becomes an enjoyable task. And once it's done, you might never need to do it again on the same saw. When a saw has well-shaped teeth, maintaining the shape of each tooth is simply a matter of pushing the saw file through each gullet evenly, letting the weight of your hand alone provide enough pressure to cut effectively. Simple.

There is very little more to learn about sharpening and maintaining your saws now. The speed and efficiency with which you master these skills depends entirely on practice, perseverance and careful attention to detail. Once you acquire a good pair of rip and crosscut saws (7ppi), your general purpose panel saw (10ppi) and a reasonable tenon saw (14ppi), you will never buy another plastic handled, disposable saw again. Take pride in your efforts, and enjoy the rewards of total self sufficiency, as artisans have for centuries.

16 Sharpening scrapers

The scraper has been used for centuries to create some of the finest handwork in all areas of woodworking. We rely on this simple tool to refine any wood surface. A scraper will level and smooth the most difficult gnarly and knotty wood grains and any opposing grain directions, where the sharpest of finely set planes, would simply tear out the surface fibres. In surfacing and levelling work, scrapers have no equal.

Flattening a small table top using the No.80 cabinet scraper

"It is in fact, a highly refined, surgically sharp cutting edge..."

Scrapers are radically misnamed in that they never scrape and nor are they ever used for 'scraping'. Only when you examine the fine cutting edge and understand how this delicate edge is formed, can you comprehend its real value. Not only do they never 'scrape' the wood, but what is often referred to as a burr along the cutting edge, has not the slightest similarity to any kind of ragged burr type edge.

It is in fact, a highly refined, surgically sharp cutting edge, infinitely controllable and supremely versatile. It is definitely not the ragged edge suggested by the word 'burr'. I refer to the 'burr' as the 'cutting edge', or 'turned edge', for the purposes of clarity. Even the sharpening process, often referred to as 'raising the burr', could not be named any more inappropriately.

The perpetuation of these misconceptions has led to a sense of perceived elitism, where the realms of scraper use have been elevated beyond the reach of supposedly average, everyday woodworkers. The following pages debunk the myths and mystery through practical hands-on teaching. Scrapers are simple to sharpen, easy to use, and so versatile that I ensure all my students master the fundamentals within the first few days of enrolling on the course.

Two types of scraper

I've used two types of scraper for more than forty years. Both types can be sharpened in minutes using similar methods. Each type of scraper, however, is sharpened in its own distinctive manner.

- One has no handles or holder, and comprises a single piece of thin plate steel, and is known as the **bench scraper** or **card scraper.** The bench or card scraper is the simplest of all woodworking tools. It has no working parts and is made from a single piece of thin plate steel, around .032" thick. We usually use this scraper more for fine surface shaving, normally on relatively small, localized surfaces.
- The other type of scraper is best known as the **cabinet scraper**, further identified as a **No.80 scraper**, following a numbering system established by Stanley Tools. The cutting action is the same as the bench scraper, but the cutting edge is guided by a flat-bottomed, cast-steel frame, with side handles similar to the spokeshave...

Simple as they are, these tools bring the surface of even the most wildly configured wood grain to a glassy smooth finish. They are absolutely not to be confused with scrapers used for paint removal. Our scrapers are, in contrast, exceptionally fine and precise hand tools for furniture making, instrument making, and many other woodworking disciplines.

The bench or card scraper is highly versatile.

The cabinet scraper will create a glassy smooth finish on large areas with ease.

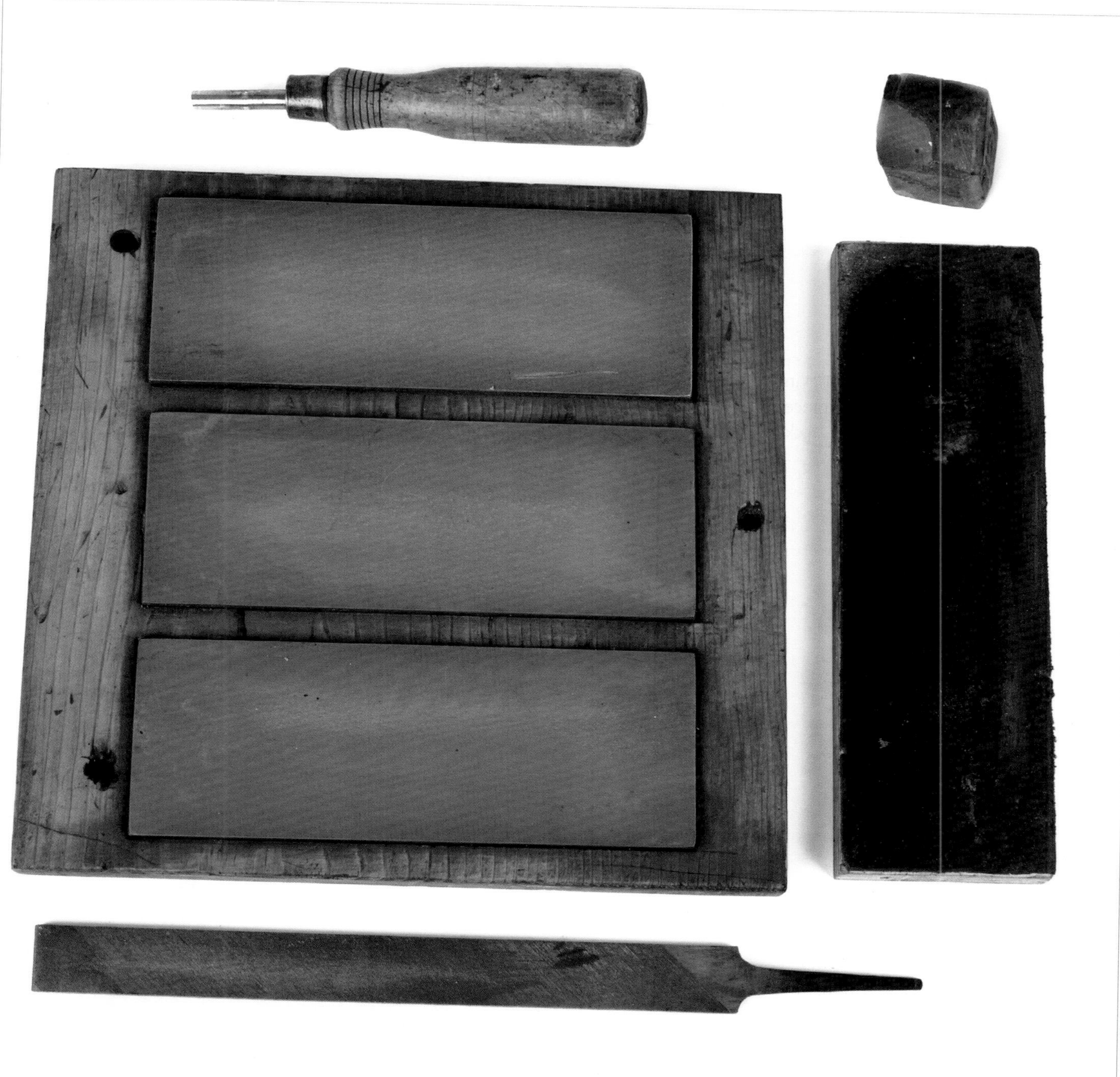

The burnisher, top, is only used for sharpening scrapers, but the other items are multi purpose.

Sharpening equipment

You generally only need these items from your sharpening kit to develop a keen cutting edge:

- A flat, single-cut, 10" mill file.
- Diamond sharpening plates.
- The leather strop block, charged with 15,000 grit buffing compound.
- A round, oval or triangular burnisher. I use a burnisher because the steel is uniformly harder than the scraper blade. You can also use a screwdriver, which is usually hard enough to act as a burnisher.

Bench scrapers

These scrapers vary in size, thickness and shape. Rectangular is the most common shape, but different shapes are also available. I cut my own semi-elliptical, round and multi-shaped scrapers for hollowed work such as bowls, spoons and the arc of coved moldings, but these can be purchased in readymade curved sets.

Due to the simplicity of design, this type of scraper is infinitely controllable by using a combination of hand and eye coordination. Depending on how it is sharpened and used, it can produce shavings of much less than one-thousandth of an inch thick when required. The thickness of shavings produced is governed by:

- The angle of presentation.
- The size of the turned edge.
- The amount of pressure applied.
- The curvature applied to deliberately focus the cutting area. (Straight 'card' shaped only).

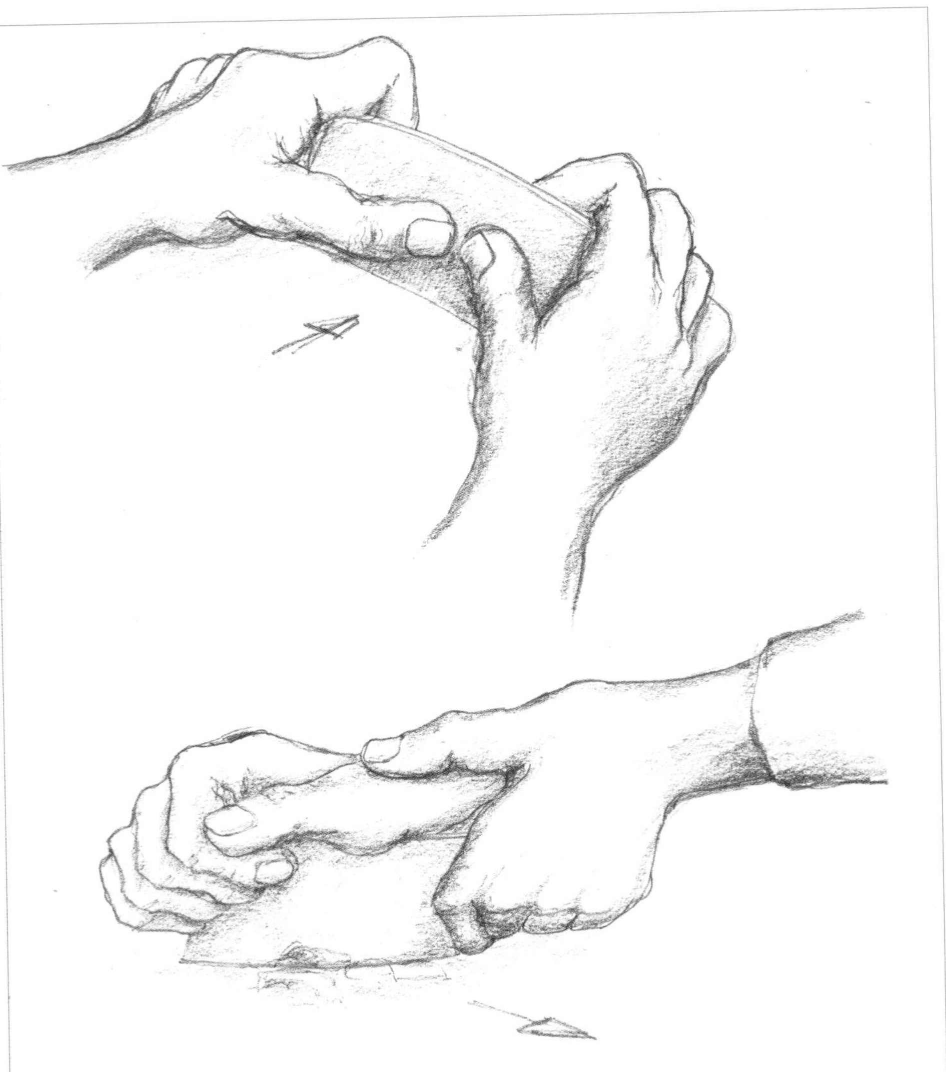

There are many ways to hold and use a card scraper. They may be pulled or pushed, changing the angle as required.

Sharpening bench scrapers

The structure of the cutting edge is similar to a sharp and well refined plane iron, in that two polished edges intersect. However, the edge is formed by a process known in the metal working industry as 'cold working'. Using pressure but no heat, the steel edge is 'worked' to form a cusp, similar in section to half a crescent. The pressure is provided by a hardened steel tool known as a burnisher. When using the burnisher, the crystal structure of the sharp 90 degree edge is subjected to extremely high pressures, similar to the action of an hydraulic press in a steel working factory. The concentrated forces cause the steel to deform and flow into the new cusp shape, critical for efficient shaving.

Terminology

There are four stages to sharpening a bench scraper, and I will describe each one in turn:

FILE: A single cut file is used to completely remove the turned edge. The sharp cusp, after repeated use, becomes blunt and is in a way, disposable. A file will quickly restore a new square edge.

HONE: From your knowledge of edge tool sharpening, you will recognize this as a refinement process, where the new edge is reduced to a flat and relatively smooth surface.

BURNISH TO CONSOLIDATE: This term refers to the first part of the burnishing process. The hard steel of the burnisher is used to actually compress and deform the microscopic undulations and scratches in the surfaces left by the honing process. This is a form of 'cold working' where the steel of the scraper edge, under immense pressure, behaves like window putty and is 'stroked' smooth. This actually produces an extremely polished surface, impossible to relate to any grit size.

BURNISH TO TURN THE EDGE: This step forms the microscopic cusp that shaves with precision. It follows directly on from the process of consolidation and is effected by slowly raising the angle of the burnisher, concentrating the force on the sharpened edge with every pass of the burnisher.

All bench scrapers are sharpened, by filing and honing, and then burnishing to consolidate and turn the steel to form a cutting edge. I will now explain the practical method to show you how to attain a good, working edge. Although there are special devices for sharpening scrapers, I prefer hand methods because of their speed and versatility. I can form an edge for an aggressive or fine cut, by feel, in as little as three minutes.

New scrapers come with cleanly cut square edges, but they are not honed or burnished ready for forming the edge. For simplicity, we will assume your scraper is used. If it's new, skip the first step.

1. File both long edges of the scraper square to the large flat face using the 10" mill file. This removes the mushroomed, cusp shaped edge from any previous sharpenings. Start at one end and, keeping the file square, file a continuous stroke from one end to the other using three or four stokes until you have created a straight clean edge.
2. Filing the edges square leaves a rough burr that must be removed before we can refine the edge any further. Grind the edges on a 250 grit stone as the second stage in refining the edges. Hold the scraper upright and move the edge back and forth until any file marks are removed. Take care to minimize any sideways rocking because this will round over the edge and make it difficult to form the fine cutting edge you need.

TOP TIP: *If you have difficulty keeping the scraper perpendicular, place a wooden block of 1½" stock on top of the sharpening plate and clutch the two together. This will serve as a guide to press the scraper against as you hone the edge back and forth.*

File the edges square to remove the blunt edge.

Use the 10 inch mill file held at 90 degrees.

Refine the 90 degree edges.

Take care as the corners become refined and sharp.

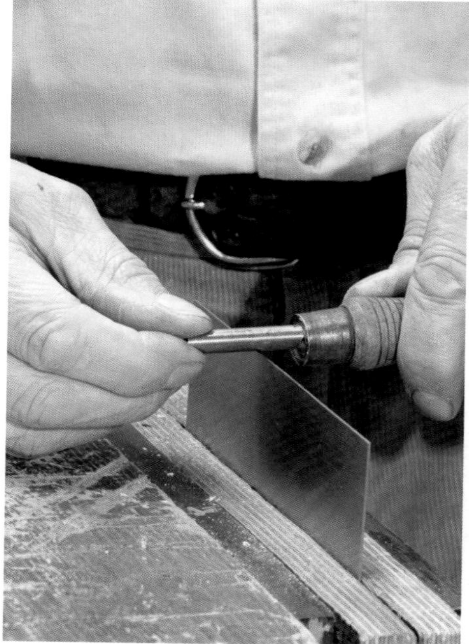
Consolidation is a form of high level polishing.

You can hold it in the vise or in one hand.

3. Further refine the edges on a 1200 grit stone, taking care with the newly formed sharp corners.
4. Burnishing is a two step process. Firstly, hold the scraper using a cloth to protect your hands and cushion the scraper. Hold it by one end, standing it upright with the opposite end braced against the bench. Then place the burnisher square across the edge and swiftly pull the burnisher upwards along the long edge several times. Make sure to keep it square with each stroke. This consolidates the steel, polishing the surface as previously described.
5. After several heavy passes, pressing firmly against the edge each time, begin to alter the angle of the burnisher with each stroke, aiming for about 10 degrees. This will 'turn' the consolidated edge to form a cusp, similar to a hook in cross section. Now reverse the scraper, return the burnisher back to the 90-degree position and work from square to 10 degrees on the opposite corner of the same edge. This puts a sharp cusp on both sides of the edge, similar to a 'T' shape.

TOP TIP: *You can also secure the scraper in the vise with the edge you plan to work on, uppermost. Then follow the same procedure.*

TOP TIP: *On really fine work, you may want to simply use the first level consolidation and turn only a small 2-degree edge. This works well on refined work such as thin veneers and inlay work, marquetry, violin making and so on.*

I would recommend using a cabinet scraper to finish all large, flat, hardwood surfaces.

Cabinet scrapers

Cabinet scrapers are made with a single-piece cast-iron body, which holds the blade at a fixed angle of approximately 70 degrees; similar to a plane or spokeshave, but at a much steeper pitch. Unlike a plane or spokeshave, the cutting blade of the cabinet scraper is housed in the cast-iron body in a forward leaning presentation, offering the razor-sharp, hooked edge as if dragging the hooked cutting edge over and into the surface of the wood—very different to a bench plane… As the cabinet scraper is pushed over the surface, the ultra-sharp edge actually shaves off fine layers of wood cells, curling them over with virtually no lifting to tear off the wood grain. This results in a pristine surface.

Cabinet scrapers offer the cutting edge of the blade at an extremely low angle to the wood's surface. The metal-cast body enables you to use much greater force on the forward thrust to progress each cutting motion and give consistent angle presentation every time. Because of the position of the handles, the thumbs are positioned right at the base on either side of the blade area. This means the force of the stroke is directly in line with the cutting edge, making the tool highly effective. Though this type of scraper is ideal for dense-grained hardwoods, it's not always so versatile on softer woods such as spruce, pine, basswood and fir. On most No.80 type scrapers, the cutting iron is ground at 45 degrees along both of the long edges and these cutting edges are then honed and burnished to a high polish following the same 45-degree angle.

Many people find it difficult to sharpen scrapers at first because the methods are unusual. The term scrapers suggests a pulling or dragging action, rather than the broad and often skewed slicing cut that really takes place on a pushing motion. The only time the tool truly scrapes is when its cutting edge becomes dull and it leaves powdery, fibrous scrapings rather than curly shavings.

Pinch up the retaining bar screws.

Make sure the cutting iron is just level with the sole.

Fully tighten the retaining bar screws.

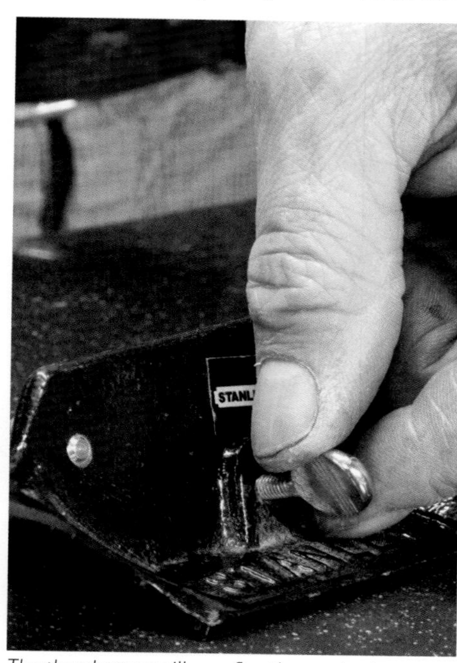

The thumbscrew will now flex the cutting iron.

Setting the cutting iron:

With the cutting iron removed, withdraw the thumbscrew until it no longer protrudes past the inside face of the scraper body. Now install the cutting iron and pinch up the screws, which hold the retaining bar, finger tight, while holding the retaining bar, blade and scraper body together with the other hand. Place the assembled scraper, sole-down, on a flat surface and carefully press the blade into the mouth so that it lies dead flush with the sole across its entire length. Tighten the two setscrews to clamp the blade securely and then turn the thumbscrew to flex the cutting edge into the mouth opening. A quarter turn should be enough to test. Adjust the depth of cut by turning the thumb screw as needed.

Sharpening cabinet scrapers

To sharpen the cabinet scraper you must carry out the same basic steps of filing, honing, burnishing and turning the edge. However, instead of this edge being square and then turned, we first create a 45-degree bevel, similar to a plane bevel.

Note: The cutting irons are double sided and I usually sharpen up both at the same time, but this is just a preference.

1. Use the 10" mill file to file along the edge of the scraper at 45 degrees to the larger flat face. This removes the previously formed bevel to establish a fresh edge. Keeping the file angled at about 45 degrees, file a continuous stroke from one end to the other, three or four times until you achieve a flat, inclined surface. I generally check my filing angle to maintain a close 45-degree bevel.

   TOP TIP: *It's also a good idea to plane a 45-degree edge on a ¾" piece of wood to clamp the blade against and hold in the vise. Use this to guide the file so that you can cut a very precise 45-degree angle. This will guide the file as you define the bevel.*

2. Filing the edge at 45 degrees creates a rough burr on the out-filed edge. This must be removed before you can refine the beveled edge further. The simplest way is to continue refining the bevel edge, but now on the sharpening stone. Hold the scraper at 45 degrees and follow the established bevel as you move the edge back and forth along the stone until any file marks are removed. Take care to minimize any rocking as this will only round the bevel and make it more difficult to form the razor edge you need.

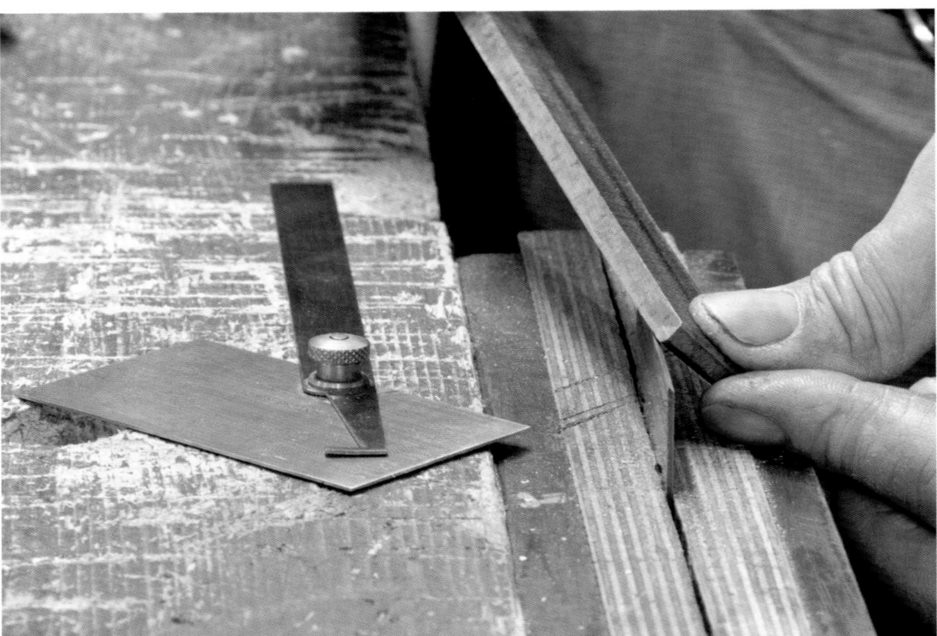

File the edges square to remove the blunt edge.

Refine the edge with successive grades of abrasive.

Polish the flat face on the strop.

Consolidate the back of the cutting edge.

Consolidate the chamfered edge and gradually form the cusp shaped cutting edge.

3. Place the scraper on its side on the 15,000 grit strop and pull the flat face (the face with the burr) of the blade away from the cutting edge until the burr is removed. Don't pull the edge towards the strop or it will dig in and shred the flat leather. Take care not to lift the scraper which will round the flat face along the edge.
4. We must now consolidate the steel along the cutting edge. Place the cutting iron on the edge of the benchtop and draw the burnisher firmly back and forth several times along the flat face adjacent to the bevel. Flip the iron over and do the same on the opposite face.

TOP TIP: *If you have difficulty keeping the scraper at 45 degrees, clamp the 45-degree guide you used for filing on the bevel side of the blade. Then use the sharpening plate like a file and follow the rake of the block guide as you hone back and forth. At this point the edge needs no further refining beyond 1,200 grit.*

5. Now we use the burnisher to consolidate and burnish the bevel at 45 degrees. Use the vise, because the smaller blade is difficult to burnish while holding it as you did with the bench scraper. By consolidating the steel and burnishing the edge, you polish the surface at the same time. After several heavy strokes taken while pressing firmly against the bevel, begin to alter the pitch of the burnisher with each stroke, aiming for a final change in angle of about 10-15 degrees. This will 'turn' the consolidated bevel to form a hooked edge.
6. Follow the procedure for setting the cutting iron (page 295).

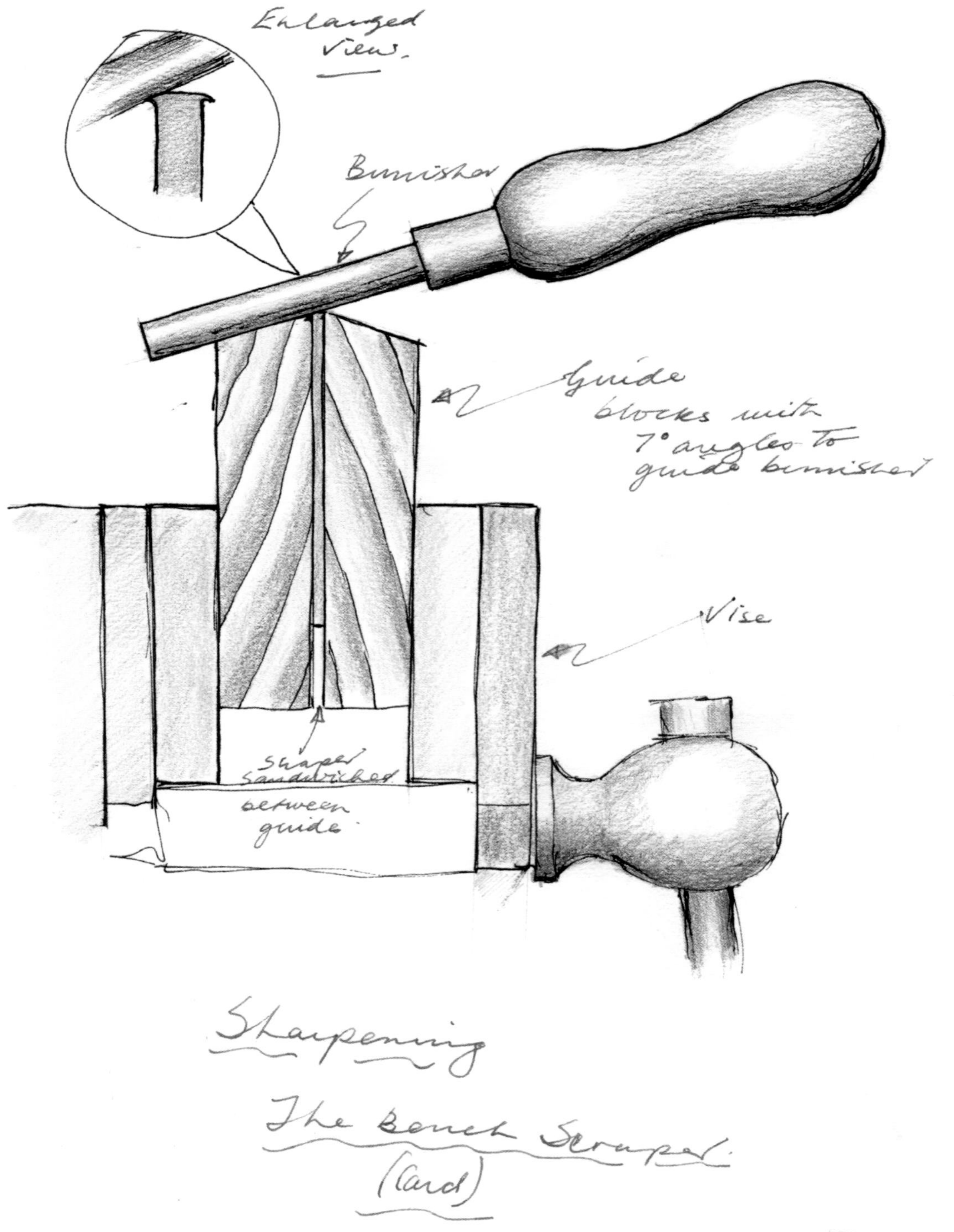

This guide can help you to get consistent results when sharpening your card scraper.

Using burnishing guides

A common problem in sharpening scrapers is turning the bevel too far and fracturing the fragile cutting edge. To prevent it, use the guide block clamped to the blade to allow full access to the bevel. This provides a very definitive starting reference for the burnisher to ride along. After a few successive passes the cutting edge will begin to form.

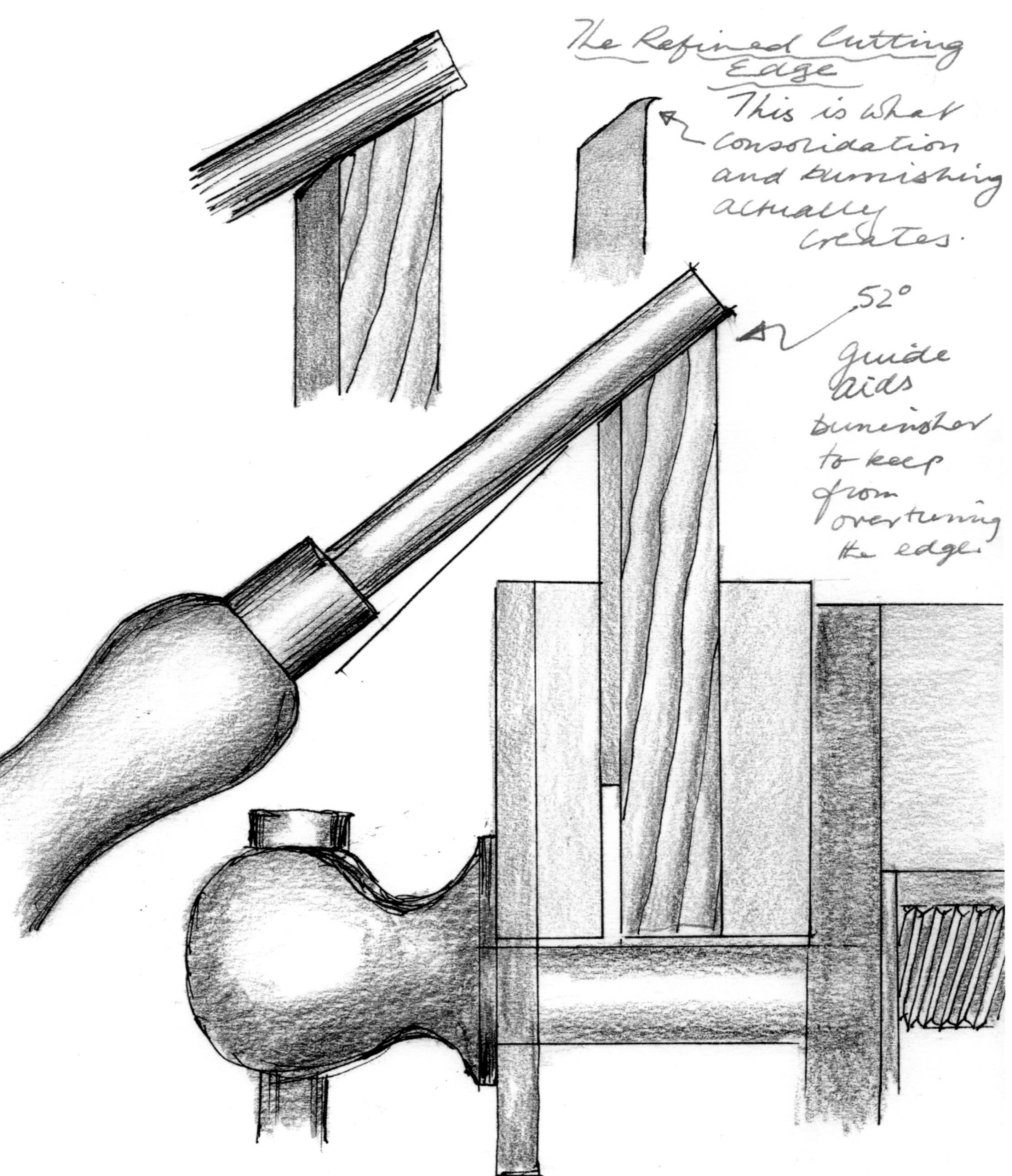

The Refined Cutting Edge
This is what consolidation and burnishing actually creates.
52°
guide aids burnisher to keep from overturning the edge

Guides are no substitute for skill but I devised this guide to help you to learn to sharpen your cabinet scraper. The guide piece is 52 degrees and so the burnisher stops when the edge is turned 7 degrees from the 45 degree bevel.

Cabinet scrapers: Questions & Answers

Question 1

My scraper judders across the surface of the wood instead of cutting. What causes this problem and how do I resolve it?

Answer 1: The most common cause of all is that the blade is housed in the scraper upside down (bevel facing down).

Solution 1: *Disengage the cutting iron and flip it over so that the bevel of the iron faces upwards and towards the back of the scraper. The back of the scraper is where the thumbscrew is located.*

Answer 2: A misaligned blade, is another common cause, but it could also be the grain of the wood or lack of confidence on the part of the user. Technique plays an important part too, so here are likely causes with suggested solutions.

Possible cause 2: Too much cutting iron protruding through the mouth of the scraper sole.

Solution 2: *Follow the instructions outlined on page 295 for correctly setting the cutting iron.*

Possible cause 3: Soft grain fibers compress under the pressure of the sole just ahead of the cutting edge and the cutting edge misses the surface fibers.

Solution 3a: *Try using the scraper at an oblique angle and with a lighter but still firm pressure. Some wood fibers rather than cutting and slicing cleanly will compress at the very edge and then bulge up behind the cutting edge. Remember also that softer less dense woods will often not cut with scrapers.*

Solution 3b: *Try using the scraper in the opposite direction.*

Possible cause 4: A gap at the leading edge allows flex between the blade and the body because of an uneven casting in the bed of the scraper body.

Solution 4: *Flatten the bed of the scraper using a flat file, abrasive paper or a rotary grinding disc.*

Possible cause 5: A misaligned cutting iron causes thicker shavings on one side of the scraper than the other.

Solution 5: *See page 295 for setting the cutting iron.*

Question 2

I get no shaving at all from my scraper. What causes this and how do I fix it?

Possible cause 1: Your cutting iron is set too shallow.

Solution 1: *Turn the cutting iron adjustment thumbscrew until the cutting edge barely catches the surface of the wood. If it still doesn't catch, see instructions for setting the cutting iron above (page 295).*

Possible cause 2: The board has a hollow section.

Solution 2: *Scrape the high points first until the cutting iron reaches the lowest sections of the board.*

Possible cause 3: Dull scraper blades, which glide and slide rather than cut and shave.

Solution 3: *Sharpen the scraper iron.*

Possible cause 4: The edge of the cutting iron is turned too much, causing the rounded bevel to ride the wood.

Solution 4: *Re-establish the 45 degrees ground bevel and hone, burnish and turn the edge as shown on pages 296 and 297.*

Question 3

My shavings are thicker on one side of the scraper than the other. How do I correct this?

Answer: This is quite common, even for experienced woodworkers. Resolving the problem is usually quick, provided you know where to look.

Possible cause 1: The cutting edge might not be lying perfectly parallel to the sole of the scraper.

Solution 1: *Follow the procedure outlined on page 295.*

Possible cause 2: You're applying uneven hand and arm pressure on the scraper handles.

Solution 2: *Even out your grip and keep a fairly rigid pressure. Try to correct the tendency to lean by feeling for the pressure you use and centralizing your scraper evenly on the wood, especially when scraping narrower edges and surfaces. Develop sensitivity through practice.*

Possible cause 3: Part of your scraper iron is dull.

Solution 3: *Check the cutting edge for sharpness and sharpen as necessary.*

Possible cause 4: The wood's surface is highly irregular and the scraper reaches only part of the surface of the wood.

Solution 4: *Surface scrape all the high spots until level with the lowest area.*

Question 4

My scraper leaves undulations and other marks that resemble chatter marks after I have finished scraping a surface. Why?

Answer: There are many causes for this. All too often woodworkers use the generic term 'chatter' to describe such surfacing problems. In most cases, the culprit is actually stammer, jarring, bouncing, shocking or scudding. Chatter is a fairly specific and a common phenomenon with scrapers because there is some degree of flex in the thin blade.

Possible cause 1: The most common cause is having the cutting iron protrude too far through the mouth of the scraper. This extra leverage allows a consistent series of close chatter marks to occur.

Solution 1: *Check the depth of the cutting iron through the sole and adjust following instructions on page 295.*

Possible cause 2: Timidity when scraping.

Solution 2: *You must gain greater confidence when presenting the scraper to the surface, and then use enough upper body force to make the cut. Any faltering will result in stammer. Practice to gain experience and increase your confidence.*

Possible cause 3: Insufficient pressure on the cutting iron from the thumbscrew.

Solution 3: *Apply more pressure by turning the thumbscrew at the back of the scraper. You may need to readjust the depth of cut following Solution 2 to Question 1 above.*

Possible cause 4: The retaining bar is loose.

Solution 4: *Loosen the thumbscrew and retighten the setscrews at the ends of the retaining bar. You may need to follow the steps on page 295, a procedure which should become second nature.*

Possible cause 5: The scraper cutting iron is assembled in the scraper upside down (bevel down).

Solution 5: *For full instructions on setting the blade correctly see page 295.*

Possible cause 6: Unevenness in the body casting of the scraper causes inconsistent support or pressure between the body of the scraper and the cutting iron.

Solution 6: *Flatten the bed of the scraper with a flat file, abrasive paper or grinding disc so that the whole cutting iron closely fits to the bed of the scraper.*

Possible cause 7: Shavings have become jammed in the throat of the scraper causing skips and jumps.

Solution 7: *Remove any shavings from the throat and check for jamming. This often necessitates removing the iron, so remove the blade, clear any shavings and follow the procedure outlined on page 295 to replace the blade. It's best not to use a knife or metal point as this can damage the fragile edge.*

Possible cause 8: The wood grain is too awkward and difficult to scrape. This is extremely rare on dense grained hardwoods but often occurs on softer woods.

Solution 8: *Some woods just will not scrape because they are too soft, no matter how good you are or the scraper is. If you find yourself in this position, I suggest careful and light sanding instead.*

Possible cause 9: The cutting iron is dull.

Solution 9: *Sharpen the iron.*

Possible cause 10: You're holding the scraper too limply when scraping.

Solution 10: *Grip it more firmly, moving the scraper into the cut while at the same time feeling for the right amount of pressure.*

17 Sharpening auger bits

Auger bits evolved through a series of slow but steady changes. Over the course of some 200 years, blacksmiths produced bits and augers of many different shapes, sizes and designs. Some of these designs have never been surpassed and yet are no longer made. This evolution did however provide us with the twisted auger bit, which allows us to bore holes to any length, with the only restriction being the length of the bit. These early developments prefaced the bits we now use in electric drills and drill-drivers. The auger bits made to the Irwin and Jennings patterns became standard. Thirteen bits in a complete set, increasing in size from ¼" to 1", in $\frac{1}{16}$" increments, will cater for most modern woodworking needs.

"Some of these designs have never been surpassed..."

When combined with the swing brace, these bits are infinitely controllable by hand power alone, provided that you keep them well maintained and sharp.

Cutting Efficiency

Efficient cutting with this type of bit relies on three aspects of the cutter's geometry:

The 'spur' point, which defines the cutting diameter, must be sharp to allow it to slice through multi directional wood fibers with ease. Sharpness alone however, is not enough for efficient cutting.

Cutting Diameter: The spur cutter is formed with the outside edge in line with the cylindrical shape of the main body of the bit. The path that the spur cuts along must be the full width of the bit otherwise the fibers may be sliced cleanly, but the auger will bind and jam as the main body of the auger is forced into a hole too small to allow the bit to continue to cut. For the spur cutting edge to work effectively it must be sharp, but also it must be sharpened so that the cutting edge is perfectly aligned with the outside diameter of the bit. This is only possible if the spur edge is sharpened from the inside face only.

The secondary cutters, located between the spur points and the central conical thread known as the snail, must also be very sharp. The action of these cutters is different to the slicing action of the spurs. These rotating chisel-shaped cutters actually slice the waste wood in a paring motion, which then lifts away the waste from the cutting face by the helical twist in the main body of the auger bit.

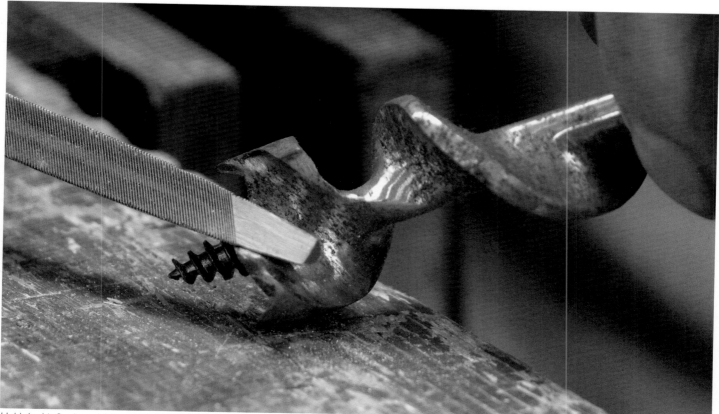

Hold the bit firmly and follow the bevel of the secondary cutter.

Sharpening Method

Larger auger bits are more easily filed than smaller augers because you have more room to access the cutting edges.

Secondary Cutters:

I use a small triangular saw file and hold the bit in one hand and the file in the other to sharpen the secondary cutters, between the side spurs. Remember that there are two halves to the twist which must be sharpened identically. Hold the bit, and with the snail (the threaded point in the center) pointing down on the bench top, angle the bit away from you and begin filing the top side of the cutting edge. File at a very shallow angle following up the angle of the twist of the bit. You will know when you have filed enough because a burr will form along the underside of the cutting edge. Flip the bit over and file between the snail and the spur, filing as close to the flat face as possible until the edge is clear of any burr. I find it best to file with light strokes on this underside. Repeat this process to the opposite side.

This step is only to remove the burr.

Spur Points

Next file the insides of the two spurs. You must file only the inside faces. The spurs must always protrude past the secondary cutters that remove the waste because the bit relies on these spurs defining the wall of the hole first, otherwise the fibers will tear and cause a ragged edge around the hole.

File only the inside of the spurs.

Conclusion

With a little practice, you will soon appreciate the simplicity of this process, which will allow you to always maintain your augers in good order.

18 Conclusion

To conclude this chapter on sharpening, I would encourage you to read and practice every step of sharpening the tools in the preceding chapters. The level of understanding and technical ability required to keep all your tools in pristine condition, should go hand in hand with these three habits:

> Keep your sharpening equipment together and close to hand in one place. Sharpness is so essential to your everyday handwork that you should be able to locate each piece of equipment without faltering.
>
> Aim for maintenance sharpening only. Never let a chisel, plane, saw, scraper or any other hand tool become so dull that it requires more than a few minutes to sharpen. That said, when it comes to performance sharpening, it's important you become thorough and proficiently accurate before increasing your speed.
>
> I try not to put tools away dull. I like the confidence of reaching for any tool, and knowing it will cut as well as any other tool I'm using. Look after your edge tools, protect the edges from other tools and they will serve you well.

It is my hope that the sharpening methods and procedures I have described in this book, will enable you to become totally self sufficient and discover the truth in this quote.

"The validity and value of woodworking hand tools relies on one simple fact: when they are truly sharp, they really work."

Chapter 2, page 28.

Join the quiet revolution.

Paul Sellers

WORKING WOOD 1&2

The Artisan Series with Paul Sellers

Master Woodworker, Paul Sellers presents the Working Wood series, teaching you the application of his woodworking principles.

Working Wood 1 & 2 provides a structured series of seven films (available on DVD and for download) and accompanying 320-page, full-color book with 880 color photos and diagrams.

This series of structured and integrated training courses will enable woodworkers of all ability levels to easily master Paul Sellers' essential skills that can be used for a lifetime of woodworking projects.

The series is produced at the Artisan Media studios in Penrhyn Castle, a prestigious, historic property in North Wales.

Working Wood 1, 2 & 3

If you have progressed through this course and completed the projects to a satisfactory standard, you will now understand the rudiments of quality craftsmanship. If you have enjoyed the process of learning the methods and procedures, and you are prepared to consolidate them through practice and diligent repetition, the next level, Working Wood 3, will increase your skill and confidence. The course is tried and tested, and so too the character of those who persevere to maintain high standards of quality craftsmanship.

You will build on your mortising skills to make a beautiful quarter-sawn oak hope chest, with an inset drawer, shaped legs and a hinged raised panel lid.

From the humble three legged stool and shaker box, you will progress to chairmaking and a fine office desk or dining table.

The essential techniques in Working Wood 1&2 are transferable throughout the entirety of the course, and you will certainly enjoy using them as foundational building blocks to progress through higher levels of accomplishment and satisfaction.

Glossary

This glossary has been compiled to explain the use of terms in the context of woodwork. It does not represent the full and exhaustive meanings of any of the terms.

ABRASIVE COMPOUND
Abrasive particles generally suspended in a solid or liquid substance and used for abrading metals to various levels ranging from coarse cutting to fine polishing.

ADJUSTMENT WHEEL
Bailey and Bed Rock pattern cast metal planes have an adjustment wheel attached to the frog of the plane that sets the depth of the cutting iron which controls the thickness of the cut.

AGGRESSIVE RIPSAW
Ripsaws with an aggressive tooth rake.

AGGRESSIVE TOOTH RAKE
A rake angle for saw teeth that allows very fast, but unrefined cutting.

ALLOY
An intimate combination of different metals and other elements developed to create a metal with specific characteristic properties.

AMATI
The name of a family of Italian violin makers producing violins in Cremona during the 16-17th century.

ANGLEPOISE
A spring-mechanized, counterbalanced table or floor lamp.

APRON
The part of a framed and jointed structure that is placed horizontally, in between legs of a table, a workbench etc.

ASSEMBLY HAMMER
A semi-hard or hard hammer usually made of plastic, leather or metal used for assembling component parts. These hammers are designed to minimize damage on impact. I use the soft end of my panel beater's mallet.

AUGER
A drilling bit with a helical body. Auger bits are held in a swing brace and used to bore holes.

AXE-HEWN
This term describes a workpiece shaped with an axe.

BACK IRON
The back iron is part of the cutting iron assembly in a cast metal hand plane. It has several functions discussed on pages 239.

BACKLASH
During depth adjustment of a hand plane, this is the momentary loss of movement of the cutting iron, as the direction of rotation of the adjusting wheel is changed. The adjustment wheel usually turns with less effort until the slack in the mechanism is taken up.

BACK SAWS
A generic name for all handsaws, regardless of length or size, with a rigid steel or brass spine (US).

BAILEY-PATTERN
A plane type developed by Leonard Bailey in the 19th century.

BARN CROOKS
Component parts in timber-framed barns are often formed from naturally occurring bends in tree branches and trunks.

BEARERS
Support pieces of wood used in woodworking to carry or distribute weight. I use them in the workbench as a simple means of securing the bench top.

BED ANGLE
The angle of presentation that supports the cutting iron at a fixed angle. This angle varies according to different plane types.

BENCH DOGGING SYSTEM
Any system or method of anchoring component parts being worked to the benchtop.

BENCH DOGS
Pegs or blocks inserted into the benchtop to allow clamping or some method of holding the workpiece.

BEVEL
The short, inclined face of an edge tool that forms the cutting edge.

An angled plane, cut using a tool on a corner where two faces meet.

BEVEL ANGLE
The angle between the bevel and the flat face of an edge tool.

BEVEL-DOWN CUTS
The presentation of any cutting edge to the wood with the bevel facing down.

BEVEL-EDGED CHISELS
A chisel with the long sides beveled along the full length.

BLADE
A woodworking tool part used to cut, plane or saw wood. In the context of edge tools, it is also called the cutting iron.

BLANK
A workpiece, pre-shaped by some process, enabling further shaping operations to transform it into different, or different forms of a finished product.

BLIND MORTISE
A mortise that does not go all the way through to the opposite side.

BOTTOM OUT
This term is used to describe the occurrence of an over length tenon preventing a joint from seating correctly.

BOW
The bend of a board along its length.

BRACE
In the context of this book, this is an abbreviation for a swing brace.

BREAKOUT
Tearing or splitting of unsupported fibers as a result of cutting towards an edge.

BREASTED
This describes a convex line of saw teeth.

BUFFING COMPOUND
See abrasive compound.

BURR
A misleading term referring to the highly refined cutting edge formed on the corners or bevels of woodworking scrapers.

A deformed growth on the outside of tree stems and branches, the inside of which is highly prized for its unique and distinctive grain configuration.

Deformation of metal wherein, after filing or grinding, a rough edge forms on the unsupported outer edge.

CABINET SCRAPER
A two-handled surfacing tool used extensively in woodworking to shave and refine the surface grain of wood.

A simple, single-piece plate steel surfacing tool used in woodworking to shave and refine the surface grain of wood, also known as a card scraper.

CALIBRATED MOISTURE METER
A digital electronic device used to measure the moisture content of wood.

CAP IRON
See back iron.

CARD SCRAPERS
See cabinet scraper.

CELLO BOUTS
The thin, curved sides of a cello.

CENTRAL THREAD
The conical thread forming the point of auger bits, also called the snail.

CHAMFER
The bevel formed between two adjoining surfaces. If the surfaces are at right angles, the chamfer will typically be symmetrical at 45 degrees.

CHEEKS
The wide faces formed on each side of any tenon.

CHIP BREAKER
A cap- or back-iron attached by a setscrew to the cutting irons of bench planes (US).

CHIP-CARVING KNIVES
A unique group of specialist knives used to make incised cuts in carving and lettering.

COACH SCREWS
Threaded bolts with very coarse screw threads to fix directly into timber.

COARSE SAWS
Large toothed saws used for either ripcutting or crosscutting wood depending upon the tooth configuration.

COMPLEMENTARY GRAIN CONFIGURATION
Grain positioned for a visually appealing balanced color and grain figuring.

CONCAVE BEVEL
A hollow ground bevel used to form a cutting edge on edge tools.

CONVEX BEVEL
A traditional bevel formed in the sharpening process to create a strong, long-lasting cutting edge on edge tools.

COPY CARVER
A CNC (computer numerically controlled) machine designed to replicate shapes in wood.

CORACLE
A small, ancient design of water craft made from thin staves of wood heated and bent to shape and covered with cloth or animal skin.

CROSSCUT SAW
A saw used in cutting across the grain of wood.

CROSSCUT PATTERN
A type of tooth pattern for cutting across the grain of wood.

CROSS-GRAIN
At an angle to the longitudinal wood cells constituting the grain.

CROSS-GRAIN PARING
Use of a sharp chisel to slice across end grain fibers of wood.

CROSS-RAIL
Any rail spanning from one part to another part of a wooden frame or structure.

CUP
One of several common forms of distortion associated with drying out timber: The cup forms a 'U'-shaped distortion across the width of a board. On one side the board cups and on the other it forms a camber.

CUTTING IRON
The part of a plane or spokeshave that is sharpened to form a cutting edge.

CUTTING IRON ASSEMBLY
The assembly of two key components, the cutting iron and the cap or back iron, used in bench planes.

DEPTH LINE
A gauge or pencil line marking the lowest level to which a tool cut should go.

DIAMOND PLATES
Flat plates of steel coated with abrasive diamond particles and generally used for sharpening edge tools. Traditionally, abrasive stones are called whetstones and bench stones.

DIPPERS
Wooden ladles and large, bowled spoons used for cooking and serving meals.

DISPOSABLE HANDSAWS
Saws with impulse hardened teeth that are too hard to sharpen saw files and must be discarded when dull.

EARLYWOOD
The early-formed portion of an annual growth ring formed during the season of spring to early summer when sap rises at optimal levels to promote growth. The earlywood is characterized by larger, less dense cells than those formed in the later, summer growth.

EBAY
Internet consumer-to-consumer corporation managing an online auction and shopping website.

EDGE TOOLS
A wide group of traditional hand tools with cutting edges used to slice, split, chop and shave wood.

EGGSHELL PAINT
A non-gloss, low shine paint used to coat materials such as wood, fiber board and metal.

END-GRAIN
An edge resulting from cross-cutting wood.

FACE MARK
An '𝒻' mark used to indicate a trued and flattened surface of a board used to register further layout tools from.

FACE-EDGE MARK
A unique ' Λ ' mark used in woodworking to denote a trued edge of a workpiece.

FIGURED WOOD
Any surface of wood with distinctive surface marking, either interesting grain configuration and structure, or diverse changes of color. This may result from the natural growth or by a variety of influences ranging from defects to disease and fungal attack such as spalting.

FINENESS INDEX
A system developed to address the tooth sizing used to define handsaws.

FIR
A type of coniferous softwood tree.

FLARE
In the context of furniture, the widening or appearance of a widening of table/chair legs towards the floor.

FLAT BEVEL
A bevel formed between two flat surfaces.

FLAT FACE
In the context of edge tools, this refers to the face of the chisel or plane iron that is always maintained dead flat and polished. The beveled surface meets this face to form a cutting edge.

FLEA MARKETS
A variety of market venues and shops used for the sale of both new and secondhand goods of all kinds.

FLEAM-TOOTH
A uniquely designed saw tooth formed into a pinnacle point and used specifically for crosscutting wood.

FLOAT GLASS
Thick plate glass known for its near perfect flatness.

FLUSH-CUT
To saw off a protrusion near to the same height as its surroundings.

FOREBEARS
The earlier generation of a family, group or nation of people.

FORE KNOB
The front, round knob of a plane.

FOURSQUARE
The straightening and squaring of four sides of any section of wood along its entire length.

FROG
The cast iron component used to mount the cutting iron in metal-cast planes.

FROG RETAINING SCREW
Setscrews used to secure the frog to the sole of a bench plane.

FRONT JAW
The outside, moveable, flat iron plate of a vise.

FULLY SEATING
The final full entry of one part of a joint into another, the result of which is to set all shoulders tightly up to one another.

GARAGE SALES
A private sale of personal and household goods from the garage of a home.

GLUE FREEZE
The premature grab of glue within a joint that prevents a joint from closing together before the parts are fully seated.

GOUGE
A rounded chisel used in carving and shaping wood.

GRADE
Sandpaper grit size.

GRAIN CONFIGURATION
See figured wood.

GRAIN RAISED (RAISED GRAIN)
The uneven surface of planed or sawn wood usually becoming more prominent through the differences in absorption of moisture between earlywood and latewood. The higher resin content in darker, denser latewood of softwood annual rings, is less hygroscopic than the more open, lighter colored earlywood.

GREEN OR SAPPY WOOD
Newly cut wood having moisture levels above saturation point retained in the wood in an unseasoned state. Also, in more recent years, a term referring to environmentally conscious woodworking using sustainable practices.

GRIT (GRIT SIZE)
Particle size used to make various grades of abrasive paper. Defined by a mesh density per linear inch.

GUILDS
A group of people formed into a union of craftsmen and women.

GULLET
The 'V' formed in between each of the saw teeth of a handsaw.

HAND ROUTER
A special plane designed to remove waste from within a recess.

HAUNCH
Reduced portion of a tenon used at the 90-degree corner of a frame or door.

HAUNCHED MORTISE AND TENON
A joint used at the corner of a frame that allows the enclosure in the tenon in the mortise joint on all four sides.

HEARTWOOD
The mature centrer-wood of the tree that no longer has growing cells or conducts sap as distinct from the outer sapwood of living cells. (This confusing term has no designation of the hardness or density in wood).

HEEL OF THE PLANE
The back, half-moon corner of the plane on the underside of the sole.

HEPPLEWHITE
A furniture maker and designer from the mid 1700s, known for creating a particular style of fine furniture.

HINGE FLAPS
The two flat faces of any hinge are known as the flaps.

HOLLOW GROUND
A concave shaped bevel of a cutting iron or chisel.

HOMOGENEOUS
Having the same properties in all directions

HONE
To refine a cutting edge by abrasion at different levels of fineness.

HONING GUIDE
A device used to hold a cutting edge tool or blade at a predetermined angle during sharpening.

HOUSING DADO JOINT
A long recess cut across the grain of one part to retain a second component across its width.

HYGROSCOPIC
Having a tendency to readily absorb moisture from the atmosphere.

INDUCTION HARDENING
The hardening of saw teeth by magnetic induction of a controlled current of electricity through each tooth to harden the outer surface portion of the steel.

INLAY
A decorative technique often using contrasting pieces of wood to make patterns or shapes that are then recessed into the surface of the surrounding wood.

INLAY RECESSES
Recesses formed in the surface of wood to receive an inlay.

JIG
A guide used to allow a repetitive procedure to be carried out with accuracy and ease.

JOINERY GRADE SOFTWOOD
Spruce, fir or pine suitable for joinery construction products and architectural millwork such as doors, windows, stairs and a wide range of other construction trade products.

JOINTING
The restorative process of leveling uneven saw teeth

The truing and squaring of long edges of pieces of wood for edge gluing together.

KERF
The width of the channel created by the saw teeth.

KILN
A large container used for drying wood in different forms by the controlled management of temperature, humidity and air circulation.

KILN DRIED LUMBER
Artificially force-dried wood, processed by kiln drying using a heat source.

KNIFE LINES
Knife cuts used for precise layout and defining all cross-grain shoulders for joinery. Also used for defining inlay recesses.

KNIFEWALL
An initial knife line made with a sharp knife, and deepened with a chisel to delineate all cross-grain cuts in joinery and woodworking.

LAMINATING
The process of gluing up sections of wood to create larger sections or panels.

LANDING THE PLANE
I use this term to describe the point during the planing process where the sole, having been lifted off to stop the stroke, is decisively brought into contact with the workpiece once more in a forward motion during the next stroke.

LAPPING
The process of abrading metal to straighten and flatten the surface.

LATE-WOOD (AUTUMN-WOOD)
The late growth of every annual ring in a tree resulting in smaller cells and thereby denser (finer) grain.

LATERAL ADJUSTMENT LEVER
The lever used on hand planes to align the cutting edge of the cutting iron to the face of the sole.

LEATHER STROP
Leather used to polish cutting edges, often but not always charged with abrasive compound.

LEVER CAP
Securing mechanism on hand planes to lock the cutting iron assembly to the main body of the plane.

LONG-GRAIN EDGE
An edge of a board or workpiece, mostly running parallel with the grain direction of the wood.

LONGLEAF PINE
Species of pine known for its extremely long pine needle leaves, also known as Pitch pine.

LOW-TACK ADHESIVE
An aerosol spray adhesive having low adhesive properties providing easy removal of materials glued.

MACHINE MARKS
Any of a variety of marks left by the cutting edge of machines such as planers and saws.

MACHINE SCREW
Refined screw thread with low or zero tolerance between engaged threads.

MAHOGANY
Species of hardwood having rich reddish brown grain color and no apparent growth rings and few or no knots.

MECHANICAL GRINDERS
Machines used for abrading metal.

MEMORY IN THE STEEL
The ability of steel to return or partially return to its former shape after bending.

MESQUITE
A slow-growing drought-resistant hardwood which grows in the south of North America.

METAL-CAST PLANES
Planes made from cast metal as opposed to wooden bodied planes.

MICRO-BEVEL
A small secondary bevel ground at a slightly steeper angle than the main bevel.

MICRON
Measurement equal to one millionth of a meter.

MITER
A line of intersection where two components meet in such a way that the joint line bisects the angle between them.

MOISTURE CONTENT
The percentage of water contained within the wood.

MORTISE ALIGNMENT GUIDE
A guide developed by the author to align the mortising chisel parallel to the face of the wood being mortised.

MORTISE CHISELS
Specific group of heavy chisels used specifically for chopping mortise holes.

MORTISE GAUGE PINS
Twin pins of a mortise gauge, one adjustable to the other, used to score the surface of wood to define the limits of the mortise hole in preparation for mortising.

MORTISE HOLE
The square or rectangular hole cut to receive a tenon.

NAIL PUNCH
Same as nail set. Used to set the nail flush or below the surface of the surrounding wood.

NEGATIVE RAKE
Any angle used on the front cutting edge of saw teeth that is less than 90 degrees.

NICHOLSON
North American file manufacturer.

OFFSET LINE
A line running parallel to an adjacent edge or other line, curved or otherwise.

OVERCUT
Cutting beyond the depth or gauge line.

PANEL SAW
Short handsaw used for ripping and crosscutting small or thin sections of wood. Usually around 10 points per inch.

PARE
To slice surface wood fibers with a wide chisel, often using the wood itself as a support or guide.

PASSIVE RAKE
A negative rake angle of saw tooth, usually around 20 to 30 degrees. This allows very smooth cutting but tends to be slower than more agressive, steeper teeth.

PASTE WAX
Any mixture of hard wax substances combined with solvents to create a soft wax for polishing wood.

PILOT HOLES
Pre-drilled holes that prevent wood from splitting when driving a screw but allow the thread of a screw to bite the walls of the hole.

PIN PIECE
The section of wood in which the pins of the dovetail joint are cut.

PIN RECESS
The gaps between the dovetails that receive the pins in a dovetail joint.

PINS
The parts of the dovetail joint that interlock with the dovetails.

PLATE
The blade of a handsaw.

POINTS PER INCH
The number of teeth points per inch of saw length, indicating the fineness index.

PRESENTATION ANGLE
The angle a plane iron or cutting edge is offered to the surface of wood.

PROGRESSIVE PATTERN
The varying size or angle of a tooth pattern used in saw sharpening.

PROGRESSIVE TOOTH PATTERNS
A pattern of saw tooth cutting that changes in configuration along the length of the sawblade.

QUADRANT MOLDING
A molded form of stock with a sectional quadrant shape.

QUARTER-SAWN
A method of sawing timber where the annular rings are at a steeper angle than 60 degrees to the saw cut. 90 degrees is perfect quarter sawn.

RACK
To force a jointed frame out of square.

RAIL
This is a term used to denote a part of a framed structure that usually runs horizontally and is jointed at both ends.

RAKE
See Rake angle, Pitch, Negative rake.

RAKE ANGLE
This is the angle swept from a vertical line below the point of the sawtooth, to the front edge of the sawtooth. It is usually represented as a negative number, in degrees.

REAR HANDLE
This refers to the handle of a bench plane, located behind the cutting iron assembly.

REAR JAW
The jaw of a vise, nearest to the bench top.

RECESS
A well defined slot or hole tailored to fit a corresponding part of a joint, such as a dovetail, or shelf.

REGISTER
I use this as a verb to describe the precise alignment of layout tools with each other or with layout marks.

REVERSE GRAIN
Wood grain inclined upwards against the direction of cutting, shaving or splitting.

RIPCUT
A sawcut going with the grain.

RIPCUT PATTERN
A saw sharpening pattern where the teeth are shaped like chisels.

RIVE
To split wood along the grain, usually referring to freshly felled lumber.

ROUGH SAWN LUMBER
Timber that has been sawn, usually by an industrial machine, but not planed.

ROUNDOVER
A curved aesthetic detail on the edge of a wooden part.

RULE OF THUMB
A general rule based on common sense and experience, not science.

RUST PITTING
Corrosion of a steel surface causing an eroded, rough texture.

SAPWOOD
The outer part of the tree trunk or branches, used by the tree for conduction of sap.

SAW DOCTORS
A term used to describe a specialist in saw restoration and maintenance.

SAWFILE
A triangular file used for the purpose of sharpening saw teeth.

SAWSET
A mechanical hand tool used to accurately set saw tooth configuration.

The geometrical arrangements of all the facets that form the saw tooth.

SCALLOP
A scooped cut, used to form a concave, bowl shaped surface.

SCROLL
A convolute carved section, used to decorate violins and other stringed instruments.

SEASONING
The process of slowly air drying timber to lower the moisture content ready for use.

SECONDARY-BEVEL
Otherwise known as a micro-bevel. A smaller bevel ground on the main bevel of an edge tool.

SECONDARY CUTTERS
The internal cutters on an auger bit, that split and lift out the cut waste as the auger rotates.

SET
The amount by which a saw tooth is bent outwards away from the blade.

SETSCREW
A threaded machine screw used to secure parts of a plane.

SHALLOW-SET
With reference to a plane or spokeshave blade, this means having minimum protrusion below the sole which takes the finest shavings.

SHARPENING MEDIA
The collective term for all materials used as sharpening abrasives.

SHELLAC
A traditional finishing and sealing compound, naturally occurring and requiring dissolution in alcohol before application.

SHERATON
Thomas Sheraton (1751 – 22 October 1806) was a furniture designer, one of the "big three" English furniture makers of the 18th century, along with Thomas Chippendale and George Hepplewhite.

SHOULDER
The sharply defined, end grain face, cut back to form part of a joint.

SHOULDER CUT
A cross-grain cut defining the part of a workpiece requiring removal.

SHRINKAGE
The reduction in size of a wooden component as it dries out.

SINGLE-CUT MILL FILE
A conventional engineering file, with a single oblique line pattern, as opposed to a double cut file that has coarse diamond shaped points.

SKEW OR SKEWED
Angled or at an angle.

SLIPSTONE
An abrasive sharpening stone with a curved profile.

SMOOTHING PLANES
A type of bench plane, typically the last to be used to smooth a surface, after previous leveling with perhaps a larger bodied plane.

SNAIL
The threaded part in the center of an auger.

SOLE
The underside of the cast metal plane body, normally polished to reduce resistance.

SPALTED
This describes the visual appearance of wood as a result of partial decay due to fungal attack. It can result in very attractive patterns and contrasting lines.

SPLAY
The angle of a leg, inclined outwards from the center of a stool or chair.

SPOKESHAVE
A form of hand plane, with a very short sole and side handles.

SPRUCE
A type of fast growing softwood with distinctive orange/brown cones. It has many uses in the construction industry, being light, abundant and reasonably strong.

SPUR CUTTERS
The outer cutters of an auger that determine the cutting diameter (hole diameter).

SPUR POINT
Alternative name for spur cutter, see above.

STARVING THE JOINT
This expression is used with reference to gluing up a joint, where there is a danger of failure if insufficient glue is used.

STOCK (LAYOUT TOOLS)
The body of a square or marking gauge that is used as a reference point from which to measure angles or score lines.

STOCK (WOOD)
A general term used to mean wood suitable for joinery.

STONES
I use this term to mean the sharpening abrasive plates that I use, which happen to be diamond coated plates, not related to the stones from which the name originates.

STOP-CUT
A saw cut made into the waste, at 90 degrees to the grain, down to a predetermined line allowing removal of the waste with a chisel. This is fast and reliable.

STOPPED CHAMFER
This is a regular chamfer that is brought out to the corner either by an abrupt change in angle or a gradual sweep.

STOPPED HOUSING DADO JOINT
This is a type of housing dado joint where the channel is not cut all the way through to the front face of the piece.

STRADIVARIUS
The name Stradivarius has been associated with excellence in the field of violin making for over 300 years. Antonio Stradivari made violins around 1700AD which today sell for millions ($US or £Sterling).

STROP
A leather charged with buffing compound for refining edge tools to a surgically sharp condition.

STUB TENON
A short tenon that generally fits into a blind mortise.

STYMIE
Literally means to thwart the efforts of someone to achieve something.

SWEEP
An even graceful curve.

SWING BRACE
A hand powered, crank shaped device for holding and rotating auger bits.

SWIPE
I refer to taking a quick pass over a workpiece with a plane as 'taking a swipe'.

TAIL PIECE
The part of a dovetail joint that you cut the tails in.

TAIL RECESS
The spaces between the pins, carefully cut to match the dovetails in a joint.

TAILS
The parts of a dovetailed joint that resemble the tails of a dove (hence dovetailed joint).

TEAR-OUT
The unwanted occurrence of surface fibers of a workpiece being torn out rather than cut cleanly.

TEETH PER INCH
This is the same as Points Per Inch (ppi) and is an index of the fineness of a saw.

TENON HAUNCH
The cut out section in the tenon that allows the tenon to fit into a haunched mortise.

TENON SHOULDERS
The clean cut end grain edges remaining after the waste has been removed to form the tenon.

THREADED KNOB
The part of a spokeshave used to tighten the cutting iron into the main body.

THROAT
The gap in front of the cutting iron allowing shavings to pass through the sole of a plane.

THROUGH-MORTISE
A mortise hole that passes all the way through a workpiece.

TOOTH LINE
The line described by the tops of the teeth on a particular saw.

TOPPING
The process of standardizing the heights of the teeth on a particular saw blade.

TRANSLUCENT
A wood finish that is semi-transparent, usually colored.

TRIMMING
The process of carefully removing wood fibers that appear to be likely to prevent a joint from fitting together as it should.

TUNE UP
The process of preparing your hand plane or spokeshave for active service, through making careful adjustments and alterations to aspects of the set up.

TURNBUTTONS
A means of holding table tops onto a rigid leg frame of a table.

VENEERING
The process of applying a thinner decorative wood onto a cheaper, stronger or less attractive base wood.

VIOLIN BELLY
The thin carved middle section of the violin body.

WASTE
The part of the wood that needs to be removed when shaping or cutting.

WELL
The section of a workbench that is lower than the bench top. Used to keep the bench top clear and prevent tools from rolling off the bench.

WILD GRAIN
Wood grain where the fibers do not follow the more usual uniform pattern but instead dip and dive, twist and turn in all directions making working the surface very difficult.

WINDOW SASHES
The sliding parts of traditional style windows, usually assisted by counterbalanced weights.

WINDSOR CHAIRS
A traditional style of chair, where the back and legs are fixed into holes in the seat, as spokes in a cartwheel would be fitted to the hub.

WITH THE GRAIN
Working the wood in a way so that the fibers are not lifted and torn but cut cleanly.

WOOD GRAIN
The term denoting the arrangement of the wood fibers.

WORKPIECE
A general term for any part or component of any project requiring shaping by some means.

YOKE
The pivoting part of the depth adjustment system on a cast steel plane that transfers the movement in the depth adjustment wheel to the cutting iron assembly.

ZERO NEGATIVE RAKE
This means that the rake of a tooth is zero. i.e. the leading edge of the tooth is vertical.

Index

Index *continued*

T

V

W

Y

Z

Pattern Page

All patterns on this page are 50% of actual size.

If you photocopy this page and then enlarge the required section by 200%, your patterns will be ready to use to make permanent templates.

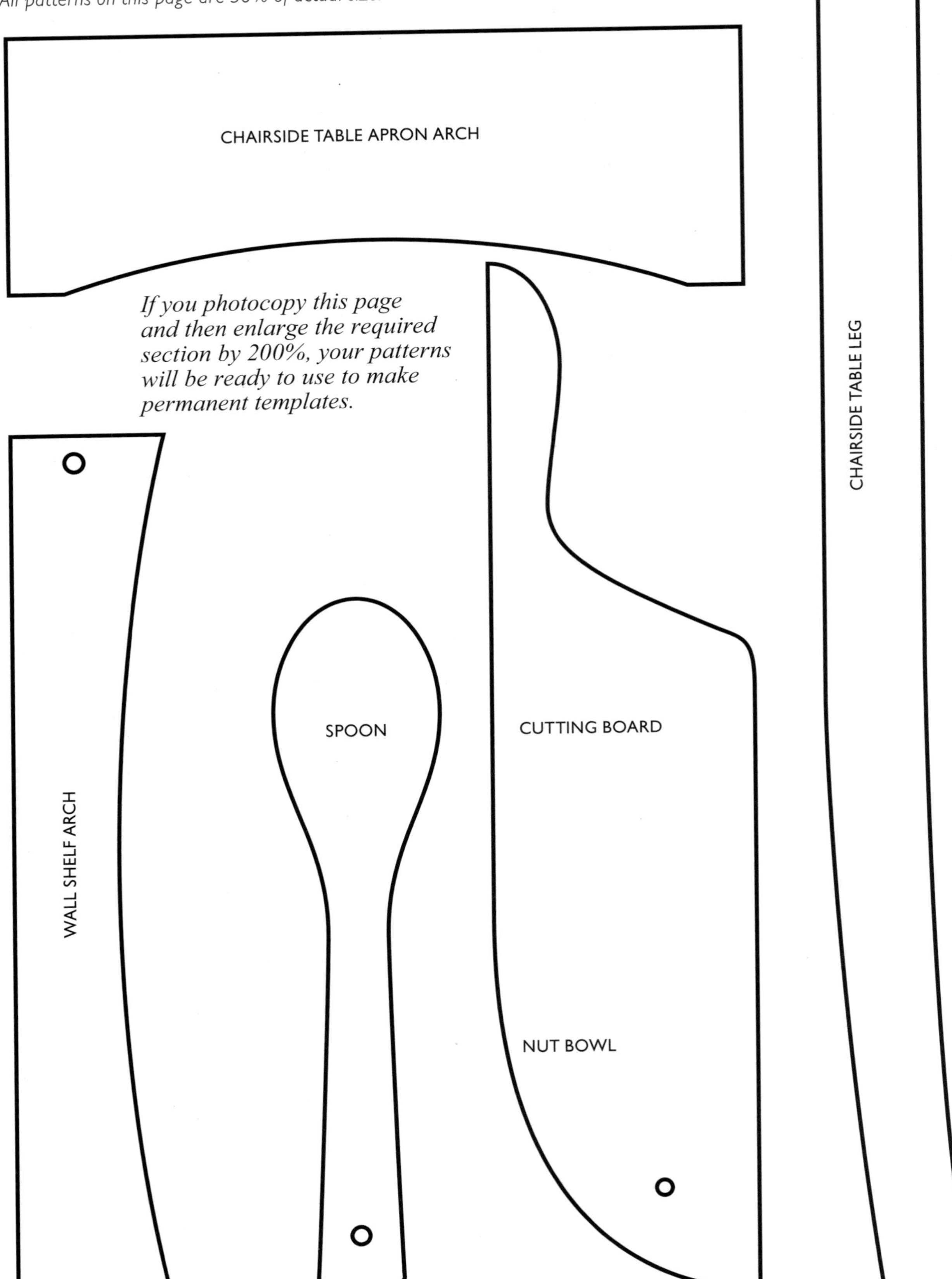